China on Screen

CINEMA AND NATION

FILM AND CULTURE SERIES: JOHN BELTON, GENERAL EDITOR

Film and Culture: A series of Columbia University Press

EDITED BY **John Belton**

What Made Pistachio Nuts? Early Sound Comedy
and the Vaudeville Aesthetic
HENRY JENKINS

Showstoppers: Busby Berkeley and the Tradition
of Spectacle   MARTIN RUBIN

Projections of War: Hollywood, American Culture,
and World War II   THOMAS DOHERTY

Laughing Screaming: Modern Hollywood Horror
and Comedy   WILLIAM PAUL

Laughing Hysterically: American Screen Comedy
of the 1950s   ED SIKOV

Primitive Passions: Visuality, Sexuality, Ethnography,
and Contemporary Chinese Cinema   REY CHOW

The Cinema of Max Ophuls: Magisterial Vision
and the Figure of Woman   SUSAN M. WHITE

Black Women as Cultural Readers
JACQUELINE BOBO

Picturing Japaneseness: Monumental Style, National
Identity, Japanese Film
DARRELL WILLIAM DAVIS

Attack of the Leading Ladies: Gender, Sexuality,
and Spectatorship in Classic Horror Cinema
RHONA J. BERENSTEIN

This Mad Masquerade: Stardom and Masculinity in
the Jazz Age   GAYLYN STUDLAR

Sexual Politics and Narrative Film: Hollywood
and Beyond   ROBIN WOOD

The Sounds of Commerce: Marketing Popular
Film Music   JEFF SMITH

Orson Welles, Shakespeare, and Popular Culture
MICHAEL ANDEREGG

Pre-Code Hollywood: Sex, Immorality, and
Insurrection in American Cinema, 1930–1934
THOMAS DOHERTY

Sound Technology and the American Cinema: Perception, Representation, Modernity
JAMES LASTRA

Melodrama and Modernity: Early Sensational
Cinema and Its Contexts   BEN SINGER

Wondrous Difference: Cinema, Anthropology, and
Turn-of-the-Century Visual Culture
ALISON GRIFFITHS

Hearst Over Hollywood: Power, Passion, and
Propaganda in the Movies   LOUIS PIZZITOLA

Masculine Interests: Homoerotics in Hollywood Film
ROBERT LANG

Special Effects: Still in Search of Wonder
MICHELE PIERSON

Designing Women: Cinema, Art Deco,
and the Female Form   LUCY FISCHER

Cold War, Cool Medium: Television, McCarthyism,
and American Culture   THOMAS DOHERTY

Katharine Hepburn: Star as Feminist
ANDREW BRITTON

Silent Film Sound   RICK ALTMAN

Home in Hollywood: The Imaginary Geography
of Hollywood   ELISABETH BRONFEN

Hollywood and the Culture Elite: How the Movies
Became American   PETER DECHERNEY

Taiwan Film Directors: A Treasure Island
EMILIE YUEH-YU YEH AND DARRELL WILLIAM DAVIS

Shocking Representation: Historical Trauma,
National Cinema, and the Modern Horror Film
ADAM LOWENSTEIN

Chris Berry and Mary Farquhar

China on Screen

CINEMA AND NATION

COLUMBIA UNIVERSITY PRESS / NEW YORK

Columbia University Press wishes to express its appreciation for assistance given by the Chiang Ching-kuo Foundation for International Scholarly Exhange in the publication of this book.

Columbia University Press
Publishers Since 1893
New York Chichester, West Sussex

Library of Congress Cataloging-in-Publication Data

Berry, Chris, 1959–
China on screen : cinema and nation / Chris Berry and Mary Farquhar.
p.   cm. — (Film and culture series)
Includes bibliographical references and index.
ISBN 0–231–13706–0 (alk. paper) — ISBN 0–231–13707–9 (pbk. : alk. paper)
1. Motion pictures—China—History.   I. Farquhar, Mary Ann, 1949–   II. Title.
III. Film and culture.
PN1993.5.C4B44 2006
791.43'0951—dc22   2005053930

Printed in the United States of America

Designed by Lisa Hamm

c 10 9 8 7 6 5 4 3 2 1
p 10 9 8 7 6 5 4 3 2 1

Cover and title page photo: From *Hero* (2002 / 2004),
directed by Zhang Yimou, visual effects by Animal Logic © EDKO Film.
Used with permission. Special thanks to Jet Li, Elite Group Enterprises, and Animal Logic.

Contents

List of Illustrations .... *vii*

Acknowledgments .... *ix*

A Note on Translation and Romanization .... *xiii*

1 Introduction: Cinema and the National 1

2 Time and the National: History, Historiology, Haunting 17

3 Operatic Modes: Opera Film, Martial Arts, and Cultural Nationalism 47

4 Realist Modes: Melodrama, Modernity, and Home 75

5 How Should a Chinese Woman Look? Woman and Nation 108

6 How Should Chinese Men Act? Ordering the Nation 135

7 Where Do You Draw the Line? Ethnicity in Chinese Cinemas 169

8 The National in the Transnational 195

Chronology *223*

Notes *233*

European-language Bibliography *265*

Chinese-language Bibliography *287*

Film List *293*

Index *301*

List of Illustrations

FIGURES 2.1a–2.1d. The fisherwoman confronts the foreign merchant in *Lin Zexu* (1959) 26

FIGURE 2.2 Li Quanxi's *The Opium War* (1963) 27

FIGURES 2.3a–2.3c The ending of *Yellow Earth* (1984) 34

FIGURE 2.4 Wen-ching threatened in *City of Sadness* (1989) 35

FIGURE 2.5 Communicating by notes in *City of Sadness* 37

FIGURE 3.1 The lovers in *Love Eterne* (1963) 52

FIGURE 3.2 The woman warrior in *A Touch of Zen* (1971) 54

FIGURE 3.3 Tan Xinpei in *Dingjun Mountain* (1905) 57

FIGURE 3.4 The heroine in *The White-haired Girl* (1950) 61

FIGURE 3.5 Ke Xiang in *Azalea Mountain* (1974) 63

FIGURES 3.6a–3.6e On the execution ground in *Azalea Mountain* (1974) 65

FIGURE 3.7 *Twelve Widows March West* (1963) 68

FIGURE 4.1 *Tomboy* (1936) 84

FIGURE 4.2 Xiao Yun from *Street Angel* (1937) 87

FIGURES 4.3a–4.3c Deathbed scene in *Street Angel* (1937) 88

FIGURE 4.4 On the town walls in *Spring in a Small Town* (1948) 89

FIGURE 4.5 Family reunion in *Spring in a Small Town* (1948) 90

FIGURE 4.6 Xianglin's wife in *New Year's Sacrifice* (1956) 93

FIGURE 4.7 *Oyster Girl* (1964) 94

FIGURES 4.8a–4.8h Family reconciliation in *Beautiful Duckling* (1964) 97

FIGURE 4.9 A family meal in *Yellow Earth* (1984) 103

FIGURE 4.10 Cuiqiao's wedding night in *Yellow Earth* (1984)   105

FIGURE 5.1 The ending of *Two Stage Sisters* (1964)   114

FIGURE 5.2 Yuehong shows off her ring in *Two Stage Sisters* (1964)   116

FIGURES 5.3a–5.3d Inspired by her teacher in *Song of Youth* (1959)   117

FIGURE 5.4 Joining the Communist Party in *Song of Youth* (1959)   118

FIGURES 5.5a–5.5c Admiring glances in *The New Woman* (1935)   121

FIGURES 5.6a–5.6f At the nightclub in *The New Woman* (1935)   123

FIGURE 5.7 Deathbed scene in *The New Woman* (1935)   124

FIGURE 5.8 Gong Li in *Raise the Red Lantern* (1991)   128

FIGURE 6.1 Kwan Tak-hing as Wong Fei-hung   146

FIGURE 6.2 Jackie Chan as Wong Fei-hung in *Drunken Master* (1978)   147

FIGURE 6.3 Chow Yun-fat in *A Better Tomorrow 1* (1986)   154

FIGURE 6.4 Celebrations in *The Story of Qiu Ju* (1992)   161

FIGURES 6.5a–6.5g The final scene in *The Story of Qiu Ju* (1992)   162

FIGURE 6.6 Execution in *Hero* (2002/2004)   166

FIGURE 7.1 Airport good-byes in *The Wedding Banquet* (1993)   177

FIGURE 7.2 Simon and Mr. Gao in *The Wedding Banquet* (1993)   179

FIGURE 7.3 The young master rides Jampa in *Serfs* (1963)   182

FIGURES 7.4a–7.4f Jampa rides the horse in *Serfs* (1963)   183

FIGURE 7.5 The sky burial in *Horse Thief* (1986)   185

FIGURE 7.6 Religious observance in *Horse Thief* (1986)   186

FIGURE 7.7 Adopting Dai ways in *Sacrificed Youth* (1985)   187

FIGURE 8.1 Bruce Lee in *The Big Boss* (1971)   199

FIGURE 8.2 Belt action in *The Way of the Dragon* (1972)   202

FIGURES 8.3a–8.3c Imitating Bruce Lee and John Travolta
    in *Forever Fever* (1998)   221

Acknowledgments

WITHOUT THE support of various funding bodies, this project would not have gotten off the ground. We are grateful to the Australian Research Council, which supported our work with a three-year Large Grant; and to the Chiang Ching-Kuo Foundation, which supported our research in Taiwan. Mary Farquhar's preliminary work on the project was also supported by the Griffith University Research Grant Scheme. Chris Berry received support from the University of California Berkeley Humanities Research Grant program and the Chinese Studies Center at Berkeley. We would also like to thank David Desser for inviting and persuading us to undertake the project in the first place.

The cooperation of both the Taipei and Hong Kong Film Archives was invaluable and fulsome. Their spirit of public access is an inspiration to us all. At the Taipei Archives, successive directors Edmond K. Y. Wong and Winston T. Y. Lee facilitated our access, and Teresa Huang Hui-min helped us daily and in more ways than we can detail here. At the Hong Kong Film Archive, director Angela Tong opened all doors, and Pinky Tam helped us repeatedly and with great patience. Our colleague and friend Hu Jubin both acted as our intermediary with the China Film Archives in Beijing and also helped us to compile our Chinese-language bibliography and film list.

Various colleagues and friends gave us invaluable support and feedback on earlier drafts of chapters: Vishal Ahuja, Gerémie Barmé, Yomi Braester, Louise Edwards, Kim Soyoung, Lydia Liu, Kam Louie, Ralph Litzinger, Sheldon Hsiao-Peng Lu, Fran Martin, Murray Pope, Sue Trevaskes, Valentina Vitali, Paul Willemen, and Yeh Yueh-Yu. To all of them we are extremely grateful. We know how busy they were and we are grateful for the time they took to read our drafts. A number of research assistants worked on the project at various times and in various roles, all of them important and greatly appreciated. They are Salena Chow, Darrell Dorrington, Hong Guo-

Juin, Rosemary Murray, and Maureen Todhunter. Hu Jubin both worked on the manuscript as a research assistant and offered us his generous and fulsome intellectual response and advice. Sue Jarvis compiled the index for us. To them, we offer special thanks.

Earlier versions of sections of some chapters were presented as conference papers and public presentations at the Chinese Cinema Conference at the Baptist University of Hong Kong in 2000; the 18th Law and Society Conference in Brisbane in 2000; Duke University in 2001; the Asian Studies Association Conference in Chicago in 2001; the Modern Chinese Historiography and Historical Thinking Conference at the University of Heidelberg in 2001; the New England Association for Asian Studies Conference at Williams College in 2001; Fudan University in 2002; the University of California, Santa Cruz, in 2002; Carleton College in 2002; the University of Washington, Seattle, in 2002; the Center for Chinese Studies at the University of California, Berkeley, in 2002; the Asian Screen Culture: Mobile Genres conference at the Korean National University of Arts in Seoul in 2003; the Global/Local/Exotic: Transnational Production and Auto-Ethnography conference at the University of Hawaii in 2003; the Berkeley Film Seminar in 2004; the "A Lifetime of Dedication: Colin Mackerras and China Studies" conference at Griffith University in 2004; Haverford College in 2004; the Center for Chinese Studies of the University of Michigan, Ann Arbor, in 2004; and as the 2004 Mcgeorge Cinema Lecture at the University of Melbourne. We are grateful for the invitations to speak, and for the questions and discussions in response to these presentations, all of which helped us to further develop the work.

Earlier versions of sections of some chapters have also been published elsewhere, and the responses we received helped us to improve them. An earlier version of chapter 1 appeared as "From National Cinemas to Cinema and the National: Rethinking the National in Transnational Chinese Cinemas," in *Journal of Modern Literature in Chinese* 4.2 (2001). Sections of chapter 3 appeared as "Shadow Opera: Towards a New Archaeology of the Chinese Cinema," in *PostScript* 20.2–3 (2001). A section of chapter 5 appeared in an earlier version and in Chinese as "Look Again: Using Chinese Examples to Rethink Gender in the Cinema," in *Ershiyi Shiji* (*Twenty-First Century*, Hong Kong), no. 68 (2001). An extended reading of Zhang Yimou's *Hero* in chapter 6 is to be published as a chapter in Graeme Harper and Jonathan Rayner's *The Landscapes of Film: Cinema and Its Cultural Geography* (Detroit: Wayne State University Press). An extended analysis of the discussion of Bruce Lee in chapter 8 will appear as "Stellar Transit: Bruce Lee's Body, or, Chinese Masculinity in a Transnational Frame," in *Modernity Incarnate*, edited by Larissa Heinrich and Fran Martin (Honolulu: Hawaii University Press, 2005).

We thank our editors at Columbia University Press (Jennifer Crewe and Roy Thomas) and at Hong Kong University Press (Colin Day) and their colleagues for their promptness, detailed attention, support, and patience. We also thank the editors at other presses that showed interest in this project and gave us much good advice, and the university press anonymous readers for their reports. Any remaining problems are, of course, our own responsibility. Finally, we'd like to thank each other! Coauthorship is a difficult task, but we both learned enormously from each other and stayed friends throughout this long and demanding project.

A Note on Translation and Romanization

THIS BOOK uses the *pinyin* system for romanizing Chinese characters unless common usage makes an alternative more familiar and therefore user-friendly.

Regarding film titles, there are many different ways of translating Chinese film titles into English and many different ways of romanizing Chinese characters into Latin letters. In this book, we have decided not to include any Chinese characters in the main body of the text. For film titles, we have used the English export titles of the films wherever they are known. However, because these titles often vary from the original Chinese titles, we have included a pinyin romanization of the Mandarin Chinese rendering of the original title in parentheses after the first appearance of each Chinese-language film title in the text. There is also a film list appended at the back of the book, which does include the Chinese character version of the original title.

For books, articles, and other bibliographical items, pinyin romanization of Mandarin Chinese is used in the endnotes for Chinese-language items. The bibliographies at the end of the book are divided into European and Chinese-language bibliographies. Items in the Chinese-language bibliography are ordered alphabetically, according to the pinyin romanization of the author's name. However, the full Chinese-character version of each entry is given.

Finally, for the names of internationally known places and people, we have used the version of their name in general circulation rather than the pinyin romanization, e.g., Hou Hsiao Hsien rather than Hou Xiaoxian. For all terms, pinyin romanization has been used.

China on Screen

CINEMA AND NATION

Introduction: Cinema and the National

JACKIE CHAN'S 1994 global breakthrough film *Rumble in the Bronx* is a dis-locating experience in more ways than one. This is not just because of the gravity-defying action, or because Jackie is far from his familiar Hong Kong. Set in New York but shot in Vancouver, the film shows a Rocky Mountain backdrop looming between skyscrapers where suburban flatlands should be. The film also marks a watershed in Chan's efforts to transform him-self from Hong Kong star to global superstar and his character from local cop to transnational cop. Funded by a mix of Hong Kong, Canadian, and American companies, *Rumble in the Bronx* is an eminently transnational film. In its North American release version, it cannot even be classified us-ing the currently fashionable term for films from different Chinese places, "Chinese-language film" (*huayu dianying*):[1] not only are the settings and locations far from China but all the dialogue is in English.[2] Indeed, one fan claims *Rumble in the Bronx* for the United States when he complains that, "From the very start you will realize that this film seems to be trying to set a record for worst dubbing in a supposedly 'American' film."[3]

While it might seem a stretch to imagine even the North American re-lease version of *Rumble in the Bronx* is an American film, *Rumble in the Bronx* certainly illustrates how futile it can be to try and pin some films down to a single national cinema. However, although *Rumble in the Bronx* demands to be understood as a transnational film, the *national* in the trans-national is still vital to any account of its specificity. It says something both about the importance of the American market to Chan and the aspirations of Hong Kong's would-be migrants in the run-up to China's 1997 takeover that Chan's character, Keung, visits the United States (rather than Nigeria or China, for example).

Even though Jackie Chan successfully vaulted to global stardom in the wake of *Rumble in the Bronx,* his cultural and ethnic Chineseness and his

Hong Kong identity remain—not only recognized by fans but also as significant elements that he exploits for the jokes, action, and narratives of his films. In *Rush Hour* (1998), Chan's first commercially successful Hollywood film, his cop persona is again assertively from Hong Kong, as he saves the PRC (People's Republic of China) consul's daughter in Los Angeles from Hong Kong gangsters with the help of a maverick black LAPD sidekick. As will be discussed in chapter 6, *Rush Hour* blends regional, cultural, and political Chinese nationalism. This Hollywood movie proclaims both Hong Kong Chinese and blacks as outsiders, who nevertheless save the day for the great and good: the USA, the PRC, and Hong Kong as well as the consul, the FBI, the LAPD, and even China's archaeological heritage, on display in Los Angeles after being saved from a corrupt, British colonial administrator in league with Hong Kong triads.

This book examines some of the many and complex ways the national shapes and appears in Chinese films. Our core argument is twofold. First, the national informs almost every aspect of the Chinese cinematic image and narrative repertoire. Therefore, Chinese films—whether from China, Hong Kong, Taiwan, the diaspora, or understood as transnational—cannot be understood without reference to the national, and what are now retrospectively recognized as different Chinese cinematic traditions have played a crucial role in shaping and promulgating various depictions of the national and national identity. Second, as the challenge of locating *Rumble in the Bronx* and *Rush Hour* demonstrates, the national in Chinese cinema cannot be studied adequately using the old national cinemas approach, which took the national for granted as something known. Instead, we approach the national as contested and construed in different ways. It therefore needs to be understood within an analytic approach that focuses on cinema and the national as a framework within which to consider a range of questions and issues about the national.

Why is the national so central to Chinese cinemas? Put simply, ideas about the national and the modern territorial nation-state as we know them today arrived along with the warships that forced "free trade" on China in the mid-nineteenth-century opium wars. Both the national and the modern territorial nation-state were part of a Western package called *modernity*, as was cinema, which followed hot on their heels. Like elsewhere, when Chinese grasped the enormity of the imperialist threat they realized that they would have to take from the West in order to resist the West. The nation-state was a key element to be adopted, because this modern form of collective agency was fundamental both to participation as a nation-state in the "international" order established by the imperialists and to mobilizing resistance.[4]

However, as Mitsuhiro Yoshimoto pointedly indicates, scholars are less sure about how to study cinema and the national than they used to be:

"Writing about national cinemas used to be an easy task: film critics believed all they had to do was to construct a linear historical narrative describing a development of a cinema within a particular national boundary whose unity and coherence seemed to be beyond all doubt."[5] Once, it might have been possible to produce a list of elements composing something called "traditional Chinese culture" or "Chinese national culture," or even some characteristics constituting "Chineseness." Then we could have tried to see how these things were "expressed" or "reflected" in Chinese cinema as a unified and coherent Chinese national identity with corresponding distinctly Chinese cinematic conventions. This would then constitute a "national cinema."

In this era of global capital flows, multiculturalism, increasing migration, and the World Wide Web, it is clear that the national cinemas approach with its premise of distinct and separate national cultures would be fraught anywhere. But in the Chinese case, its difficulty is particularly evident. Today, "China" accommodates a multitude of spoken languages, minority nationalities, former colonies, and religious affiliations. Until 1991, it designated a territory claimed by two state powers: the People's Republic of China with its capital in Beijing and the Republic of China currently based on Taiwan. Even when President Lee Teng-hui of the Republic of China made reforms in 1991 removing the Republic's claim to the territory governed by the mainland, it was still stated that, "the ROC government recognized the fact that two equal political entitles exist in two independent areas of one country."[6] A glance at the Chronology at the back of this book shows that China has been through numerous territorial reconfigurations over the last century-and-a-half, and has spawned a global diaspora.

With these circumstances in mind, how do we need to rethink the cinema's connection to the national and ways of studying it? This introduction attempts to answer this question. On the basis of our exploration of the issues discussed below, we argue for the abandonment of the national cinemas approach and its replacement with a larger analytic framework of cinema and the national. Instead of taking the national for granted as something known and unproblematic—as the older national cinemas model tended to—our larger analytic framework puts the problem of what the national is—how it is constructed, maintained, and challenged—at the center. Within that larger framework, the particular focus of this book is on cinematic texts and national identity. But we hope this book can serve as both an embodiment of our larger argument and a demonstration of the kind of studies that can come out of such a shift.

Although it may sound odd at first, the transnational may be a good place to start the quest to understand what it means to speak of cinema and the national as an analytic framework. As if taking a lead from Mitsuhiro

Yoshimoto's critique, Sheldon Hsiao-Peng Lu begins his introduction to *Transnational Chinese Cinemas* by characterizing the anthology as "a collective rethinking of the national/transnational interface in Chinese film history and in film studies."[7] He goes on to trace how the cinema in China has developed within a transnational context. As in most of the world, it arrived in the late nineteenth century as a foreign thing. When Chinese began making films, they were heavily conscious that the Chinese market was dominated by foreign film, and increasingly they saw the cinema as an important tool for promoting patriotic resistance to Western and Japanese domination of China. Following the establishment of the People's Republic, most foreign film was excluded and an effort was made to "sinicize" the cinema. Meanwhile, the cinemas of Taiwan and Hong Kong came to depend on diasporic Chinese audiences. Most recently, Chinese cinemas have participated in the forces of globalization through coproductions and the work of émigrés in Hollywood. With this history in mind, Lu concludes, "The study of *national* cinemas must then transform into *transnational* film studies."[8]

This is a very suggestive insight. The essays in Lu's anthology focus on the transnational dimension of transnational film studies. But to use this insight as a way into our project, we need to ask where the national is in transnational Chinese cinemas and in transnational film studies. This question can be addressed by spinning a number of questions out of Lu's comment.

What does "transnational" mean and what is at stake in placing the study of Chinese cinema and the national within a transnational framework?

The term *transnational* is usually used loosely to refer to phenomena that exceed the boundaries of any single national territory. However, there is a tension around the term, which stems from its relation to the idea of "globalization." In many uses, "transnationalism is a process of global consolidation" and transnational phenomena are understood simply as products of the globalizing process.[9] For example, while the multinational corporation is headquartered in one country and operates in many, "a truly transnational corporation ... is adrift and mobile, ready to settle anywhere and exploit any state including its own, as long as the affiliation serves its own interest."[10]

In contrast, other writers use "transnational" to oppose the rhetoric of universality and homogenization implied in the term *globalization*. For them, the "transnational" is more grounded. It suggests that phenomena exceeding the national also need to be specified in terms of the particular places and times in which they operate, the particular people they affect, and the particular ways they are constituted and maintained.[11]

The focus on China in Chinese film studies precludes assumptions about global universality (although certainly not the impact of capitalist "globalization"). However, the issue of homogeneity versus specificity remains crucial to the question of how we might understand the transnational in "transnational Chinese cinemas." One possibility is that the territorial nation-state and national cinema as sites of Chineseness are being eclipsed by a higher level of unity and coherence, namely a Chinese cultural order that is transnational. This would be the kind of culturalism that supports Western discourses ranging from Orientalism (as critiqued by Edward Said) and Samuel Huntington's "clash of civilizations" to Chinese discourses on Greater China (*Da Zhonghua*) and Tu Weiming's "Cultural China."[12]

The alternative is that the transnational is understood not as a higher order, but as a larger arena connecting differences, so that a variety of regional, national, and local specificities impact upon each other in various types of relationships ranging from synergy to contest. The emphasis in this case is not on dissolving the distinctions between different Chinese cinemas into a larger cultural unity. Instead, it would be on understanding Chinese culture as an open, multiple, contested, and dynamic formation that the cinema participates in. Key to understanding these two different trajectories for the deployment of the "transnational" is the question of what the "national" in the word *transnational* means. This leads to a second question.

What does the "national" mean?

Understandings of Chinese transnationality as a higher level of coherence above the nation-state reinstate the modern nation under a different name. Whether Chinese or Western in origin and whether praising or critical, they simply deploy culture or ethnicity rather than territorial boundaries as the primary criterion defining the nation. The distinction here is between an ethnic nation and a nation-state. Yet both forms retain the idea of the nation as a coherent unity. This coherent unity is also usually assumed in the concept and study of national cinemas. But it is precisely this understanding of the nation that has come under interrogation in English-language academia over the last twenty years or so, and the directions this critique has taken must guide efforts to transform the study of national cinemas into the study of cinema and the national.

The rethinking of the nation and the national in a general sense has produced a very large body of literature. However, three major outcomes are especially relevant to the arguments in this book. First, the nation-state is not universal and transhistorical, but a socially and historically located form of community with origins in post-Enlightenment Europe; there are other ways of conceiving of the nation or similar large communities. Second, if this form of community appears fixed, unified, and coherent, then that is an effect that is produced by the suppression of internal difference and blurred boundaries. Third, producing this effect of fixity, coherence, and unity depends upon the establishment and recitation of stories and images—the nation exists to some extent because it is narrated.

Before elaborating on these points, the implications of these outcomes must be briefly considered. For those committed to the nation, the idea that the nation is constructed can seem to be an attack on its very existence. And for those opposed to the nation, this can seem to presage its imminent demise. Yet if the metaphor of construction implies potential demolition, it also suggests that new nations can be built and existing nations renovated. In other words, how this more recent discourse on the nation gets used is not immanent to that discourse, but dependent upon social and institutional power relations.

One reason for the frequent assumption that recent thought constitutes an attack on the nation is the title that looms over this entire field: *Imagined Communities* by Benedict Anderson.[13] In a recent survey of writing on national cinemas, Michael Walsh finds that "of all the theorists of nationalism in the fields of history and political science, Anderson has been the only writer consistently appropriated by those working on issues of the national in film studies."[14] However, Anderson does not use "imagined" to mean "imaginary," but to designate those communities too large for their members to meet face-to-face and which therefore must be imagined by them to exist. He also distinguishes between the modern nation-state as one form of imagined community and others, including the dynastic empire. For example, he points out that empires are defined by central points located where the emperor resides, whereas nation-states are defined by territorial boundaries. Those living in empires are subjects with obligations, whereas those living in nation-states are citizens with rights, and so forth.[15] After Anderson's watershed intervention, the nation no longer appears universal and transhistorical but as a historically and socially located construction. Indeed, if Michael Hardt and Antonio Negri are right, our transnational era is already a new age of empire.[16]

Anderson's intervention also demands attention to distinctions all too easily collapsed in the thinking that took the nation for granted and long characterized the national cinemas approach. As well as the distinction between an ethnic or cultural nation and a territorial nation-state made above, there is also the question of the concept of a biologically distinct nation. However, although most cultural nations and nation-states retain links to ideas of race, it is difficult to assert that they are one and the same after the notorious example of the Holocaust and Nazi rule in Germany. This then raises the issue of internal divisions and blurred boundaries of nations, both ethnic and territorial. Although members of nations are (supposedly) constituted as citizens with equal rights and obligations, this individual national identity is complicated by citizens' affiliations to other local and transnational identity formations, including region, class, race, religion, gender, and sexuality, to name but a few. These issues and the questions and problems arising from them are foreclosed upon in a national cinemas approach that takes the national for granted as something fixed and known. But with the shift to a framework of cinema and the national that puts the focus on the national as a problem, they take center stage.

Why does this proliferation of different affiliations for citizens create tensions within the modern nation-state and provoke efforts at containment, when the same situation was commonly accepted in empires? In empires, agency is understood to lie with a deity, an absolute monarch, or a hierarchy of differently empowered subjects. In these circumstances, the various differences among the people in an empire are not so crucial. But the modern nation-state is understood as a collective agency composed of its citizens, whether acting through the ballot box, the dictatorship of the proletariat, or some other mechanism. In these circumstances, loyalties to other collectivities created by diverse identity formations threaten the ability of "the people" to act as an agent, and must be managed either through suppression or careful containment.

However, this is a "catch-22." As Homi Bhabha points out, quite apart from all the other tensions, producing the nation as collective agency in itself leads to a split between the people as objects and as subjects of the discourse that depicts them.[17] So, in addition to the differentiation of nations according to defining criteria such as culture, territory, and race, we also need to distinguish between nation as subject or agency and nation as object. This distinction cannot necessarily be reduced to that between the state (subject) and people (object), as neither of these entities is a stable given, nor is there always a clear line between them.

It is the need to produce and maintain citizenry as a collective national subject in the face of competing and challenging forces that leads Ann Anagnost to write that the nation is "an 'impossible unity' that must be narrated into being in both time and space," and that "the very impossibility of the nation as a unified subject means that this narrating activity is never final."[18] To understand this endless narrating activity in the case of the collective national subject, Judith Butler's work on the individual subject—"me"—may be useful. She argues that the individual subject is not a given but produced and, furthermore, that it is produced through the rhetorical structures of language. Here she notes the Althusserian idea of *interpellation*. Interpellation is the hailing of the subject, where language calls upon us to take up positions that encourage psychological identification and social expectations of who we are. An example might be when heterosexual couples repeat the marriage vows read out to them by the celebrant. Butler terms this process "performative"—doing is being. Her particular contribution to the understanding of this performative process is to ground it in history. She notes that each citation of a subject position is part of a chain that links different times and spaces. This causes it to be necessarily different from the previous citation in locally determined ways. Butler's privileged example is drag as a citation of gender that undermines the citation it repeats. Another clear example would be the way in which some members of the Chinese business and political communities cite Confucianism today. Although the rhetorical form of their citation declares continuity, there must be difference because premodern Confucianism despised commerce.

Butler's ideas on performativity and citation give us tools for analyzing the paradox of discourses that declare the national subject as fixed and transcendent yet are marked by contradiction, tension, multiple versions, changes over time, and other evidence of contingency and construction.[19] Furthermore, her insight about the impact on the citation of the different times and spaces it occurs in is particularly pertinent to colonial and post-colonial environments. When the European concept of the modern nation-state is imposed onto and/or appropriated into other environments, it is likely to be made sense of through a framework composed of other already circulating concepts of imagined community. For example, Tsung-I Dow has given an account of the impact of the Confucian environment upon Chinese elaborations of the modern nation-state.[20]

What happens to "national cinemas" in this new conceptual environment?
The rethinking of the nation discussed above has combined with changes in cinema studies to undermine the expressive model of national cinemas. It is no longer possible to assume that the nation is a fixed and known bundle of characteristics reflected directly in film. In cinema studies itself, there is growing awareness of the dependence of nationally based film industries upon export markets, international coproduction practices, and the likelihood that national audiences draw upon foreign films in the process of constructing their own national identity.[21]

In these circumstances, it becomes proper to talk about the reconfiguration of the academic discourse known as "national cinemas" as an analytic framework within which to examine cinema and the national. Just as Anderson's work grounds the nation as a particular type of imagined community within Europe, national cinemas reappear in this framework as a set of institutional, discursive, and policy projects first promoted by certain interests in Europe and usually defined against Hollywood. The framework of cinema and the national extends beyond these specific national cinema projects. It also includes the idea of a national cinema industry, which concerns film production within a particular territory and the policies that affect it but might not include participation in the production of a national culture. Other areas include the activities of a national audience within a particular territory, censorship, regulation within a particular territory, and so on. This broadening of work on national cinemas to include the cinema as an economic and social institution shapes Yingjin Zhang's important new chronological history of Chinese national cinema.[22]

Unlike Yingjin Zhang's book, many other examples of the institutional approach to national cinemas also abandon analysis of films, their dissemination of images and narratives about the national, and their role in the construction of national identity. There is no question that the challenge to the expressive model of national cinemas has drawn interest away from national imagery and identity. Some writers have even claimed that with the discrediting of national identity as something fixed and transcendent, it would be better to abandon the examination of cinema and national identity, and just speak about common cinematic tropes and patterns as "conventions" within the cinema of certain territorial nations.[23]

However, such a move would perform a sort of short circuit that forecloses consideration of what is most crucially at stake in cinematic significations of the national, namely the production of the collective identity and, on its basis, agency. Relying on the rethinking of the national subject as located and narrated into existence outlined in the previous section, this book returns to national identity in the cinema, not as a unified and coherent form that is expressed in the cinema but as multiply constructed and contested. Furthermore, just as preexisting Chinese ideas of community provide a framework through which the imported European nation is made sense of, we are also interested in how the imported discursive techniques of the cinema work with and are worked upon by existing local narrative patterns and tropes, creating cinematic traditions in which Chinese national identities are cited and recited. Each chapter considers a particular aspect of this process.

The scope of the book is wide, both socially and historically. This is necessary to capture the complexity of the national in its various Chinese configurations. Efforts to recast China as a modern nation-state coincide with the century of cinema, making it desirable to range from among the earliest surviving films to the most recent. Two intertwined themes became increasingly clear as we watched film after film. First, there are patterns that appear and reappear in new forms across Chinese-language cinemas over the last century. Martial arts movies are just one example: banned in mainland China in 1931, they remorphed in Hong Kong and Taiwan from the middle of the twentieth century to be reclaimed by the People's Republic in the 1980s with the ascendancy of Jet Li. Filmmakers and audiences are aware of this heritage. Thus, for example, bamboo forest fight scenes in both Taiwan-American director Ang Lee's *Crouching Tiger, Hidden Dragon* (2000) and mainland director Zhang Yimou's *House of Flying Daggers* (2004) pay homage to the extraordinary combat scene in the bamboo forest in King Hu's *A Touch of Zen* (1971). Second, the transformations in these patterns that cut across the cinema are linked to different ideas about the national and nationhood that have appeared in different Chinese places at different times. The range of these ideas cannot be grasped by only attending to one Chinese space and cinema, such as the People's Republic or Taiwan or Hong Kong. Therefore, we have attempted to bring films from different Chinese societies and cinemas together in each chapter.

The topics of each chapter emerged in the process of exploring both the Chinese and English-language writings on Chinese cinema, and the films themselves. The most significant and consistent intersections with the national formed the basis for the following seven chapters. In the next chapter, we look at the intersection of cinematic time and the time of the nation. Chapters 3 and 4 focus on the intersection of the national with indigenous and imported cultures to produce distinctive modes of cinema opera and melodramatic realism. Chapters 5 and 6 examine the intersection of gender and the national in the production of modern Chinese femininity and masculinity. Chapter 7 extends that discussion into the intersection of the national and ethnicity in Chinese cinema, and our final chapter returns to the transnational to examine how the national is recast in a globalizing cinematic environment. In order to understand these topics, we have explored recent work in cinema studies, Chinese studies, and other related fields. We begin each chapter with a section that explains the framework of thought that we have developed to approach the topic under consideration.

Chapter 2 examines time in the cinema. Where many have focused on cinematic time as a philosophical concept, our interest is in time and the formation of nation and community. We demonstrate that cinematic time and the national are configured in at least three major ways. Each corresponds to a different perspective on the nation-state and modernity. First, national history films operate from within the logic and vision of the modern nation-state to produce time as linear, progressive, and logical. Often, as in the example of the Opium War films examined, these narratives start from a moment that produces national consciousness in humiliation. Prompted by crises in modernity, a second group of films takes a critical look back at the projects of the modern nation-state. Our primary examples are the post–Cultural Revolution film *Yellow Earth* (1984) in the People's Republic of China and the post–martial law film *City of Sadness* (1989) in Taiwan. Finally, and possibly most radically, our third group registers a yearning for lost pasts before modernity—and maybe new futures—from within modernity itself. Films like *In the Mood for Love* (2000) engage haunted time, running wormholes in and out of modernity to ruin the linear logic of national progression and mark the persistence of nonmodern formations.

Chapters 3 and 4 turn to Chinese cinematic modes. A *mode* transcends individual films, genres, periods, and territories as the broadest category of resemblance in film practice. We argue that the Chinese cinema exhibits two main modes whose variations must be explained within contexts of different formations of the national: the operatic mode, which began with opera film as a statement of cultural nationalism, and the realist, which was intimately linked to modernity and nation-building.

Chapter 3 explores the operatic mode as the syncretic core running through Chinese cinemas. We call this mode "shadow opera." It relies on cultural spectacles that link the premodern and the modern in a Chinese cinema of attractions, and appears in a range of genres from opera film to martial arts movies over the last century. These genres are seen as explicitly Chinese, but they vary according to different—and often contested—understandings of Chineseness. The earliest opera films sinicize the foreign art form of the cinema for cultural and commercial purposes, just as the nation-state itself had to be made Chinese in the process of appropriation. Later revolutionary operas, like *The White-haired Girl* (1950) and *Azalea Mountain* (1974), appropriate and transform opera as a national cultural form in the pursuit of a proletarian nation. Shadow opera operates below, within, and beyond the idea of the nation-state. Early Taiwan films, based on a local operatic form called *gezaixi*, were reinterpreted in the 1990s as a nationalist form that projects an independent Taiwan identity. *Crouching Tiger, Hidden Dragon* borrows a mythic sense of the Chinese national to originate a new form of transnational and diasporic identity, while *Hero* (2002) borrows the same generic form to promote a vision of the territorial and expanding Chinese nation-state back in the mists of time.

In chapter 4, we argue that Chinese reformers adopted realism as the hegemonic and "official" mode of modernity in the Chinese cinema. Operatic modes were frequently proscribed as "feudal" or dismissed as crassly commercial. Realist modes were considered both contemporary and modern. However, realist modes were almost always qualified by melodramatic conventions that, in their different forms, proffered different views of the national through stories of the family and home. In pre-1949 China, films of divided families, such as *Tomboy* (1936), *Street Angel* (1937), and *Spring in a Small Town* (1948), reflect the deep anxiety about a China divided by migration, war, and politics in conservative, leftist, and politically nonaligned film. After 1949, Mao Zedong's People's Republic of China on the mainland and Chiang Kai-shek's Republic of China on Taiwan each separately "prescribed" realist modes with melodramatic happy endings for different national purposes: socialist construction and class justice on the mainland and small-scale capitalist construction in Taiwan's countryside. The final section looks at realist aesthetics in films from different Chinese New Waves, including *Father and Son* (1954; 1981) from Hong Kong and *Yellow Earth* from the People's Republic. The happy endings required by national aesthetic codes become social critique through the "unhappy ending." These films rewrite the local and the national outside received linear versions of modernity by reinventing realism and melodrama as a form of nostalgia. Nation, community, and the promises of Chinese modernity all fragment through images of the "emptied out" family home.

Not only culture but also gender is transformed in modernization. Most discussions about gender in the cinema have focused on Hollywood's various ways of communicating heterosexual desire within the modern patriarchy of North America. However, in chapter 5 we argue here that dominant images of Chinese women in the cinema can be understood better in relation to different configurations of modernity and the nation-state. To understand this, we develop a framework showing that debates about how a modern Chinese woman should act in life appear in the cinema as images showing how she should look. We examine three senses of the look—the look of the camera upon the woman, the woman's subjective look, and her appearance or how she looks before others. Ruan Lingyu, Xie Fang, Gong Li, and Maggie Cheung's star images are manifested in these different senses of the look. They respectively embody the contestation of Confucianism and values appropriated from the West in the effort to produce China as a modern nation-state in the 1930s; the political passion of the Communist heroine who represents the proletarian nation in the People's Republic; the libidinal woman who represents the desiring subject of the "marketized" post-Mao People's Republic; and the cosmopolitan woman who signifies the "world city" of Hong Kong.

In chapter 6 on masculinity and ordering the nation, we examine how men should act. We argue that Confucian legal codes that privileged masculinity in governing the nation and the family are reinvented across Chinese cinemas as a moral measure of masculinity, honor, and leadership in modern times. These codes—filiality, brotherhood, and loyalty—are ethnosymbolic myths that link contemporary struggles over masculine identity with various constructions of the colonial and the national in Hong Kong and China, respectively. Other chapters look at Taiwan cinema. We suggest that Jackie Chan's early films, such as *Drunken Master II* (1993), are about the liminal state of adolescence that mirrors the liminal status of Hong

Kong as a colony that constantly reasserts its right to semiautonomous identity; that John Woo's film on Hong Kong brotherhood amongst gangsters and cops, *The Killer* (1989), depicts a vanishing world of honor within a violent and lawless society caught between paternal systems in London and Beijing; and that Zhang Yimou's ambivalent attitudes to patriarchy and the state in his early and mid-career films are revisited as mandatory loyalty to the ruler who, as we said, promises unification of the territorial nation-state in *Hero*.

The circulation of signs of ethnicity in the cinema is examined in chapter 7. However, here we go beyond the dominant understanding of ethnicity and nationality as the drawing of a line between national self and foreign other. Instead, we demonstrate some less noticed but equally important configurations of ethnicity and nationality. First, in films like Ang Lee's *The Wedding Banquet* (1993), the line is drawn around the good foreigner to accommodate him within the Chinese family. We argue this is a modern transformation of a pattern that can be traced back to practices like the imperial tribute system. A second pattern appears in the People's Republic after 1949. Faced with the tension between the Chinese ethnic and territorial nation embodied by the minority nationalities, films tried to stabilize the situation by depicting minorities as "little brothers" to the Han Chinese "big brother." Finally, a third pattern consists of lines drawn between different Chinese groupings. We examine how these intra-Chinese distinctions appear in films made in Taiwan and Hong Kong following the influx of refugees after the establishment of the People's Republic.

Our final chapter returns to the transnational. If the national is to be thought of now as part of transnational film studies, it seems fitting to close the book by examining how the national and the transnational interact. The focus on the transnational in Chinese cinema so far has been a celebration of export success as a kind of resistance to the forced opening up of China in the opium wars. We acknowledge these successes, but ask what price has been paid for them by examining three instances: Bruce Lee's recasting of Chinese masculinity by borrowing from Hollywood, the appropriation of the blockbuster concept to counter the threat posed by Hollywood imports today, and the use of the transnational cinema market to support the revival of Singapore's film industry.

What does it mean to think about "transnational film studies" as an academic field?

Finally, Sheldon Lu's remark suggests that not only Chinese cinema but the field of film studies itself is now to be understood as transnational. Yingjin Zhang has trenchantly criticized Chinese film studies in English and its frequent complicity with orientalism.[24] Therefore, in this final section of the introduction, we must address the position of this book within that transnational field and also our position as researchers and authors.

It is noteworthy that Lu's conclusion is phrased as a general remark. He does not say that the study of *Chinese* national cinemas needs to be transformed into transnational *Chinese* film studies, but simply that the study of national cinemas needs to be transformed into transnational film studies. Although Lu himself does not explicitly make the claim, this implies that Chinese cinemas can stand as exemplary sites in the study of cinema and the national.

This is an important point. For, as Rey Chow has noted, "while [authors dealing with Western cultures] are thought to deal with intellectual or theoretical issues, [authors dealing with non-Western cultures,] even when they are dealing with intellectual or theoretical issues, are compulsorily required to characterize ... their intellectual and theoretical issues by way of a national, ethnic or cultural location. Once such a location is named, however, the work associated with it is usually considered too narrow or specialized to warrant general interest."[25]

So long as the expressive model of national cinemas reigned, privileged locations for their study were places that troubled the assumed unity and coherence of the nation the least. For the most part, these were the European nation-states and Japan. As Yeh Yueh-Yu has pointed out, while this national cinema paradigm was dominant, the difficulty of fitting Hong Kong and Taiwan cinemas into it contributed to their neglect in English-language academia and helped people to write about mainland cinema as Chinese "national cinema" in a seemingly unproblematic way.[26] The recent attention to the transnational has reversed the bias in the other direction, with the Maoist period of national isolation and socialism-in-one-country suffering from relative neglect today.

Within the framework of cinema and the national, the national appears as multiple and constructed. Therefore, places that have the most evidently complex relation to the national are likely to emerge as privileged sites of analysis now. Many people would agree that few places have a more complex relation to the national than the combination constituted by the People's Republic, Hong Kong, Taiwan, and the Chinese diaspora. Therefore, Chinese cinemas can emerge as key sites in the intellectual shift to cinema and the national, and also be part of the urgently needed attack on Eurocentrism in English-language film studies as that field also becomes transnational.

For if "English-language film studies" really exists, it certainly does not exist as a world unto itself. The rapid increase in the international circulation of scholars studying Chinese cinema in various academic disciplines over the last few years stands as evidence for the emergence of transnational film studies as a field. What are the implications of this? In this in-troduction we have argued in our discussion of the nation for an under-standing of the transnational not as homogenization but as the connection of difference, and of knowledge itself as located rather than universal. In these circumstances, we need to address our readership and our location as scholars.

First, although transnational connection may exist in film studies, lan-guage is still a divider. The main readers for this book will be speakers of English and located outside most Chinese societies. In writing the book, we have tried to take their needs into account, supplying background where needed, citing English-language materials wherever possible, and focus-ing in particular on films which are either known in the English-speaking world or available with English subtitles. However, at the same time and in order to present a fuller picture of the topics we have decided to address, we have included other materials and films wherever necessary.

Even though we have certainly tried to include reference to important films less well known in the West and the writings of Chinese scholars, there is no question that we ourselves are Western scholars. Again, Rey Chow raises an important issue:

> It is … important for us to question the sustained, conspicuous silence in the field of China studies on what it means for certain white scholars to expound so freely on the Chinese tradition, culture, language, history, women and so forth in the postcolonial age.... The theorization of Chineseness, in other words, would be incomplete without a concurrent problematization of whiteness within the broad frameworks of China and Asia studies.[27]

In making a claim for placing Chinese cinema at the center of an analysis of cinema and the national within the emergent field that Sheldon Lu has proposed as transnational film studies, we hope it is clear that we are mov-ing outside sinological orientalism. By drawing upon the work of Chinese scholars, we are not setting ourselves up as the subjects and China as the object of analysis. Rather, we are invoking an environment of transnational scholarly exchange and discussion around an analytic project that we be-lieve could and should be extended to include the cinemas of other nations, including Western nations. Of course, we do not expect the connection of differences constituted through such a transnational exchange to lead to homogenization or to invalidate our perspective from outside China. How-ever, in this era when some forces in both China and the West seem deter-mined to construct a confrontation between two separate "civilizations," we hope this contribution to the arena of transnational film studies can constitute a step, however small, in the opposite direction. As we move into a new century when global economics, politics, and war demand new ways of imagining community, we believe that Chinese cinemas, which have always been transnational and challenge conventional understandings of the national in so many ways, will take an ever more central position both in global popular culture and in scholarship around the world.

2

Time and the National

HISTORY, HISTORIOLOGY, HAUNTING

IN THE MOOD FOR LOVE (2000) is Wong Kar-wai's tale of infidelity and frustration among the Shanghai émigrés of 1960s Hong Kong. It ends at Angkor Wat in Cambodia, where Mr. Chow hides his secret by whispering it into a crevice in the ruins. He is a journalist, and the transition to Cambodia is marked by what looks like documentary footage of the visit of French president General Charles de Gaulle. We discuss *In the Mood for Love* again at the end of this chapter, and in particular the evocative image of history as a secret hidden in the ruins. But the significance of the transition to Cambodia sequence is that it highlights some ways cinema "brings the past to life." The documentary footage is a direct recording of public events, replayed in the eternal present tense of the cinematic now. If real, it is a historical document. However, even if it is only a dramatization, it can still be understood as another cinematic form of history writing—an attempt to narrate events that really did happen in the past. But what of the fictional narrative that surrounds this footage? The characters are not representations of real individuals, but much energy has gone into evoking a particular period of time through settings, costumes, music, hairstyles, and so on. If this is not history, what kind of a narration of the past is it?

Most writing on cinema opposes historical representations of real events like the documentary or mock-documentary footage in *In the Mood for Love* to fictional narratives of the past like the rest of the film. History is what happened, and analysis of historical films emphasizes questions of accuracy—is it really fact or just fiction? Our approach is different in two ways. First, we emphasize the narrative quality of all stories about the past, no matter how grounded in fact. In the next section, we do not ask about accuracy. Rather, we examine the national history genre in Chinese filmmaking as a narrative form. The shift from dynasty to modern nation-state has produced a quite different understanding of the past and movement through time, with linear progression replacing the cyclical pattern of the rise and fall of succeeding dynasties.

This linear progress often follows the logic of recovery from a wound. In China, a key trope for this relation to the past has been "speaking bitterness" (*suku*). But the drive to elaborate this logic of the wound as the singular truth of China is undercut by the tendency of different regimes to speak bitterness according to their particular political needs. To illustrate this, we examine four different cinematic versions of the Opium War story: one produced during the Japanese occupation, one made in the People's Republic in the Maoist era, a third made in Taiwan in the 1960s, and the final version made to mark the reversion of Hong Kong to Chinese rule.

Second, we do not draw a line between different historiographical modes and fiction. Instead, as the discussion of the Cambodia sequence from *In the Mood for Love* indicates, we draw a line around them. We put them under one umbrella because they are all ways of telling stories about the past and linking them to the nation. In the second section, we uncover a mutually reinforcing ideological relationship between modern academic historiography, the nation-state, and national history films like the Opium War films. We then dismantle the wall between modern historiography and fictional modes of apprehending the past to reveal alternative ways of narrating the past beyond the requirements of the nation-state. In the third section, we consider films that mix fact and fiction to build subaltern memory. These films distinguish the experiences of the ordinary folk from those of their rulers, running against the rhetoric of the nation-state by separating nation as people from nation as state. Some subaltern accounts of the past are narratives of alternative nation-state projects. But others insist on retaining the gap between the people and the state. For example, Hou Hsiao Hsien's films explore material suppressed and neglected during the martial law years in Taiwan. We examine his unique cinematic language in *City of Sadness*, which took the Venice International Film Festival's Golden Lion for Best Film in 1989, to show how it produces subaltern memory without being drawn into a nation-state model of history.

Films such as *City of Sadness* may emphasize fictionalized characters over recorded facts, and they produce an alternative vision of time within modernity as one of repeated ruination rather than progress. However, they continue to work largely within the parameters of modernity and the nation-state. In the fourth and final section, we turn to films that imagine nonmodern time as persistent within modernity, ruining it by undermining its very foundations. Haunting is the trope that opens the door to nonmodern time because, by breaking down the barrier between past and present, haunting confounds linear progress and the definition of the modern itself. Ghost films constitute an obvious site for the examination of haunted time. But by figuring haunting as supernatural and therefore unreal, they often contain the challenge that nonmodern time poses and maintain the distinction between the modern and the premodern. Films like Wong Kar-wai's *In the Mood for Love* are haunted without being ghost films. Furthermore, they are doubly haunted, from both the past and the future. To account for this particular temporal condition, we look to Hong Kong's status as a former colony and now a Special Administrative Region, but never a nation-state. Excluded from the linear progress of the modern temporal order, it is caught between anxiety about the future and melancholic dwelling on what might have been. But, paradoxically, hanging on to that mixture of anxiety and melancholy (just as Mr. Chow hangs on to his secret by hiding it safely in Angkor Wat) inscribes the power of memory as resistance to modern progress.

The Logic of the Wound: The Opium War and National History

Regardless of their political affiliations, most Chinese historians and politicians, including Mao Zedong, date modern Chinese history from the mid-nineteenth-century opium wars.[1] Therefore, it is not surprising that there are at least four extant versions of historical epics on the topic, each with a very different provenance. The earliest surviving feature on the topic, *Eternal Fame,* was made in Shanghai in 1943 during the Japanese occupation and as a Japanese-initiated project. The second version was the best known internationally until recently. Directed in 1959 by Zheng Junli and Cen Fan, *Lin Zexu and the Opium War* was the approved People's Republic version of the narrative. It was superseded there in 1997, when Xie Jin made *The Opium War* to mark the handover of Hong Kong. In between came a Taiwanese-language film also called *The Opium War,* directed by Li Quanxi in Taiwan in 1963 and the third version of the film.

It is commonly said that the appeal of such historical epics lies in their ability to "bring history to life." As Robert Rosenstone puts it, "our presence in a past created by words never seems as immediate as our presence in a past created on the screen."[2] In the case of historical events that no one actually remembers, the mimetic qualities of film are certainly a powerful tool for constructing cultural memory. However, it is the function of all dramatic narratives to "bring things to life." Opera, oral storytelling, and historical novels also bring history to life. What does differentiate film from live performances or relatively low-cost media like literature is its susceptibility to control. High costs, the use of complex machinery that only well-trained people can operate, the scale of production, and the special conditions required to exhibit a film all contribute to this. Furthermore, once finished, a film is not subject to the variations of live performance.

This combination of "bringing things to life" and easy control makes film particularly appealing to governments, as they try to disseminate historical narratives that mobilize the population by promoting shared identity through shared history. Andrew Plaks notes that the act of communication (which he calls "transmission" or *chuan/zhuan*) is the main function of historiography and fiction in the Chinese dynastic era.[3] This function is still linguistically embedded in the modern Chinese term *xuanchuan,* used interchangeably to mean both "propaganda" and "publicity," and in terms for a range of narrative forms that blur historiography and fiction.[4] In these circumstances, we should not be surprised to read that during a period of high state control like the seventeen years between the foundation of the People's Republic in 1949 and the outbreak of the Cultural Revolution in 1966, at least 87 percent of historical films focused on revolutionary history.[5]

In the move to appropriate and participate in modernity, the use of history as part of the effort to transform China into a nation-state was a matter of survival. For, as Prasenjit Duara points out, "it was only territorial nations with historical self-consciousness which, in the world of competitive capitalist imperialism in the late nineteenth and early twentieth centuries, claimed rights in the international system of sovereign states. Such nation-states claimed the freedom, even right, to destroy non-nations such as tribal polities and empires."[6] As a prerevolutionary event, the Opium War has been deemed a suitable topic for all Chinese filmmakers engaged in this project of producing national history, and not only those from the People's Republic.

But from a contemporary perspective, the Opium War is a low point in Chinese history—a time when the survival of China, whether as dynasty or as future nation-state, seemed in peril. Why have Chinese filmmakers returned to this dark episode again and again, and in such different ways? To begin to answer this question, we need to look at historiography as a narrative mode and grasp some of the structural differences between dynastic and national historiography, as well as some of the internal contradictions in the latter mode.

The modern historiographical mode that supports the nation-state is different from the preceding dynastic mode of historiography. Maureen Robertson argues that an assumption of continuous ongoing flux underlies most Chinese historiography prior to nineteenth-century appropriations from the West. Change was acknowledged but it was not understood as directed, whereas modern Western models imagine stages and a causal logic of development.[7] Q. Edward Wang points out that dynastic historiography was dominated by the "annals and biography" mode of writing, where information was piled up as a general repository of knowledge to be drawn upon and inform current decision-making at the court.[8] On the other hand, models of modern national history are linear and teleological, integrating the past into a coherent cause-and-effect–based narrative of progress, and leaving out material that does not fit (or seem "relevant").[9] While the cyclical concept of time and change is understood as a force of nature or the cosmos, the idea of history as progressive requires agency or a motor of that history. This agent is the nation as a people (*Volk* in German or *minzu* in Chinese), and the modern nation-state is the vehicle through which the people realize their agency.

However, although the availability of mass media (including newspapers, radio, and cinema) helped disseminate this new form widely, narrating the modern nation still has to confront internal contradictions. In an essay entitled "Narrating the Nation," Homi Bhabha cites Benedict Anderson. "If nation states are widely considered to be 'new' and 'historical,'" Bhabha points out, "the nations to which they give expression always loom out of an immemorial past and ... glide into a limitless future."[10] This inherent contradiction begs the question of where to start a linear national narrative, and how to stabilize the contradiction.

Rey Chow's comment that Chineseness is often imagined according to "the logic of the wound" provides an answer. It also draws attention to the parallels between the individual subject and the collective national subject as constructions of modernity. The idea of the "the wound" is derived from psychoanalytic theory.[11] In what follows, we examine the "logic of the wound" and its operation in modern Chinese historiography. Then we show how each film on the national wound of the Opium War—when Western powers invaded China—works to produce the Chinese nation as a unified collective subject. But we also show how the differences between them expose the inherent contradictions and instability of all such projects.

The "logic of the wound" implies a disruption of a supposedly eternal preexisting nation, and it also demands diagnosis and remedy. This is a version of the basic formula for narrative: a movement from disturbance of stasis toward its restoration. In the Chinese context, the idea and practice of "speaking bitterness" (*suku*) also works according to the logic of the wound. Ann Anagnost has examined this as a powerful trope in Chinese revolutionary discourse that transforms local stories of personal suffering into collective narratives of blood and tears based on class identity. In the class-based nation of the People's Republic, it simultaneously constructs nation and subject, blending individual stories into collective memory that claims—or counterclaims—to be "truth written in blood."[12] In accordance with the progressive logic of modern history, "remembering [past] bitterness" (*yiku*) is balanced by "appreciating [present] sweetness" (*sitian*) in the ritual formula *yiku sitian*.

National histories are usually also a kind of "speaking bitterness" that conforms to the logic of the wound. Examples range from the anchoring of the modern Zionist narrative in the biblical flight from Egypt to 1066 and the foundational status of the Battle of Hastings in English history. The Opium War is one of the most widely cited wounds in Chinese historiography. The British forced the Qing empire to accept opium products. This event is not written up as one distant border skirmish amongst others being handled by the dynasty. Instead it is narrated as a humiliation felt by a national "people" whose sense of shared identity it simultaneously produces. For example, the opening title of the 1943 film version of the Opium War, *Eternal Fame,* concludes with the comment, "This was the biggest national disgrace in Chinese history." And many years later, a critic writing about the most recent film version of the story also notes, "The Opium War was an incident that brought terrible disgrace to the entire Chinese nation and was a watershed in Chinese history, because this war inaugurated China's long century of humiliation."[13] Made to mark the end of British rule in Hong Kong, Xie Jin's *Opium War* implicitly fulfills the logic of both the wound and the remedy (as marked by its closing title, which notes the return in 1997 of Hong Kong).

Because the phrase "logic of the wound" draws parallels between the individual psychoanalytic subject and the collective national subject, it also points to another contradiction. In psychoanalytic theory, the wound refers to castration anxiety. This notoriously controversial phenomenon is allegedly stimulated in the infant male by misrecognition of the female genitalia as a wound.[14] However, beyond the gender politics and the dubious metaphors, castration anxiety is provoked by anything that reminds the subject of her or his ontological vulnerability. In Freudian psychoanalysis, the penis threatened by castration anxiety is only a material signifier of the phallus, which symbolizes the autonomy, freedom, and power of the modern individual subject. But ironically, in the Freudian narrative of the production of the individual subject this phallus is only attained by the boy child upon submission to a larger symbolic order beyond himself, or, as it is referred to in Lacan's elaborations of Freud, the Law of the Father. However, this submission must be hidden or denied to produce the effect of mastery characteristic of the modern subject.[15] These ideas can be translated to the political collectivities under discussion here, where a similar paradox is found. From this perspective, Qing dynasty China and other non-nation-state polities facing the European imperialist order had to transform themselves into nation-states to attain agency within the new order imposed from the West, because that order recognized only nation-states. But although this transformation leads to a proclamation of sovereignty as a nation-state, it simultaneously constitutes a submission to that new order.

In Freudian psychoanalysis the little boy responds in two ways to the threat of castration: he either pretends there is no threat or he destroys that which symbolizes the threat.[16] Anderson's reference to attempts to project national identity back into an "immemorial past" and forward into a "limitless future" can certainly be understood as an example of the former method of allaying anxiety. The national narrative that speaks bitterness and follows the logic of the wound and remedy corresponds to the latter method by producing a threat to be destroyed. As Prasenjit Duara puts it, "national history secures for the contested and contingent nation the false unity of a self-same, national subject evolving through time."[17]

The Opium War Films: Four Versions

The Opium War is commonly understood as a national "wound" marking the beginning of "modern history" (*xiandaishi*) in China. The basic narrative is fairly consistent. British and other foreign merchants are importing opium into China through the southern port of Guangzhou (also known as Canton). Previous imperial bans have been subverted, because merchants have corrupted local officials. Addiction is creating growing social problems. In 1838 the emperor sends Lin Zexu south to enforce the edicts against the import of opium. Lin is able to discover which officials are corrupt and enforces his authority. He then blockades the merchants, forcing them to give up their opium, which he destroys in public. However, the British respond with war, not only forcing open the empire but also leading to the surrender of Hong Kong.

Beyond this basic narrative, however, different state formations require different tellings of historical events at different times, according to their current needs. One way in which Duara's "contested and contingent" quality of the modern Chinese nation can be seen is by looking at the different Chinese films that have been made about the Opium War. All four film narratives follow the logic of the national wound. However, there are significant variations.

The earliest example, *Eternal Fame*, is particularly intriguing. It might seem odd that an occupying regime would endorse what is conventionally understood as a Chinese nationalist story. However, as Cheng Jihua and his colleagues—authors of the official People's Republic account of pre-1949 film history—are quick to note, the Japanese government was actively promoting a pan-Asianist rhetoric of common resistance to Western imperialism, and so the behavior of the English in the Opium War made it appropriate.[18] The film features racist representations of the English, played by Chinese actors wearing exaggerated nose prostheses and curly wigs. Indeed, as David Desser points out in his analysis of a 1942 Japanese film about the Opium War shot entirely on location in China but with an all-Japanese cast, there was a tradition of anti-Western films in Japan that *Eternal Fame* fits into.[19]

Existing scholarship on *Eternal Fame* concentrates on how to judge the Chinese filmmakers: are they traitors, or did they act to minimize the propaganda appeal of the film.[20] However, what distinguishes *Eternal Fame* from the other Chinese Opium War films is a subplot about a young girl who sells candies in the British-run opium den. She reveals that opium addiction ruined her family and sings of its dangers, leading to an altercation with the merchants. A Chinese addict and former friend of Lin Zexu intervenes. They are both thrown out, but then she helps him to overcome his addiction. They fall in love and marry. This is more than a romantic digression. The girl is played by Li Xianglan. Known as Ri Koran in Japan, Li was the main star of the Japanese-owned Man'ei film company of Japanese-occupied Manchuria. In her Man'ei films, Li usually played young Chinese girls rescued by fine Japanese officers who she then falls in love with. Here, the gender roles are reversed, with Li signifying Japanese affiliation and saving the Chinese man. This is ironic; at the end of the war it became

---

ETERNAL FAME (WANSHI LIUFANG)

DIRECTED BY BU WANCANG, ZHU SHILIN, MAXU WEIBANG, AND YANG XIAOZHONG

China United Film Company, China Film Company, and Manchukuo Film Company, 1943

SYNOPSIS

Jingxian falls in love with the young Lin Zexu. But Lin falls out with her father and leaves. The county commander recognizes Lin's talent and takes him in, allowing him to continue his studies and become an official. The grateful Lin marries the commander's daughter. Because Jingxian's younger brother becomes addicted to opium, she experiments and develops a cure, which Lin uses to save his addicted mother-in-law. But Lin's childhood friend Pan Danian is hopelessly addicted. One day, the girl hawker Feng sings a song in the opium den, warning against addiction. Pan flees with her and she helps him kick the habit. Pan reports the English opium traders' plans to Lin Zexu, who has been sent to Canton. Lin consequently seizes and burns the opium. This sets off the Opium War and leads to Lin's dismissal. At this moment, Jingxian comes to the area. Seeing the marauding English soldiers, she and the locals resist them, and she is killed. Lin is reappointed. On his journey south, he visits her grave, which has the epitaph, "Eternal Fame."

known that although she had been promoted as a genuine Chinese star eager to help Sino-Japanese relations, Li was actually ethnically Japanese.[21]

Another minor subplot in *Eternal Fame* features the resistance to the British of ordinary villagers. This helps to communicate that the wound of the opium wars was not inflicted on a dynasty so much as on a national people. This element is emphasized more strongly in the 1959 People's Republic film, *Lin Zexu and the Opium War*. In accordance with a class analysis of Chinese history, the majority of the Chinese ruling class is shown as corrupt and devoid of any patriotic sense. Where other films make Commissioner Lin a lone hero, in this film he shares the limelight with the *laobaixing*, the ordinary people, who have an instinct for what is right. Lin learns from the people on his arrival in Guangzhou, when a local fisherwoman pilots his boat past the British merchant quarters and recounts their evil behavior. In this way, Lin's journey mimics the Communist "going down among the people" and learning from them as a way for intellectuals to combat their bad class background.

When one merchant tries to escape disguised as a Chinese after Lin has laid siege to their quarters, the same fisherwoman pursues and catches the fleeing foreigner, to the accompaniment of rousing music. She towers above him. The camera looks down at him from her point of view as he cowers in a dark corner and claims the privilege of being a foreigner. Cut to a shot looking up at her from his point of view as she replies, "I know you are a foreigner," and smacks him across the face. The camera cuts again to look down at him as he desperately tries claiming, "I am Chinese." Another reverse shot, and she smacks him again. In a film with a contemporary setting, this could easily be a scene between a peasant and a landlord, but here class struggle is combined with nationalism and anti-imperialism.

The distinctive element of Li Quanxi's 1963 Taiwan film, *The Opium War*, is not to be found in the plot. The film also narrates a modern and national Chinese consciousness by showing the suffering and struggles

---

LIN ZEXU AND THE OPIUM WAR (LIN ZEXU)

DIRECTOR, ZHENG JUNLI

Haiyan Film Studio, 1959

SYNOPSIS

The emperor sends Commissioner Lin Zexu to Canton to combat the drug trade. In disguise, Lin goes down among the masses to find out what is really going on. When he blockades the foreign opium traders, one tries to escape but is apprehended by the local fishing folk. When Lin seizes and destroys the opium, the British send warships. The emperor gives in to their demands and Lin is removed from his post, but the local people continue to resist the British.

FIGURE 2.1a *Lin Zexu* (1959): "I am a foreigner!"

FIGURE 2.1b "I know you are a foreigner!"

FIGURE 2.1c "I am Chinese ... "

FIGURE 2.1d The fisherwoman smacks the English merchant.

of ordinary and patriotic Chinese—the people—in the face of imperialism and corrupt feudal dynastic officials. Such a narrative fit with the worldview of the ruling nationalist and republican KMT Party (Kuomintang Chinese Nationalist Party). However, unlike the other films, this version is not in Mandarin. It is in the Taiwanese variant of the Minnanhua language of Fujian Province, whence most long-standing inhabitants of the island trace their origins. The Chiang Kai-shek KMT regime was trying to emphasize Taiwan's cultural unity with the rest of China, despite fifty years of Japanese colonial occupation, and the Opium War was a wound inflicted before Taiwan was ceded to Japan by the Qing dynasty. The public use of Taiwanese was usually discouraged in favor of the decreed national language, Mandarin. However, its use here indicates the film was aimed specifically at the formerly colonized islanders, who had not been exposed to Chinese national historiography before.

Finally, what differences follow from the production of Xie Jin's *The Opium War* to celebrate the handover of Hong Kong in 1997? The People's Republic is now eager to promote links with previously despised overseas Chinese plutocrats to fuel its burgeoning economy. One result is a widening gap between rich and poor. The overtones of class struggle and learning

---

THE OPIUM WAR (YAPIAN ZHANZHENG)

DIRECTOR, LI QUANXI

Tailian Film Company, 1963

SYNOPSIS

The emperor has banned opium but his own officials are corrupt, making it hard for Commissioner Lin Zexu to enforce the ban. Opium den proprietor Williams molests a blind singer's sister and shoots her when she resists. An addict is so destitute he sells his own son. His wife commits suicide, but Lin arrives, returns the son, gives him money to bury his wife, and tells him to turn over a new leaf. Lin discovers the foreigners' and corrupt officials' island opium depot, seizes the opium, and accuses the officials of being "foreigners' running dogs." Lin burns the opium and executes the traitors. The recovered addict is among the spectators. But the blind singer has to be rescued by her sister's boyfriend, who says this is a new era and any invasion will be resisted. Lin notes the invaders will return and everyone must protect the country.

FIGURE 2.2 Caught red-handed in Li Quanxi's *The Opium War* (1963)

(COURTESY CHINESE TAIPEI FILM ARCHIVE)

from the common people so prominent in *Lin Zexu and the Opium War* are entirely absent. Instead, the film resonates with debates around free trade, rights, and sovereignty, which were current during production. At the end of one scene, Lin Zexu announces his demand that the British give up the opium trade. Much as the Chinese government emphasizes the principle of noninterference in the internal affairs of other countries and respect for each country's laws, Lin notes that the British should respect the laws of the Qing empire within its boundaries and quit the opium trade. The film promptly cuts to a meeting of the merchants insisting that free trade will not be constrained.

The film displays perfidious Albion and its hypocritical use of high-sounding principles to justify warfare. However, it also features secondary characters from the West who have a sense of justice and morality more in tune with the values of the film, including a priest. This also resonates with the contemporary values of the period in which the film was made, because the Chinese government was eager to juggle its criticisms of the West with a continuing desire to engage the West and do business. As Rebecca Karl asks in her extended comparison of *Lin Zexu and the Opium War* with Xie Jin's *The Opium War*, "is it not ironic that markets are celebrated ... for was it not the 'success' of the opium market itself that kicked off the whole 'humiliating' chapter of modern Chinese history?"[22]

In conclusion, each of these cinematic accounts of the Opium War follows a different logic. *Eternal Fame* produces it as part of a common trauma or series of traumas experienced by the "yellow race" at the hands of the "white race," and therefore as grounds for supporting the Japanese East Asian Co-Prosperity Sphere. *Lin Zexu and the Opium War* places it as a national rather than race trauma, but also shows the ordinary working people of China as the only class that has the correct response. Li Quanxi's Taiwanese *The Opium War* downplays class dynamics but emphasizes common Chineseness across intra-Chinese differences and historical separations. Finally, Xie Jin's *The Opium War* also downplays class dynamics in favor of echoes with current issues in the conduct of international trade.

Despite these differences across the four films that demonstrate the instability and contingency of such accounts, each individual film deploys similar techniques to suppress awareness of this contingency. Each one pursues a linear and logical account that leaves no room for contradiction or information that does not fit. Each one addresses the Opium War as a wound that can be redressed. Each one also encourages identification between the people and a nation-state as a combination of collective subjectiv-

---

THE OPIUM WAR (YAPIAN ZHANZHENG)

DIRECTOR, XIE JIN

Emei Film Studio and Xie Jin Hengtong Film and Television Company, 1997

SYNOPSIS

The emperor despatches Lin Zexu to end the opium trade. The British opium merchant Danton thinks Lin can be bribed. He seeks out the girl singer and opium addict, Rong'er, in an opium den. Lin arrives and tests his officials' loyalty, then blockades the British merchants in Guangzhou, demanding they hand over their opium and abide by Chinese laws. The merchants resist, demanding free trade. British Navy Captain Elliot arrives and tells the merchants he will guarantee the value of their goods, but that they should hand them over so they can leave Guangzhou. This guarantee, however, means the opium can be seen as British government property, stoking the fires of war in England. The British attack China successfully, causing the emperor to dismiss Lin. Rong'er dies in an attempt to assassinate Elliot. Hong Kong is ceded to Britain, and Lin is exiled to Xinjiang because of his failure.

ity and agency that might pursue redress, using the individual protagonist as a vehicle for this identification.[23] Finally, each one uses the techniques of classical realist filmmaking to draw attention away from their status as discourse and make them appear transparent and real.[24] However, our prior discussion of dynastic historiography has noted that this modern mode is not the only form of historiography. Indeed, as we discuss below, historiography is not the only mode of apprehending the past.

Counter-Memory and Subalternity: *City of Sadness* as Historiology

Hou Hsiao Hsien's *City of Sadness* tells the story of ordinary people swept up in the turmoil of modern history driven by nation-states. But unlike some versions of *The Opium War,* where the villagers of Sanyuanli are heroic representatives of the national people and protagonists making that history, for the most part in *City of Sadness* ordinary people are on the receiving end of history. Furthermore, the structure of the film is very different from the transparent and linear form preferred in the various Opium War films. Instead, events are narrated through diary entries and letters, scenes pop up on screen only to be made sense of retrospectively, and major public events occur offscreen. Clearly, this is a different mode of apprehending the past. To understand what is at stake here, we need to investigate the seemingly natural form of historical films like the Opium War films—a form whose taken-for-granted quality makes a film like *City of Sadness* seem strange and difficult to many audiences. We will show a hidden link between the form of apprehending the past that we now call history and the promotion of the nation-state. This implies that different forms, such as that found in *City of Sadness,* may have a different and critical relation to modernity, progress, and the nation-state.

To begin this investigation, we detour to the island of Ibatan in what is today the nation-state of the Philippines, then to the People's Republic of China film *Yellow Earth,* and then back to *City of Sadness.*

> Written language gave us a way to capture our history and compare ourselves to people everywhere. Now that we have a past, I find that I think only of the future. I always feel a clock ticking and rushing by. But Joaquin, he lives always in the present. He hears no clock. Once, that's the way we all were.

Frank Simon's poignant statement about events on Ibatan since the arrival of missionaries in 1977 reveals that the nineteenth century may not be over yet, never mind the twentieth. It divides thinking about the past in a manner typical of the Euro-American modernity the missionaries brought

---

CITY OF SADNESS (BEIQING CHENGSHI)

DIRECTOR, HOU HSIAO HSIEN

Central Motion Picture Corporation, 1989

Written by Chu T'ien-wen and Wu Nien-jen

SYNOPSIS

In the mountain town of Chiufen in northern Taiwan, a son is born to the eldest son of the Lin family, Wen-heung, as the Japanese empire falls. The second and third sons, Wen-sun and Wen-leung, had been drafted into the Japanese army and are missing. The fourth son, Wen-ching, is a deaf-mute photographer. His friend Hinoe's sister Hinomi comes to work as a nurse in Chiufen. Hinomi and Hinoe's Japanese friends are repatriated, and Hinoe meets with his intellectual socialist friends to discuss what is happening to Taiwan. Wen-leung returns shell-shocked. When he recovers, he gets involved with Shanghainese gangsters, who later denounce the Lin brothers as collaborators with the Japanese. Wen-leung is arrested, tortured, and returns insane. Wen-ching and Hinomi become close. On the eve of the February 28 Incident, Hinoe and Wen-ching go to Taipei. The wounded from the incident come to the Chiufen hospital. Wen-ching returns after narrowly avoiding a beating. Hinomi's parents send Hinoe into hiding. Wen-ching is temporarily arrested, narrowly avoiding execution. He visits Hinoe in the mountains, where he and the other radicals are hiding. Wen-heung is killed in a fight with gangsters. Soon after his funeral, Wen-ching and Hinomi marry. She gives birth to a son, but hears soon after that Hinoe and his friends have been killed by the military. Wen-ching is arrested again.

---

with them. On one side lies writing and "history"—a modern way of thinking about the past, measured by the clock, and felt as a headlong rush along a line of progress from past to future. On the other side, the article explains, lies oral memory and endless cycles of day and night illuminated by a body of stories about the past—"legends." This division is ideological: it comes from the modern world's outlook that legitimates history as part of civilization and dismisses other ways of approaching the past as nothing, absence, and lack. The statement is poignant not only in its nostalgic sigh for a time when things were simple. Frank Simon is not European but a member of the younger generation on Ibatan, where Joaquin is an elder. So his sigh may also be for the precolonial as well as the premodern.[25]

What Frank Simon's statement does not reveal is modern history's connection to the nation-state and the cinema, both also products of the long nineteenth century. Yet modern history was invented as a way of promoting the nation-state in both the West and China, where it was part of the local appropriation of modernity. The cinema has been one of the primary vehicles for the promotion of national history and the nation-state. Furthermore, the division between valorized and disparaged ways of apprehending the past also plays out in film and film scholarship. History films are defined as representations of true events, whereas genres such as the costume drama and the ghost film are dismissed as mere fictions of the past. Scholars interrogate the truthfulness of history films but do not even consider that fiction films might also convey a truth about the past.[26]

Vivian Sobchak argues that by now it is "common knowledge" that "historiography is about arranging and telling stories, not about delivering objective truth."[27] However, she may be overoptimistic, as the long-running schism between professional historians and cultural theorists is persistent. The former tend to emphasize objective facts in their discipline, whereas the latter treat history as a genre of storytelling. Ann Curthoys and John Docker trace a series of key critiques of objective history delivered by FIGUREs such as Roland Barthes, Claude Lévi-Strauss, and Hayden White, but also point out that historians tend to see work on the discursive nature of their activity as attempts to reduce the "truth" of history to the "fiction" of literature.[28] Furthermore, what is less often pointed out is that this betrays an anxiety about the ideological links between the origins of modern historiography itself and those of the modern nation-state.

Distinguishing historiography as the production of scientific knowledge and fiction as a flight of fantasy is relatively recent. Until the late eighteenth century, historiography was seen as literature in Europe. Plaks notes the same was true in early China, but historiography was so dominant there that "it is fiction that becomes the subset and historiography the central model of narration."[29] In both places, modern professional historiography is created by rejecting the literary and redefining historiography as a science, with an emphasis on objectivity and knowledge verification.[30] To insist on the common discursive status of historiographical and fictional apprehensions of the past is to question the foundations of the modern discipline and its privileged status as the only legitimate mode of apprehending the past.

Moreover, as Q. Edward Wang points out in his study of modern historiography in China, this scientific history is simultaneously national history. The link, according to Nicholas Dirks, is "irrevocable."[31] The doyen of scientific history, Leopold von Ranke, was motivated by his drive to write national histories.[32] The claim to scientific objectivity was useful in the contemporary European struggle between the competing state forms of monarchy and nation. Modern historians used science to project the nation as a people and culture—an ethnos—back in time, simultaneously territorializing history in the name of the modern nation-state and undercutting the authority of monarchical bloodlines as a principle for the formation of territorial states. To have understood both monarchy and the nation-state as equally human inventions—and the nation-state as a much more recent one—would have weakened the argument for the sole legitimacy of the nation-state. Modern historiography's self-proclaimed scientific status supports its narrative practice, while at the same time disavowing its very status as narrative.[33]

The various Opium War films discussed in the previous section are prime cinematic examples of modern historiography that supports nation-states. To examine alternatives to this model impels consideration of fiction films. For example, whereas official history builds the past as the deeds of famous men—and sometimes women—these counterhistories aim to convey the experiences of the nameless ordinary people whose lives are not recorded in preserved documents, like the family in *City of Sadness*. Only fiction enables the imagination of this subaltern experience. Such fictionalized subalterns do appear in nation-state historiography—for example, the girl singer in the opium den in *Eternal Fame* and the Taiwan version of *The Opium War*, or the brave fisherwoman who briefs Lin Zexu and seizes the fleeing foreigner in *Lin Zexu and the Opium War*. But they tend to be secondary characters in films whose main emphasis remains on documented real individuals.

Nation-state historiography also prefers its truth in the singular. Therefore, it presents history transparently as objective fact. In contrast, subaltern accounts of the past use tropes such as memory to emphasize the multiplicity of individual experiences and resist the complete fusing of individuals into the collective body of the nation-state. Furthermore, their rhetoric may promote empathy and reflection on the part of the spectator more than wholesale identification with the protagonist as embodiment of the nation-state. We suggest Johannes Fabian's term "historiology" for these subaltern counterhistories. In his discussion of popular culture in Africa, Fabian uses "historiology" for popular and inventive tales about the ordinary people's experience of colonization and modernity as something visited upon them. He distinguishes this from the official historiography of both the colonizer and the postcolonial nation-state.[34]

Turning first to the People's Republic, we see that the disasters of the Cultural Revolution (1966–1976) were not only associated with political violence but also with central control and the command economy. Starting in the mid-1980s, winding down of central control led to the appearance of films produced more autonomously by film studios on their own initiative.[35] They still had to pass censorship, but many are historiologies. Probably the most famous are "Fifth Generation" films such as *One and Eight* (1983), *Yellow Earth* (1984), *Horse Thief* (1985), and *Red Sorghum* (1987), which are set in the prerevolutionary era but use it as a metaphor to speak of the postrevolutionary era. We discuss most of these films in detail in later chapters, but here we briefly consider their features as historiology.

The use of the prerevolutionary past as a metaphor for the postrevolutionary era and the Cultural Revolution in particular is an audacious stroke that challenges official Chinese historiography and dismantles the FIG-URE of modernity as progress. State-sponsored revolutionary history is a conventional national historiography of the wound. The prerevolutionary world is the bad "old society" where the wound is located. The revolution is the therapy that promises a cure. The result is a revolutionary progress toward Communist perfection. Revolutionary history films encourage full identification with this trajectory, gazing toward the future with bright eyes just as the lead character in *Song of Youth* (1959) gazes over and past the camera at the end of that film (discussed in more detail in chapter 5). Within this logic, to use the prerevolutionary era as a metaphor for the postrevo-lutionary era is scandalous. It demolishes history as progress, replacing it with a criticism of the revolution for failing to produce the promised prog-ress. It locates the metaphorical wound in the postrevolutionary present as much as in the prerevolutionary past, producing modernity as repeated ca-tastrophe rather than recovery from disaster. It is retrospective rather than prospective. The promotion of detached critique rather than identification has led scholars to identify these films as examples of critical modernism.[36] Yomi Braester calls such literary and filmic texts that register the ruination inherent in what is proclaimed as progress "witnesses against history."[37]

For example, in *Yellow Earth* (which we discuss in more detail in chapter 4), the metaphor linking the prerevolutionary to the postrevolutionary may be recognized through the parallel between the protagonist's and the film-makers' experiences.[38] Most members of the "Fifth Generation" were ur-banites sent down to the countryside during the Cultural Revolution. They had been led to expect—by films and other media—flourishing sites of so-cialist modernization. But what they actually discovered shocked them.[39] The main character in *Yellow Earth* is a Communist soldier sent down to the countryside in 1939. His mission is also to engage in a cultural revolution of sorts, collecting folk songs so their lyrics can be rewritten for propaganda purposes. He discovers immense poverty and an older generation of peas-ants that, instead of being the vanguard of the revolution, shows no interest in it.

The final shots of *Song of Youth* show the heroine joining the Commu-nist Party in a shot–reverse-shot rendering of her dewy-eyed gaze at the red flag. After this, we cut to her leading a demonstration, gazing over and past the camera. In contrast, the closing shots of *Yellow Earth* show the soldier returning to the countryside to find the farmers praying to the Dragon King. As he appears over the horizon, a reverse shot shows all the farmers run-ning in the opposite direction. The final shot cuts back to the horizon, but the soldier is gone. The visual language of *Song of Youth* conforms to the logic of history as progress by showing the people coming together and moving forward to overcome their enemies. The visual language of *Yellow*

FIGURE 2.3a *Yellow Earth* (1984): The soldier returns.

FIGURE 2.3b The farmers run away.

FIGURE 2.3c The soldier is gone.

Earth communicates a critical modernist vision of history by showing the inability of the people to come together and the absence of any vision of the future.

The ending of another early Fifth Generation historical film, *One and Eight,* features a similar negative use of the gaze and the shot and reverse-shot structure. Like *Yellow Earth,* it is set in the Communist base areas during the late 1930s. Political Commissar Wang finds himself under suspicion and imprisoned with local bandits by Section Chief Xu. After Japanese attacks, Xu is injured. Wang leads him and gangster Eyebrows to join other Communist troops, demonstrating his continuing loyalty. But just as the film seems headed toward a scene of Communist union (like the ending of *Song of Youth*), Eyebrows stops. He promises to continue fighting the Japanese and not to rob the poor anymore. But he explains that he is a bandit and cannot join the Communist Party. The film presents his departure as a series of shots–reverse-shots between Wang and Xu, propped up against each other, and Eyebrows as he walks away from them. The final shot in the exchange catches Eyebrows turning back for a last look at Wang and Xu.[40]

Subaltern historiology that eludes the nation-state is also central to the Taiwan New Cinema of the 1980s and early 1990s. The most famous example may be Hou Hsiao Hsien's *City of Sadness,* which, like *Yellow Earth* and *One and Eight,* takes a critical look back at the project of building modern Chinese nation-states.[41] *City of Sadness* focuses on the "February 28 Incident," a topic politically taboo in Taiwan from its occurrence in 1947 to the lifting of martial law in 1987. Following recovery of the island in 1945 after fifty years of Japanese colonial occupation, the postwar corruption and economic dislocation that destroyed the KMT government's reputation on the mainland also swept over Taiwan. This was exacerbated by misunderstandings. As Taiwanese intellectuals point out in one scene of the film, the officials' Mandarin Chinese and the Hokkienese-derived language spoken by the islanders were mutually incomprehensible. When islanders demonstrated, the regime responded brutally, killing thousands and relentlessly pursuing all involved.[42]

This trauma has clear potential to become a wound in an alternative nation-state historiographical project to narrate the origins of modern Taiwanese national consciousness and, depending on future events, the birth of a Taiwanese nation-state. However, *City of Sadness* speaks the bitterness of the islanders' memories, but it does not articulate them according to a national logic of the wound. Although it was the only Taiwan film to make the local top ten in its year of release, some critics expressed frustration about its "failure" to produce such a Taiwanese nationalist perspective.[43]

FIGURE 2.4 Wen-ching is threatened during the February 28 Incident in *City of Sadness* (1989).
(COURTESY ERA COMMUNICATIONS)

First, the film is literally located at a distance from the nation-state, in the hill town of Chiufen near Keelung, north of Taipei. Although the main characters are deeply affected by the February 28 Incident, it is never shown on screen. Hou's film takes the position of those to whom national history happens rather than those who make themselves its agents. The film's characters do include some based on real participants in the uprising, such as the teacher who leads the rebels when they retreat to the hills. But they are secondary, and the main focus is on the fictional Lin family.

However, being on the periphery of nation-state history does not lessen its effects. Indeed, in different ways, all four Lin brothers are destroyed by it. Before the film even begins, two have been conscripted into the Japanese imperial forces, as many Taiwanese men were. One never returns. The other comes back mad. The eldest brother is a victim of the corruption unleashed on the island by the arrival of the KMT, as it is his inability to avoid dealings with Shanghai gangsters that leads to his stabbing. The fourth brother, who is in many ways the main character, survives until the end. But then we learn from a poignant letter narrated over a shot of a family photo that he has been arrested for suspected involvement in the February 28 Incident, presumably never to return.

These narrative elements of the film placing us at a distance from the February 28 Incident itself are extended by Hou's cinematic techniques. Some writers have compared his style to Japanese directors Ozu Yasujiro and Mizoguchi Kenji. Hou's measured and regular style that operates almost autonomously from the characters and plot may be reminiscent of Ozu's "parametric" narration.[44] His favoring of long shot–long take aesthetics may also recall Mizoguchi.[45] However, as Nornes and Yueh have pointed out, such similarities are superficial; Hou's films have their own linguistic system.[46]

In *City of Sadness,* the camera position is not literally that of the fourth brother and Hinomi, his fiancée. Nonetheless, as a silent onlooker, its status is similar to theirs. The fourth brother is deaf and mute, and makes his living as a photographer. For communication, he is dependent on Hinomi, who writes notes to him. Their relation to the fevered politics of the day is conveyed in a scene where Hinomi's brother and his friends come to visit, engaging in an energetic discussion of the politics of the day. The camera focuses on the animated debaters for a long time. But then, at a moment when we may have forgotten about fourth brother or his inability to hear what is being said, the camera pans slowly over to where he is sitting with Hinomi, on one side of the main group. The conversation fades away on the sound track as we watch them engage in their own conversation through an exchange of notes. Those notes appear on the screen in the manner of intertitles, becoming more and more detached from the conversation of the brother and his friends and drawing us into the intimate space of their romance. Some see this as suggesting that the couple's romance is more important than politics. But there is another way of understanding this. While the brother and his friends are not aware of the contents of the notes, and the couple is increasingly detached from the debate, we see both. In this way, the film does not construct the Taiwanese experience as a monolithic, unified, abstracted, and seemingly objective national history, but as a multiplicity of distinct experiences, sometimes shared, sometimes separate. This is the historiological mode.

By putting us in a position that is not that of any particular character, we are distanced. This perspective is also maintained in various scenes of conflict and violence between characters, usually connected to various sectarian disputes. In one notorious scene, a knife attack occurs by the side of a road amongst high grasses. The film does not follow the conventional pattern of cutting into the exchange and taking up the positions of the combatants, cutting back and forth between them. Instead, the camera moves back to the distance of an extreme long shot, making the violence a small disturbance in a verdant setting.

Writing about *The Puppetmaster* (1993), the second film in the historical trilogy that starts with *City of Sadness*, Nick Browne notes that narrative episodes are punctuated by shots of empty landscape. In *City of Sadness*, narrative episodes are broken up with shots over the rolling hills, taken from the

FIGURE 2.5 Wen-ching and Hinomi communicate by writing notes in *City of Sadness* (1989).
(COURTESY ERA COMMUNICATIONS)

heights where Chiufen is situated. Browne argues such shots echo the aesthetics of Chinese landscape painting, with its use of empty spaces and its decentering of human affairs within the larger cosmos.[47] Elsewhere, Esther Yau has made similar observations about the aesthetics of *Yellow Earth*.[48] However, Rey Chow has resisted any interpretation of this as a "preservation" of "tradition" through the cinema, insisting that the very cinematic rendering of such aesthetics and cosmology must be understood as specifically modern and syncretic.[49] Maybe the counterhistory of *City of Sadness* does not separate the state and the people who suffer at its hands in order to retreat from the modern to nature or "tradition." Perhaps it inscribes both human and natural spaces that resist being subsumed into the nation-state modernity to point to different relations of modernity and the nation-state and to the possibility of different futures.

Postcolonial Postmodernity: Haunted Time in the Films of Wong Kar-wai

The historiological cinema discussed in the last section disrupts the objective and transparent perspective of national history films to produce multiple perspectives, suggesting that the modern imagination of time and nation may not be universal after all. Historiological films do not take progress for granted, nor do they assume modernity is positive. They do not assume that the people form a unified collectivity or that they are necessarily aligned with the state to form a homogeneous nation-state. However, the historiological mode does not necessarily imagine nonmodern time. For this we turn to the idea of haunting and, in particular, Wong Kar-wai's mysterious *In the Mood for Love*. Set in the 1960s, but resonating with possible meanings for the present, *In the Mood for Love* is often described by viewers and reviewers alike as a "haunting" film. Although it is not literally a ghost film, it shares many of the properties of the ghost film that interest us here. There can be a special relationship between the time of the ghost film and the time of the postcolonial condition. The return of the dead suggests trauma, violence, and the unfinished business produced out of colonial violence and cultural disjuncture. Furthermore, the disruption of linear progress by the ghost's appearance from the past into the present can also constitute a refusal of the sequential logic of modern "progress" and an assertion of coevalness. Transferring these ideas to Wong Kar-wai's haunting films, we argue that they characterize the postcolonial postmodernity of Hong Kong—once a colony, now a Special Administrative Region, but never a nation-state—as a temporal condition incommensurable with and peculiarly resistant to modernity's progress.

Various scholars have used ghostliness to consider modern time and its subset, colonial time. Drawing on Walter Benjamin's insight that modernity is characterized by the shock of the new and a radical disjuncture with the past, Françoise Proust has argued that history appears in modernity as specters that haunt it.[50] Benedict Anderson's *The Spectre of Comparisons* uses the ghost metaphor to argue that colonial modernity is always haunted by the culture of the colonized.[51] These insights have also been extended to the ghost film itself. Citing Korea's forced and rapid modernization under colonialism and neocolonialism, Kim Soyoung notes that, "The fantastic mode of cinema in its powerful conjuration of the obstinate past also provides a rich platform on which to think about non-synchronous synchronicity and the working of the premodern in modernity."[52] Bliss Cua Lim gives extended consideration to these questions in her article on "spectral times," and analyzes two films that use the wronged female ghost to signify a past that returns to demand justice.[53] One is the 1987 Hong Kong film *Rouge*, which others have also analyzed in relation to Hong Kong's postcolonial culture.[54]

These insights into the cinematic imagination of nonmodern time and the postcolonial condition can be extended in at least two directions. First, as we will briefly discuss below, ghosts can signify the explosion of linear time as a blast not only from the past but also from the future. This occurs in both Taiwan and Hong Kong films. Second, time structures that explode modern progress are not confined to the ghost film. We use the phrase "haunted time" to designate this wider realm of films where past, present, and future collapse into each other. And we demonstrate this point through Wong Kar-wai's films. Contrary to those who argue that Wong's films are stranded in the present, we examine *In the Mood for Love* as a haunted film. The copresence of past and future in the cinematic now of *In the Mood for Love* destabilizes the very idea of a clearly demarcated present, which is the cornerstone of modern linear time. In this way, it signals the cultural persistence of Hong Kong's distinct and non-national status even after 1997 as one that resists incorporation into the linear progress of the nation-state.

Specters that haunt from the future can be found in both Hong Kong and Taiwan films. In Taiwan director Chang Tso-chi's films, the ghost is an anticipated and longed-for FIGURE rather than a repressed threat. However, at first sight, Chang's films do not seem like ghost films. As Feii Lu points out, among the younger generation of Taiwan directors Chang's work inherits the commitment to a realist depiction of everyday life that characterized the Taiwan New Cinema. Having worked as assistant director to Hou Hsiao Hsien on *City of Sadness* and on other Taiwan New Cinema films, he maintains the practices of realist cinema. He never uses the conventional signifiers of a move into the supernatural realm such as dissolves, superimpositions, or special effects. However, at the end of his most recent films, characters who died earlier in the film suddenly appear again, apparently alive. In *Darkness and Light* (1999), using conventional realist style, the protagonist's point-of-view shot suddenly shows her father—who has died in hospital—and her boyfriend—who was stabbed—returning from the hospital to her home.[55]

Chang develops this pattern further in *The Best of Times* (2002). At the end of a gritty working-class narrative about two teenage friends and their involvement with gangsters, one is stabbed to death in retribution for an accidental killing. On the run, his friend comes to the scene of his death and finds him apparently alive and waiting. They run off again, only to be stranded on a bridge with their attackers approaching from both ends. The two friends jump into the water, reminding the audience of an earlier scene in which a retarded boy claimed to have seen two young men who looked just like them jumping into the water. The film ends with the two protagonists swimming in the water like the fish in the aquarium that have fascinated them throughout the film. In Chang's films, the present is not haunted by the past, but by the better future the characters have been cheated out of. Ghosts are not threatening FIGUREs that must be eliminated, but FIGUREs of wish fulfillment.

Furthermore, the persistence with realism even when the film moves toward the supernatural may signal a more radical disturbance of modern time than the conventional special effects representation of the supernatural in the ghost film genre itself. The use of a single style for both a conventional modern milieu of secular and linear time and a coeval world where the dead and the living coexist pulls the carpet out from under the conventional distinctions between modern and nonmodern time and between realism and the fantastic. In retrospect, we may remember all the scenes in *The Best of Times* before the return from the dead, and notice the frequency of scenes featuring small neighborhood shrines. This is at once a realistic representation of everyday life in modern Taiwan and an everyday postcolonial practice that defies the modern attempt to distinguish the so-called feudal, primitive, and superstitious from the modern, scientific, and secular by consigning the former to the past.

Simultaneous haunting from the past and the future is also a feature of Hong Kong cinema. In the case of *Rouge,* the nostalgia for a disappeared past is made more poignant by the audience's knowledge that Hong Kong itself was earmarked to disappear into the People's Republic in 1997. This cultural condition of anticipation, where the present becomes an almost-already-past, has been widely commented on. Ackbar Abbas has encapsulated this with his term, the *deja disparu.* As he notes, writing before 1997, "Almost every film made since the mid-eighties … seems constrained to make some mandatory reference to 1997."[56] Abbas's numerous examples demonstrate that this double haunting, where the past and the future both break down the barriers separating them from the present and operate as metaphors for each other, is by no means confined to the ghost film.

Two questions arise. First, does the passing of 1997 mean that Hong Kong's temporal condition is still characterized by double haunting? And second, how can cinema produce haunted time without the FIGURE of the ghost? We answer both of these questions by analyzing Wong Kar-wai's *In the Mood for Love*. Wong Kar-wai is widely considered the cinematic poet of the 1984 to 1997 period between the Joint Declaration when Hong Kong's fate was announced and the change of government itself. We disagree with interpretations of Wong's postmodern films as devoid of any relation to the past—a charge leveled against postmodern culture in Europe and North America. As Tony Rayns insists, Wong "is never a postmodernist brico-leur."[57] Instead, Wong's films produce Hong Kong's simultaneously post-modern and postcolonial condition as a historically and socially specific one where present, past, and future are constantly collapsing into each other.

In the Mood for Love is Wong's long-awaited first film after 1997. Be-fore 1997, Hong Kong was a colony, not a nation-state in its own right. According to the rhetoric of the People's Republic of China, after 1997 it "returned" and was integrated into the Chinese nation-state. However, we argue here that *In the Mood for Love* also narrates the post-1997 mood through a nostalgic allegory haunted by both past and future. In this way, it produces Hong Kong's post-1997 temporal condition as one that continues to resist incorporation into the linear time of the nation-state.

Three tropes are crucial in the production of this double haunting with-out ghosts. Bliss Cua Lim identifies two of them at work in the ghost film: nostalgia and allegory. Like the ghost itself, both explode the sequential time of progress. As Lim puts it, "The selfsame distance that allows nostalgia to appropriate the affective value of an object for another time is that very distance that enables allegorical objects to be seized, rescued, and invested with new meanings."[58] But of course, films can use allegory and nostalgia without using ghosts, and Wong's films do. A third trope also blurs the boundaries of time and place to produce a haunted effect in Wong's films. This is doubling, where there is an echo between one element and another, confusing the lines between ostensibly different places and times.

It is not surprising that all three tropes play with time: whatever their differences, everyone agrees that Wong Kar-wai is, as Tony Rayns puts it, a "poet of time."[59] In addition to formal tropes, time is emphasized in the narratives of his films. For example, characters set deadlines for themselves, and the "use-by" dates on cans of pineapples in *Chungking Express* play an important role in the narrative. Time also peppers the mise-en-scène, for

---

IN THE MOOD FOR LOVE (HUA YANG NIAN HUA)

DIRECTOR, WONG KAR-WAI

Block 2 Pictures, Jet Tone Production Company, and Paradis Films, 2000

Written by Wong Kar-wai

SYNOPSIS

Hong Kong, 1962, and new inhabitants who fled mainland China after the Communist takeover in 1949 live in crowded tenements. Newspaper editor Chow Mo-wan and his wife move into a building full of Shanghai migrants at the same time as secretary Su Li-zhen and her husband. Chow's wife and Su's husband travel on business, and the two neighbors become friends. Gradually, they realize their spouses are having an affair. Despite many shared interests and frequent opportunities to emulate their errant partners, they resolve not to descend to their level. New opportunities lead Li-zhen to emigrate from Hong Kong. On a return visit, she discovers that Mo-wan has also left Hong Kong. On a trip to Cambodia, he whispers his secret love into a crevice at Angkor Wat.

---

example in the numerous clocks of all kinds that appear everywhere. Finally, it appears in the visual devices cinematographer Christopher Doyle has deployed for Wong's films, such as slow-motion sequences, freeze frames, and "step-printing" or "smudge-motion"—ripples in the smooth linear progress of the cinematic now.[60]

Opinions vary on whether to interpret Wong Kar-wai's time obsession allegorically as saying something about Hong Kong. David Bordwell notes, "This Romantic and romantic cinema, however concerned with the city in history, is centrally about being young and in love."[61] He relates Wong's time obsession to missed dates, the agonies of waiting for phone calls, and fleeting flirtation. "To treat these lovelorn films as abstract allegories of Hong Kong's historical situation," he concludes, "risks losing sight of Wong Kar-wai's naked appeal to our feelings about young romance, its characteristic dilemmas, moods, and moves."[62] Powerful though this argument is, the opposite is also true. To abstract these films so resonant with Hong Kong's condition from their origins risks losing sight of their local meaning.

However, most commentators do not hesitate to read Wong's films in relation to Hong Kong itself. The ticking clocks, the use-by dates, and the deadlines all resonate with 1997 and its associated anxieties, making these films participants in the production of Abbas's *deja disparu*.[63] However, whether these allegorical inferences add up to a message is more contested. In his discussion of *Happy Together*, Jeremy Tambling is critical of those who want to understand allegorical structures as parables with direct and single meanings. Instead, he draws on Benjamin to contrast the symbol and the allegory. He argues that the meaning of the symbol is constrained because it is directly related to the thing it symbolizes. In contrast, in allegory, there is no direct relation between the allegorical text and what it alludes to. *Happy Together* takes place entirely outside Hong Kong, in Argentina and Taiwan: there is no direct reason to read Hong Kong through Buenos Aires. In these circumstances, Tambling concludes with Benjamin that in allegory, "there is not a single buried narrative to be retrieved, only fragments and interrupted moments."[64] This is what we mean when we talk of "resonances."

In the Mood for Love is set entirely in the 1960s: there is no necessary relationship between it and present-day Hong Kong. Yet it resonates with the mood and concerns of post-1997 Hong Kong. This appears in something as obvious as the hotel room Mr. Chow rents when he wants to find a space to write his martial arts comic books. The number of the room, 2046, is the same as that of the year when Hong Kong's new status as a "Special Administrative Region" will end, followed by fuller integration into the People's Republic. In this way, the anxiety about 1997 is replaced with a new "use-by" date, and the continued presence of clocks and concerns about time in *In the Mood for Love* resonates with 2046 rather than 1997.

Furthermore, the entire film is a story not exactly about a lost love but, more precisely, about an obsession with what might have been. This extends not only to Mr. Chow and Mrs. Su's speculations about the details of their spouses' affair but also to the affair that they themselves might be having if only they had not decided not to be "like them."[65] Furthermore, this "what might have been" combines allegorical potential with nostalgia and the desire for different futures. Extracts from the original novella appear as intertitles narrated in the past tense. Just as the narrative reveals that Mr. Chow and Mrs. Su cannot forget each other long after they have lost contact, it seems this obsession with "what might have been" has been taken over by the narrator and continues in the present. The entire film is stuffed with fondly remembered iconography from the Hong Kong culture of the sixties, ranging from pop standards sung by Nat King Cole to Maggie Cheung's vibrant cheongsam fabrics. Is this nostalgic "what might have been" resonant with the difficulty some Hong Kongers are having reconciling themselves to the present and their continuing thoughts about what might have been?

Finally, the "what might have been" in *In the Mood for Love* is reinforced by the third trope of time that Wong Kar-wai deploys consistently—doubling. This doubling occurs in the mostly commonly understood manner of character doubles, who often play out what David Bordwell calls "interwoven" and "spliced" plots.[66] For example, in *Chungking Express* there are two cops, 223 and 663, and in *Ashes of Time* there is the double-character of Murong East and Murong West. Although we stick to one plot in *In the Mood for Love,* the film is not exceptional, because there are the two couples. The couple we never see has an affair, the other doesn't. But when Mr. Chow and Mrs. Su rehearse the details of their spouses' affair, the film often refrains from revealing that they are only acting until late in the scene. This leads the audience to think for a moment that they have succumbed, further blurring the moral line they try to uphold.

However, in *In the Mood for Love,* what we call "doubling" here has a wider significance. As both Stephen Teo and Audrey Yue have discussed in detail, the title of the original novella from which it is adapted refers to a *tête-bêche,* or stamp with a double-headed image.[67] If the progress of modern history looks forward and the critical stance of historiology looks back, the *tête-bêche* is an image that refuses the idea of a singular, unified body of people (the nation) moving in any particular direction, and instead insists on multiple and simultaneous possibilities. If this is understood as a vision of Hong Kong's modernity in relation to the order of the nation-state, it provides a third cinematic vision of time under modernity. The narrative structures of Wong's films manifest this radical alternative.

The *tête-bêche* leads both Teo and Yue to emphasize the idea of intersection in the film. And indeed, in the early stages of their acquaintance, when Mr. Chow and Mrs. Su pass each other on the stairs and the film slips into slow motion, the idea of two intersecting trajectories through time catching on each other and generating ripples in time is powerfully conveyed. But these intersections can also be uncanny and haunting in other ways. For example, long after they have gone their separate ways, both Mr. Chow and Mrs. Su return to the neighboring apartments where they rented rooms. The film gives us a close-up of Mrs. Su's face as she looks out at what was Mr. Chow's room. Her eyes fill with tears and her lips tremble slightly, while her former landlady Mrs. Pan prattles on unaware. Later, when Mr. Chow looks out at what was Mrs. Su's room and hears that a woman—Mrs. Su?—and her son live there, we are privy to his smile. Together, the scenes communicate the nostalgic pull of the "what might have been," drawing past possibilities into the present, doubling a present absence with a past presence and imagining a possible future. By using these techniques from his earlier films made during the pre-1997 period in his first post-1997 film, Wong makes Hong Kong's new SAR status similar to its previous status as a colony with a use-by date, and makes its culture unassimilated into that of the People's Republic. What should we make of this particular and persistent status of Hong Kong?

In addition to understanding Wong's films before *In the Mood for Love* as allegories for 1997, other writers relate the manipulation of time in Wong's films to the temporal condition known as postmodernity in Hong Kong.

This is implicit in Janice Tong's essay on *Chungking Express*. Tong sees the film as cinematic realization of Gilles Deleuze's time-image. Deleuze relates the emergence of the time-image to the post–World War II situation. This suggests a correlation to Jean-Françoise Lyotard's ideas on postmodernity as characterized by loss of faith in modern progress. Ewa Mazierska and Laura Rascaroli explicitly relate the "compression of time and space," "loss of longterm memory," and "end of history and obsolescence of time" in Wong's films to Fredric Jameson's, Lyotard's, and David Harvey's characterizations of postmodernity.[68]

However, Tong takes issue with Mazierska and Rascaroli's argument that the characters in Wong's films are "trapped in the present," as the title of their article puts it. "Resnais' protagonists are overburdened by their often traumatic recollections and their memory is a creative force, shaping their present lives," they argue, "while for Wong Kar-Wai's heroes … the past and memory matter very little. Instead, they live in the present."[69] They support these contentions with an Orientalist "life is cheap" characterization of Hong Kong as a "throw away" society, and argue that in Wong's films characters live lightly with little need for enduring relationships. For them, nostalgia in Wong's films lacks any genuine connection to the past and is a mere consumer object. In contrast, Tong's final section is entitled "This is Not of the Present." She argues that an inability to be fully in the present because of anxiety about the future and obsession with the past is precisely what characterizes Wong's films. In *Chungking Express,* she points out that Cop 223 is always focused on the future, such as the use-by dates on cans of pineapples. In contrast, the Faye Wong character is drawn back to the sixties, when her signature tune "California Dreaming" was written.[70]

In the Mood for Love is set entirely in the 1960s and filled with icons of the era as experienced in Hong Kong, but is narrated from the present. Its evident obsession with the past and the future seems to further undermine Mazierska and Rascaroli's argument and extend Tong's argument. It may be counterproductive to try and decide whether to assign *In the Mood for Love* to the past, present, or future. Every scene in a film is experienced in the present tense. But in *In the Mood for Love,* nostalgia and allegory burrow wormholes from the past and the future into the cinematic now. A supernatural FIGURE like a ghost gestures to the clear line between the modern and the premodern at the same time that it challenges it. But haunting without ghosts does not recognize that foundational distinction at all. Double haunting from the past and the future scrambles the entire linear time scheme of modernity.

Tong's argument implies that Wong's films are part of the time-image associated with the postmodern condition, but that they do not match the model of postmodernity described in Europe and America. The double haunting trope in Wong Kar-wai's films may help to grasp the distinctive quality of Hong Kong's postmodernity. Hong Kong may be rich and brimming with high technology. But first as a colony and now as an SAR, Hong Kong is postcolonial but not a nation-state. In these circumstances, it is not so easy to indulge the nation-state fantasy of the people of Hong Kong as a collective sovereign agent on a journey of linear progress.

In *In the Mood for Love,* most of the characters are on a journey. They have come from China to Hong Kong. And then, in what Audrey Yue calls a "re-turn," they move out again into the wider world. But they travel as lone individuals and without clear destinations, once again producing the multi-headed and multidirectional image of the *tête-bêche*. Mr. Chow goes to Singapore, Cambodia, and then back to Hong Kong. Mrs. Su's landlady, Mrs. Pan, migrates to the United States, offering to rent her apartment to Mrs. Su, who finds a way to visit Mr. Chow's apartment while he is in Singapore but does not make the effort to meet him again. Mr. Chow himself returns to Hong Kong and visits his old apartment. His landlords, the Koos, have also moved on. And of course, Mr. Chow and Mrs. Su's spouses head to Japan to pursue their affair on "business trips." As they all move toward their various futures, the absence of any apparent end-point to the journey generates anxiety and memories, producing a postcolonial postmodernity that confounds the very distinctions of premodern, modern, and postmodern that ground these time schemes in Europe and North America. Furthermore, their journeys are largely responses to the actions and anticipated actions of nation-states, from which they are fleeing and to which they hope to migrate. Like many of the sojourners who move through Hong Kong itself, Hong Kong's cinema and the films of Wong Kar-wai in particular haunt and trouble the time schemes of national modernity.

When Mr. Chow hides his secret in a hole in the wall of Angkor Wat, is he trying to give it up or is he putting it somewhere safe, like a treasure that must be protected for future use? And does the choice of a ruin like Angkor Wat also suggest the persistence of that which has supposedly disappeared, itself ruining the time schemes of modernity as progress and repositioning what is supposedly past as already present? To investigate these themes further, we turn now to the relation of cinematic styles and modes to nation in Chinese cinema. Where most critics have related modernity to realism, in the next chapter we write an alternative history of style and mode in Chinese cinema that emphasizes the persistence and transformation of a premodern form—Chinese opera—as a key marker of Chinese cinematic modernity.

3

Operatic Modes

OPERA FILM, MARTIAL ARTS, AND CULTURAL NATIONALISM

CROUCHING TIGER, HIDDEN DRAGON (2000) is a blockbuster that defies generic labels. According to the director, Ang Lee, it belongs to the Hong Kong martial arts genre. But Lee also calls the film a Daoist *Sense and Sensibility* that tries to recapture his favorite operatic romance as a boy in Taiwan. It blends Chinese and Western melodrama, psychological realism, and martial arts.[1] At the end of this chapter we return to *Crouching Tiger* in more detail, commenting on the particular rhythm of many Chinese films. We argue that this rhythm rests in part on an operatic aesthetic, which forms a distinctive mode of the Chinese cinema.[2] But we first trace the lineage of this mode back to the earliest films across Chinese-language cinemas: opera film.

Opera film is one of the most neglected genres in academic writing on the Chinese cinema. This neglect is predicated on assumptions that we argue here are false. First, it is still widely assumed that cinema is inherently mimetic or realistic, and that therefore becoming cinematic entails a progression away from stylized or expressionist art forms to the allegedly realist language of film.[3] Second, it is assumed that opera films are largely recordings of opera, manifesting a problematic interaction between cinema and opera. From this perspective, opera film appears as a historic anachronism. It was long considered a feudal remnant unsuitable for the new national culture of a modern Chinese nation. Yet, following new Chinese and Western scholarship on early cinema, we argue for an alternative understanding of opera film that places it at the center of a Chinese "cinema of attractions." We call this nonmimetic mode of Chinese cinema "shadow opera." It includes all the genres and subgenres of the Chinese cinema spun out of opera conventions, including opera film itself as well as martial arts, costume film spectaculars, and the long tradition of opera within film. Shadow opera is not anachronistic but the living core of a distinctive Chinese cinema. It is the site where opera and film interact to produce forms at once culturally familiar, hybrid, and locally distinct. This provides the basis for a new archaeology of Chinese cinemas based not on Chinese appropriations of Western-style realism but on the dynamic extension of local popular cultural forms. In this sense, the mode is culturally nationalist. It represents an ongoing sinicization of cinema, which came into China as a foreign import.

A Chinese cinema of attractions continues as a major cinematic mode. The crux of this cinema, even when radically transformed in the People's Republic, is a cultural identity that is read through China's changing tradition of the popular and performing arts, especially but not only opera and its transposition into film. Geremie Barmé, for example, sees opera and popular fiction as the constant influence on all twentieth-century Chinese cinema, with opera as "the backbone not only of film itself but also of the viewing habits of the public."[4] Lu Hongshi claims that the merger of opera and film produced a distinctive and dynamic cinema in China that has enriched the world.[5]

This mode hails viewers first and foremost as Chinese people seeing a Chinese spectacle. Its core genre, opera film, is an example of commercialized entertainment where film transformed opera into a "national infatuation," according to Sek Kei, disseminating major works beyond their former regional and linguistic boundaries. He traces its origins to operatic displays of Han ethnic identity during the Mongol Yuan dynasty when opera first flourished. Changes in the genre may therefore signal changed perceptions of national identity during times of crisis.[6] The twentieth-century transformation of opera into film was part of the early KMT Republican nation-building project in China, which included transforming local forms, such as Beijing opera, into national cultural forms. Hence, opera film is a form of cultural nationalism that may be transformed by state directive into political nationalism.[7] It is also appropriated into martial arts and revolutionary movies. The different forms within different settings relate to different modern Chinese formations of the national, as we saw in the context of time in chapter 2. However, viewers are not necessarily addressed as homogeneously Chinese in this cinema. They may be a particular teahouse clientele (China's first films), members of regional language-cultures (Taiwanese *gezaixi* or Cantonese operas and *kung fu* martial arts), a social class such as workers, peasants, and soldiers (revolutionary operas), or a global audience (such as Bruce Lee and Jackie Chan movies from Hong Kong, *Crouching Tiger, Hidden Dragon,* and *Hero*). Until the revolutionary model, the perceived problem with this cinema earlier last century was its feudal content and regional diversity, the flip side of the grand narrative of an imagined modern nation. Traditional arts including shadow opera were considered popular but feudal; early reformist arts were modern but lacked "a common language with the Chinese working people," according to China's first Marxist literary theorist, Qu Qiubai.[8] Qu—and later Mao Zedong—advocated that popular art forms become the common language for revolutionary mobilization. The popular was to be popularized and made revolutionary in pursuit of a socialist nation state. In practice, opera constituted a common Chinese language for conservative, entrepreneurial, revolutionary, regional, and transnational filmmakers alike. So it was variously criticized, censored, celebrated, and reformed last century, all in the name of the abstract citizen-spectator. When flesh-and-blood spectators could choose, they flocked to this cinema that surfaced, again and again, across the Chinese world.

Opera film and martial arts movies in colonial Hong Kong (see chapters 6 and 8)—which produced more of these films than either China or Taiwan—have been the subject of excellent studies.[9] Our emphasis on shadow opera in China and Taiwan supplements this work, recasting it under the rubric of a cinema of attractions. In this chapter, the first section sets up the theory of shadow opera through the concept of *shadowplay*. The second section on early opera films deals with the issue of making cinema, a foreign import, Chinese by turning to films of opera. The third section deals with the production of a class-based nation—a People's Republic that privileges the masses—through revolutionary opera film. The final section explores two instances of shadow opera that operate under and above the level of the nation-state, respectively. First, we examine the wave of local Taiwanese opera films made in the island's own *gezaixi* opera form. Made in the 1950s, they then consolidated local identity. But today they are remembered as the cultural heritage of a potentially independent nation-state. Second, we look at the Chinese martial arts blockbuster. This global product circulates Chinese cultural identities for consumption by Chinese and non-Chinese alike. Ang Lee's *Crouching Tiger, Hidden Dragon* takes advantage of the genre's global reach to produce a Greater Chinese diasporic cultural identity marked by diversity, difference, and absence of affiliation to a state power. Zhang Yimou's *Hero* (2002) demonstrates that the need for a global audience does not preclude reproducing territorial nation-state nationalism in this new genre.

Shadow Opera: A Chinese Cinema of Attractions

Until the 1980s in the West, early cinema was seen as "immature babblings" within a linear approach to film history.[10] The view was that primitive cinema matured into classical cinema, exemplified worldwide by Hollywood. Scholars—such as Thomas Elsaesser, Robert Allen, Noël Burch, André Gaudreault, Tom Gunning, and Miriam Hansen—have since transformed our view of early cinema, claiming it represents an alternative, not primitive, approach to filmmaking. Thomas Elsaesser calls this "a new archaeology of the art."[11]

Within this new archaeology, Tom Gunning's work on early American cinema is one of many areas that have been extended to other cinemas, including Chinese. Gunning rejects the realist prejudice that disparages early cinema as theatrical, and therefore somehow not really cinematic at all. He recasts it as "a cinema of attractions," which aggressively addresses the spectator akin to vaudeville. Gunning states:

> To summarize, the cinema of attractions directly solicits spectator attention, inciting visual curiosity, and supplying pleasure through an exciting spectacle—a unique event, whether fictional or documentary, that is of interest in itself. The attraction to be displayed may also be of a cinematic nature, such as the early close-ups.... Theatrical display dominates over narrative absorption.[12]

Film-vaudeville coexhibition determined that viewers first saw early film as spectacle. This mode was supposedly then displaced by classical (Hollywood) cinema's narrative mode, which absorbs spectators into the story as they sit isolated in dark theaters. Early Chinese cinema was clearly a cinema of attractions, screened in public spaces (teahouses, markets, parks, and theaters) used for a variety of traditional performances such as acrobatics, opera, peep shows, and the many performing arts known as *quyi*. Such similarities between early Western and Chinese cinemas are not surprising given that Western, especially American, films long dominated the Chinese market in the first half of the twentieth century. Our point is that early cinema fitted neatly into the exhibition context of China's indigenous aesthetic of attractions, including the strong tradition of curiosity that rapidly exploited any technological innovation as novel entertainment.

Tom Gunning's cinema of attractions fits with recent Chinese archaeological studies of their own cinema. Post-Mao historians in China have been delving into film archives and rethinking early Chinese cinema outside the mandatory Marxist-Leninist framework of former years. One strand is dominated by an evolutionary approach. Li Suyuan and Hu Jubin claim, for example, that early film progressed through a number of stages: "from the making of traditional opera films to the making of documentaries and short fiction films and finally to the completion of a number of feature films."[13] Maturity arrived with the making of realist feature films from the late 1920s in Shanghai. As in the West, the rich archival studies have also led to alternative approaches to early Chinese cinema, often by the same scholars. Zhong Dafeng and Chen Xihe, for example, claim a distinctive Chinese film theory called "shadowplay" (*yingxi*).[14] "Shadowplay," the earliest term for film, combines *ying* (shadow or film) and *xi* (play or drama or opera). Thus, many scholars claim that early "film *is* drama": *yingxizhe, xi ye.*[15] Over the next sixty years, theater was so enmeshed with film that leading critics in the post-Mao period exhorted Chinese filmmakers "to throw away the walking stick of drama."[16] As in the West, theatricality has been viewed pejoratively. But what sort of theater? *Xi* and its synonym, *ju,* more commonly mean "opera" or "performance" to ordinary Chinese rather than the Western-style realistic theater familiar to urban elites. Hence, one valid translation of *yingxi* is "shadow opera."

However, the earliest reading of *xi* is as "play" or "show." Like Gunning, Li Suyuan looks at text-spectator relations and finds that the *xi* in *yingxi* initially related to viewer perceptions of film as vaudeville or variety show. As in the West, shadowplay was a novel performance "far removed from [traditional or modern] drama."[17] At the end of the nineteenth century, according to Li, *xi* was a common linguistic ending in the Shanghai region where the term was first used. Thus, *xi* denotes variety shows, such as *baxi* for acrobatics, *xifa* for magic shows, and *maxi* for circuses. *Yingxi* specifically refers to China's ancient lantern shadowplay (*dengyingxi*) that used a lantern to throw shadows of puppets against a screen. The fuller terms for film were "electric shadowplay" (*dianguang yingxi*), "western shadowplay" (*xiyang yingxi*), or "moving shadowplay" (*huodong yingxi*), the modifiers differentiating the film show from traditional shadowplay technology. Indeed, as Li argues, the first Chinese film appreciation, published in 1897, emphasizes *yingxi* as marvelous spectacles, rather than onscreen drama. The illusory and elusive nature of American shadowplay was said to condense the world and clearly conjure up "the secrets of the universe," making life seem as "dreams and bubbles."[18] Film technology was itself part of the attraction. Later in the 1920s, when Chinese were making their own films, film was perceived by some—not all—filmmakers as primarily drama but even then not necessarily as the realistic Western-style "civilized plays" that Zhong Dafeng calls the stepmother of many early Chinese films.[19] According to Li, early film theory was richly diverse. So, too, was early Chinese cinema.

In fact, China's first films were opera films (*xiqupian*). Classic operas were selected or adapted for the screen. Thus, the display of well-known operas onscreen was a crucial attraction of early Chinese cinema. If civilized plays are cinema's stepmother, then opera is the mother in terms of first film productions, whether on the mainland (1905) or in Hong Kong (1909).[20] Opera films were also the first productions in major regional-language films in Cantonese (1933) and Taiwanese (1954).[21] There is no doubt that opera film was popular, familiar, and obviously Chinese, comprising a substantial slice of the films produced in the embryonic period (1905–1921). With opera excerpts as the exception, early feature films were essentially fragments, slapsticks, folktales, short features, and magical illusions as in the West. Of these genres, Luo Yijun argues that opera films represent the earliest merger of Western cinema and Chinese aesthetics and are still favorites, especially in the villages. He claims this genre (along with animation) is the most successful in Chinese film. But, he writes, the aesthetics of West and East clash and they are always "incomplete."[22] However, as a cinema of attractions, opera films are not incomplete works but a style of cinema where "narrative coherence is supplied in the act of reception rather than inherent in the film itself."[23] And if, like Ang Lee, we see the martial arts genre also as a site that blends West and East, then shadow opera has gone global as Jackie Chan's body-on-the-line, John Woo's ballets of blood, and Ang Lee's action-poetry. The stylized choreography of violence displays operatic origins and gives genres like martial arts and gangster movies their distinctive rhythm.[24]

Unlike the West, China's cinema of attractions did not decline with the rise of classical realist cinema in the golden age of the late 1920s and the 1930s. Opera film was a staple, even though there were successive crazes for more exciting hybrid genres. Opera film was also a pioneer. In 1931, opera scenes, songs, and music delighted audiences of China's first sound film, *Sing-Song Girl Red Peony*, directed by a founding father of Chinese film, Zhang Shichuan.[25] China's first color film in 1948 was a full opera (*Remorse at Death*), starring China's foremost opera and film actor, Mei

FIGURE 3.1 The lovers Xue Pinggui and Wang Baochuan in *Love Eterne* (1963).

(COURTESY CHINESE TAIPEI FILM ARCHIVE)

Lanfang, as the main attraction.[26] In the 1950s and 1960s, after World War II and the founding of the People's Republic, opera film again became very popular with mainland, Hong Kong, and Taiwanese audiences, so it is not surprising that the first PRC–Hong Kong coproductions in the 1950s were opera films.[27] Indeed, opera film is more than a genre; it is the core genre of a vital cinema of spectacle-attractions.

A few famous examples demonstrate this cinema's resilience, diverse forms, and complex intertextuality. Across China—whether mainland, Hong Kong, Taiwan, or the diaspora—various film versions of the operatic melodrama *Liang Shanbo and Zhu Yingtai* began in 1935 and climaxed in the Shaw Brothers' box office hit and most frequently revived movie, the Li Hanxiang and King Hu production of 1963 known in English as *Love Eterne*.[28] It made the young Ang Lee cry and was so popular in Taiwan at the time that some viewers saw it five hundred times.[29] Film critic Lin Nien-tung describes such "catering to vulgar tastes" as "pernicious."[30] Nevertheless, the Li-Hu film began a fad for "yellow-plum-melody" (*huangmeidiao*) opera films outside the People's Republic. By the mid-1960s, Hong Kong audiences tired of opera film romances, with effete heroes, and seriously turned to action heroes in swordplay martial arts films (*wuxiapian*).[31] Yet this genre too derived much from diverse regional operas in terms of performance and from popular stories of knights-errant. In Cantonese martial arts movies, Kwan Tak-hing—whose role is synonymous with the hero in the famous Huang Feihong series directed by Hu Peng from 1949 onward—was a Cantonese opera star.[32] This series established the *kung fu* subgenre that Bruce Lee later brought to global prominence. King Hu's movies, directed from both Hong Kong and Taiwan, boast the first opera-trained martial arts choreographer that is now such a staple of this genre. Hu's movies belong to the swordplay subgenre. Stephen Teo calls King Hu's films "cinema opera" because of their operatic style, especially in the spectacular combat scenes.[33] Hu credited the success of these scenes to Han Yingjie, a Beijing opera star, who played the villain in *A Touch of Zen* (King Hu, 1971) and also in Bruce Lee's 1971 *kung fu* blockbuster, *The Big Boss*. Hu said:

> That [the martial arts in my films are so new] has a direct link with my martial arts director Han Yingjie. The term "martial arts director" actually started with me using Han Yingjie. It has a lot to do with his ideas. During the making of *Come Drink with Me* [1966], it was quite difficult for me to handle the action. I had no problems with handling the story because I had read many martial arts stories. I have never had any training in the martial arts and I don't know how to fight, so I called in Han Yingjie, a Beijing opera actor, to help me out. I studied his martial arts moves and selected the best.[34]

FIGURE 3.2 The woman warrior, Yang
Huizhen, flies through the air in
A Touch of Zen (1971).

(COURTESY YUNG-FONG SHY)

Han Yingjie attributes the stunning effects in the combat scenes of *A Touch of Zen* to revitalized martial arts styles, costumes, realistic performances, and film editing. Apart from editing, all other factors relate to bodily spectacles in which movement, costume, and stylized combat converge as dance and poetry. Editing adds surprise and speed, stretching cinematic time, space, and performance to the outer bounds of credibility.

We are not arguing here that the shadow opera mode *is* opera. Rather, we suggest that this mode appropriates an operatic aesthetic that choreographs performance as spectacle. In "shadow opera," the combat scene is the main spectacle-attraction. But it is also narrative heartbeat, bodily display, and choreographed rhythm of stillness and motion. Combat scenes often also encapsulate the moral essence of a film, the site where embodiments of good and evil fight to the death.

In Hong Kong and Taiwan, opera film lost audiences in the 1960s to martial arts movies, such as those by King Hu, Zhang Zhe, and Bruce Lee. However, Maoists under Jiang Qing in the People's Republic of China returned to Beijing opera to develop revolutionary models (*yangbanxi*) from the 1960s onward. Revolutionary opera films were a specialized art with special committees during the Cultural Revolution. Their famous forerunner was the Shaanxi *yangge* opera, *The White-haired Girl*, written in Yan'an and filmed in 1950.[35] Yet, even today, these works are frequently dismissed as political propaganda. The long tradition of opera as attraction *within* films resurfaced in the post-Mao period.[36] Chen Kaige's *Farewell My Concubine* (1993) is a recent example. It too attracted criticism, this time for exoticizing old China for foreign viewers.[37]

Despite censorship and criticism, a constantly changing cinema of attractions continued across China where shadow opera flourished last century. Whereas Elsaesser has speculated on a return to such earlier modes in late-twentieth-century Western media, Chinese viewers have continuously enjoyed a vibrant cinema of attractions throughout a turbulent last century.[38]

Early Opera Film: Making the Cinema Chinese

Early opera films no longer exist. Therefore, scholars are still archivists and historians as well as analysts of film texts. Indeed, when Lu Hongshi investigated China's first films made by Ren Qingtai between 1905 and 1909, he described himself as a paleontologist, reconstructing the films' look from a few skeletal remains.[39] As isolated texts, these films are usually described as documentaries. However, within the framework of a cinema of attractions, Chinese audiences would view them as glimpses of traditional complex narratives performed onscreen. These traditional narratives sinicize foreign film technology, creating a syncretic Chinese modernity onscreen as part of the transition from empire to modern nation-state. As a cinema of operatic attraction, the novelty is threefold: film as technology, the origins of the Chinese story, and performances by the "King of Beijing Opera" in the first films.

Film as Technology Li Suyuan argues that Chinese first saw film as a marvelous spectacle. But it was a *foreign* spectacle. Ren Qingtai made film a *Chinese* spectacle. A photographer and entrepreneur, he screened films at his own entertainment centers in Beijing—Dongan Market and Daguanlou. Daguanlou was a theater built in the traditional teahouse style of horizontal rows of seating, with women (upstairs) segregated from men (downstairs). The seats were always full, offering a variety show format that included opera and short foreign films of slapstick, magic, and Chinese and foreign scenery. This commercial exhibition mode is central to a cinema of attractions. Ren included moving pictures of opera—an extension of his business selling photos of opera stars through his photography shop—as a novel Chinese addition to the repertoire. "So China's first films were born!"[40] *Dingjun Mountain* was the earliest and apparently so popular that Ren continued to film more favorites, after first performing the stage versions at Daguanlou. He selected excerpts such as fighting and acrobatics which emphasized the spectacle of early silent film technology: visuality and movement.

The Origins of the Chinese Story By the time Ren Qingtai made his opera films, narrative was a feature of foreign films exhibited in China. According to Charles Musser, these films adopted three overlapping strategies for clarifying the narrative: audience familiarity (the spectator), simple but self-sufficient narratives (the film), and the lecturer/narrator (exhibition).[41] Ren adopted the first audience-centered strategy. China had a vast treasury of raw narrative to be reworked onscreen; opera is merely one of the performing arts that retell long, complex, and multilayered stories from popular fiction such as *Romance of the Three Kingdoms* (history, statesmen, and heroes), *Water Margin* (heroes, outlaws, martial arts), *Journey to the West* (monks, super-warriors, gods, and demons), and *Strange Tales of Liaozhai* (scholars, beauties, fairies, flower spirits, ghosts, demons, goblins, and foxes).[42] But much popular fiction itself originated as oral folktales and story cycles that not only continued alongside the written works but are also inscribed in their form. Thus chapters are story cycles or *hui*. Popular performances are usually story cycles familiar to the audience. Opera is considered the richest and most complex of these traditional performing arts. But it is also regional. Ren made his films in Beijing. He chose story cycles from the most loved operas in the most widespread but also local style—Beijing opera with its repertoire of 1,220 stories—and featured China's most famous Beijing opera stars.[43] This began the tradition of opera film as a national film form.

Dingjun Mountain, for example, is a classic opera based on the seventieth and seventy-first story cycles of *Romance of the Three Kingdoms*, China's first novel, which came out of the oral storytelling tradition. It is a favorite source for opera. As a film text, *Dingjun Mountain* is rudimentary narrative. As a text in a specific cultural context, the film is a novel glimpse of a rich narrative familiar to Chinese viewers. This is true for all Ren's opera films that followed.[44] If early Western cinema is approached as media intertext in the new archaeology, then so too is this Chinese cinematic mode. It is difficult to talk of definitive sources for a given film, but we can talk of intertextuality as a dynamic relationship between film and other art forms. Shadow opera is neither traditional art nor documentary; it selects, transposes, and transforms traditional arts in its voracious appetite for novel displays of well-known stories, and these arts in turn animate Chinese film. Ren did not adapt opera for the screen; he selected bits of cycles best suited to the silent film medium.

The Performance Opera stars were China's first film stars. They were the billing attraction in these first films. *Dingjun Mountain* featured Tan Xinpei (1847–1917), one of China's foremost actors, who specialized in *laosheng* or mature male, and especially military, roles that dominated the stage from the 1830s.[45] These roles replaced the previous emphasis on *dan* (or boy actor) female roles which again became prominent from the 1920s through the virtuoso performances of famous actor and film star Mei Lanfang (1894–1961).[46] Thus, Beijing opera was not a static art, and opera film extended its reach deep into the urban populace. Audience tastes in opera previously roamed among fads for civilian dramas of righted injustice, love, and the family to military dramas of war, rebellion, and heroic adventure.

FIGURE 3.3 The famous opera star, Tan Xinpei, in *Dingjun Mountain* (1905).

(COURTESY CHINA FILM ARCHIVE)

So, too, film fads first exploited military operas and, by the mid-1920s, developed into successive crazes for costume spectaculars (*guzhuangpian*, incorporating the notion of opera, also called *guzhuangxi*), and martial arts films, which challenged Western cinematic modes.[47] The stories are found in popular literature and art and performed in a variety of modes, especially opera. Ren's opera films are embryonic shadow opera.

Dingjun Mountain belonged to the military category of opera, with battle scenes and "spectacular acrobatics."[48] It is a foretaste of the martial arts genres to come. Tan was so famous for his military male roles, his martial arts, and his swordfighting that the famous reformer Liang Qichao wrote, "His name evokes a roar like thunder everywhere in the world."[49] Acting was far from the naturalistic or realist civilized play performances. The whole point was capturing the essence (*xieyi*). Spectators understood operatic conventions, such as "painted faces" denoting character and symbolic, stylized movement. For Huang Zuolin, operatic performance is not a question of audience-character identification but a Brechtian audience-character distance.[50] This feature of spectator-text relations is a core difference between a cinema of attractions and realist cinema. It is certainly a feature of Tan's performance in *Dingjun Mountain*. It was shot outside to music. Ren used a fixed camera, natural light, and no scenery, just a plain white cloth. The film was presumably shown accompanied by a live orchestra as part of Ren's variety show. Audiences experienced the film as a performance:

The human figure was clear and everyone could see that it was Tan Xinpei. But once the sword was brandished, all one could see was the moving of the sword; the human figure was nowhere to be found. In another scene, the upper half of the boot was missing. Even so, people enjoyed the film very much.[51]

This early filmmaking ended when Ren Qingtai's Fengtai Studio burned down in 1909. Chinese began making films again in 1913 and, by the 1920s, film and cinemas were established features of urban cultural landscapes. By this time film technology had matured beyond anything that could be displayed onstage or in the marketplace, simultaneously sustaining and displacing the traditional performing arts. The box office hit at this time was *The Burning of Red Lotus Temple,* made by Zheng Zhengqiu and Zhang Shichuan in 1928. Audiences were so excited by the intricate plot, the mysterious events, the special effects, and the filmic spectacle of "the unimaginable"—flying swords spat out of mouths, thunder produced by hands, flying swordsmen, and cartoon characters interspersed among the real—that seventeen sequels were made.[52] This began the martial arts genre and a complex and more covert intertextuality. *Red Lotus Temple,* for example, had its performance origins in opera (such as acrobatics and fighting), its story from a best-selling novel, and its sensation from the "unimaginable" capacities of foreign filmmaking and fantastic exploits of gods and spirits. The Hong Kong *Ghost Story* series is a modern version of the "god-spirit martial arts movies" (*shengui wuxiapian*).

The *Red Lotus Temple* sagas no longer exist. Reformist writers from the late 1920s criticized the entire corpus of costume films as feudal, and the state eventually banned them in 1931 as unrealistic, unethical, and generally unsavory, especially in their influence on the uneducated masses. The push for modernity allegedly required a clear rejection of traditional views of Chinese national identity. The Chinese Communist Party continued this rejection of the feudal as state policy after 1949 and in model operas, which explicitly promoted proletarian heroes and heroines as representative of a new socialist modernity and a class-based national identity in the 1960s. Chinese opera and martial arts film is an instance of a contested, multiple, and dynamic popular culture, variously linked to nation, society, class, and regional communities.

Revolutionary Operas: Making the Nation Proletarian

At the very same time that costume films and martial arts movies were banned, Chinese revolutionaries were reassessing such popular arts in terms of audience, ideology, and nation. Their concern is a continuation of the ethical dimensions of shadowplay aesthetics.[53] If the KMT Republicans condemned opera and martial arts film because they were superstitious and not scientifically modern, the Communists were eager to appropriate and transform opera as a tool of class struggle in forging a class-based nation—the People's Republic. For Marxist-Leninists, the primary function of all the arts was revolutionary education of the masses, envisioned as masters of a socialist state. This cinema is produced by political elites, not the market. Yet in theory and in practice, the revolutionary line on film resonates with features of a proletarian cinema of attractions.

The theory is political. From the late 1920s, revolutionaries reviled traditional and urban commercialized entertainment in general as inimical to the revolution, which needed art to mobilize the masses throughout the nation against imperialism, especially Japanese invasion. Audience is fundamental. Qu Qiubai considered reformist arts of the May Fourth period to be Europeanized, a banquet for the gentry while "the laboring people were still starving." The answer was "new wine in old bottles": to fill popular art forms with revolutionary content. Qu specifically advocated the use of a street vernacular in popular old and new forms—including cinema and comic books, which were accessible to the illiterate—to attract the masses. Hence, intertextuality is also crucial. This cinema exhorts the spectator to move from film viewing to revolutionary action. To save China from its enemies, Qu told artists to take revolutionary arts to the people, to "the streets, factories, slums, teahouses, and bookstalls," and to infiltrate the film industry.[54] This urban strategy became rural under Mao when Qu Qiubai became commissar of education in the Jiangxi soviet in 1934. The definitive statement is in Mao's "Talks at the Yan'an [Yenan] Forum on Literature and Art" in 1942. Artists were to produce works "which awaken the masses, fire them with enthusiasm, and impel them to unite and struggle to transform their environment."[55] Finally, then, this art is not self-sufficient but one that consciously hails the spectator as a member of a class-based nation. Audience acknowledgment, intertextuality, and performativity are core elements of a proletarian cinema of attractions.

A proletarian cinema of attractions had to be Chinese. To achieve this, a Marxist-Leninist archive of "Chineseness" was formulated that inherited earlier Republican efforts but transformed them along class lines. The theory and practice is still about sinicizing all the arts, including cinema, but is now a subcategory of sinicizing Marxism itself. In rural Yan'an the question of national form (*minzu xingshi*) in the arts was again fiercely debated from 1938 to 1940. At its core was the old tension between Chinese and Western art forms. David Holm states that the Yan'an solution of "new wine in old bottles" led not to transformed Chinese art but to a "patchwork," a "bricolage," a "hodge-podge." The model revolutionary genres—Yan'an's new

EVOLUTION OF *THE WHITE-HAIRED GIRL*

I. ORAL FOLKTALE (1940)

Supposedly, *The White-haired Girl* originated as a 1940 folk story about a "white-haired goddess" spreading from northwest Hebei and reaching Yan'an in 1944. In the folktale, a 17-year-old peasant girl is abducted by her landlord in payment of her father's debts, raped, becomes pregnant, and escapes the landlord's attempt to kill her by running away and living in a cave for nine years. Her hair turns white and locals believe she is a goddess. She is liberated by an Eighth Route army officer and the landlord is exposed.

II. OPERA AND FILM

1945: Yan'an Local Opera and Beyond

The folk story is the basis for a five-act opera by He Jingzhi and Ding Yi first performed in Yan'an in April 1945. The operatic form is adapted primarily from local *yangge,* a mixture of song, dance, and ribald comic action in the Yan'an region and beyond, in accordance with precepts in Mao's "Talks." From 1945 to 1949 the new opera was widely performed in liberated areas and adapted into other forms of local opera. In 1958 it was performed as a Beijing opera. It has also featured as a spoken play (*huaju*) and a comic book (*lianhuantuhua*) by Hua Sanchuan, which followed the film, not opera, version. The He-Ding opera is the classic text.

1950: Feature Film
Directed by Wang Bin and Shui Hua, Northeast Film Studio, 1950

This feature film is adapted from the He-Ding opera with some revisions, particularly the downplaying of Xi'er's baby. This version is now seen as a classic work of early revolutionary cinema, produced by the first Communist-run film studio. When Xi'er is rescued by the Communist Party, her hair returns to black.

III. BALLET AND FILM

1955: The first ballet was made in Japan, and performed in Beijing in 1957.

1964: The Shanghai Dance School performed a half-hour ballet version, approved by Jiang Qing.

1965: Model Ballet

The full revolutionary ballet, *The White-haired Girl,* was performed in Shanghai. It was based on the 1945 local opera and the 1950 film. The ballet was later adopted as one of the few model dramas (*yangbanxi*) performed during the Cultural Revolution. In this version, Xi'er fights the landlord, is not raped, and so has no baby. Nevertheless, her hair still turns white.

1971: Film of the 1965 Ballet

This is a faithfully filmed version of the model ballet, featuring *The White-haired Girl* Troupe of the Shanghai Dance School (Shanghai Film Studio, 1971).

yangge opera, such as *The White-haired Girl,* and the Cultural Revolution's model ballets and model operas—are, Holm rightly states, "single, hybrid model genre(s)."[56] When adapted to film, however, it is precisely this hybridity and theatricality that hail and attract the spectator.

In practice after 1949, opera film became an archetypal national film form under Mao's Yan'an line on the arts. But here, national film form is redefined in class-based terms. In this context, the 1950 film, *The White-haired Girl,* is a textbook case of intertextuality, performativity, and spectacle. Its genre transposition (see box: "Evolution of *The White-haired Girl*) mirrors traditional narrative performances and spans the evolution of revolutionary cinema in Maoist China. With some modifications, the 1950 film basically follows the classic opera version, a somewhat sanitized reworking of local *yangge* opera into hybrid form. The opera and then the film were displayed as models for class struggle during land reform. Like Ren Qingtai's films, the opera was first tested on the local populace. A Yan'an dress rehearsal in which the landlord, Huang, escaped punishment evoked strong local criticism. Holm reports:

> There was a cook in the kitchens who emphasized what he was saying by continuing to chop vehemently at the cabbage on his chopping block, "The play's all right, but not to shoot that evil bastard Huang Shiren, that's just too unjust!" As Zheng Gang remarks, "At the time [of the United Front] we still felt that basically one should work for solidarity with the landlord class. If he were to be shot, that would certainly have gone against government policy. So we didn't change it."[57]

The cook was right. Huang had to be shot. There was to be no compassion for class enemies. After a public performance before Mao and other Yan'an leaders, the Central Secretariat approved the opera and passed down the following policy decision: "Huang Shiren is a character so steeped in evil that it would not be right not to have him shot (*sic*). The broad mass-

FIGURE 3.4 The heroine in *The White-haired Girl* (1950)

(COURTESY CHINA FILM ARCHIVE)

es will definitely not tolerate that."[58] In the fighting *yangge* of communist Yan'an, peasant audiences could empathize with their own world, their own wounds, their own people, in their own language, and stylized in their own operatic form. A 1947 observer reported that village audiences stood and shouted "kill, kill," like the cook, while women in particular wept.[59]

The film of *The White-haired Girl* was a model for later cinema.[60] Lee Haiyan argues that class background was "racialized" early in the People's Republic so that it becomes a fixed, political—not economic—category that is inherited.[61] Class struggle includes class purification, a process that is exemplified in the film by the gradual writing out of the landlord's rape of the peasant girl, Xi'er, and the resulting baby: "vile spawn" (*niezhong*).[62] Thus, Xi'er is depicted in film reviews in the 1950s "not as an ordinary, victimized character but an embodiment of the unyielding, anti-feudal fighting spirit of China's laboring people."[63] It is a militant opera film.

Azalea Mountain (1974) is an example of opera film form toward the end of the Cultural Revolution and so representative of the corpus of works filmed in this period. All are militant, celebrating class struggle as the key to producing a socialist nation-state. Revolutionary operas therefore continued the Republican transformation of China's best-known regional form, Beijing opera, into a national form, but this time as a class-based nation. The filming principle was "to restore the stage but improve on the stage," and a three-month conference in 1973 studied film adaptations of opera.[64] *Azalea Mountain* was filmed after the conference, and—while too late to be designated a model work—was nevertheless considered not only one of the best at the time but also "a mirror" of peasant uprisings over two thousand years of Chinese history.[65] The opera distinguishes failed traditional peasant rebellions from successful peasant revolution, led by the Communist Party under Mao Zedong. In this sense, it is the ongoing cinematic correction of *The Life of Wu Xun*, a 1951 historical costume film much criticized for defiling the revolutionary peasant struggle, the linchpin of revolutionary history.[66] As narrative, then, *Azalea Mountain* is familiar and sprinkled with quotations from Chairman Mao.

Like all revolutionary Beijing operas, *Azalea Mountain* as a text shows appropriations from the West in linear plot, music, scenery, and costume.[67] It is therefore within the modern tradition of appropriation and hybridization that began a century earlier. The work also retains many vestiges of operatic artifice, such as symbolic props (chains and bayonets, for example, that abound in revolutionary cinema), "the [painted] face denoting character," stylized movement, and a mixture of song, dialogue, dance, and martial arts. Film adds powerful techniques lacking in drama. Revolutionary opera films perfect a rhythmic visual movement from establishing shot to full close-up of the hero. This rhythm realizes the then-current artistic policy of

AZALEA MOUNTAIN (DUJUAN SHAN)

DIRECTED BY XIE TIELI

Beijing Film Studio, 1974

Adapted from the opera of the same name by Wang Shuyuan

The film is set in 1928; Lei Gang leads a local peasant guerilla group to rescue Ke Xiang from civil guards as they lead her to execution. Lei Gang is shocked to learn that this Party member is a woman. Ke Xiang, whose husband was executed before her arrest, brings sound Party leadership to the peasant partisans. She leads a force to rescue Lei Gang and others who have been captured because of Lei's impetuosity. The peasants under Ke and Lei finally go to Jinggang Shan to join Mao's guerillas.

FIGURE 3.5 Ke Xiang confronts the guards in *Azalea Mountain* (1974).

"the three prominences," which prescribed overwhelming focus on heroes, far more successfully than any other art form. The rule was "close, big, and bright" (*jin, da, ming*) for heroes and heroines; "far, small, and black" (*yuan, xiao, hei*) for villains.[68] This rule was achieved by marrying the operatic *liangxiang* with the cinematic gaze. A *liangxiang* is a frozen, sculptural pose that visually conveys "archetypal images and emotions" onstage.[69] In film, the full *liangxiang* close-up on the character's face (and especially the eyes) intensifies the emotional impact; we call this cinematic look the *liangxiang* gaze. The *liangxiang* gaze was already systematized in many opera and feature films during the 1950s and 1960s. In the 1970s the camera fully exploited this convention.

The second scene in *Azalea Mountain*, when Ke Xiang first appears on her execution day, is an example of its use. This scene pulsates with the dance-freeze-dance-freeze rhythm of the operatic mode (which we noted at the beginning of this chapter), varied here by music and interspersed with song. The camera position is also frozen with Ke Xiang consistently centered high in the frame or in the center of a cowering circle of black-clad villains. They are always below her. The camera focus on Ke Xiang, however, moves back and forth within a restricted depth of field akin to a stage. The rhythm of Ke Xiang's first appearance begins with an establishing shot of the yamen (local government office) next to the market square, cutting to a close-up of the yamen's forbidding gates as Ke sings unseen. In a long shot, the gates open, the guards run out, and then Ke Xiang briefly moves into the gateway. The camera cuts to a medium shot of Ke framed in the gateway in a *liangxiang* of defiance with one arm stretched up, the other with a clenched fist, holding chains (fig. 3.6a). Her eyes gaze over the unseen crowd. She then moves, tossing back her hair and tossing back the chains. Her face in close-up fills the frame, light, young, robust in a brief *liangxiang* of dedication and defiance (fig. 3.6b). Looking beyond her captors, she sings. Her eyes never flicker, her head stays still as bayonet tips point toward her heart (fig. 3.6c). With an exaggerated tilt downward of her head, her unflickering eyes focus on the enemy. This is a *liangxiang* of distilled hate (fig. 3.6d). The camera tracks back, and so do the enemy, as Ke Xiang proudly walks down the yamen steps, moving from prison to the people (fig. 3.6e). The musical accompaniment is the Internationale.

The scene ends when the people, under Lei Gang, fight and free Ke Xiang, and the rebels are together under Party leadership. This scene illustrates screen techniques that dominated the production of revolutionary film—both realist and performative—from the 1950s to the 1970s in the People's Republic. The basis is Xia Yan's essays, the definitive working statements on the dramatic structure and techniques of film within the shadowplay tradition.[70] Ke Xiang's first appearance fulfills the three essentials required by Xia Yan. First, as the principal character, she is previously mentioned in scene 1. Second, her character is certainly distinctive. Third, she is immediately involved in dramatic crisis—her own execution. Indeed, as Xia Yan insists, she "strikes a pose" and "briefs" us through action, dialogue, and song. Action is emphasized, as he suggests, by close-ups and smooth, rhythmic editing, or montage.[71] The whole point is viewer identification so that emotion is aroused. This, for Xia, is national form and national style.[72]

This expressive rhythm comes out of opera. In *Planet Hong Kong*, David

FIGURE 3.6a Ke Xiang, framed in the yamen gateway in *Azalea Mountain* (1974)

FIGURE 3.6b Ke Xiang gazes over the crowd in the marketplace.

FIGURE 3.6c Ke Xiang sings as bayonets point at her heart.

FIGURE 3.6d Ke Xiang's *liangxiang* of distilled hate for her enemies

FIGURE 3.6e Ke Xiang walks toward the people.

Bordwell comments on the "pulsating expressive intensity" of Hong Kong cinema from the 1970s.

> Films correlate gesture, composition, color, and music more exactly than we expect in Western live-action cinema.... An actor turns, and holds the pose.... Such bold expressivity surely owes something to Cantonese Opera. In this dance-like theatre virtually every gesture is matched by musical passages, particularly

percussion, and a cascade of movement will be accented by a flash of color in the garments.[73]

As we see in *A Touch of Zen, Azalea Mountain,* and later in this chapter in *Crouching Tiger, Hidden Dragon* by Taiwan director Ang Lee, this dancelike "bold expressivity" is a central feature of the operatic mode more generally. The rhythm comes from a range of operatic forms, especially Beijing opera, which became national operatic form. Certainly, action choreographers such as Han Yingjie (*A Touch of Zen*) and Yuen Woping (*Crouching Tiger*) were trained in Beijing opera, as was Jackie Chan and the various actors in revolutionary operas. As *Azalea Mountain* is clearly opera, viewing habits would simultaneously distance and collapse the spectator-text relationship. At this time, a mass popularization movement to perform operas was in vogue so that people of all ages learned the arias, mimicking the filmic representation. Ordinary spectators became everyday actors in a mimetic circulation from stage, to screen, to nationwide performance in public and private spaces.[74] Hence, a crucial point of the play is the performance. In *Azalea Mountain* this is film form. The cinematic rhythm is a complex dance between revolutionary movement and perfect stillness, of camera, pose, and gaze. This is expressive and expressionist (*xieyi*) cinema, which freezes revolutionary action and universalizes the particular. Stylized movement and stillness counterpoint each other. Luo Yijun claims that *xieyi* in traditional aesthetics is about expressing emotion (*qing*).[75] It is also about expressing cosmic energy (*qi*), transformed into class energy. Ke Xiang's *liangxiang* gaze combines *qing* and *qi*. It says very clearly, very expressively, and very definitely—again and again—*we are* the rightful masters of new China and *we do* control our destiny. This is the success of China's revolution. This is the performance and pride that is constantly reiterated in China's proletarian cinema of attractions. But it lacked a crucial component—novelty—finally boring spectators with its relentless politics, limited repertoire, and black-and-red characters.

Local and Transnational Shadow Opera: Regional Opera, Global Martial Arts

The instances of shadow opera we have discussed so far have often been associated with Chinese nation-state formations. However, shadow opera also operates below and beyond the national. We now move to ongoing regional Chinese cinemas with martial arts as the exemplar of the shift from regional to global markets. The *kung fu* Cantonese-language tradition of Bruce Lee and Jackie Chan is the best-known example. The work of both actors is discussed in detail in later chapters. In comparison to the Hong Kong *kung fu* tradition, Taiwan cinema is neglected. Yet at the local level, a homegrown Taiwanese operatic form—*gezaixi*—has recently been rewritten as the beginnings of Taiwanese-language film and an autonomous Taiwanese identity. Meanwhile, on the global scene, Ang Lee's *Crouching Tiger, Hidden Dragon* is the Taiwan-American director's first foray into the martial arts genre. It scooped most regional film awards and won an Oscar for best foreign film. It spawned a host of copies, aimed at projecting a pan-Chinese national identity to both Chinese and Western markets because it "created a [worldwide] audience for this kind of film".[76] That identity is mythic; Lee calls the sword-fighting film a "dream of China, a China that probably never existed, except in my boyhood fantasies in Taiwan."[77]

Gezaixi and other Taiwanese-language opera films occupy the provincial end of the spectrum from the mid-twentieth century on. Given the search of many Taiwanese for an identity that differentiates them from the mainland Chinese, especially after the first Taiwan-born president was elected in 1990, the history of Taiwanese-language movies is said to reflect Taiwan's national history. Both flourished around the 1950s with the end of Japanese colonization.[78] *Gezaixi* is now celebrated for the provincialism that once attracted its suppression and neglect; it is now part of a new Taiwan protonational identity. According to Zeng Yongyi, *gezaixi* developed from its rural origins in Taiwan into a major operatic form by adapting elements from theater, by absorbing music from folksong and opera, and by establishing professional troupes as the form moved from countryside to city.[79] Because *gezaixi* represented the culture of the native Han-Taiwanese, who had their own 400-year history and comprise the majority of the population, the form was popular and over three hundred troupes were quickly established throughout the island. Two of these troupes supplied the actors in the first Taiwanese-language film(s). There is some debate as to the first film although both contenders were *gezaixi*. The Taiwan-made and Taiwanese-performed film *Xue Pinggui and Wang Baochuan* (1956) is usually credited as the first because its precursor, *Six Scholars of the Western Chamber* (1955), was performed by a troupe from mainland Xiamen. Besides, *Six Scholars* was a box office flop while *Xue Pinggui and Wang Baochuan* was a hit, featuring the premier opera troupe under Chen Chengsan. Taiwanese critics now celebrate *gezaixi's* difference and its history of bans, censorship, and neglect under both the Japanese and the KMT as emblematic of a suppressed Taiwanese identity. Ye Longyan wrote that *Xue Pinggui and Wang Baochuan* finally allowed "we Taiwanese to hold our heads up high."[80] A 1993 documentary traces the history of this theatrical and film form through Chen Chengsan's pioneering opera troupe as crucial to Taiwan's local identity in the post–martial law era.[81]

The failure of *Six Scholars* shows that early box office success relied on more than operatic form alone. It was a poor-quality film. In contrast, *Xue Pinggui and Wang Baochuan*'s director, He Jiming, was a trained filmmaker. Bai Ke, an influential Taiwanese-language director, praised the film highly at the time for its cinematic values.[82] As with other opera-film traditions, the regional language, shrewd advertising, local form, a well-known folk story, and local stars were acknowledged factors in its success. Indeed, the star cult, according to Miriam Hansen, is part of an "aesthetics of display," and stars have been used in successful opera film from Beijing to Tokyo.[83]

While these early films are no longer extant, later Taiwanese-language opera films from their heyday in the early 1960s profile their theatricality, including the much-criticized tradition of female actors in male roles.[84] This alleged flaw is, in fact, an advantage in women warrior films, such as *Twelve Widows March West,* in which twelve widows from the Yang family save both the Northern Song dynasty and the two remaining Yang male descendants from annihilation by northern barbarians. At a time when the Communists and KMT both claimed China, Taiwan film celebrates an inclusive Chinese cultural heritage as part of its claim to national power, while China rejects tradition as feudal, and therefore inimical to the Maoist vision of a modern socialist state.

All ends happily in *Twelve Widows* as the grandson and heir of the Yang clan is captured and imprisoned by the barbarian chief's daughter.

BARBARIAN PRINCESS: I haven't killed you because I want you to be my husband. Your parents arrive today and if you marry me I'll spare their lives.
GRANDSON: Will you love me?
BARBARIAN PRINCESS: Yes or heaven will punish me.

The grandson agrees and the two kiss, a Western feature that made its debut into popular Chinese visual culture in the May Fourth period. The

FIGURE 3.7 The barbarian princess proposes to the imprisoned Yang family grandson in *Twelve Widows March West* (1963).
(COURTESY CHINESE TAIPEI FILM ARCHIVE)

magical kiss is also, we will see, a feature of *Crouching Tiger*. Like many early mainland opera films and martial arts movies, obvious magical moments abound: bats drop from trees during fighting, the cooks (costumed as operatic clowns) turn into dogs, and the princess transforms swords into snakes. The props are rich, the scenes are frequently middle and long frontal shots, and the fights are stagy, accompanied by music from Holtz's *The Planets*.

At the global end of the Taiwan spectrum is *Crouching Tiger, Hidden Dragon*, the originator of the new global sword-fighting martial arts genre. The film projects a mythic, cultural version of Chineseness for Chinese and non-Chinese audiences. However, the film also responds to contemporary circumstances. First, it displays an ethnically diverse China that mixes accents and origins, as is the case in the diaspora itself. Second, it shows a Chinese cultural nation in which Western-style individualism is celebrated by younger generations to the dismay of older generations. Indeed, youthful rebellion and female liberation are central to the storyline, to the combat scenes, and to the generational tussle between Chinese and Western lifestyles that is part of the diasporic Chinese experience.

Yet the package is very much the martial arts genre, enhanced through high-tech visual effects. Global stars from the region are part of the martial arts attraction, performing "an epic love story and a thrilling action drama

---

CROUCHING TIGER, HIDDEN DRAGON (WO HU CANG LONG)

DIRECTED BY ANG LEE

Action choreographer Yuen Woping

Asia Union Film and Entertainment, China Film Co-Production Corporation, Columbia Pictures, EDKO Film, Good Machine, Sony Pictures, United China Vision, and Zoom Hunt, 2000

The story is adapted from the novels of Wang Dulu (1909–1977). King Lear-like, the legendary swordsman Li Mu Bai (Li Mubai) gives away his sword, Green Destiny, to retire from the chaotic outlaw world for life with woman warrior Shu Lien (Xiulian).* A daughter of a Manchu aristocrat, Jen (Xiao Long or Little Dragon), steals the sword from its new home "for fun." Jen's swordsmanship has already surpassed that of her teacher and governess, the notorious Jade Fox, who has previously killed Li Mu Bai's master. In seeking to regain the sword, Li also seeks to avenge his master's death and tame Jen's rebellion by making her his disciple. In the end, both Li and Jade Fox die. Jen is reunited with her outlaw lover from the desert, Lo (Xiao Hu or Little Tiger), in the mythic home of knights-errant on Wudang Mountain. But she leaves her lover too, enacting an ancient legend as she leaps from a bridge into the clouds and floats into the vast unknown.

---

*Note that the Chinese and English names often differ.

set against the breathtaking landscapes of ancient China, filmed entirely on location" in the People's Republic.[85] The main attraction, however, is the combat scenes. In *Crouching Tiger,* martial arts conventions sit alongside Western and Chinese melodrama. This creative challenge to generic norms is a feature of martial arts movies in the later twentieth century.[86] But the film is nevertheless about China and Chineseness. According to Ang Lee:

> My team and I chose the most populist, if not popular, genre in film history—the Hong Kong martial arts film—to tell our story, and we used this pop genre almost as a kind of instrument to explore the legacy of classical Chinese culture. We embraced the most mass of art forms [cinema] and mixed it with the highest—the secret martial arts as passed down over time in the great Daoist schools of training and thought.[87]

Yuen Woping, an action choreographer from Hong Kong with a vast knowledge of Beijing opera, martial arts, and cinema, worked behind the scenes with Ang Lee to create "an abstract form of filmmaking, where the images and editing are like dance and music."[88]

This is the expressive intensity of the operatic mode, which we discussed in relation to *Azalea Mountain.* In *Crouching Tiger,* eight combat sequences punctuate the drama and extend the rhythm to the entire form of the film. The dancelike sequences display diverse weapons, with Jen's rebellious presence or absence central to each fight. The scenes are the *kung fu* fight in courtyards and on rooftops after Jen steals the sword at night (about 5 minutes); the short appearances of Jen and Li Mu Bai at the end of the nighttime fight between Jade Fox and her pursuers from the hinterland which establishes Jen's mastery of the sword (various weapons, including the sword); the fighting scenes (on and off horseback) between Jen and Lo in the desert, which function as foreplay to love and passion (pursuit and close body "fighting"); Lo's horseback skirmish during Jen's wedding procession to an aristocratic husband chosen by her parents; Jen's swordfight against numerous warriors with various weapons in the inn (3.5 minutes); the fight between Jen (sword) and Shu Lien (a range of weapons) in Shu Lien's house (4 minutes), immediately followed by Li Mu Bai and Jen's dreamlike sword-fighting confrontation in the bamboo forest (3.5 minutes); and, finally, the computer-enhanced fight *fantastique* (lasting only 40 seconds) between Li Mu Bai (sword) and Jade Fox (poison).

Just as the sword Green Destiny dominates the plot, so too swordplay dominates the combat. *Crouching Tiger* therefore belongs to a main subgenre of Hong Kong martial arts movies—the swordplay film—rather than the *kung fu* film. Scenes oscillate between so-called civilized society in the heart of Beijing and the anarchic, reckless underworld, a mythic but violent landscape governed only by codes of chivalry. The underworld law is simple in this film: "Kill or be killed." It leads, says Li Mu Bai, to endless sorrow.

Ang Lee acknowledges the debt that martial arts movies owe to opera, including their distinctive rhythm. He said in an interview: "They are all choreographed in the same way. Pose, re-establish position, pose again. It is all the same." He also acknowledges *Crouching Tiger*'s debt to King Hu, particularly in the bamboo forest and inn scenes that King Hu made so famous. Stephen Teo claims that Lee's aerial combat in the bamboo grove is the most "elegaic tribute" to Hu's legacy.[89] The same can be said of the inn scene in *Crouching Tiger*. The fighting in this scene is performed as dance-like poetry in motion.

The inn-scene drama builds through a series of confrontations that can only erupt in a crescendo of violence. Jen—now cross-dressed (as is common in opera)—escapes her arranged marriage and arrives at the inn. Two outlaw fighters accost her. She disdainfully defeats them. As she later awaits her dinner, they return with a line of male warriors who mount the stairs to test their skills against Green Destiny, which Jen falsely claims to have won from Li Mu Bai. Guests scatter in fear. After a lead-up and humorous fight against Iron-arm Mi, she confronts Shining Phoenix Mountain Gou. Gou unfortunately shares a surname with her abandoned husband. Gou's introduction is combined with a prolonged operatic gesture, a large, fluttering, metal fan. On hearing his surname, Jen says, "Gou? I hate that name. It makes me puke!" and leaps into action to the accompaniment of drum and flute. The frenzy stills as Warrior Monk Jing demands, "Who are you?" She responds in classical poetry:

"Who am I?
I am the Invincible Sword Goddess
Armed with the Incredible Green Destiny.
Lower your head
And ask for mercy.
I am the desert dragon.
I leave no trace.
Today … I fly over Emei Mountain,
Tomorrow … I kick over Wudang Mountain."

Ang Lee plays with generic conventions even as he cites them with exquisite timing. The dancelike beat requires both action and stillness of varied intensity, especially at the end of the battle sequence. In this scene, bold operatic movements begin and end the battle. Demure girls, not gigantic warriors, usually flutter fans. From this gesture onward, Jen's actions—flying, leaping, slashing, twirling, maiming, and posing—are all modulated to the rhythm of her poem. The poem progresses through three musical movements marked by rhyme and visual signifiers, such as close-ups and ironic poses. After chanting "I leave no trace," she executes a combat move that crosses the frame, cutting to a close-up of the sword tip at her enemy's belly, and finally cutting again to a close-up of her enemy's horrified face. The final *liangxiang* is both climax and cadence, signaling the end of the action to her drawn-out chant of "Wudangshan." She acts out kicking over the sacred mountain in a medium close-up that cuts to a back-on long shot as Jen freezes, arm raised, and surveys the inn's wreckage. This is a *liangxiang*, frozen frenzy. A balustrade collapses, moving to a final scene of the inn from outside. The effect is of grace and power. Ang Lee consciously melds martial arts action with the feminine style of such old, operatic melodramas as *Love Eterne*. He said, "It is so beautiful."[90]

If Ang Lee plays with cinematic moments in the history of both opera film and martial arts movies, he also subverts classic norms of both genres through a third element: Western-style psychological realism. Despite the action and the historical settings, this film is as much about generational and gender conflict as about Confucian values, such as chivalry, filiality, and brotherhood (represented here by Li Mu Bai and Shu Lien). It is therefore as much about both globalized Chinese culture and modern Chinese society as about mythic, traditional China. This aspect of the plot is character-driven in two ways. First, the revenge motif that is so central to martial arts movies is triggered by Jade Fox's killing of Li's master, who thinks she's good enough to sleep with but not good enough to teach. Women are not allowed to be disciples at Wudang, so Jade Fox poisons him. To a modern audience, her murderous behavior is perhaps understandable, even if inexcusable. Second, this motif is subordinate to the mainspring of the drama: Jen's quest for individual freedom. She steals, cheats, maims, and disregards everyone—parents, elders, governess, husband, lover, and respected warriors whether it be Li, Shu Lien, or the fighters at the inn who declare her to be the most uncivil person they have ever met. She rejects both the Confucian and underworld codes of conduct. She should be the villain, as Ang Lee says. But the sympathetic psychological treatment of her rebellion and romance adds dramatic depth. Jen is not a villain but a very modern heroine. The focus on Jen and the dilution of the martial arts format has led to complaints: there is no *wu* (physical fighting) or *xia* (heroic chivalry) in this so-called martial arts movie (*wuxiapian*).[91] The complaints ignore the restrained and chivalrous love between Li and Shu Lien. Their love is consummated with Li's dying breath—the kiss that promises eternity together in this life and the next. These two love affairs juxtapose tradition and modernity as coexisting codes of conduct that impact, through the stolen sword, on the core of national government in Beijing.

As we said at the beginning of this chapter, *Crouching Tiger* spawned many look-alike films. The most successful is Zhang Yimou's historical epic, *Hero* (see chapters 6 and 8), which the director claims was planned before *Crouching Tiger's* release in 2000 and then nearly abandoned because Zhang feared "people would accuse him of riding on Ang Lee's coattails."[92] Although the storylines are very different, comparison between the two films is inevitable,[93] with their similar exploitation of cultural resources in terms of genre, musical director, combat visuals, star-studded transnational Chinese casts, and luxurious Chinese settings. At issue in this transnational cinema is ownership of particular versions of both mythic nationhood and populist genre. The subtext in many film reviews is, who best realizes such mythic projections of the Chinese nation: Lee or Zhang? The jury is out but both Lee and Zhang's film narratives have generated considerable controversy about what it is to be "Chinese" in a global world. We have noted that some critics claim that *Crouching Tiger's* love story is too individualist and too westernized. *Hero's* so-called "fascinatin' fascism" has been criticized as too nationalistically Chinese in its emphasis on self-sacrifice to ruthless leaders.[94] *Hero's* sequel, *House of Flying Daggers* (2004), is more akin to *Crouching Tiger* in that it too "is a film about [star-crossed] love", which Zhang says means that "American audiences may find it easier to understand (than *Hero*)".[95] *Daggers* was also a blockbuster in the United States. National culture is being made more palatable for foreign audiences.

It is clear from these films that Chinese national identity is not fixed or homogeneous. Tim Edenson states that "globalization promotes the mutation of national identity," which may "become detached from the nation-state ... proliferate in diasporic settings ... [and] appear in syncretic cultural forms and practices."[96] This is arguably the case with martial arts blockbusters since the work of King Hu, Bruce Lee (see chapter 8), and Jackie Chan (see chapter 6) began celebrating a Chinese cultural nationalism in non-mainland films, aimed at local, regional, and transnational audiences. However, pleasing transnational audiences is not the same as pleasing regional Chinese audiences. *Crouching Tiger* flopped at China's main movie house in Beijing while Shanghai audiences hissed at the famous bamboo fight scene. As Henry Chu reports:

> Director Lee has said he tried to combine both Eastern and Western concepts in *Crouching Tiger* to fuse a Bruce Lee film with the style of one of the director's earlier art-house hits *Sense and Sensibility*. Critics in both North America and Europe have applauded the result. The Chinese, who seem to guard their movie genres as jealously as they guard their cuisine, are not interested. "Since it's a kung-fu movie, you can't just make it according to your own sensibility," said theater manager Xu Zhongren. "You have to adjust for a mainland Chinese audience".[97]

The Western-style romance and psychological realism in *Crouching Tiger* brings us to a second mode of the Chinese cinema, discussed in the next chapter: realism. Realist modes dominated discussions of Chinese cinema as a national cinema for much of the twentieth century. Indeed, realism was often officially prescribed as the mode of modernity and nationhood on both the mainland and in Taiwan. But operatic modes, especially in martial arts and action movies, are arguably more popular among local audiences and recognizably Chinese to foreign audiences. In Chinese film history, shadow opera and realist filmmaking are often cast as opposites, as tradition versus modernity. In film practice, however, the modes often intertwine to produce classics works in the Chinese cinema, whether revolutionary operas on socialist nation-building or such martial arts movies as *Crouching Tiger* which present a mythic version of China with a very modern twist.

4

Realist Modes

MELODRAMA, MODERNITY, AND HOME

YELLOW EARTH (1984) is one of the most famous Chinese films. While it is not usually considered a realist work, we argue later in this chapter that it is a reflection on the Chinese nation that belongs to a realist lineage in two ways. Stylistically, it generates new standards of realism at a time when socialist realism had lost its credibility. Visually, as with all the other films we examine here, it also imagines the national through the family and home. The "yellow earth" of the title is the real location of both ancient and revolutionary Chinese civilization. The location speaks of China; the richly colored earth is the "ancestral home" of all Chinese peoples which shapes their lives over centuries. *Yellow Earth*'s story of one peasant family is the story of all peasants in a harsh landscape that is transformed by light, color, and song into the mother of the Chinese people.

Yellow Earth constitutes one moment in a century of filmmaking in China. Looking back, Chinese cinematic realism is as diverse as else-where. The styles and conventions are various, heterogeneous, and always qualified by some sort of prefix, such as social, socialist, new, old, or even healthy. Hence, realist cinema is understood in this chapter as "moments" in context, explored through seminal texts.[1] This approach feeds into the various debates on realism as the allegedly dominant mode of classical Hollywood—or socialist cinema for that matter. Linda Williams suggests that realism is not only a mixed mode but also a lesser mode in American cinema that transforms the melodramatic mode in different ways, at differ-ent times, and in different places. She writes that "melodrama may prove central to who we are as a nation."[2] Similar claims have been made of the Chinese cinema: Yin Hong and Ling Yan consider moral melodramas a major tradition in Chinese cinema during the first half of the twentieth century.[3] Other scholars suggest that melodrama spans a century of Chi-nese filmmaking.

In the first section of this chapter, we argue that realism is hailed as the dominant mode of twentieth-century Chinese cinemas for ideological reasons that link realism, modernity, and nationalism. In practice, however, Chinese cinematic realism is a mixed mode that is highly melodramatic.[4] In this chapter, we call this mixed mode "melodramatic realism."[5]

In the following sections, we link different modes of realism and the national to different onscreen representations of the family and home, which we call "family-home" (*jia*). The second section looks at films from the 1930s and 1940s—*Tomboy* (1936), *Street Angel* (1937), and *Spring in a Small Town* (1948)—when Chinese cinema came of age as allegedly realist and overtly nationalist. These pre-1949 films criticize the Chinese present and look forward to a better or worse future through the metaphor of the divided family-home and, by extension, the divided nation. But they adopt different realist styles according to views of China's past and the politics of imagined national futures in these films. The third section is on cinema of the 1950s and 1960s, when state-prescribed realisms dominated film production on the mainland and in Taiwan. Both *socialist realism* in the PRC and *healthy realism* in Taiwan convey a faith that the present is the road to national utopia through the metaphor of the reconstructed family and rediscovered home. The final section discusses New Wave films from the 1980s and beyond, focusing on *Father and Son* (1981) and *Yellow Earth*. In the 1980s, a new generation of filmmakers reworked realism outside the parameters of earlier state cinemas or, in Hong Kong's case, commercial cinema. A loss of interest in a monolithic state-prescribed modernity is played out through the trope of the "emptied out" family-home.[6]

Several related themes therefore emerge from the films themselves. The first is that realism is ideologically linked to debates on Chinese modernity and national survival in the first half of the twentieth century. The second is that realism is always qualified as social, socialist, and so on, and these prefixes point to a mixed aesthetic that is often melodramatic. The third theme is the focus on family-home as the site at which these complex changes are played out. Indeed, many of the films under discussion imagine the "family-home" (*jia*) and link it to the "nation" (*guojia*) onscreen through melodramatic conventions, such as elaborate mise-en-scène (which functions as national allegory) and happy endings (which project different visions of China's future).[7] New Wave Chinese filmmakers rejected—but nevertheless played out against—many of these accepted conventions. After decades of staged settings, Chinese films like *Yellow Earth* are shot on location. And instead of celebrating the reunion of the family, these films challenge dominant state narratives and utopian endings through nonlinear plot, complex characterization, and scenes of disunity, nostalgia, death, and alienation. They describe, in this way, "the emptied-out" family-home.

Realism, Romanticism, and Melodrama

Despite the melodrama of much cinematic realism, realism was nevertheless the hegemonic mode of the Chinese cinema. It was approved as the mode of modernity. Realism's power lay in its explicit links to the making of a modern Chinese nation or—in Ted Huters' words—to bringing "imagined worlds into existence."[8]

This section outlines the shifting contours of realism in Chinese film. Overall we can say that realism in the Chinese cinema was variously linked to modernity and nationhood until the late twentieth century, when globalized modernity changed the terrain, often reconfiguring local identity through the past. At the same time, realism is often mixed with romantic and/or melodramatic conventions in cinematic practice.

Our first position, then, is that realism is constructed as the aesthetic counterpart of the quest to make China a modern nation-state. Realism was originally hailed as a radical aesthetic that was grounded in secular cosmologies whose core is social transformation. Transformation as *telos* is the crux of scientific and supposedly universal meta-narratives that dominated twentieth-century Chinese thought and cinema: Social Darwinism and then Marxism-Leninism. These are founding and often competing meta-narratives of Chinese nationhood.

Both evolution and Marxism came into China from nineteenth-century Western culture, along with realism and the cinema itself. Gillian Beer argues that growth and transformation and its counter-possibilities retrogression and extinction were two elements in evolutionary theory that shaped much thought and fiction, including "dark fantasies" of extinction as "a fate more probable than progress."[9] The hope of national transformation and the fear of extinction are the Janus-faced fantasy that drove early Chinese efforts to modernize. Revolutionary social transformation is also the crux of Mao Zedong's worldview, inheriting Marx's statement that the task of philosophy is not only to interpret the world but also to change it. While evolution and revolution were appropriated as universal theories, they were discussed in aggressively Chinese terms as ways of explaining China's territorial crisis as a nation-state under threat from Japanese imperialism. When social realist filmmaking emerged in the 1930s, the veteran filmmaker Zheng Zhengqiu called for revolution: "China is at the crossroads of survival and extinction. There are only two roads before us: the brighter road of life and the narrow road of death."[10]

At this time, cinematic realism was linked to national crisis, leading to a dualist discourse of life and death, new and old, progress and extinction, oppressed and oppressors. The discourse included a debate around old or *social realism,* a reformist aesthetic based on evolutionary change and liberal-democratic nationhood, and new or *critical realism*, a revolutionary aesthetic based on Marxism-Leninism and socialist nationhood. The two aesthetics projected different views of national transformation and survival, particularized onscreen as debates over the home, family, and nation. These dualisms operated until New Wave cinemas, in the People's Republic and in Taiwan, deconstructed the teleologies of transformation in the 1980s. *City of Sadness* (1989), as we have seen, is one such example. *Yellow Earth* is another. Allen Fong's film, *Father and Son* (1981), is a personal example of rethinking Hong Kong's colonial past through his family.[11]

This understanding is embedded in the main Chinese term for realism. Realism or *xianshizhuyi* ("present reality-ism") is clearly a counterpart of the words for modernity and modernism, respectively *xiandai* and *xiandaizhuyi* ("the present era-ism"), through the common character *xian*, meaning "the present."[12] Other terms, such as *xieshi* (a traditional term for realism) or *zhenshi* (the real), relate to aesthetic practices and are subordinate to *xianshizhuyi* as ideology. Modernization (*xiandaihua*) is so integral to Chinese twentieth-century experience as a nation that it is now enshrined as "the four modernizations" in the 1982 Constitution of the People's Republic. Realist filmmaking was harnessed to this process.

Scholars of Chinese literature Marston Anderson and Ted Huters have written at length on realism as a foreign concept in a literary context where realism was read as modernity but debated in its national Chinese context. The terms relating to realism in this chapter are therefore familiar to Western readers, but their usage differs across time, place, and territories, and they are variously applied to films by Chinese critics. Social realism is a term that relates location and identity to character development and social change, as in *Tomboy*, often with a nationalist but not necessarily a reformist or revolutionary agenda. Critical realist films such as *Street Angel* are distinguished from social realist films by their political alignment to pre-1949 revolutionary nation-building. Socialist realism in the Chinese cinema is modeled on that of the Soviet Union. It claims critical realism as its heritage, but it is a state aesthetic that promotes a socialist nation-state, mass audience accessibility, idealized images of Chinese society, positive messages, and stereotyped class heroes or heroines.[13] The example is *New Year's Sacrifice* (1956) in this chapter and, as we explain later below, Taiwan's healthy realism is similar to socialist realism, except for the class analysis. Huters writes that realism's utopian national project to modernize was never quite realized because it was about "imagining something into existence" while "mired within the horrible reality of twentieth-century China." In left-wing discourse, failure was attributed to tradition and not to realism, which retained its status as the fixed signifier of modernity, including postmodernity.[14] Thus, nostalgia for the past was repressed or severely criticized in mainland critical realist and socialist realist cinema. Despite this suppression, it emerges again and again as poetic realism in many Chinese films, such as *Spring in a Small Town, Father and Son,* and *Yellow Earth. Poetic realism* takes its name from a movement in French art cinema of the 1930s that gives an "early-optimism, later-pessimism message" that parallels the rise and fall of the leftist Popular Front in France in the interwar period.[15] In the Chinese context, *Yellow Earth* for example documents the promise and failure of the Chinese Communist Party in its founding years. These films are often politically nonaligned, stylized, and imbued with poetic symbolism, fatalism, and a sense of degeneration or death.

In contrast to the People's Republic, nostalgia flourished in Taiwan realist cinema after 1949. Loss of China surfaced as sentiment and sorrow for many decades: "tears abounded in books, films, and records, even in newspapers."[16] Unlike mainland cinema, tradition was celebrated as integral to Taiwan modernity. Hong Kong's colonial status gives the Hong Kong cinema its own realist lineage with its own "gaze towards China."[17] The 1949 film that inaugurated Cantonese realist cinema, *Tragedy on the Pearl River,* was made by left-wing filmmakers from Shanghai on a common antitraditional theme: feudal oppression of peasant families, especially women. With no nation-state agenda or prescribed aesthetic, Hong Kong cinema diverged from that of Taiwan, turning "sorrow into strength" in allegedly more realist martial arts movies—the *kung fu* film—that rework Confucian values, or producing Hollywood-style melodramas around questions of family and identity in Hong Kong's own brand of cosmopolitan capitalism.[18] All this changed with New Wave cinemas that document the end of the utopian project on the mainland and in Taiwan, and the end of the colonial era in Hong Kong, leading to a cross-border renaissance in cinema, in politics, and in thinking about family, home, and nation—and realism.

Our second position in this chapter is that the utopian quest to make China a modern nation-state also impels cinematic realism to become a mixed mode. It incorporates romanticism and melodrama in a variety of forms and under various labels. Before we turn to European romanticism and melodrama in China, we note that China has its own history of romantic literature and of melodrama, including a whole range of operas that often became film.

Unlike China, a common contrast in the West is between realism and romanticism. Like realism, romanticism describes a European literary movement that emerged in the late eighteenth century and was central to national revivalism and cultural regeneration.[19] In China, early European romanticism was concerned with liberating the imagination from centuries of Confucian thought and was crucial to reconceptualizations of the individual within the family and society. Romanticism was perceived as revolutionary in the fight against tradition, a view inherited by the People's Republic of China. Raymond Williams argues that realism and romanticism were originally "interlocking interests" that were later disassociated in the West.[20] In China realism and romanticism came hand in hand and were not disassociated until later in the twentieth century. Jaruslav Prušek states:

> The modern revolution in China is thus, first and foremost, in the sphere of ideas, a revolution of the individual and of individualism in opposition to traditional dogmas. In this context, we can then realize the immense importance of subjectivist and individualistic [Romantic] tendencies in modern Chinese thought and art. It is equally natural, however, that this consciousness of self ... must go hand in hand with realism, with the ability to look at oneself and the facts of existence without the spectacles of tradition.[21]

Just as Chinese distinguished between old and new realism in the 1930s, so too various left-wing intellectuals distinguished between "passive" romanticism as reformist and "active" romanticism as revolutionary. Again, both versions were linked to conflicting ideas of transforming the nation, Republican or socialist, respectively. Left-wing thinkers reformulated "passive" romanticism into a collective, nationalist, and active aesthetic. Hence, in Chinese terminology, realism is often romanticized. Realism may be seen through changing romantic spectacles (such as old, new, social, socialist, healthy, and so on) except when romanticism has equal billing in the Maoist prescription for all the arts in the late 1950s: "revolutionary realism and revolutionary romanticism." Thus, romanticism evolved into an active, utopian, and mythic imaginary of China's future. According to Ma Junxiang, nationalism informed early cinema as a realist and mythic art that spoke symbolically of China's destiny as victim of Western modernity. Linda Ehrlich and Ma Ning further argue that this art depicts the fate of the nation through the fates of family-clan (*jiazu*) for much of the twentieth century.[22] However, as the following sections demonstrate, the family-home as a dominant trope was used in different ways with different realisms to project different projected fates of the nation and of the nation-state.

This mixed allegorical mode is a distinctive feature of Chinese film language. The mix is now seen as central to melodrama. Realism and melodrama have also been cast as opposites in the West, contrasting realism's alleged emphasis on authenticity and truth with melodrama's theatricality, exaggeration, and sentimentality. Realism was approved; melodrama was not. It is now recognized that realism, romanticism, and melodrama share many basic conventions.[23] In the classic work in the field, Peter Brooks calls melodrama the "mode of the modern imagination" while Thomas El-saesser calls it a "mode of experience." The mode enacts spiritual crises in a secular world and, by extension, enacts national crises.[24] In Brooks's words, melodrama is about "the confronted power of evil and goodness, the sense of hazard and clash, [and] the intensification and heightening of [everyday] experience corresponding to dream and desire."[25] In Western cinema studies, melodrama has become a floating signifier of modernity, whether as genre, mode, or ideology. It is a persistent critical "chameleon" and "catalyst."[26]

As a critical catalyst, melodrama has been extended to Chinese cinemas with their own melodramatic traditions.[27] Scholars claim, for example, that the origins of early realist cinema in China are Hollywood cinema, Chinese spoken drama, and a popular literature called the Mandarin Duck and Butterfly School.[28] These are modern cultural forms. When we look more closely at these forms and at early Chinese cinema itself, the dominant mode is realist melodrama. Characteristics that Li Suyuan assigns to early Chinese cinema as *Chinese*—linear narrative, simplified plot, and happy endings (*da-tuanyuan,* meaning "reunions of the family")—are also recognized features of Western melodrama and of traditional Chinese melodrama.[29]

In the 1980s, Ma Ning and others applied Western theories of melo-drama to mainland Chinese cinema, claiming that family melodrama is a "vital form of social representation." The analyses converged on the so-called political melodrama of the director Xie Jin, whose work spans five decades.[30] Other scholars apply Western theories to Taiwan and Hong Kong cinema. A problem for all these scholars is that melodrama (vari-ously called *qingjieju, tongsuju, shangyinpian,* or *wenyipian*) does not (yet) have a clear Chinese terminology and lineage. Where melodrama is used, it usually refers to a genre rather than a mode. The Taiwan scholar Cai Guorong claims that modern Chinese melodrama (*wenyipian* or "literature-art-films") developed in two directions—family melodramas (*lunli qinqing pian* or "ethical family feeling films") and romances (*langman aiqingpian* or "romantic love films")—but a search through the literature shows that these two directions often merge.[31] However, Law Kar's extension of Cai's analysis to Cantonese melodrama points to characteristics of melodrama as mode, not just genre:

> Melodrama has two conditions: the first being that films of this genre use con-temporary or recent society as a backdrop and, second, they dealt with human emotions and are therefore lyrical to an extent. Melodrama functions as a bridge between everyday life and fantasy, and it is for this very reason that this genre has such continued vitality. [32]

These two conditions summarize melodramatic realism as we understand it in this chapter. Romanticism and melodrama are intrinsic to realist practices in the broad sweep of the Chinese cinema. Its visual poetry reveals the moral dimensions of the everyday world. The mode favors the dispossessed and was therefore tailor-made for early Chinese reformers who often saw themselves as victims of a modern *and* traditional world order that had to be transformed. All in all, melodramatic realism is a major strain in the Chinese cinema because its central theme of outraged innocence was often perceived as real in national, and not just personal, terms.[33] Realism (with its melodramatic core) is a dominant mode of the Chinese cinema because, in China as elsewhere, it is what Raymond Williams calls "a lived hegemony"—active, inclusive, transformational, and continually contested.[34] In this sense, melodramatic realism is the mixed mode of the national.

Divided Families, Divided Nation

The interwar period was when realism in Chinese film came of age. Film after film presents pictures of divided families and homes across a divided nation. Many are now classics of the Chinese cinema. They include *Big Road, Tomboy, Street Angel,* and *Crossroads* from the "golden age" of 1930s Shanghai cinema. They also include films from the civil war period in the late 1940s, such as *A Spring River Flows East, Faraway Love, Spring in a Small Town,* and *Crows and Sparrows.* With the exception of *Tomboy* and *Spring in a Small Town,* all are famous left-wing, critical realist texts. Without exception, they all employ melodramatic conventions. The films merge together as a story of a nation divided—by imperialism, by war, by class, and by gender in cities, towns, and countryside.

These divisions emerge as actual and symbolic architecture in three paradigmatic family films—Shanghai mansion in *Tomboy,* Shanghai ghetto in *Street Angel,* and gentry courtyard house in *Spring in a Small Town.* The architecture displays three different families as real yet transcendent, linking family dramas to national narratives. The families are a patriarchal Confucian clan in *Tomboy,* an exploitative foster family in *Street Angel,* and a gentry household in *Spring in a Small Town.*[35] The national background at this time is war, from 1931 to 1949. This outside world is invisible (or barely visible) but omnipresent as architecture in all three films. The architecture symbolizes entrapment in turbulent times, visually displaying walls as metaphors of China's imprisonment and death. Except there is some hope, some agency; there are parks, gardens, windows, alleyways, and gaps in walls. And all explicitly link class-based family narratives to competing national narratives.

These three films employ common melodramatic conventions within different realist aesthetics, although they were not considered melodrama until recently. Mainland Chinese film criticism of the three revolved around constructions of realism in which only *Street Angel* was approved until the post-Mao period. Indeed, cinema overall was not considered correctly realist in orthodox Marxist film histories until the 1930s, a time when global cinema was turning to realism and, in China, when the Communist Party infiltrated the film industry and left-wing social realist films were produced.[36] Contemporary reviews of the three films therefore reflect the Marxist-Leninist position on critical realism as a patriotic duty. Yet all have melodramatic elements. The first film, *Tomboy*, is similar to Hollywood middle-class family melodramas within a classic realist mode. The film was much maligned by left-wing critics in the 1930s. *Tomboy* was called "soft film," "opiate for the masses," "ice cream for the eyes," and a "sofa for the soul." Indeed, *Tomboy* opposes—"traitorously" it was said[37]— revolutionary film discourse and the overriding patriotism required of all films on the eve of the Anti-Japanese War. In contrast, Yuan Muzhi's *Street Angel* is "new realism." It is considered a left-wing classic and "hard film," exposing Japanese aggression and class exploitation through the stories of two displaced Manchurian sisters living in the underbelly of Shanghai. While the film's aesthetic is said to be akin to Western realist forms, such as social realism, new realism, and and Italian neorealism and German Expressionism,[38] Ma Ning claims that populist Chinese elements give a nationalist allegory to the film's predominantly melodramatic form.[39] *Spring in a Small Town* evokes a different aesthetic, the lyricism of traditional poetry. In Marxist-Leninist film criticism, *Spring in a Small Town* was long considered a "wan," "morbid" work of the degenerate bourgeoisie that was "entirely out of step with the times."[40] However, the film is now acknowledged as a masterpiece by all critics, and Tian Zhuangzhuang remade it in the People's Republic in 2002. The 1948 original was praised for recording the mood of an era "beyond words" and "beyond realism."[41] It has been called "shadow poetry" and shadow painting, but not shadowplay.[42] Its film language is realist, poetic, melodramatic, and transcendent.[43] According to Ginette Vincendeau, poetic realism and melodrama both evoke "the world of the everyday" that is "dominated by fate, coincidence, circularity, and nostalgia."[44] This is the style of *Spring in a Small Town*.

Within either evolutionary or revolutionary Chinese frameworks, the rich extended family in *Tomboy* is minimally modern. The grandfather finally acknowledges his granddaughter's filial virtue and is immediately rewarded with a traditional heir: a grandson. He is oblivious to "the invasion and murder by our [Japanese] enemies."[45] He is also a capitalist; the wealthy family lives in a mansion and "forbids one drop of fertile water to

---

TOMBOY, A.K.A. GIRL IN DISGUISE (HUASHEN GUNIANG)
<hr/>

DIRECTED BY FANG PEILIN

Yihua Film, 1936

A beautiful 18-year-old granddaughter, Liying, disguises herself as a grandson when the family patriarch calls her home from Singapore—because the family lied about her being a girl to satisfy his desire for a male heir. This disguise is the excuse for romantic suspense, a series of comic incidents (such as sleeping in the same bed as her grandfather), and moments of recognition. Finally, however, the grandfather accepts Liying as a girl and immediately receives news of the birth of a real grandson. The closure is a family *datuanyuan*—recognition/reunion, a grandson, and marriage for the "tomboy." In a sequel soon after, an evil nephew kidnaps the baby boy and substitutes a baby girl to inherit the family business. But Liying disguises herself as a male (again) and rescues the boy from the thieves' lair. The latest sequel was made in Hong Kong in 1956.

---

fall on outsiders' fields," according to a contemporary critique.[46] In left-wing readings, *Tomboy* is an escapist film that incorporates three popular genres of the times: comedy through Liying's cross-dressing, romantic love as the subplot, and detective fiction in the sequel.[47] *Tomboy* directly opposes hard film, according to contemporary left-wing critics, which "takes its themes from living reality, stirring national consciousness, and fulfilling the mission of national defense: this is the sole duty of contemporary film

FIGURE 4.1 A girl flirts in the park with Liying, disguised as a male in *Tomboy* (1936).

(COURTESY CHINA FILM ARCHIVE)

in China."[48] While *Tomboy* was called "poisonous," "frivolous," and "worthless," it was nonetheless a box office hit. [49] Urban audiences loved it.

As both family and romantic melodrama, *Tomboy* uses the trope of the family's angst about male heirs to communicate a national angst about the future. In terms of the expressive conventions that govern melodramatic realism, hysteria is embodied in the grandfather in this film. He collapses in the early scenes because he has no grandsons, and this motivates the family's deceit and Liying's disguise, which in turn motivates the twists and turns of the film's plot. The denouement pivots on moments of recognition, of publicly acknowledged filial virtue. These moments take place in privileged bourgeois spaces: parks, garden, and bedrooms. There are two climactic bedroom scenes. The first is when the grandfather discovers that Liying is a girl (in *her* bedroom). The second is when the grandfather accepts Liying (in *his* bedroom). Both scenes are told through gestures, an intimate "semiotics of the body."[50] The first scene takes place at ten o'clock at night when Liying is ill in bed from a "woman's illness." She cries out, waking her grandfather from his sleep.

> *Medium shot:* Grandfather hurries to his "grandson's" bedroom, embraces Liying, and then sees her breasts.
> *Full close-up:* A lingering shot of Liying's breathing chest from the grandfather's point of view.
> *Full close-up:* A point-of-view shot that cuts to Liying's face, eyes closed, as she collapses back onto the pillow.
> *Medium close-*up: Grandfather withdraws, hand to head in horror, and says, "You're a girl!"
> *Long shot:* Grandfather points an accusing finger at Liying and then he faints to the floor.
> *Long shot:* Liying collapses across the bed.

This scene is high melodrama as the grandfather stares in horror at Liying's scantily covered breasts and faints! It acts out the unspeakable—a voyeuristic fear of liberated femininity, family extinction through lack of male heirs, and free choice in marriage—and highlights troubled themes in early films as in Chinese society. The unspeakable is often cast as illness, a common metaphor for social disease throughout early-twentieth-century literature and film.[51] Within this framework, the grandfather's illness in *Tomboy* is healed with a traditional panacea: a male heir. This happy ending is a sign of the times in Kuomindang (KMT) versions of China's destiny, which include Confucian values as central to the Republic's national identity. With the imminent Japanese takeover of Shanghai, Ma Junxiang claims that film closures became utopian: "Chinese must win—the future belongs

STREET ANGEL (MALU TIANSHI)

WRITTEN AND DIRECTED BY YUAN MUZHI

Mingxing, 1937

Two sisters, Xiao Yun and Xiao Hong, are homeless refugees from Manchuria after the Japanese takeover of Shanghai in 1931. They are adopted by an evil couple among Shanghai's underclass. Xiao Yun is beaten and forced to work as a street prostitute; Xiao Hong works for them as a "sing-song girl" (or entertainer/courtesan). The couple sells Xiao Hong to a local gangster, Gu, but she escapes with Chen Xiaoping, a musician, who loves her but disapproves of her prostitute sister. Chen and Hong marry. Xiao Yun and Chen's friend, Lao Wang, fall in love. However, Xiao Yun is killed by her so-called father when he pursues Xiao Hong with Gu and his thug. Thus, Xiao Yun dies to save her sister, and her sacrifice is recognized by her friends and sister at her deathbed.

to the people" as a nation.[52] In *Tomboy,* the wealthy family survives as an elite institution in Shanghai, but it is not the inclusive family of the dispossessed that was required of all left-wing films of the 1930s and 1940s.

Street Angel captures the architecture of Shanghai modernity as literally upper and lower classes in its opening sequence: walls and windows, streets and alleyways, open and closed rooms, skyscraper, park, church, and ghetto. As dark and light, as a long establishing sequence of mismatch shots, or as shadowy ghetto, architectural imagery dominates this film. As Ma Ning explains, the realism in *Street Angel* is complemented by Soviet-style montage and by the original 1928 Hollywood melodrama of the same name.[53]

Characters have various levels of agency in negotiating Shanghai's urban spaces. Xiao Chen, the hero played by Zhao Dan, comes and goes through the public and private spaces of Shanghai's underclass (streets, barber's shops, teahouses, roofs, and rooms) but is barred from the lawyer's white penthouse because he is poor. He nevertheless gives agency to Xiao Hong—through their facing windows across the alleyway where they sing their love, but also through stairways, squalid rooms, streets, and hideaways when she escapes her foster parents. Xiao Hong is all movement, usually alone or with others in medium shots: singing, pouting, crying, smiling, wriggling, walking, and hiding in the loft. She escapes. Her sister, Xiao Yun, is a street prostitute. She only has agency as a sacrificial victim. Her isolation and despised status are frequently rendered in stillness, silence, and full close-up. Her unmoving gaze contrasts with the exaggerated eye movements of Xiao Chen and Xiao Hong. She is confined by the architecture. On the street, in the pouring rain, in dark alleyways, and in closed rooms, her presence is the accusatory social force of this film. The

FIGURE 4.2 Xiao Yun, a prostitute on the streets in *Street Angel* (1937).

short scene where her foster mother is about to beat her with eager sadism is a powerful example. The foster father leaves. The door closes. The mother (holding her stick) dominates the center of the small room, seeking information on Xiao Hong's hiding-place. Xiao Yun presses against the walls. Shot–reverse-shots of Xiao Yun and her mother are overlaid with loud, harsh commands: "Shut the door." "Come here." "Tell me the truth or I'll kill you." "Strip off." "Did you hear?" "Strip everything off." "Hurry." Xiao Yun never speaks.

Xiao Yun, like prostitutes in nearly all Chinese films of the 1930s, dies in the closing scene despite being loved by Chen's friend, Lao Wang. The moral conflict, but not the social conflict, is clearly resolved in this film. Xiao Yun is united on her death with Xiao Chen and his friends, who surround her with Xiao Hong as her new family (fig. 4.3a). This is a reunion, a *datuanyuan*. In the best melodramatic tradition it is also a public recognition of private virtue; in the revolutionary tradition, it is a moral claim by the poor to be the new rulers of the Chinese nation. Xiao Yun's sacrifice allows her to pronounce on society. Recognition belongs to a new class—a prostitute, not a patriarch as in *Tomboy*. Semidelirious and dying, Xiao Yun starts and speaks as she sees a shadow at the window: "Lao Wang, is Lao Wang back? ... He's good, he helps the poor ... we're all just ants, ants ..." (fig. 4.3b).

Xiao Yun dies (fig. 4.3c). Her friends surround her in a tableau shot of solidarity in a dark room, seen through a barred window that symbolizes entrapment. But they look out. This is social accusation, reinforced in the

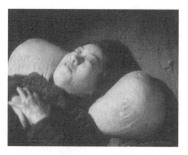

FIGURE 4.3a Xiao Yun on her deathbed, surrounded by her friends in *Street Angel* (1937).

FIGURE 4.3b Xiao Yun makes her deathbed accusation ...

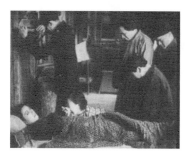

FIGURE 4.3c ... and then she dies.

final image of a white skyscraper that presses down on the poor as a symbol of the rapacious capitalism promoted under the KMT Nationalists. The Law resides in this heaven, but any justice except revolutionary justice is denied to China's poor.

Architectural ruins dominate *Spring in a Small Town*. They reflect the deep melancholy of the times that Chen Mo retrospectively sees as a type of realism.[54] The film merges the characters' inner melancholy—narrated as voice-over by the wife, Zhou Yuwen—with their everyday world in a walled-in gentry household. Long, slow establishing shots of the town, and especially the town walls, set the mood. This shot sequence suggests that "the picture is larger than the frame, [and] there are pictures outside the frame."[55] Zhou Yuwen's young sister-in-law, Dai Xiu, explains: "The walls go on and on in an endless circle. You look out as far as the eye can see and realize the world is big." Inside, the imagery shifts to the bombed ruins of the house that, in Dai Xiu's words again, "hardly lets you breathe." The household is made up of the sick husband Dai Liyan, his wife who lives "without hope," the servant, and Dai Xiu. Then Zhang Zhichen, a doctor friend of the husband and former lover of the wife, passes through the gate in the town walls, clambers over the garden walls and into the lives of the

> *SPRING IN A SMALL TOWN (XIAOCHENG ZHI CHUN)*
>
> DIRECTED BY FEI MU
>
> Wenhua Film Studio, 1948
>
> An estranged gentry couple, Dai Liyan and Zhou Yuwen, live in a small town with Dai's schoolgirl sister and an old servant. Their daily monotony is broken by the arrival of Zhang Zhichen, Dai's friend and the wife's former lover. Zhang is blown home by "the east-west-north-south winds" of China's war of resistance and brings with him the excitement of revolutionary changes in the outside world. Zhou and Zhang fall in love again. Her morbidly melancholy husband, Dai Liyan, attempts suicide so his wife may reunite with her lover but he fails. At the climactic reunion, Zhang and the family surround Dai's bedside, recognizing that Zhang, a doctor, must save his friend and that life must go on. In the end, Dai Liyan's wife stays with him in the small town; the lover leaves.

Dai family, bringing with him life outside the frame: wartime China. The love affair rekindles and Dai attempts suicide. This act brings the household to reunion and recognition through wifely anguish at his bedside. Psychic excess is enacted through tears and tableau as Zhou Yuwen lies sobbing on her husband's unconscious body, surrounded by Zhang and the family. Thus ruined walls in this film enclose the action as visible and yet also invisible "ghost walls" that, for Lu Xun and for Fei Mu, are symbols of old China's past isolation and glory and present decay.[56]

In the end, Zhang leaves the house and the town. In the final sequence, Dai Liyan joins Zhou Yuwen on the walls in a long shot of marital harmony. Li Cheuk-to finds this "happy" ending "imperfect."[57] Yet the ending—as is common in melodrama—is ambiguous. An acknowledged strength of melodrama is its capacity to display contradictions, to uncover the re-

FIGURE 4.4 Dai Liyan walks on the town walls in *Spring in a Small Town* (1948).
(COURTESY CHINA FILM ARCHIVE)

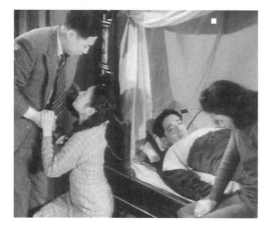

FIGURE 4.5 Family reunion at the husband's bedside in *Spring in a Small Town* (1948).

(COURTESY CHINA FILM ARCHIVE)

pressed, to retain a sense of the past, and to focus desire (and viewer pleasure) on "the unattainable object."[58] Geoffrey Nowell-Smith claims that the
happy ending is frequently impossible and, what is more, the audience
knows it.[59] The town wall in Fei Mu's film is a site for dreaming and for
nostalgia, a landscape of loss. Husband and wife may be reunited in the
frame. But they are reunited on ruins. As a national metaphor in this film,
walls symbolize the end of the scholar gentry and the end of an era. A new
nation is being born, under Mao Zedong's leadership of the revolutionary
classes.

The unspeakable in all these films is family division, represented as patriarchy's loss of future generations in *Tomboy*, as loss of homeland, loss of
family and, indeed, loss of life in *Street Angel* and, finally, as loss of an era
in *Spring in a Small Town*.

Reconstructed Families, Reconstructed Nations

In the People's Republic after 1949 and the Republic of China in the 1960s,
realism was elevated to the official aesthetic. This is the major difference
between the films discussed in this section and the preceding section. In
the state-supported cinemas of the People's Republic and of Taiwan, film is
explicitly harnessed to national reconstruction. Ashish Rajadhyaksha calls
such cinemas of social purpose "nationalist realism-modernism"; they promote national "reconstruction agendas adopting economic programs based
on the principles of scientific rationalism and its aesthetic counterpart of
realism."[60] The mode in both the mainland and Taiwan is melodramatic,
enacting dramas of good and evil within fictional families—whether bound
by blood, work, or class—as the foundation of the state. These works come

complete with endings that herald a new social order. The crucial difference between the imagined social orders in China and Taiwan is the attitude to Chinese tradition. Mainland socialist realist cinema fiercely rejects tradition; Taiwan's healthy realist cinema celebrates it.

In the People's Republic the agenda was called "socialist reconstruction" until China's post-Mao leader Deng Xiaoping introduced the socialist market economy in the late 1970s. Its aesthetic counterpart was socialist realism, based on the Soviet model from 1949, with the addition of revolutionary romanticism to socialist realism in 1958. Both promoted an idealized image of social progress, based on class struggle, and stereotyped class heroes and villains. In many ways, both socialist realism and socialist realism and revolutionary romanticism borrowed representational techniques from literal melodrama, where social issues are simplified for their full pathos and ethical import. For Brooks, literal melodrama and realism come together as

> the polarization of good and evil [that] works toward revealing their presence and operation as real forces in the world. Their conflict suggests the need to recognize and confront evil, to combat and expel it, to purge the social order.... While its social implications may be variously revolutionary or conservative, it is in all cases radically democratic, striving to make its representations clear and legible to everyone.[61]

Good and evil were cast within historical as well as class frameworks, with a line drawn between preliberation and postliberation China. An explicit message across films of this era was the need to purge society of the old feudal order, embodied in the old family system. The well-known adaptation of a famous May Fourth short story by Lu Xun, *New Year's Sacrifice,* makes this message quite clear.

Lu Xun's original story is vehemently anti-Confucian. It exposes a Confucian family system that tortures its victims beyond death. The narration is personal, told by a scholar of the Lu family who is complicit in Xianglin's wife's death and haunted by her questions of the afterlife. Finally, the scholar forgets her in the New Year festivities at dawn that signal the "boundless good fortune" coming to the hometown of the Lu clan. This "happy ending" is ironic. Lu Xun's fiction is an explicit "call to arms" against tradition. For Lu Xun, Chinese modernity is "the path of evolution" while tradition is a retrogressive "suicidal turning back."[62]

In the film, the personal voice disappears, a linear plot replaces the narrator's retrospective reconstruction of the widow's life, and the message is explicit and collective. The film's final scene is powerful, ending rather than beginning with the dying widow's question: "After death, is there such a

---

NEW YEAR'S SACRIFICE (ZHUFU)

DIRECTED BY SANG HU

Beijing Film Studio, 1956

Based on the story by Lu Xun, *New Year's Sacrifice*, 1924

A young peasant widow, Xianglin's wife, runs away from her mother-in-law, who plans to sell her. She works in the wealthy Lu household until recaptured and is forcibly remarried despite the Confucian proscription on the remarriage of widows. Tragedy follows: her second husband dies and a wolf eats her young son. Destitute, she returns to the Lu household but, twice-widowed, she is considered unclean and becomes a beggar. She dies in the snow on New Year's Eve. The settings—peasant and literati homes—accentuate class difference. There is a double closure. The first points to past "tragedy" through the widow's death. The second is a happy ending: a voice-over recognizes the widow's virtue, claiming that the era of class exploitation and feudal superstition has gone forever.

---

thing as a soul?" This death scene follows the rich red interior shots of the Lu household during the New Year festivities. In contrast, a medium close-up of Xianglin's homeless wife sitting outside alone on a cold snowy night is muted in shadow (fig. 4.6). On the verge of death, she slowly stands up and staggers offscreen. A long shot tracks to a close-up as she approaches the camera, asking the unknown spectator (not the scholar-narrator) about life after death. A final long shot shows her dark silhouette collapsing and dying in the snow as an omniscient male voice retrospectively recognizes the widow's class virtue on behalf of the nation:

> Xianglin's wife was an honest hardworking woman, but after sufferings and humiliations she died tragically. This happened forty years ago in the old society. Happily for us such a time has gone forever and will never ever return.

The socialist message is clear. Such family-national tragedies, the voice-over claims, cannot happen in the new China. Socialist realist film in China demonizes the feudal past and romanticizes the revolution within a melodramatic mode that polarizes rich and poor, past and present, and exploiters and victims. The revolutionary poor are new heroes and masters of the new China.

Taiwan cinema, in contrast to socialist realism, draws on the past as integral to its modern identity. National reconstruction agendas were based around small-scale state capitalism. Together with the Taiwan government, Taiwan's major film studio (Central Motion Picture Corporation, CMPC) introduced "healthy realism" (*jiankang xieshizhuyi*) in the 1960s as a mode that endorsed these family values and family enterprise. Its foremost ex-

FIGURE 4.6 Xianglin's homeless wife sits outside in the snow in *New Year's Sacrifice* (1956).

(COURTESY CHINA FILM ARCHIVE)

ponent is the director Lee Hsing. Lee is little known in the West, but all Chinese scholars consider him a major figure across Chinese-language cinemas.[63] He has a distinguished role in Taiwan film production, beginning in the late 1950s with Taiwanese-language films (see chapter 7) and then shifting to Mandarin-language films.

The level of realism in such work has been the subject of some debate. When the realist element is judged according to modern usage, it is found wanting. Indeed, healthy realism was renamed "healthy (reformist) strategy," acknowledging that "realism" is a misnomer. Lu Feii, for example, claims healthy realism adopted the *Reader's Digest's* editorial style, making it closer to socialist realism than to the social critique in critical or neorealism. Lu lists the "six nots" that guided healthy realism: "do not publicize the dark sides of society, do not stir up class hatred, do not have a pessimistic tone, do not express romantic sentiment, do not produce trivial works, and do not express incorrect thinking."[64] Such criticism evaluates realism as *xianshizhuyi,* the modern Western-derived term. Healthy realism, however, uses the traditional term for realism (*xieshi*) plus "ism": *xieshizhuyi. Xieshi* is an aesthetic, not an ideological, term and is understood in relation to its aesthetic counterpart, *xieyi* or expressionism, as the privileged aesthetic of traditional Chinese arts.[65] Despite similarities with socialist realism, the addition of "ism" (*zhuyi*) indicates a recasting of traditional realism into the modern. As a term, *xieshizhuyi* distinguishes its aesthetics, ideology, and social order from that of the enemy, the Chinese Communist Party, which had refashioned realism (*xianshizhuyi*) as socialist realism on Soviet models. Thus, when critics evaluate "healthy realism" on traditional Chinese criteria around *xieshi,* a more positive view places the style within a grand and evolving Chinese lineage that is populist, plot-driven, utopian, and moralistic. Given that the Lee Hsing lineage ostensibly includes famous traditional writers, then Taiwan's healthy realism embraces China's entire populist and classical heritage. Indeed, both sides of the debate acknowledge healthy realism's traditional family values as—in Lee Hsing's own words—"typical of traditional conservative Chinese people and greatly influenced by my strong belief in China's feudal ethics."[66]

Healthy realism extends the Chinese genre of family melodrama (*jiating lunlipian*). It was inaugurated in 1963 by the Kuomindang's (KMT) Central Motion Picture Corporation under the leadership of the former deputy of the government's Information Office. CMPC produced two box office hits in 1964 and 1965—*Oyster Girl* and *Beautiful Duckling.*[67] These films exemplify healthy realism's espousal of small family enterprise cemented by family feeling. The setting is pastoral, a lyrical evocation of the Taiwan countryside. The realist element is ordinary rural families overcoming problems in the Republic's new home, Taiwan. The healthy element is the triumph of so-called traditional family values. Good and evil in Lee's films are polarized and personalized around the dual ethic of family love and hard work.

FIGURE 4.7 *Oyster Girl* (1964).

(COURTESY CENTRAL MOTION PICTURE CORPORATION)

BEAUTIFUL DUCKLING (YANGYA RENJIA)

DIRECTED BY LEE HSING

Central Motion Picture Corporation, 1964

Xiaoyue (Little Moon) is an orphan. Her mother died at birth and her father is sent to Hainan by Japanese warlords, where he dies. Without knowing this family history, Xiaoyue is brought up by a widowed neighbor, Lin Zaifeng, as his own daughter. The film opens with scenes of father and daughter working together on their experimental duck-breeding farm; if the experiments are successful they can keep the ducks. Her blood brother Zhaofu arrives, first blackmailing Lin to keep the secret of Xiaoyue's birth from her and then trying to make her join his opera troupe as a star when she finds out that she's an orphan. In the end, Xiaoyue recognizes both her father's sacrificial love and Zhaofu and his wife's greed. Xiaoyue falls at her father's feet, crying again and again, "I'm your real daughter." They walk into the distance, holding hands and planning their future prosperity.

Beautiful Duckling is a romance with the Taiwan countryside and the nuclear family at its center, The melodramatic conventions of excessive mise-en-scène and tearful reunions naturalize the new family into its postwar Taiwan home. The abundance of the mise-en-scène in *Beautiful Duckling* communicates the fecundity of the countryside. The human drama is interspersed with scene after scene of rural prosperity—experimental duck farms, plump pigs, fish, babies, ducklings, town fairs overflowing with produce, and golden harvests where the reapers sing "grains glisten in the sun, paradise is here on earth." Lee Hsing employs a wide lens, close-ups, montage within the shot, and editing to suggest the plenitude of postwar Taiwan.

This plenitude is visually reinforced through repetition. The opening scenes, for example, set the bucolic tone with a kaleidoscope of duck shots. A voice-over states, "Ducks are everywhere in Taiwan. Ducks are popular subjects in vivid watercolor paintings and, in an artistic sense, have inspired *Beautiful Duckling*." The film opens with multiple images of ducks from watercolors by a famous Taiwan painter and then cuts to more multiple images of real ducks on the Lin family's pond. The rural family is then painted into the picture as Xiaoyue feeds the ducks, linking landscape, ducks, and girl in a series of single frames. At the end, this pastoral idyll is transformed into propertied idyll because Xiaoyue's father earns the land, his adopted daughter, and the ducks (previously on loan from the state for experimental breeding). He is the good father of the soil and of the family.

The "good father" is the recurring motif in Lee Hsing's healthy realist films. At the family level, *Beautiful Duckling* is a romance between adopted father and daughter, replete with secrets, misunderstandings, reunions, and lots of tears. The Lin family's crisis is resolved through emotion-charged scenes that resolve the moral dilemma around the treatment of the adopted daughter, Xiaoyue: a sacrificial paternal love (the good father) versus fraternal exploitation of blood ties (the bad brother and his wife).

However, the crux of the plot is private ownership. Capital replaces blood in unifying the new Confucian family in a nation of small capitalists. When he lets out the secret of Xiaoyue's adoption, the neighbor's son says : "Your ducks don't belong to your family and neither do you." Xiaoyue runs away to her blood brother. Property in turn pivots on the distinction between produce that is earned (good) and money for its own sake (bad). The successful breeding program means that Xiaoyue's father eventually owns the ducks, which he converts to cash and gives to brother and sister to finance a small business that will set them on the "right path" in life. In other words, cash converts back to produce. This moral is quite explicit in the final sequences as the father and his blood son confront Zhaofu, his wife, and Xiaoyue in their rented room. The message ends with a close-up of the father in tears as he says to Xiaoyue, "You're not my blood daughter but I can never get you out of my heart. How can I not care for you when I brought you up? Go with your brother and his wife. I'll visit you." To sobs, father and son leave. This triggers a mute, tear-filled reunion that transmutes the package of money on the table into pure love (figs. 4.8a–4.8h).

The message about the evil of money is then reiterated. Zhaofu and his wife come to blows over the money. In contrast, Lin, his son, and Xiaoyue are reunited as a family on the farm together. The last scene begins with a close-up of three pairs of legs walking along a road with Xiaoyue asking how they will live without any ducks. Her father replies, "Don't worry. We have lots of eggs to hatch." His son then says that he is leaving his factory job to come home to the farm. The film ends with the family walking away from the camera into the countryside, holding hands. The prosperous countryside is now mirrored in the overflowing love of this small united family.

Beautiful Duckling claims tradition but in fact espouses an emerging capitalist modernity with all its problems. Lee Hsing's films boldly dramatize family secrets, such as adoption, alcoholic fathers, premarital pregnancies, the disabled, and infanticide. Conflict is simplistically resolved onscreen through cathartic tears. The Lee Hsing model works as literal melodrama around the metaphor of a reconfigured family-home. However, the family values in this model are not those of traditional patriarchy that devalue the young and the female. The young dominate these movies. Lin sacrifices even his livelihood for his daughter who is not his daughter. Xiaoyue is allowed to leave home, she will have a say in her marriage partner, and she is a full family member who is explicitly valued in the film for her economic

FIGURE 4.8a Xiaoyue calls out "Papa" in *Beautiful Duckling* (1965).

FIGURE 4.8b Xiaoyue falls at her father's knees.

FIGURE 4.8c Xiaoyue's father sobs.

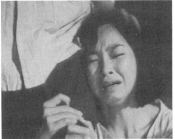

FIGURE 4.8d Xiaoyue sobs at her father's knees.

FIGURE 4.8e Xiaoyue's adopted brother sobs.

FIGURE 4.8f Zhaofu sobs.

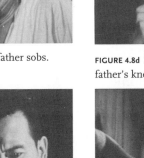

FIGURE 4.8g Xiaoyue says she wants to go home.

FIGURE 4.8h Zhaofu hangs his head in shame.

productivity, not her reproductivity. This family is not founded on blood and lineage. Scene after scene in *Beautiful Duckling* shows the family working together. The adopted family is a nuclear family unit bound by work, upbringing, and pooled capital, not by blood. The film belongs to the popular genre of family melodrama, reshaping a humanist Confucian tradition into a Confucian ethic and a spirit of capitalism as the foundation of the Republic of China in Taiwan.

All the nontraditional elements are transfigured by the utopian setting and tearful reunions, legitimized as tradition but economically bourgeois. Lee Hsing's healthy realism therefore endorses small-scale rural modernization as the backbone of modern society. This is therefore a cinema of its times that ideologically affirms Taiwan as the home of its people. The theme of emerging capitalism is explicit. The visual pairing of land and people is implicit. It naturalizes an adopted family of Mandarin-speaking peasants as part of the rural landscape, a microcosm of the KMT Nationalist takeover of Taiwan as both home and nation following the Japanese loss of the colony at the end of World War II. Healthy realism is therefore a proto-national reunion or *datuanyuan:* "coming home" to Taiwan.

The "Emptied-Out" Family-Home

Reenvisioning the family-home by rejecting the codes of literal melodrama is common across late-twentieth-century Chinese cinemas. In this section we apply the notion of the "emptied-out" family-home to specific New Wave films from Hong Kong and the People's Republic: Allen Fong's *Father and Son* (1981) and *Yellow Earth*.

The phrase "emptied-out family-home" describes fundamental changes in late-twentieth-century Taiwan society. The term "emptied-out" was coined by Chang Hsiao-hung to explain *Vive L'Amour* (1994), one of a *fin-de-siècle* Taipei trilogy by Tsai Ming-liang. Fran Martin extends the concept, explaining that Tsai's other two films in the trilogy—*Rebels of the Neon God* (1992) and *The River* (1997)—"deal directly with the family-home at the level of the story." She links memory of the plenteous family-home to other Taiwan films of the same period, notably Ang Lee's *Wedding Banquet* (1993).

> It is in *Amour* that the idea of the *jia* (family-home) and its apparent absence is most arrestingly present at a symbolic level, in the metaphor of the empty apartment. Taiwan feminist scholar Chang Hsiao-hung argues convincingly that what we see in *Amour* is not so much a dramatisation of the tragic breakdown of some mythic "traditional family," as has been suggested by some, but rather an "emptying out" of the *jia* itself that compels a fundamental re-thinking of

its significance in relation to current transformations in Taiwan's society and culture.[68]

If we consider this shift in the light of the fictitious fecundity of the family-home in Lee Hsing's films, then its representation through emptiness records the loss of monolithic and utopian state narratives of social change. This loss is often cinematically represented through ambiguous or lack of family reunions.

Emptiness in the "emptied-out" family-home is variously conceptualized in New Wave films beyond Taiwan. In Hong Kong, emptiness is part of a "nostalgia cinema craze." Yingjin Zhang analyzes this craze against the dual tropes of disappearance and dislocation in which the 1997 handover of Hong Kong to the People's Republic plays a political role. In temporal dislocation, Hong Kong itself is the star.[69] Zhang argues that many of the nostalgia films prefer the past of the 1950s and 1960s as "the golden age of the colonial period." They invest this period with emotion, sentiment, and yearning. Thus, disappearance and dislocation work alongside reinscription—an attempt to make sense of past, present, and future as local identity outside the utopian formulations of the previous era.[70] Or, as Fran Martin writes, there is eloquence in emptiness.[71]

Allen Fong's *Father and Son* exemplifies the eloquence of loss in Hong Kong's New Wave cinema. Law Kar calls the style poetic realism.[72] The actual title is *Fuzi Qing:* the "feelings" between father and son. In a very real sense it is a visual funeral oration, celebrating the memory of Fong's father with a tenderness that he rarely displayed to him in life. Reminiscence fills up the space emptied by his father's death.

The film has a nonlinear structure. The opening scenes that accompany the credits set the tone. From an establishing shot of Hong Kong, the camera focuses on an old man, reading a letter with joy as he hurries home. He

---

FATHER AND SON (FUZI QING)

DIRECTED BY ALLEN FONG

Fenghuang Film Studio, 1981

The setting is Hong Kong in the 1950s, 1960s, and 1970s. The film begins with the death of the narrator's father, just as he is reading a letter of his son's graduation from an American college in the diegetic present: the 1970s. The son, Ah Hing, flies home for the funeral. From this time perspective, the son recalls his difficult relationship with his father through flashbacks into the 1950s and the 1960s. The whole film is an extended moment of recognition of the father's dedication to his son. The film closes with a melodramatic recognition/reunion/nostalgia through death, the funeral, the airport farewell, and the son's story of his father's efforts to fund his overseas studies.

runs up the stairs and then pauses, jerks, and, in slow motion, falls backward from the camera, then forward into the camera and away. He dies of a heart attack. A close-up shows the letter that has fluttered from his hand. It is his son's graduation certificate in cinema studies from San Francisco University. The camera cuts to the sound of a plane over Hong Kong, bringing the son Ah Hing back for the funeral. Ah Hei, his sister, meets him and says of their father, "He loved you the most … we got the leftovers." The feelings of the father for his son are announced at the outset. Back home, family members look at old photographs showing the family together. Soft music plays. The photos trigger Ah Hing's flashback to collecting them with his father in the 1950s. In contrast to the photos' fixed fullness, the flashbacks record Ah Hing's ambivalent attitudes to his father as he grows up, including resentment, anger, and disobedience. In the end, his father funds his overseas studies through a semiarranged marriage for the eldest daughter. Sons come first. The final scene links diegetic present and ambivalent past; it shows Ah Hing at the airport, leaving for America. After bidding his family farewell, he returns to hug his father, who smiles and nods. The plane takes off, followed by the credits and a silent sound track.

The naturalistic performances and realist mise-en-scène mask the contrived circularity of the narrative, and the muted melodrama of the final hug and following silence. Just as realism reappears in the ambivalence and elegiac mood of poetic realism, so does melodrama, which thrives on crisis and sentiment. The film revolves around more than the death of the father. As Stephen Teo notes, intergenerational conflict and the crisis of death is resolved through Ah Hing's ambiguous but final acceptance of paternal authority, or "father knows best." This sentiment gives the film its poetic power and melodramatic text of muteness.

Teo links theme and sentiment in *Father and Son* to a cycle of father-son melodramas in the Cantonese cinema, beginning with such classics as Ng Wui's *Father and Son* (1954), *Parents' Hearts* (1955), and an early Bruce Lee performance in *The Orphan* (1960). We would add the recently restored print of Bruce Lee's debut, *The Kid* (a.k.a. *My Son Ah Chung*, 1950). All these early films tell of paternal care for sons. For Teo, they evoke "a time when social conscience was a cinematic composite of realism and melodrama, while the film's heart is firmly located in its portrayal of the father and son relationship and the survival of the family unit."[73] In terms of lineage, *Father and Son* sits between these earlier melodramas of family survival and later twentieth-century films of loss and betrayal in father and son relations, such as Fruit Chan's *Little Cheung* (1999). These father-son melodramas in Hong Kong cinema map tensions in a changing Hong Kong through family narratives. Ah Hing's transnational identity mingles with his Chinese childhood cultural identity through his father. His de-nationalized status results not so much because he does not have a national cultural origin but because he is so successful at crossing cultures, just as Hong Kong is a cultural crossroads in many ways. The death of the father records the death of Hong Kong's colonial era; the son's mourning pays tribute to its syncretic Chinese and colonial legacy; but the son's home is de-territorialized—it is both Hong Kong and America.

In Fong's film, the full family unit has not survived. As Linda Williams states, "melodrama is fueled by nostalgia for a lost home."[74] It is reconstituted by memory as a place of tension, not plenitude. There is also a realist edge to the narrative, reinforced by location shooting in a range of urban settings, which are not romanticized. Apart from the crowded apartments the family calls home, public spaces reflect the struggle of everyday life for poor families. These spaces include concrete stairs, streets, shantytowns, the schoolyard, the office toilets where the struggling father steals toilet paper, and a movie palace that ejects Ah Hing and his friend because they don't have money for the ticket. These settings have the docudrama feel that characterizes Fong's background in television. The mix of real locations and melodramatic moments in the narrative suggest that this film still works within the framework of melodramatic realism.

The realism in *Father and Son* nevertheless prefigures a more gritty realism, in later Hong Kong cinema. A prime example is Fruit Chan's neorealist aesthetic in his 1990s films. Fruit Chan uses covert location shooting, hidden cameras, nonprofessional actors at times, and no rehearsals for his films on the lost, helpless, and poor in his Hong Kong trilogy and in *Durian Durian* (2000). These films show Hong Kong empty of paternal care and, by extension, of national belonging. Then Chan became bored with realism and reverted to stylized farce in a film about rich and poor, fantasy and reality: *Hollywood Hong Kong* (2001).[75]

Nevertheless, Chan's films are also part of the lineage of Hong Kong father-son films that map Hong Kong's changing and ambivalent identity within larger nation-states. The final film in his Hong Kong trilogy, *Little Cheung,* has exactly the same Chinese title as the 1950 Bruce Lee vehicle, *The Kid.* There is the same focus on a poor but loving family as the ethical foundation of Hong Kong society. The narrator in Chan's film, the boy Little Cheung, tells a story of everyday life through his impoverished family, living on one street in Hong Kong. Subtitles point to big national events such as Hong Kong's 1997 return to China. Hong Kong politics and everyday life finally come together as Little Cheung and his friend Little Fan celebrate the Hong Kong handover in a pastoral harbor-side scene. He shouts, "Hong Kong is mine!" Little Fan shouts, "Hong Kong is ours!" As an illegal immigrant from the mainland—colloquially called "snakes" in the film— Little Fan now believes that she and her family are safe from police arrest and forcible return across the border. In mainland rhetoric, Hong Kong had come home to China, where it always belonged. In the end, however, Little Fan does not belong. The police arrest her family and load them onto a bus. Little Cheung fails to find her to say good-bye. The grand political reunion of Hong Kong and China contrasts with everyday disunion: the separation and disillusion for the children of both the mainland and Hong Kong. As Little Fan concludes, "this was the end our childhood," the end of personal joy, political innocence, and national reunion.

As we said, the Bruce Lee connection is explicit in *Little Cheung* and invoked to highlight the ambivalence about Hong Kong's political identity as it is swapped between great powers. Watching a film of *The Kid* on television, a character asks who is the real and who is the false Little Cheung: Bruce Lee's "kid" or Little Cheung himself? The question is not answered but it extends to Hong Kong's own identity. Which is the "real" Hong Kong: the former colony or the new autonomous region of China?

Despite the exploration of realism in Hong Kong New Wave cinema, there is some debate as to its aesthetic breakthrough. Many scholars see the movement more as a reinvigoration of existing cinema (such as the father-son lineage) and contemporary Hong Kong as a location for realist genres. For Chinese commentators, there is no such question surrounding the aesthetics of new or Fifth Generation cinema in the People's Republic. *Yellow Earth* launched mainland China's new wave, first in Hong Kong and then worldwide.[76] The Fifth Generation director Tian Zhuangzhuang said in 1986: "If it wasn't for *Yellow Earth,* then there wouldn't be the whole debate about film aesthetics [in China.... The film] represents the future of Chinese cinema now."[77] Dai Jinhua wrote that the film relies on "viscerally realistic cinematic images new to Chinese cinema" even as it lays bare the cinematic frame itself through "the use of stationary shots, deep focus, de-

---

YELLOW EARTH (HUANG TUDI)

DIRECTED BY CHEN KAIGE

Guangxi Film Studio, 1984

The setting is northern Shaanxi in the spring and summer of 1939.
Gu Qing, a soldier from the Eighth Route Army Propaganda Team based in Yan'an, visits a poor region in northern Shaanxi to collect folksongs. He stays with a family who lives in a cave: the daughter Cuiqiao, her father, and her brother Hanhan. Cuiqiao and Hanhan are enthralled by the possibility of liberation in Yan'an. Cuiqiao's mother and sister have already died or left. But there is no liberation, revolution, or family reunion (*datuanyuan*). Cuiqiao dies, Gu Qing is late returning to the village, and the peasants resort to ancient rainmaking rituals to "save the people."

centered perspective, postmodern shot composition, and monochromatic color schema."[78] *Yellow Earth* brought a new look to the Chinese cinema.

There is much written on *Yellow Earth* as art house cinema. The film-makers inaugurate Fifth Generation film by rejecting the conventions of socialist realism and revolutionary romanticism that ruled mainland cinema in the previous decades. We nevertheless argue that *Yellow Earth* still belongs to the realist mode of Chinese cinema and, more particularly, to the lineage of poetic realism. First, the film's narrative is anchored in real historical events in 1939 and in the real problems of an impoverished peasantry.[79] Second, the mise-en-scène is realist through a verisimilar acting style and location shooting so that the "real, physical world [of place and people] is actually, iconically represented"[80] (fig. 4.9). At the same time, it is symbolically stylized in a way that is reminiscent of traditional landscape painting: a river, a single tree, a simple cave dwelling, a lone ox, a vast sky. As in traditional painting and poetry, the landscape dwarfs the characters in many frames. Third, the film also reproduces the mournful mood of French poetic realism—political ambivalence, personal disappointment, melodious sadness, and a sense of degeneration and death.

Yellow Earth plays with the conventions of socialist melodrama. It begins as familiar, political melodrama, then slowly unscrolls as vast national allegory reaching back to the dawn of Chinese civilization. It ends in death and disharmony, the opposite of the clear-cut melodramatic endings of socialist

FIGURE 4.9 Gu Qing and Cuiqiao's family eat together after ploughing the yellow earth (*Yellow Earth*, 1984).

realist cinema. It confounds melodramatic expectations by "emptying-out" the revolutionary myth from within. The resulting emptiness is enchanting, screening images of the yellow earth that echo to ancient folksongs. The filmmakers move beyond melodrama to critique melodramatic codes themselves and, in so doing, they extend the mythic spaces of China and the social question of the revolutionary family-home and nation.

Yellow Earth explicitly criticizes Maoist history and socialist realist narratives. It begins with official revolutionary history, written in white words and scrolled slowly on a black screen.

> In September 1937, a national united front was established to fight the Japanese. Chiang Kai-shek was forced to recognize the [Communist guerilla base at Yan'an] in the Shaanxi-Gansu-Ningxia border region, bringing about a Nationalist Party–Communist Party alliance after years of fighting. But deep-rooted feudal habits and Nationalist political power meant that some people in northern Shaanxi still suffered cruel oppression.

> Folksongs have reverberated over this ancient land down through the ages.

> Several members of the Eighth Route Army's Propaganda Team form a group that disperses throughout the region to find the source of these folksongs [in] early spring, 1939.[81]

The screen dissolves into mystical images of the yellow earth at dusk. The audience sees familiar set pieces from revolutionary cinema—a handsome Communist Party cadre, a poor peasant family, and a traditional arranged marriage. They expect yet another retelling of the Yan'an story, a cinematic version of the power of revolutionary action led by the Party. But these expectations are confounded; the cadre fails the people, the peasantry fall into even direr poverty, and the marriages continue. There is no resolution within the human framework of official history, sung here by Gu Qing, Hanhan, and Cuiqiao as "only our Party can save the people." Instead, earth, water, and sky nurture and destroy as springtime hope turns to summer, drought, and death. The river drowns Cuiqiao as she tries to reach Yan'an on the other side. The desperate peasants resort to age-old rituals.

In this film, the real yellow earth beside the real Yellow River becomes cosmic China. Emotions are inscribed onto sky, water, and earth, as well as transmitted through the people. *Melos* (music) and mise-en-scène are the two elements of melodrama that absorb emotional excess, expressed here as the desire for liberation that runs throughout mainland Chinese cinema from the 1930s. The songs carry this desire, but the men's songs are public

FIGURE 4.10 Cuiqiao on her wedding night (*Yellow Earth*, 1984)

whereas Cuiqiao's are personal; she sings to herself. So the ending of the story (as well as the song lines) is separation, a reverse reunion (*datuanyuan*), as we discussed in chapter 2. The patriarchal Party, which long voiced the dream of liberation and claims its inevitable fulfillment, has failed in its peasant heartland—the loess plateau across the Yellow River from Yan'an, cradle of Chinese civilization and birthplace of the revolution. People and Party are kept separate in the story, in the location, in the frame, in the sound track, and in the end.

Yellow Earth was so different from socialist realist melodrama that it was initially ignored in China. When replayed domestically to a curious public after its international success in 1985, many local moviegoers were "very dissatisfied, very confused, and very unhappy."[82] The film lacked the pre-scribed plots, clear-cut characters, and happy endings of literal melodrama that peasants were said to like.[83] Instead, the plot is minimal and the ending is multiple and ambiguous, features of art cinema in general and Fifth Generation cinema in particular.[84]

If emptiness operates as ambiguity—through metaphor, memory, or mise-en-scène—across late-twentieth-century Chinese cinemas, then *Yellow Earth*'s aesthetic of emptiness operates as a philosophy of the Dao. The

Dao, we have argued, reinvests "nothingness" or emptiness with a postmodern significance. This philosophy and symbolism is vital to all levels of the film's aesthetics and central to the "concealed" message: the emptied-out family-home, the emptied-out nation, and the emptied-out revolutionary mandate.[85] There are numerous scenes of a landscape emptied of people. The significance of this emptiness lies in its juxtaposition with revolutionary claims of fulfillment and fullness, symbolized by Gu Qing's presence alone on the yellow earth in the opening shots. A series of absences and "empty" shots follow. The first major absence is Gu Qing himself, who leaves for Yan'an. Cuiqiao sees him off with a song and then disappears from the ridge as she returns home across the plateau, singing of the tragedy of girls' lives. The "empty" image is of a glowing, elemental earth that fills the frame. The second absence is Cuiqiao's death after her enforced marriage; she sings a revolutionary song as she drowns in the Yellow River at night. Her disappearance is followed by a sequence of magical dissolves of the "empty" river at day, dusk, night, and dawn. The river fills the frame. Later, when Gu Qing finally returns, he finds an empty cave-home in tatters. He leaves and a blank shot of an indistinct sun fills the frame before moving to the riverside rain ceremony to ancient gods. The final scene is a full tableau of earth and sky:

> From the high heavens [the camera] pans down to the vast yellow earth. As if from the earth itself, Cuiqiao's faraway song soars to the sky over a stretch of still land … the yellow earth sinks silently into serenity.[86]

Her song joins all the other "sour" songs of suffering, reverberating "over this ancient land down through the ages."

> Sickle, axe, and hoe,
> Build a road for peasants and workers to go,
> The spotted rooster flies over the wall,
> Only our Party can save the people, one and all[87]

Thus emptiness becomes a world devoid of nurture, females, water, and hence humanity itself.

However, there is a grander reunion in this film—the return of the land to the people who lived on it for centuries. In several long shots, the people are shown as red, black, and white dots seemingly emerging from the earth and then disappearing back into it. In a famous quote, director Chen Kaige said:

> In January, I came with my cinematographer and art director to Shaanbei [northern Shaanxi]. There we saw the Yellow River … [which] in Shaanbei is just like

an image of our peoples. It is these [middle reaches] of the river that nurtured the splendors of China's ancient civilization. We faced this mother river, which both nurtures and destroys our civilization, and were filled with emotion. Early one morning we saw an old man drawing a pail of water from the river. In that moment we knew how the film would be and how to film it.... In the film, the person who embodies the ideal of human endurance is the main female character, Cuiqiao.... The river that drowns her is the same river that nurtures her.[88]

Yellow Earth is a postsocialist take on Chinese modernity, recording the shift away from the enforced authenticity of state cinematic narratives in Mao's China. China exists in silence beyond the meta-narratives of modernity. Arjun Appadurai calls this postmodern phenomenon "modernity at large": no *telos*, no social engineering, and no grand narratives.[89] This is a cinematic realism that, at one level, refuses literal melodrama but retains romanticism. *Yellow Earth* reimagines China as mother of the north, expressed musically in a never-ending song cycle of its people's dreams and expressed spatially as a place of suffering and loss, generation after generation.

Realism is clearly a powerful force in Chinese cinematic narratives of the nation, whether as a nation-state or culturally marked colonial space, as we see in this chapter and the next chapter on gender. In the early twentieth century, realism emerged as a political project to help make China into a strong modern nation-state at a time of national peril. In practice, it merged with melodrama as the hegemonic mode of the Chinese cinema. By the late twentieth and early twenty-first century, the situation has changed; China is an emerging great power within the international political order. Not surprisingly, realism has become disengaged from its nation-building purposes to become a mode of address on contemporary issues that nevertheless still deal with the national: the syncretic and ambivalent identity of Hong Kong in *Father and Son*, the meaning of Hong Kong's return to China for ordinary citizens of both places in *Little Cheung*, the emptiness of the Communist revolution for generations of suffering peasants in *Yellow Earth*, and woman as an emblem of China's suffering in a remake of the story of the early film star Ruan Lingyu (discussed in chapter 5). In the international marketplace, however, operatic martial arts films like *Crouching Tiger, Hidden Dragon* and *Hero* (discussed in chapters 3 and 8, respectively) are better known than any realist film from a century of Chinese cinema.

5

How Should a Chinese Woman Look?

WOMAN AND NATION

DURING THE PRODUCTION of Stanley Kwan's 1991 film *Center Stage*, an interesting casting incident made the news pages in Hong Kong and also highlighted the importance of star image in the cinema. Anita Mui had been cast to star in the biopic about ever-suffering 1930s Shanghai film star Ruan Lingyu. Critics had often seen Ruan as a metaphor for China itself, suffering under semicolonialism, semifeudalism, and Japanese invasion in the 1930s. For a Hong Kong director to make a film about this iconic Chinese national figure using an iconic Hong Kong star already pointed to the possibility that he was going to claim the Cantonese Ruan and the Shanghai cinema as Hong Kong's heritage rather than China's. But Mui, who resembled Ruan in many ways, was forced out of the production for reasons beyond the filmmaker's control, and Maggie Cheung took her place. Cheung's cosmopolitan resilience stood in marked contrast to Ruan's image and added a new dimension to the film, drawing attention to the difference between 1930s Shanghai and the confident prosperity of contemporary Hong Kong. We return to *Center Stage* at the end of this chapter, but this incident draws attention to the intersection of gender, nation, and cinema through the visual metaphor of woman-as-place.

The intersection of gender, nation, and cinema attracted little attention in English-language academia until relatively recently. Analysts of the nation and nationalism ignored gender, and debates around gender in the cinema ignored the nation. That situation has begun to change. In the case of Chinese cinema, this chapter demonstrates that gender and nation have been inextricably but variably linked, and that Chinese examples challenge and recast existing Eurocentric thinking. In order to support our arguments, we compare the images of three female actors in some of their starring roles: Xie Fang, Ruan Lingyu, and Gong Li. Xie Fang is a postrevolutionary heroine, Ruan Lingyu the suffering icon of 1930s left-wing progressive cinema, and Gong Li the object and agent of desire in some of the most globally successful Fifth Generation films. A final section returns to Ruan Lingyu through Maggie Cheung's portrayal of her in Stanley Kwan's *Center Stage*.

We focus on women here not because men are unimportant to issues of gender, but because men are the focus in chapter 6. And the choice of actors is not determined by aesthetic judgment, but because they represent distinctly different examples among a great range. Particular attention is paid to two factors. The first is role. Analysts of gender and nation have tended to argue that motherhood is the primary role that links women and the nation. This role is present in Chinese cinema, but not so prominent; there is no Chinese equivalent of *Mother India*. Why is this so, and what takes its place? How does this challenge us to rethink the connection between gender, nation, and roles for women in postcolonial modernity?

The second factor concerns the look. This is an important trope in cinema studies, where the concept of the libidinal gaze—in particular the libidinal gaze upon the female body—occupies a central place. Yet it is widely agreed that this libidinal gaze is not so important in Chinese cinema. Therefore, we rethink the look by asking the question, "How should a Chinese woman look?" in three senses. How should she appear before others? How should the cinematic apparatus and spectators look at her? And how should her subjective look upon others and the world be articulated in the cinema?

Mothers and Daughters

The topic of woman, nation, and the cinema links two existing areas of scholarship: analysis of gender and nation and analysis of gender and cinema. In each case, Chinese examples challenge dominant paradigms. They do so in ways that might appear from English-language feminist perspectives to challenge patriarchy, too. However, some Chinese feminist scholars have been less enthusiastic. To understand why, it is necessary to examine the specific Chinese intersection of women's liberation and the invention of cultural tradition under the rubric of the national.

Taking gender and nation first, Nira Yuval-Davis states, "Most of the hegemonic theorizations about nations and nationalism ... have ignored gender relations as irrelevant."[1] She argues this is because such theorizations assume a divide between public and private and between culture and nature, placing gender on the side of the private and nature and the nation on the side of the public and culture. Although this may be true of "hegemonic theorizations," an increasing number of scholars have been paying attention to the way in which the nation is gendered and the way in which discourses of the national inform gender roles and models. Within this work, the dominant argument has been that woman is constructed in a metaphorical relation to an essential and ahistorical national identity, which supposedly men are working or fighting in history to preserve. Yuval-Davis writes: "Women are ... constructed as the symbolic bearers of the collectivity's identity and honor, both personally and collectively.... A figure of a woman, often a mother, symbolizes in many cultures the spirit of the collectivity.... As [feminist scholar] Cynthia Enloe has pointed out, it is supposedly for the sake of the 'womenandchildren' that men go to war. Women are associated in the collective imagination with children and therefore with the collective, as well as the familial, future."[2]

In the case of places subject to imperialism, this association between women, premodern tradition, and domesticity acquires an additional significance as that which must be kept pure from contamination by the imperialist. Here, Partha Chatterjee's work on late-nineteenth-century Bengal has been particularly influential. In *The Nation and Its Fragments,* he carefully traces how male and middle-class nationalists allowed themselves to appropriate elements of Western modernity in their fight against colonialism. However, at the same time, they increasingly construed women as keepers of the hearth, an inner domain seen as sanctuary for a spiritual cultural essence.[3] In cinema studies, various articles on non-Western cinemas have also attended to the frequent connection between mother and nation.[4]

Generalization is always dangerous, and one glance at Chinese cinema reveals that the patterns outlined above do not apply there. Although there are plenty of mothers in Chinese film, it is doubtful if there is any "Mother China" figure. This may in part be because the Chinese term for the nation to which one owes allegiance is already gendered male. *Zuguo* means "ancestral land," and this ancestral lineage is patriarchal. Furthermore, the following case studies will reveal that iconic Chinese female stars and the roles they play have been less associated with the hearth and home than with public space, even when they are married and mothers. Cinematic heroines appear as martial arts fighters, businesswomen, labor heroines in the factories and fields, and as guerilla fighters and Communist Party cadres.[5]

In these circumstances, the connection between women and the nation in Chinese cinema demands further examination. Indeed it is already the subject of one whole book.[6] However, here we confine our examination of the topic to the particular cinematic trope of the look, which has been a dominant paradigm in studies of gender and cinema. If Chinese women characters in film often elude dominant gendered narrative tropes by being agents in public space rather than confined to the hearth, do they also elude dominant models for gendered cinematic tropes like the look?

Maggie Humm points out in *Feminism and Film* that, "No other single essay excited and transformed contemporary film theory as much as Laura Mulvey's 'Visual Pleasure and Narrative Cinema.'" She goes on to note that "much film theory of the past twenty years revisits, challenges, or builds on Mulvey's ideas."[7] The look lies at the heart of Mulvey's 1975 article. Mulvey argues that in the classical Hollywood cinema of the studio era, woman is constructed as an object to be looked at. This effect is achieved partly by the way she is dressed, made up, and lit, and partly by the look of the camera, which is masculinized through its alignment with the look of male characters in the film.[8]

Mulvey's essay has been questioned ever since its appearance. Its failure to account for female spectatorial pleasure prompted Mary Ann Doane's investigations of female spectatorship and masquerade, Elizabeth Cowie's examination of fantasy as a model for spectatorship not determined by gender, and Kaja Silverman's work on the aural dimension.[9] Silverman has also investigated cinematic masculinities that run counter to Mulvey's model.[10] Other critics have pointed out that the dominance of gender in Mulvey's psychoanalytic model elides consideration of other axes of identification. For example, Jacqueline Bobo points to the omission of ethnicity, and Richard Dyer's work examines sexuality.[11] Finally, D. N. Rodowick argues that Mulvey's model does not allow for historical change.[12] However, this ongoing critique also underlines the continuing central position of Mulvey's essay.

Work on gender in the Chinese cinema has also frequently noted divergence from Mulvey's model, and in particular that the libidinal objectification of women characters for male spectatorial pleasure may be present but is not dominant. For example, Chris Berry's 1985 examination of socialist realist cinema in the People's Republic notes that the viewing subject is not engaged libidinally but epistemophilically in a position of heightened knowledge that is not necessarily gendered.[13] Writing in 1990, Chinese scholar Ma Junxiang shows a similar pattern at work through close analysis of Cheng Yin's 1959 film *Shanghai Girl*.[14] Ma specifies that his aim is to demonstrate divergence from Mulvey's model, and that is why he has chosen a rare example in which the libidinal gaze appears at all, although it is refused and subverted by the women characters.[15] To be fair, Mulvey never claimed application beyond classical Hollywood cinema, so perhaps it is not so surprising that post-1949 mainland Chinese cinema does not fit her model. Nonetheless, work such as this does suggest the need for greater attention to the local and historical specificity of the look in different cinemas, a project we pursue in the case studies below.

Not only do the two patterns discussed above recast existing thinking, but from English-language feminist perspectives they also seem very positive. Women in cinema of the People's Republic are neither constructed predominantly as objects of the gaze nor excluded from agency in public space. Indeed, it has also been noted that women are comparatively common as film directors in the People's Republic.[16] Yet in her article "Invisible Women," Dai Jinhua complains of the absence of any autonomous "women's cinema" there. In her opinion, most "liberated women" in cinema of the People's Republic are still inscribed within a patriarchal imaginary, and most women directors are more concerned to equal men than challenge patriarchy.[17]

Dai's work on the cinema joins a range of post-Mao scholarship that has qualified previous enthusiasm about women's liberation in the People's Republic, pointing out that the specificity and autonomy of women's interests have been sacrificed to those of the Party and the revolution.[18] Meng Yue emphasizes that Chinese Marxist thought understands the whole nation as a quasi-proletariat under imperialist oppression; therefore, the revolutionary is simultaneously patriotic.[19] And Lydia Liu comments, "In the emancipatory discourse of the state, which always subsumes women under the nationalist agenda, women's liberation means little more than equal opportunity to participate in public labor."[20] Furthermore, Tani Barlow has shown that the construction of "woman" (funü) has occurred within discourses constructing the "nation-state" (guojia) not only during the period of the People's Republic, but throughout Chinese modernity.[21]

However, what remains to be answered is how it has been possible to produce a modern model of Chinese womanhood as a national and anti-imperialist discourse that is not like the maternal keeper-of-the-hearth figure described by Chatterjee. To understand this, we need to look at the invention and reinvention of tradition as part of the narrative of the nation.[22] The Chinese cultural repertoire contains no shortage of virtuous mothers and chaste widows who could have been appropriated as exemplars for modern women. In fact, Chiang Kai-shek did cite them in this way in his 1930s New Life movement.[23] Yet for the most part, in the great sorting process that divided the past into the progressive and the feudal, these figures were consigned to the dustbin of the feudal. Instead of the mother, it was the unmarried daughter figure that provided a "traditional" role model fit for Chinese modernity.

For non-Chinese readers, Disney's film version of the Hua Mulan legend reminds us that unmarried daughters have long provided Chinese role models for women in public space.[24] The story of the girl who helps her old and sick father by taking his place when the emperor calls for conscripts is well known. It effectively licenses women to participate in public space, if male incapacity to perform usual roles warrants it. As Louise Edwards points out in her discussion of the woman warrior, although there may be an underlying tension around gender roles in this story, interpretations of it as anti-patriarchal are incorrect. Because Mulan is taking her father's place in the army to help him and the emperor, this is approved within Confucian ethics as both a patriotic and a filial act.[25]

Joseph R. Allen has traced different tellings of the legend since its inception some fifteen centuries ago.[26] However, where Allen's structuralist approach leads him to emphasize an essential core legend that persists, our emphasis on performativity and recitation focuses on the changes that he traces as the story is retold in the modern era. These take two forms. One concerns the illustrations that increasingly accompany the printed versions of the legend from the late nineteenth century on. What Rey Chow calls "visuality" becomes more important in China, as there is a growing attention to corporeal signifiers of gender and an eroticization of Hua Mulan's body.[27] For example, as Allen points out, depicting a woman in trousers allows her legs to be outlined by the clothing and allows her to take stances where her legs are visibly parted.[28] Here, then, we are already entering into a discussion of the look. The second change Allen notes concerns the growing popularity of the Mulan legend after the encounter with European imperialism, and greater emphasis on martial episodes. In other words, the patriotic and nationalistic aspects of the role are developed to at least match the filial aspects and meet the demands of the modern period as one response to imperialist incursion.[29]

The inscription of seemingly liberated models of womanhood as good daughters of the nation also inscribes the nation as a patriarchal institution modeled on the Confucian family. One response to this has been to highlight those rare women's films that do escape the hegemony of the national, as Dai Jinhua does with Huang Shuqin's *Woman, Demon, Human* (1987). Other writers have taken the same course with other so-called "women's films" (*nüxing dianying*) of the late 1980s and early 1990s.[30] Another necessary response, and one that we follow here with Xie Fang, Ruan Lingyu, and Gong Li, is to examine how the narrative model of the daughter myth has been cited and recited in different Chinese constructions of the national and through various configurations of the look.

Xie Fang: "Let Us Remould Ourselves Earnestly"

In regard to narrative role, of the three stars under consideration here, Xie Fang is the one who can be compared most directly to Hua Mulan. However, instead of playing women who fight for the nation as an extension of her father and her family in a Confucian value system, her characters fight for the nation as an extension of the Communist Party and revolution, even

---

XIE FANG

Xie Fang was born in 1935 in Hubei. Two years later, her family moved to Shanghai, where she was brought up. Both her parents were teachers in a Christian school. As she grew up, she followed her father's growing allegiance to the Communist Party. In the 1950s, she began her career as an actress on the stage, appearing in revolutionary plays like *The White-haired Girl* and classic operas like *Hua Mulan*. She is one of the best-remembered film stars from the pre–Cultural Revolution era. This is despite the fact that she only appeared in three films prior to the beginning of the Cultural Revolution in 1966: *Song of Youth* (1959), *Early Spring in February* (1963), and *Two Stage Sisters* (1965). However, all three were high-budget and high-prestige productions praised by critics. Like most others in the film industry, Xie's career went on hold during the Cultural Revolution. She attempted a comeback in the late 1970s, but her image was too strongly associated with the past era for her to recover her position.[31]

---

if this entails defying her family. Unusually, among post-1949 stars, she never played one of the soldier-peasant-worker heroes prioritized by Mao in the "Talks at the Yan'an Conference on Literature and Art."[32] Instead, her roles were as students, progressive intellectuals, and artists from the pre-revolutionary era, who overcome their less promising class backgrounds to become revolutionaries.

In the postrevolutionary era, the primary purpose of the cinema was explicitly acknowledged to be didactic. In her study of didactic fiction, Su-

FIGURE 5.1 "Let us remould ourselves earnestly and always perform revolutionary operas," Chunhua tells Yuehong at the end of *Two Stage Sisters* (1964).

san Rubin Suleiman points to apprenticeship structures in which characters function as models for the audience.[33] This idea of the apprentice as a role model for the audience and other characters is illustrated clearly in *Two Stage Sisters*. Xie Fang plays a child bride who is on the run from an arranged marriage and takes refuge with a traveling opera troupe. She becomes close to the troupe manager's daughter, and the two stage sisters perform duets together. When they grow up, they move to Shanghai and become stars. Xie's character, Chunhua, is drawn to left-wing politics under the tutelage of a woman journalist who is a Party member. However, her sister Yuehong is lured by promises of luxury to become her Shanghai manager's concubine. After the revolution, Yuehong sees the error of her ways, and the sisters are reunited. In the final scene of the film, Chunhua puts her arm around Yuehong's shoulder, saying, "Let us remould ourselves earnestly and always perform revolutionary operas."[34]

The representation of the Party authority figure by a woman is an unusual feature of *Two Stage Sisters*. While it is not unusual for women to perform as the apprentice characters in Chinese revolutionary cinema, the Party authority figures that guide them are usually male. In both *Song of Youth* and *Early Spring in February*, the Xie Fang characters are inspired in their actions by male characters. In the first film, she moves from one male teacher to another. Her character, Lin Daojing, tries to commit suicide after her stepmother responds to family bankruptcy by selling her into an arranged marriage. Beijing University student Yu Yongze rescues her. After hearing her story, he compares her to Ibsen's Nora. They marry, but grow apart when it becomes clear he supports the KMT Nationalist government line of avoiding confrontation with the Japanese invaders, whereas she is drawn to the Communist line of active resistance. Eventually, she starts working for the Party under the guidance of another man called Lu Jiachuan.[35] In this transfer from one man to another, as Dai Jinhua puts it, she becomes "the good daughter of the Party."[36] In reference to the novel on which the movie was based, Meng Yue also emphasizes that Chinese Marxist thought understood the whole nation as a quasi-proletariat under imperialist oppression, so Lin Daojing's awakening class awareness is, like Mulan's devotion to her father, simultaneously patriotic and nationalistic.[37]

The similarity to Mulan also extends to the look in the sense of how she appears before others. Just as Mulan cross-dresses to participate in public life, when Xie Fang's characters move closer to the Party they dress more androgynously. In *Two Stage Sisters*, for example, Chunhua disdains the jewels, furs, and body-hugging silks that, in Mulvey's terms, make Yuehong a fetishized object of the male gaze, in favor of more modest, dark, and plain clothes. Furthermore, by the final scene, she is in a military-style uniform. However, although Xie Fang's costumes followed the general tendency to

FIGURE 5.2 Fur-decked Yuehong shows off her ring to Chunhua in *Two Stage Sisters* (1964).

combine women's participation in public life with androgyny,[38] we must acknowledge an undercurrent of glamorization. First, the return to the pre-revolutionary era and the class backgrounds of her characters permitted her to appear in expensive silks and jewels that disappeared completely after 1949, as well as tight-fitting clothing that emphasized the body. And second, even the military-style uniform from *Two Stage Sisters* is more tailored to the body than would probably have been the case in everyday life.[39]

Turning to the topic of the camera's look and the characters' own subjective looks, Mulvey's libidinal structure of the gaze characterized by male relays and shot–reverse-shot structures is not entirely absent. However, although the appearance of Xie Fang's characters may be glamorized in some ways, these are not the key tropes here. Rather, just as the narrative teleology in her films tends toward progressive deglamorization of her appearance, the look of the camera and the spectator upon her is engaged, but then directed elsewhere. This is a pedagogical structure that aims to inspire the spectator to self-sacrifice rather than erotic indulgence. The key tropes are the admiring look, often from slightly below, much as a pupil seated at a desk might look at a teacher, followed by the character's look, either downward in reflection and thought, or off screen past the camera and the spectator in anticipation of the revolutionary future.[40]

For example, in *Song of Youth*, Lin Daojing looks up at Yu Yongze in admiration when he romances her by reciting poetry, speaking of Ibsen, and declaring the need to resist feudalism. Sometimes, the libidinal engagement is emphasized by organizing this as a shot–reverse-shot structure. At other times, the camera is positioned so that the spectator looks up at her wide-eyed expression as she looks up at him, in a position that emulates hers. The leaders of student demonstrations calling for active resistance against the Japanese are also shot from below, and Lin's inspired expression as she watches them is also often shot from below. Among those leaders is Lu Jiachuan. When he is arrested and resists by launching a hunger strike, he is consistently shot from below. By contrast, in the next scene when his friend Dai Yu is arrested and agrees to become a turncoat, Dai Yu sits down in despair. The camera maintains its position but tilts down, so the spectator goes from looking up to Dai Yu to looking down at him. In a scene that follows soon after, Lin Daojing realizes Lu has been arrested (figs. 5.3a–5.3d). Here the logic of the camera angles and the looks is the opposite of that used in the scene with Dai Yu. When Lin Daojing stands up, excited by the Communist Party flyers (fig. 5.3b), we are looking up at her (fig. 5.3c). When she remembers Lu, he appears above her, gazing down at her and urging her on. She is not returning his gaze in a romantic exchange, but is instead looking off screen and presumably toward an imagined future filled with revolutionary action (fig. 5.3d).

When characters gaze off screen into the middle distance, there is usually no reverse shot to show us what they are gazing at, suggesting that it

FIGURE 5.3a The camera tracks back from a close-up as Lin Daojing unwraps the package Lu Jiachuan left with her in *Song of Youth* (1959).

FIGURE 5.3b Lin Daojing's perspective: the package is full of Communist Party flyers.

FIGURE 5.3c Inspired, Lin stands up and looks up and off into the middle distance.

FIGURE 5.3d Lin remembers Lu.

FIGURE 5.4 Lin Xiaojing joins the Communist Party in *Song of Youth* (1959).

(COURTESY CHINA FILM ARCHIVE)

is something beyond literal representation. However, in the penultimate scene, when Lin finally realizes her wish to join the Communist Party and swears to devote her life to the Party, she is shot from below gazing off screen. The camera cuts to a close-up of the red flag with the hammer and sickle in the left-hand corner, and then back to Lin. Next, her face dissolves into the image of red flags flying in the breeze. In this scene, a shot structure that might be used to represent the formation of the couple at the conclusion of a Hollywood-style romance is used to represent a marriage to the Party, a marriage inspired by the patriotic determination to resist Japanese invasion.

Ruan Lingyu: "I Want to Live!"

Compared to Xie Fang, Ruan Lingyu's relation to models of good womanhood and patriotism is altogether more complex. This is hardly surpris-

---

RUAN LINGYU

Born in 1910 into a laborer's family from Guangzhou, Ruan Lingyu committed suicide on International Women's Day in 1935. The sensation was heightened because in her last film, *The New Woman* (1935), she had played a regretful suicide whose dying cry was, "I want to live!" There were many such parallels between her life and those of characters she specialized in. Her father died when she was a child, and her mother supported the family by working as a maid for the Zhang family. Ruan married their son, but they soon separated. Just as her character in *The New Woman* is driven to suicide by press gossip, Ruan also became embroiled in a scandal when it transpired that by living with a new lover while not legally divorced, she was technically an adulteress. Tens of thousands of ordinary citizens attended her funeral parade. To this day, she is widely regarded as one of China's finest film actors.

ing. Compared to post-revolutionary China, Shanghai in the 1930s was a more open society in which attitudes to the past and goals for the future were being contested.[41] From 1930 until her death in 1935, Ruan worked for the Lianhua Studio. "Lianhua" means "united China," and the company's founder, Luo Mingyou, launched the firm with a patriotic slogan calling for the "revival of Chinese cinema" (*fuxing guopian*).[42] However, precisely what form this nationalistic spirit would take in Lianhua's films was contested. Luo himself was a supporter of Chiang Kai-shek's Nationalist government. However, after 1932, Lianhua became one of the targets for infiltration by the Left-Wing Film movement, affiliated with the Communist Party.[43] As a result, Ruan appeared in Lianhua films that explicitly supported the government's culturally conservative New Life movement, such as *National Customs* (1935), and in films controlled by left-wing writers and directors committed to the overthrow of many traditions, such as *The New Woman, Little Toys* (1933), and *The Goddess* (1934). However, whether it is because of their quality or promotion by the current government in Beijing, or a combination of the two, it is for the left-wing films that she is most celebrated. We concentrate on those works here.

Ruan's roles display great variety. Wang Zhimin notes that she played "girls from the countryside, maids, women workers, sex workers, beggars, Buddhist nuns, and female students,"[44] thus incarnating an array of positive and negative models of femininity circulating and competing for attention in the 1930s. She also often played roles that combine these qualities. As they would seem mutually incompatible in most value systems, this is very distinctive. For example, in one of her most famous roles as the title character in *The Goddess,* she is the devoted mother to a little boy, the ideal role for a woman according to Confucian values. This ties into nationalism as her determination to pay his school fees is motivated by the hope that he will do great things for his country. However, it also leads her to become a sex worker to raise the money to pay for the fees. This is not the sort of thing for which widows got memorial arches in premodern China, but it is a remarkable condensation in one figure of different aspects of the times. These include continuing Confucian values, the quest for national modernity, capitalism and the commercialization of life, ideas about free love, and the proliferation of women alone in society, together with the anxieties this provoked for the patriarchal imaginary. Furthermore, it carried over into Ruan's star image through the press, which made it known that she was not only a film star but also a separated woman raising a daughter alone, and the mistress of a powerful man. Maybe this capacity to sum up the spirit of the times by encompassing such a range of otherwise contradictory roles and values in the one figure helps to explain her powerful charisma, demonstrated in the vast crowds that turned out for her funeral.[45]

In her analysis of Ruan's suicide and the film that preceded it (*The New Woman*), Kristine Harris emphasizes that three roles for women converge in Ruan Lingyu. She comments: "For historians, the film and the suicide expose Chinese popular culture at a moment of crisis over the degree to which women would be agents, symbols, or victims of modernity."[46] In postrevolutionary figures like Xie Fang, that crisis is decisively resolved as they become both agents and symbols of modernity characterized by patriotic nationalism and revolution. But for Ruan Lingyu, the range of roles and models she encompasses, often within one film, suggests ongoing struggle.

Despite the variety of roles, certain consistent differences from Xie Fang's roles can be discerned. First, although Ruan also often plays patriotic characters, they do not usually find any successful outlet for their ardor, and they certainly do not join the Communist Party. Shanghai in the 1930s was under the KMT Nationalist government, whose censors did not permit representation of their mortal enemies. Second, whereas Xie Fang's characters from before the Cultural Revolution usually eschew romantic entanglements for chaste revolutionary work, Ruan Lingyu's characters are often involved in various complicated romantic and sexual situations throughout the film.

Given these complications, how is Ruan Lingyu's image constructed in relation to the look? In regard to the look as appearance, William Rothman places *The Goddess* within Stanley Cavell's category of "the melodrama of the unknown woman" and compares Ruan to Marlene Dietrich. However, he claims that her physical appearance is not in any way fetishized.[47] Compared to Dietrich's appearances in von Sternberg's films, this might be true. But when Ruan's appearance is compared to that of Xie Fang and other postrevolutionary female actors, the situation is less clear. On the one hand, Ruan often wears form-fitting, slit-to-the-thigh *qipao* (also known as cheongsam) dresses made of shimmering silk. As Antonia Finnane points out, this was a nationalistic garment designed in reaction to westernization as a form of indigenous modern dress, but also one intended to emphasize sexual difference.[48] The leering gaze of her unwanted admirer in *The New Woman* on her exposed leg in shimmering silk stockings and her high-heeled shoes says as much (figs. 5.5a–5.5c). On the other hand, Ruan's *qipao* is often dark in color and not lit in such a way as to shine. Of course, this varies according to role. When she plays poorer women, as in *Little Toys,* where she is a rural toymaker, there is almost nothing to draw attention to her body. Her clothes are dark, plain, and she is often obscured by scenery. When she plays a sex worker, as in *The Goddess,* or an abandoned mother and former teacher trying to become a glamorous and modern woman author, as in *The New Woman,* the opposite is true.

FIGURE 5.5a Ruan Lingyu's admirer glances down at her legs in *The New Woman* (1935).

FIGURE 5.5b Ruan's *qipao* exposes her shapely leg.

FIGURE 5.5c A happy man.

If we turn to the question of how the camera looks at her, a great range of structures can also be found. These include the libidinal gaze mediated by male characters. For example, although she is married in *Little Toys,* she also has a rich young lover from the city, Mr. Yuan, who wants to take her to Paris. Their romantic exchanges of looks are rendered through the shot–reverse-shot structure. Yet if any one cinematic trope is particularly associated with Ruan, it is the direct look upon her face, unmediated by relay characters, in the close-ups for which she is famous. In what was still mostly silent cinema in China in the early 1930s, Ruan's expressive face registers numerous intense and fleeting emotions in these moments.

What is the significance of these close-ups of the face? The key here is not erotic objectification but empathy. Because the face is what we read to understand emotions, as we look at her face we come to feel with her. In Ruan's case, she moves through a gamut of emotions from joy to tragedy, but more often than not the narrative ends tragically. In *Woman and Chinese Modernity,* Rey Chow writes about the fascination many Chinese male authors of this period had for the figure of the suffering woman. This figure was a symbol for the Chinese nation, feminized because weak, passive, invaded, and tragic. Chow argues that this was also a figure they masochistically empathized with at the same time they distanced themselves from her by constructing her as a different gender and class.[49] These close-ups of Ruan are a cinematic equivalent of this structure. Although the libidinal gaze of male characters is usually downplayed in these films, the overall male narrative point of view is clear. For example, in *Little Toys*, Mr. Yuan embodies this class and gender difference. The toymaker turns down his suggestion that they run away to Paris, arguing that too many people depend upon her toymaking and urging him to concentrate on bringing modern techniques back to China to strengthen the nation. By his return from Europe near the end of the film, his initial libidinal engagement has been transformed into a mixture of idealization, pity, and concern.

Given this empathetic engagement with the characters played by Ruan Lingyu, perhaps it is not surprising that they have a strong subjective look of their own. In her piece on *The New Woman*, Kristine Harris rightly points out that Ruan and the other "new women" in the film "possess privileged narratorial knowledge in the film, and they initiate nearly all the subjective point-of-view shots and flashbacks."[50] Harris goes on to explain that in Ruan's case these flashbacks enable self-criticism, combining with the emotive close-ups to produce a "tension between the cathartic and didactic ... often present in left-wing Chinese cinema of the 1930s."[51] For example, Ruan's gentleman admirer in *The New Woman* takes her to a nightclub. On the way, she remembers ruefully how she was introduced to him by her school principal, who explained that he was a wealthy patron of the school, implying that she should be nice to him. These scenes play back in the frame of the car window she is looking out of. Once they get to the nightclub, a performance by a Caucasian woman entrances her beau but excites Ruan's imagination to a cross-ethnic identification with this woman in chains (figs. 5.6a–5.6f). Horrified at the implications of what she has done, she flees the scene.

Harris is correct as far as she goes. However, it should be added that not only do Ruan and other leading women characters from the left-wing cinema of the 1930s initiate subjective point-of-view shots and flashbacks, but also they often articulate visions of the future. In this way, a resolution to the tension Harris discerns between the didactic and the cathartic is often gestured toward. In the case of *The New Woman*, the Ruan Lingyu character dies after sitting up in bed and dramatically crying out to the camera, "I want to live!"—a phrase that is superimposed over her image. Here it is almost as though she sees us directly. Afterward, we see another character. This woman has already proved she can fight like a man, and combines a strongly androgynous appearance with a commitment to left-wing politics. Shot from below, she is marching forward together with the workers, gazing off screen into a mythical future over the camera and the

FIGURE 5.6a A Caucasian woman puts
on an erotic and exotic show for
Shanghai nightclub patrons in
The New Woman (1935).

FIGURE 5.6b Ruan Lingyu's admirer
is delighted, but she reacts in horror.

FIGURE 5.6c From Ruan's perspective:
the woman in chains grovels.

FIGURE 5.6d After a dissolve, Ruan
imagines herself as the woman in
chains.

FIGURE 5.6e Again from Ruan's
perspective: the woman in chains
grovels.

FIGURE 5.6f Ruan jumps up from the
table and flees.

spectator. Here we can see the early development of a cinematic structure
that becomes a fixture by Xie Fang's time.

An even more interesting example occurs at the end of *Little Toys*. Ruan's
vision here is that of a madwoman, as she mistakes the noise of New Year's
firecrackers for another attack on Shanghai one year after the actual Japa-

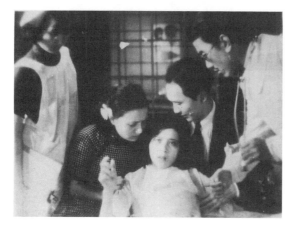

FIGURE 5.7 Ruan Lingyu cries "I want to llive!" before she dies in *The New Woman* (1935).
(COURTESY CHINA FILM ARCHIVE)

nese bombing of 1932. She has visions of scenes of war, which the spectator also sees. However, at first the Shanghai public responds with shock and no understanding. Mr. Yuan appears to stop her from being taken away by the police. Gradually, as her performance continues with imagined scenes of Chinese resistance to the Japanese, the audience begins to applaud. Given KMT Nationalist appeasement policies, perhaps it is not surprising that no intertitles explain the exact significance of their action, but we may be justified in understanding it as support for her patriotic hopes. If Ruan herself embodies a China that cannot act now, she also acts as a channel for the expression and articulation of hopes for future agency.

Gong Li: "You Are Not My Father!"

Gong Li has played a wide range of roles in various films, including mothers in *Red Sorghum, Judou* (1990), *The Story of Qiu Ju,* and *To Live* (1994),

GONG LI

Born in 1966 and brought up in Shandong Province, Gong Li was training to be an actress at the Central Drama Academy in Beijing when she was selected by Zhang Yimou for his first film as director, *Red Sorghum* (1987). A series of glamorous starring roles in other films by Zhang followed, and she became established as the only People's Republic of China film star whose name was internationally recognized. These roles included *The Story of Qiu Ju* (1992), in which she was cast against type as a dowdy peasant woman and won the Best Actress award at the 1992 Venice International Film Festival. She has also appeared in many films by directors other than Zhang, including Chen Kaige's *Farewell My Concubine* (1993) and a variety of Hong Kong and Taiwanese productions. However, none has won her acclaim and attention to equal her work with Zhang Yimou.[52]

for example. However, her star image is no more maternal than Ruan Lingyu's was.[53] In *Red Sorghum*, for example, the narrator refers to her as "My Grandma," but the figure that appears before us is a far from grand-motherly young bride. Perhaps it is fair to say that her image has been set by the roles she is still best known for internationally, namely those she played in Zhang Yimou's historical trilogy consisting of *Red Sorghum, Ju-dou,* and *Raise the Red Lantern* (1990). It is through these films that we will examine her image, in terms of both narrative role and the various senses of the look.

In terms of narrative role, Gong Li's character repeats a trope across all three films. In each case, she plays a young woman in prerevolutionary China, unhappily married to or made a concubine of an older and tyranni-cal man. In her debut role in Zhang Yimou's *Red Sorghum,* for example, she has been sold into marriage by her impoverished father and deceived about her future husband. However, she rebels against her fate, only returning to her natal home to trash it and renounce her father to his face, shouting, "You are not my father!" In narrative terms, this represents a reversal of the structure of the Mulan myth. Instead of leaving home voluntarily to help her father, she is forced out. And instead of risking life and limb out of loy-alty to the patriarchal line, she refuses her destiny and rejects her family.

In fact, there is nothing new at all in this rebelliousness itself, and by the late twentieth century the trope that Gong Li cites here was already hackneyed. The woman who resists her family's attempts to determine her marriage has been a common signifier of China as a nation rejecting ele-ments of its past in the name of modernization since the early part of the twentieth century. Ruan Lingyu appears as an abandoned or widowed sin-gle mother in *The Goddess, Little Toys,* and *The New Woman,* and Xie Fang is seen resisting or running away from arranged marriages in *Song of Youth, Two Stage Sisters,* and *Early Spring in February.*

However, there are some significant differences between Gong Li's roles and those of both Ruan Lingyu and Xie Fang. Both Ruan Lingyu's and Xie Fang's roles are structured around a contradiction between sexuality and patriotic endeavor. Sexuality is represented as simultaneously tempting and threatening, but ultimately as individualistic and selfish, whereas pa-triotism is a public endeavor that involves joining a collective cause. In both cases, the audience is implicated in this shift by structures of the look that privilege empathy over libidinal objectification. Kristine Harris notes these structures in regard to Ruan Lingyu in *The New Woman,* but explicitly es-chews the use of psychoanalytic terminology for them.[54] However, we have noted the similarity to sublimation of such structures in 1930s cinema.[55] Ma Junxiang makes a similar comparison to sublimation for the structures of the look that he finds in *Shanghai Girl.*[56] Like Ma, we note some differ-ences between the cinematic structures discerned and the precise structures of sublimation described by Freud, but we differ over whether or not to use the term. More significant than these questions of terminology, however, is the continuity of a structure that opposes libidinality to engagement in public service, nationalism, and revolution.

In contrast, Gong Li's roles are structured in such a way that sexuality free of hierarchy and the collective cause can be on the same side, but impeded by feudal patriarchs, be they her fathers or husbands. In each film she seeks out another male sexual partner to help liberate her from these patriarchs. In *Red Sorghum,* made in 1987 and released early in 1989, she succeeds in finding such a man, and they fight the Japanese invaders together at the end of the film after dispatching her unwanted husband at the beginning. But in *Judou* and in *Raise the Red Lantern* she is progressively less able to find such a figure and remains trapped.

Furthermore, whereas it is clear that Ruan Lingyu's patriotism is directed against the Japanese invaders and that Xie Fang's is structured around revolution, it is less clear exactly whom Gong Li is resisting. This is because the highly stylized and invented worlds in which Zhang Yimou sets her make it clear that these films are allegories and not realist films. We will return to the complexities arising from this issue later.

Given that Gong Li's roles do not construct her sexuality as something necessarily negative, perhaps it is not surprising that one of the hallmarks of her roles and her star image is that she is constructed not only as object of desire but also as agent. Probably, she is the first People's Republic woman star since 1949 to be constructed in this way. This distinctive characteristic was established clearly in the first scenes of her first role as "My Grandma" in *Red Sorghum*; they communicate her desire for at least one of the shirtless men carrying her bridal sedan with subjective shots of her peeking out at his sweating and naked back. This representation of erotic agency was celebrated as a liberation of female sexuality by some Chinese commentators writing around the time of the release of these films, including for example Wang Yuejin.[57]

Wang notes that for a woman to be the possessor of the desiring gaze is highly unusual in a patriarchal culture and certainly does not fit the Mulvey model. In regard to look as appearance, there is no doubt that Gong Li's body is more emphasized by clothing than that of either Ruan Lingyu or Xie Fang, and that it is a sexualized body by virtue of the presence of male relays of the cinematic look. However, in regard to how the camera looks at her and her own look, there is already a considerable and established debate. We have already mentioned the position of those mostly male Chinese critics who, around the late eighties, celebrated her sexual agency as symbolic of the liberation of female sexuality. That position was convincingly criticized by Esther Yau, who points out that this and similar such representations made by male filmmakers around this time need to be understood as part of a male fantasy of the willing and active female sexual partner. She treats *Red Sorghum* as part of a group of texts in which finding such a partner is integral to the restoration of male potency, itself a wish with national and not purely personal symbolic significance.[58]

Wang Yuejin and Esther Yau read Gong Li's image in Zhang Yimou's films in relation to the Chinese domestic situation of the late 1980s. However, more recently critics relating it to the international success and circulation of the films have roundly criticized her image as submission to neocolonialism. In this perspective, Gong Li is not just a male sexual fantasy figure, but also a fantasy figure served up by a Chinese male director as an exotic delight to tempt the jaded palates of the Western male spectator. Here, Zhang Yimou is accused of simply imitating Hollywood cinema's representations of women, and almost of pimping Gong Li to the West. There are numerous Chinese-language examples of this critique, the best known probably by Wang Yichuan and Zhang Yiwu.[59]

A later article based on this interpretation and written in English appears in a book of more recent work on the gaze.[60] Its interpretation of the representation of Gong Li simply combines Mulvey with Said's orientalism. Though this and other such writings give new examples, they tend to a mechanical application of Western theory to Chinese film. They fail to observe how the Gong Li figure in Zhang Yimou's films cites, albeit in a specific and new way, the long history discussed here of women as empathetic characters who symbolize the nation and carry the primary spectatorial involvement. For example, in the critique of *Raise the Red Lantern* in the recent article on the gaze, the author fails to note that the Gong Li character is the main protagonist in this film. While she is certainly represented as an object of the (mostly) invisible master's libido, she is also the agent with whom the audience enters the courtyard house and along with whom they are introduced to its strange rituals. Chow draws on Mary Farquhar's and Jenny Kwok Wah Lau's analyses, pointing out that Gong Li is not only looked at but also looks back. They illustrate this point with a scene from *Judou*, which Chow claims almost parodies the voyeuristic structure of Mulvey's understanding of classical Hollywood cinema. When Gong Li's character looks back, her look does not affirm the male desiring look but protests against it, drawing attention to her body, which is battered and bruised by her elderly and sadistic husband.[61] Again, what we have here is another structure that moves us away from simply objectifying the female character and toward an empathetic engagement with her based on her suffering.

However, if (as we pointed out earlier) the highly stylized and invented worlds of Zhang Yimou's films invite an allegorical or metaphorical read-

FIGURE 5.8 Imprisoned glamour—Gong Li in *Raise the Red Lantern* (1990).

(COURTESY CHINA FILM ARCHIVE)

ing, there remains the important question of who the Gong Li character's look protests against. Discussing the international circulation of Zhang Yimou's films, Rey Chow reads this metaphorically as a protest against the commodifying gaze of the West upon China and therefore as a kind of resistance to neocolonialism.[62] Though this interpretation of defiance is ingenious and stimulating, it fails to address why Zhang Yimou's films after *Red Sorghum* were placed primarily under the commodifying gaze of the West. This omission is also the structuring absence that underpins the entire mainland Chinese critique of these films, and the alternative understanding of allegory in these films. Maybe it is so obvious that some people feel it need not be said? However, the feudal patriarchal figures in these films demand to be read allegorically as the Communist Party power structure itself. This reading is plausible because the films move from optimism about challenging that power structure in *Red Sorghum* to deep despair in *Judou* and *Raise the Red Lantern,* which were made after the 1989 Tiananmen Square massacre. It is this possible reading that led to the last two films being banned in China until after *The Story of Qiu Ju* (discussed further in chapter 6). Yet for reasons of censorship, this seemingly evident reading is literally unspeakable in the People's Republic. By producing a discourse that ignores this reading and also Gong Li's defiant look back at the camera, the mainland "postcolonial" critics participate in the willful forgetting of the events of 1989 that underpins the People's Republic of China today.

However, this also reopens the issue of what Gong Li symbolizes in regard to the national. In both the "postcolonial" critique of Zhang Yimou and Rey Chow's answer to it, she symbolizes China's suffering and struggle in the globalizing marketplace. Ruan Lingyu-as-China is defined from a modernizing perspective as the struggling victim of both imperialist invasion and the shackles of feudalism. Xie Fang-as-China is defined in relation to patriotism as revolution, and in this case in relation to a position within global class struggle. Within an interpretation that returns us to the metaphor of protest against the Communist Party's hierarchy, Gong Li-as-China also symbolizes the nation, but in a different way. Here, she symbolizes a popular nation defined against its rulers and envisioned by the young educated elite of the 1980s.[63]

Epilogue: Maggie Cheung Is Ruan Lingyu, But Is Maggie Cheung Ruan Lingyu?

The preceding sections have examined narrative role and the look to trace a lineage of Chinese women in the cinema who signify the nation but are not maternal keepers of the hearth. In different ways, Ruan Lingyu, Xie Fang, and Gong Li have performed variations on the pattern of the daughter who leaves home and struggles in public space as a symbol of the vicissitudes of the modern Chinese nation. However, when Ruan Lingyu's life story was made into a biopic, it was not a mainland Chinese actor like Xie Fang or Gong Li who incarnated her. In Stanley Kwan's 1991 *Center Stage,* Hong Kong's Maggie Cheung took the role. In the context of questions about the national, what does it mean when an actor from Hong Kong plays Ruan? As Audrey Yue puts it in her writing on *Center Stage,* "If a nation and its peoples can only be defined, affirmed, and legitimated through the construction of its histories, what then can be said of the nationality and subjectivity of a 'non-nation' like Hong Kong?"[64] What kind of history does linking old Shanghai and contemporary Hong Kong through Ruan Lingyu

---

MAGGIE CHEUNG

Maggie Cheung[65] was born in Hong Kong in 1964. When she was eight, she left for England with her family and grew up there. After returning to Hong Kong and securing a modeling contract, her agency entered her for the Miss Hong Kong Beauty Pageant in 1983. She was First Runner-Up. This led to television appearances and a movie contract with Shaw Brothers. She became a star three years after her debut, when she acted opposite Jackie Chan in *Police Story* (1985). Her performance in Wong Kar-wai's first film, *As Tears Go By* (1988), made people begin to take her seriously, and in 1992 she had a breakthrough when she won the Best Actress Silver Bear Award at Berlin for her role as Ruan Lingyu in *Center Stage.* So far, she has appeared in at least eighty films, and is one of the most internationally known female Hong Kong film stars.

produce? And furthermore, what specific significance attaches to the casting of Maggie Cheung in the role?

To answer these questions, we consider the look not in the sense of the textual tropes examined so far, but in the more abstract sense of star image—the baggage of significations a known actor brings into any new film.[66] Focusing on star image enables us to show how both Stanley Kwan's deployment of the Ruan Lingyu story and the casting of Cheung make a difference. Kwan's Ruan Lingyu adds to the various ways in which the film connects contemporary Hong Kong to old Shanghai and invokes a lineage of Chinese women in the cinema who signify Chinese modernity not as the national but as the trading city. Anne Ciecko and Sheldon Lu have pointed to another lineage that invokes the trading city, namely Hong Kong's own filmic women warriors. These women warriors include not only Maggie Cheung in some of her roles but also stars like Michelle Yeoh in her resignification of the Bond Girl as action heroine rather than sex object, and Ciecko and Lu parallel their filmic struggles and triumphs with the Hong Kong industry's own battles on the high seas of international trade.[67] However, Kwan's Ruan Lingyu invokes a different lineage of women who symbolize the trading city. Permutations on the old figure of the courtesan, these women survive outside the home not because of patronage or as women warriors, but as commercial agents trading in the new economy and symbolized by a range of entertainers including the streetwalker and the female actor. Furthermore, Maggie Cheung's own star image as a cosmopolitan "free spirit" adds a twist to Ruan's tragic image, running against the grain of the analogy between Hong Kong facing 1997 and old Shanghai on the eve of its eclipse.

Some commentators see Kwan's film as just a new version of the story of Ruan Lingyu/China's noble but tragic struggle,[68] and some others simply do not ask if it is a metaphor for either China or Hong Kong.[69] However, there are good reasons for thinking that the film parallels 1930s Shanghai with Hong Kong in particular. For example, Leung Ping-Kwan notes *Center Stage*'s focus on filmmakers who later came under strong criticism from the People's Republic and were closely associated with Hong Kong cinema, including producer Li Minwei, and directors Fei Mu and Cai Chusheng, whom he refers to by his Cantonese name of Choi Chorseng.[70] Interviews with surviving film veterans currently resident in Hong Kong, such as the actor Li Lili, further underline the connection. Audrey Yue notes the significance of the dates in titles for sections of the film. For example, "1929" is the eve of Ruan's move to the newly established Lianhua Studio and the beginning of this version of her story, but the founding of Lianhua is also widely regarded as a watershed event in Hong Kong cinema, as was 1932, when the Japanese bombing of Shanghai prompted flight to Hong Kong by many filmmakers, including Ruan.[71] At the very least, this strain in "Kwan's cinematic historiography functions to ambiguate the rubric of 'Chinese cinema' by adopting it, yet shifting its ground, or center,"[72] as Wang Yiman argues, and maybe even to challenge the idea of Shanghai cinema as the heritage of the People's Republic and claim it for Hong Kong.[73]

Furthermore, the film's efforts to connect 1930s Shanghai and 1990s Hong Kong are not confined to the film industry. Julian Stringer points out that Kwan's interview question to Maggie Cheung about being remembered "fifty years from now" resonates with the fifty years without change promised Hong Kong by the People's Republic. He also notes that repeated references to fears of imminent invasion by the Japanese in the 1930s resonate with the fears many Hong Kong residents held about the People's Republic.[74]

How does Stanley Kwan's portrayal of Ruan Lingyu herself color this analogy? First, Kwan picks out details that highlight Ruan's Cantonese identity. Whereas all Ruan's films were silent and therefore did not connect her to the south of China, not only is this film in sound but Kwan has also ignored the Chinese cinema convention of using one language throughout. Instead of the whole film being either in Mandarin or Cantonese, Ruan speaks in Cantonese-accented Mandarin to most people and in Cantonese to other South Chinese, like her mother and Cai Chusheng. Furthermore, an important subplot that resonates with Hong Kong's anticipation of 1997 concerns Ruan's difficulties learning Mandarin in anticipation of Chinese cinema's conversion to sound.

Second, as Julian Stringer also notes, the film parallels the fallen woman and the fallen city, with Ruan's tragic end echoing that of 1930s Shanghai and possibly Hong Kong in the 1990s.[75] Although it has been shown above that her cinematic roles can be seen as a permutation on the Hua Mulan myth, the star image conjured up by Kwan's version of her life story is significantly different. Unlike Hua Mulan, there is nothing masculine about the image of her that Kwan constructs. In regard to patriotism, Ruan's opposition to Japanese aggression appears in various scenes. However, where Hua Mulan is an agent of the state and her own loyal and patriotic family, to which she returns after completing her mission for the state, Ruan's concern for her country in *Center Stage* is not linked to the Chinese government of the day or any political party that might aspire to government. Furthermore, although she is the breadwinner for her mother and daughter, she has no legitimate status in the patriarchal families of the men in her life, and this causes the scandal that ruins her.

The image of Ruan in *Center Stage* links her to a different lineage. Researching the 1920s and 1930s, Michael Chang notes the emergence of the female movie star as a figure initially made sense of in the light of the old high-class image of the refined courtesan supported by patrons and the more recent and more simply sexual and commercial image of the street-walker. He notes that it is only in the 1930s, with the development of professional studios and career movie actors, that women stars can move away from these images toward establishing acting as a professional activity for women in its own right.[76] Ruan's career straddled this transition, and the scandalous details of her personal life involving bigamy and adultery as shown in the film certainly dovetail into this significatory mix. Through the analogy established in the film and discussed above, the commercial streetwalker and the vicissitudes she experiences become metaphors for the Chinese entrepôts that emerged as a result of trade with the West, including Shanghai and Hong Kong.

Given the eclipse of Shanghai with Japanese invasion, and the isolation of China that followed the Communist takeover and Ruan's suicide, the analogies for Hong Kong with old Shanghai and Ruan constructed by *Center Stage* seem compatible with the "deja disparu" mentality of the "culture of disappearance" Ackbar Abbas diagnosed in Hong Kong's runup to 1997.[77] However, the casting of Maggie Cheung complicates this.

In a frequently noted interview scene at the beginning of the film, before even the credits, Kwan tells Cheung that Ruan was taken seriously as an actor only after changing studios in 1929. Cheung laughs and says, "Isn't she a replica of me?" Different commentators understand this in different ways. Some find it plausible and others do not, but none regard it as an ironic remark. Cui Shuqin, for example, takes it on face value and goes on to ask whether this achievement is the product of Cheung's female agency or Kwan's male agency.[78] Julian Stringer similarly assumes it is a direct claim on Cheung's part, but questions it.[79]

Yet the circumstances of Cheung's casting demand the consideration of another possibility. As Julian Stringer reminds us, Cheung was not Kwan's first choice for the role. This was Anita Mui, who, "apart from bearing an uncanny similarity to photographs of Ruan Lingyu circa-*New Woman*" with "her mix of erotic danger and world-weary tragedy," was also "a great fit, in both her on and off-screen images, with the politics of scandal and tragedy."[80] Indeed, her previous role for Kwan as the sad ghost of an early-twentieth-century courtesan in *Rouge* seems almost like a preparation for the role of Ruan. Yet as Stringer mentions, offscreen events including problems with gangs involved in film production forced Mui off the picture.[81]

These circumstances, which were very much in the Hong Kong public eye at the time of the film's release, lead us to favor construing Cheung's comment as ironic and acknowledging public doubts about her suitability for the role. This could be understood from the way she laughs when she makes the comment, and also from Kwan's editing decision to place this interview segment before the credits, like a prologue.

Furthermore, if one considers star image, unlike Anita Mui few Hong Kong stars could be further removed from Ruan Lingyu than Maggie Cheung. While both their backgrounds emphasize the geographical mobility associated with the market economy, Ruan's family was poor and moved north in search of work. Cheung's was middle-class and mobile. She returned to Hong Kong not as a poor country girl but from England as a cosmopolitan with a perfect English accent. If Ruan was embarrassed by her poor Mandarin, Cheung happily peppers her Cantonese with English in the interview clips in the film. Before *Center Stage*, she rarely if ever appeared in period roles. Instead, she came to fame opposite Jackie Chan in *Police Story* and was associated with popular genres such as romance, action, and comedy, all set in modern times. In these films, Cheung was the cheerful girlfriend, the upbeat girl next door, and so on. Taking on the challenge of a radically different role such as Ruan is, of course, a classic maneuver for a star wanting to be taken seriously as an actor. However, at the stage in her career when she took on *Center Stage*, it is difficult to think of a female Hong Kong star less likely to commit suicide because of a sex scandal than Maggie Cheung. If she is, as Bérénice Reynaud claims, "an icon of modernity," it is a very different modernity from that incarnated by either Ruan Lingyu or Gong Li.[82]

By the 1980s, the figure of the woman entertainer was no longer shrouded in dubious sexuality as Ruan had been. Further analysis could detail this change by tracing a lineage of what Stephen Teo calls "Les Sing-Song Girls in Hong Kong."[83] Of course, as a silent star, Ruan did not sing. But perhaps the sing-song girl type can be expanded to include the woman entertainer in general. Teo shows how figures of the 1940s and 1950s such as the tragic Zhou Xuan, "who personified the type," continued many of the qualities associated with Ruan, and he notes of the star originally intended to play Ruan that, "Anita Mui is the contemporary reincarnation of the classic sing-song girl."[84] However, the sing-song girl had long ago undergone a transformation along with Hong Kong itself. By the time of Grace Chang—the star of 1957's *Mambo Girl*—the torch songs had given way to upbeat American trends.[85] From here, it is not far to the resilient perkiness of Maggie Cheung's early image. Her beginnings in a beauty pageant are a significant part of her star image; these are events that display female beauty for the look of a spectator but have come to operate under a rhetoric that refuses to acknowledge libidinality.

If Cheung's star image adds a twist to Ruan's, how does this complicate what *Center Stage* has to say about Hong Kong? Three other authors have focused on what the slippage between star images adds as part of a comparison between *Center Stage* and French director Olivier Assayas's *Irma Vep,* in which Cheung incarnates a French silent star. As mentioned above, Wang Yiman factors it into her consideration of both films as revisionist film historiography, and Carlos Roja uses it for a discussion of "aura" in the cinema.[86] Olivia Khoo, on the other hand, takes up the metaphor of the vampire in *Irma Vep* to argue that "rather than conceive of Maggie in terms of her star *aura,* perhaps it would be more accurate to think of her as a 'spectre' or a ghost."[87] We understand the difference between *aura* and *specter* here to signify the haunting effect achieved by visible difference between star image and role; where an aura is singular and fixed, the metaphor of haunting suggests a double presence. This is registered in *Center Stage* not only in the interview segments where the "real" Cheung appears so very different from Ruan but also in the numerous scenes in which she is shown rehearsing scenes. One sequence in particular has caught the eye of many commentators. When Cheung is playing Ruan's deathbed scene in her final film *The New Woman,* Cheung's breathing registers on camera, spoiling the perfect mimicry of the original scene. On one level, Cheung's difficulty echoes Ruan's difficulty with certain parts and her stumbling pronunciation of Mandarin. But on another level, it registers the difference between them; Ruan died in real life in circumstances that echoed the film, but Cheung goes on.

Furthermore, Khoo's idea of acting as haunting suggests mobility, as she herself points out by citing Ken Gelder's discussion of the vampire as a figure of the cosmopolitan and "global exotic."[88] This then suggests a different image of Hong Kong from the "culture of disappearance" postulated by Abbas. Audrey Yue has argued for such an alternative understanding in her discussion of the 1997 "return" as a "re-turn" outward; a remobilization of Chinese diasporic culture that survives (sometimes struggling, sometimes thriving) on the seas of globalized trade, cosmopolitan and detached from the space of the nation-state.[89] Whether the deployment of Cheung's star image and the lineage it invokes in *Center Stage* can be regarded as a mark of her agency—she is the one who breathes when she should not—or of Stanley Kwan—he is the director who chooses to edit this into rather than out of the film—may be a moot point.[90] However, the simultaneous appearance of the two star images of Ruan and Cheung in *Center Stage* does signify two different versions of woman as the Chinese but non-national space of Hong Kong and its history to be added to the examples of woman as Chinese nation discussed earlier in this chapter.

6

How Should Chinese Men Act?

ORDERING THE NATION

IN 2002, CHINESE audiences and Party leaders flocked to see Zhang Yimou's *Hero*, which broke box office records around the country. *Hero* tells of the founding of the Chinese empire in the Qin dynasty (221–207 b.c.), complete with maps of neighboring states yet to be conquered and brought within its borders. While the film is a historical martial arts epic, many contemporaries, including China's leaders, read it as an affirmation of the modern, territorial, and unified nation-state. In the film, an assassin called Nameless confronts the King of Qin. The drama revolves around Nameless's choice to kill or not to kill the king, whose army had previously murdered his family. The ending suggests that sons forgo their filial duty to avenge their father's death (almost mandatory in the martial arts genre) and submit as subjects to rulers who promise national unity and future peace. All Chinese viewers know that the historical King of Qin did achieve unification but through violence and repression, not peace. The film was therefore controversial on its release in China in 2002 and internationally in 2004, stimulating a debate on the nature of heroism, nationalism, the Chinese state, and Chinese citizens' loyalty to the state in modern times.

In this chapter, we turn to three Confucian codes that circulate not only in *Hero* (whose historical events actually predate the codes' formulation) but also across a century of Chinese cinema. These codes were premodern legal, moral, and hierarchical obligations: loyalty to the ruler, filiality toward parents and ancestors, and brotherhood, the last requiring the submission of the younger to the older brother. Brotherhood has been reinvented in literature, in martial arts films, and in society as an egalitarian code of loyalty and emotional bonding between men who are sworn brothers but not necessarily blood brothers. The premodern codes were fundamental to Confucian notions of ruling the nation through virtue, rather than to modern concepts of rule by or of law. Before the twentieth century, they came together to regulate male behavior and to privilege men in governing the family as fathers and ruling the nation as emperor and bureaucrats. As "feudal" laws, their status changed in the twentieth century, but they were reinvented in various ways. For example, the idea of comradeship, while not gendered, is a Communist version of brotherhood as a political, emotional, and class-bound bond that required collective sacrifice to the revolution under the Maoists, as we saw in *Azalea Mountain* in chapter 3 and in *Song of Youth* in chapter 5. Leaders still invoke these codes in the twentieth and twenty-first centuries—in Taiwan (see chapter 4), in Singapore under Premier Lee Kwan-yew, and more recently in mainland China—as a "return to roots" in order to solve problems of crime, corruption, and moral degeneration within the social order.[1]

These codes are long gone as law. However, we argue that the codes persist as mythic symbols of national identity, ideal masculine behavior, and institutional governance that are reconstituted in various ways in films within different national and non-national settings. Their prevalence in film suggests their symbolic potency as a way of talking about society and nation, and about how men should act. *Hero* appears to commend loyalty to the state over all other moral obligations, including Nameless's filial duty toward his parents and his brotherly commitment toward his fellow assassins in their joint enterprise to kill the king and so save their own rival kingdoms from conquest. However, as Rey Chow points out, the seductive "force of surfaces" in Zhang's films challenges the viewer in "a fronting, facing, and daring of convention."[2] The assassins all choose to act individually and on the basis of very modern principles rather than through blind obedience to now bygone codes. The three male assassins—Nameless, Broken Sword, and Sky—betray their allegiance to their own kingdoms and let the enemy king live so that "the people" will no longer suffer. Flying Snow, the sole female warrior, persists in her desire to avenge her parents and save her home kingdom, but in the end she commits suicide for love. In this sense, Zhang continues his earlier cinematic "assault" on "feudal patriarchy," which he said lives on in modern China. In *Hero*, the assault continues in the assassins' confrontation with the all-conquering King of Qin. The king converts enemies into either subjects or dead enemies, according to Qin's new legal codes.[3]

In the first section of this chapter, we approach issues of masculinity and ordering the nation through the interdisciplinary field of "law and film."[4] We analyze how these past patriarchal codes are deployed in the cinema to talk about different modern social orders in both non-national and national spaces. The focus is on films from Hong Kong and the People's Republic. We argue that these premodern codes in films from Hong Kong and the mainland are not just abstract symbols. They retain normative and affective force in cinematic representations of how men should act today. While Taiwan film is not represented in this chapter, the argument applies equally to Taiwan films discussed in other chapters, such as the so-called traditional values of the "good father" in Lee Hsing's work (discussed in chapter 4) and the problems of filiality and loyalty in Ang Lee's *Crouching Tiger, Hidden Dragon* (chapter 3) and *The Wedding Banquet* (chapter 7).

In the later sections of this chapter, we turn to the work of three icons of the contemporary Chinese cinema: Jackie Chan, John Woo, and Zhang Yimou. These filmmakers in no way encompass the diverse representations of masculinity in Chinese films. Chan and Woo are from Hong Kong, a colonial and then provincial space that has marked out a local identity within larger nation-states. Zhang is from the People's Republic and his work invokes the territorial nation-state as well as the cultural nation. The transnational prominence of the works of Chan, Woo, and Zhang reveal the variety, contest, and dynamic debate around masculine *mores* and national identity that have most resonance with Chinese and international audiences today. In Chan and Woo's work, images of Hong Kong hover between the local and transnational as a fluid space of negotiation. As Kwai-cheung Lo argues, the local in Hong Kong films is the primary source of national identity, but it is never asserted as a "nationalistic entity": "the local is the transnational itself in the process of becoming."[5] Zhang's cinematic worlds, in contrast, are firmly situated in the national as nation-state, even though they aim for a wider audience.

Despite these differences, each filmmaker has a signature style that involves play with the same patriarchal codes. Jackie Chan's signature is "saving the father." We suggest that he both affirms and denies filiality, loyalty, and the national in his early films and becomes the first adolescent hero in Chinese film history. The main example is *Drunken Master II* (1993), with a coda on *Rush Hour* (1998). John Woo's gangster films are now famous for reinventing masculinity through a romantic view of brotherhood. We call this section "romancing the brother." His descriptions of brotherhood delve into traditional codes of friendship in a lawless Hong Kong world, which lacks an ultimate lawgiver. *The Killer* (1989) is a major example of Woo's Hong Kong trademark relationships, which have a changed emphasis in his Hollywood films, such as *Face/Off* (1997). Zhang Yimou's theme is "killing the father." He explores the son or subject's desire to rebel against local and national codes, both legal and customary, in the pursuit of justice, but actual rebellion commonly fails. Here, we focus on *The Story of Qiu Ju* (1992) and *Hero*. The common denominator in all these films is the transgressive nature of male heroism and its complex relationship to authority figures, who are always male.

Male Codes: Filiality, Brotherhood, and Loyalty

Codes are just one way to look at masculinity onscreen. Nevertheless, masculine codes are familiar signs in the Chinese cinema. They link the social order constructed within and across films to the wider society outside. Patrick Fuery writes that "codes order signs, as well as provide rules of exclusion, combination, and hierarchy."[6] As such, paradigmatic codes in Chinese films order representations of social justice and the moral domain within different national and non-national settings. They operate as "myth, memories, traditions, and symbols of ethnic heritage."[7]

Representations of Chinese codes—filiality (*xiao*), brotherhood (*yi*), and loyalty (*zhong*)—are therefore one way to explore the wider debates within Chinese national and other communities about social structure, gender, and nation. These codes are central to imperial Chinese law and, more recently, to Chinese film: historically, the codes were the core laws and customs that ordered the nation, both institutionally and socially. Today, they have cultural and not narrowly legal implications; as we wrote at the beginning of this chapter, they are often invoked in contemporary Chinese societies as a means to moral and social regeneration. Transgression and performance of the codes in and across films over time therefore refer to wider social debates within Chinese communities on the moral health of the nation and on local and national institutions of governance. The debates involve male hierarchies of power, competition, conflict, and consensus.

The codes traditionally reflect reciprocal family-based relationships, which privilege men. The rules were originally generational and gender-based. We focus on codes of behavior between fathers and sons, between brothers, and between ruler and subject. As anyone familiar with Chinese society knows, family codes extend to wider social and national networks of power. Martial arts movies originated as vengeance for the death of the father and, by extension, that of the warrior's master or *shifu*, who compels a disciple's heroic revenge for his slaying just as a father in the Confucian legal order compels a son's filial obedience as a right. Within the same legal order, the emperor's power mirrors that of the father, commanding a subject's loyalty as both state and natural law. These rules still operate within the hierarchies of China's mythic underworld—*jianghu*—as the mirror image of Confucian or state law. John Woo's gangster movies reinvent brotherhood (not brothers) as an egalitarian friendship in a modern and brutal Hong Kong underworld. Brotherhood involves strong customary rules that translate into a range of genres, from revolutionary comrade films to martial arts and gangster movies. The movies project a bonding around codes of honor, which applies to heroes on both sides of the law in Woo's work. In short, the Chinese cinematic imaginary provides a rich store of regimes of justice and power through which men relate to, and fight with, each other.

Issues of justice and power encompass the broadest possible notions of law, social justice, and social order in Chinese cinema, including their opposites—lawlessness, injustice, and disorder.[8] Law and film scholar David Black observes that film *"indefatigably* represents law" and both law and film "traffic in symbolic representation" of the moral and social order.[9] How then does this operate in Chinese film? Given the past and present richness of legal regimes, why do Chinese filmmakers commonly refer to the Confucian codes of filiality, brotherhood, and loyalty that are long gone as law? And what does this have to say about various cinematic views of the national?

We suggest that these codes have mythic status within modern and contemporary Chinese cultures. In *Science and Civilization in China*, Joseph Needham wrote, "unnumbered generations of Chinese had instinctively felt" that rules such as filiality were "right."[10] Filmmakers mediate their stories between the repressive and ideal order of the myth that is familiar to all Chinese and the problematic "real" world onscreen so as to criticize, modernize, and revitalize the myth, and regenerate the nation, through some sort of narrative resolution.

Furthermore, law across Chinese societies may have been richly plural during the twentieth century but, unlike the myth, modern law was foreign, diverse, top-down, individualist, and frequently in disarray if not in disrepute. After all, the West provided models of modern nation-states. These Western states often championed the rule of law even as they trampled over Chinese rights and territories, as we saw in the various film versions of the Opium War (discussed in chapter 2). In a transitional century when Chinese sought and fought for a role in the world, Confucian codes provided an ethnic symbol of a past order based primarily on moral suasion rather than legal compulsion or military might. The codes act as a foil to judge alternative means of collective organization, social justice, and power relationships. Because the codes are no longer solely aligned to a particular state, they are also available to Hong Kong and Taiwan filmmakers as a storytelling resource. Thus, the codes provide a fictional and historical anchor in China's twentieth-century transition from empire to modern nation-state, in Hong Kong's shift from colony to autonomous region, and in Taiwan's struggles for an independent identity.

Finally, both the codes and state sovereignty are, in principle, masculinist. John Hoffman writes in *Gender and Sovereignty* that men usually govern states, patriarchy arose as the "creation" of the state, and "state sovereignty is gendered by its assertion that leadership is monolithic, hierarchical, and violent."[11] However, patriarchy is a problematic notion, according to Nira Yuval-Davis, because there are "different forms of patriarchy" that operate "across different social domains."[12] This is certainly the case with Chinese nations and territories, given the profound changes in social and nation-state formations over the last century. While we turn to concrete instances in particular films in the following sections, it is clear that the social contract, whether Confucian, socialist, or capitalist, requires the state to care for its citizens. In the cinema, injustice, violence, or exclusion by authority figures (whether cast as good or bad characters) trigger retaliation, retribution, or revenge and demands resolution—usually the province of males. As Yvonne Tasker observes, "action cinema depends on a complex articulation of both belonging and exclusion, an articulation that is bound up with the body of the hero and the masculine identity that it embodies. These dramas of belonging and exclusion mobilize discourses of national, racial, and gendered identity."[13] But a hero cannot *be* a hero unless he embodies certain notions of social justice that resonate with audiences.

In other English-language work on Chinese masculinity and the cinema, there are approaches that also employ traditional gender concepts. The work includes Stanley Kwan's documentary, *Yang + Yin: Gender in Chinese Cinema* (1997). *Yang* (the cosmic male principle) and *yin* (the cosmic female principle) interact as a life force in traditional Chinese cosmology and aesthetics. While they are gendered principles, they operate from the cosmos to the human body and are not specific to one sex. For this reason, Kam Louie argues in *Theorizing Chinese Masculinity* that *yang* and *yin* theory does not explain sexual difference in terms of Chinese masculinity alone. He turns to the *wen* and *wu* dyad (respectively, cultural attainment and martial valor) as specific to men and traces its variations over the centuries. He concludes with a discussion of globalized representations of Chinese martial valor through superstars Bruce Lee (discussed further in chapter 8), Jackie Chan, and Chow Yun-fat. Both Kwan and Louie's work frequently touches on the principles of filiality, loyalty, and brotherhood. Indeed, their work brings a balance to gender studies because, as Louie laments, gender has long focused on "woman" in China studies.[14] Consequently, there is a failure to treat "man" in similar depth. When masculinity is discussed, it is usually within Western paradigms.

Both Kwan and Louie demonstrate that the scholarly gap is not reflected in the cinema itself. There is a rich array of masculine representations, including heroes and antiheroes, over the past century. Stanley Kwan's documentary, especially, focuses on a range of male relationships and their changing representations in cinema. Men and male power can be seductive. He features the martial arts actor, Ti Lung, saying:

Men relate to each other as much as they relate to women. I agree with [the martial arts director] Chang Cheh on this. Men have their own charisma, their own way of moving that can be attractive too.[15]

Hence, fathers, sons, and brothers are a focus of Kwan's work in which filmmakers discuss filiality, brotherhood (including homosexual love), and loyalty as ongoing features of Chinese society.

Kwan comments that "fathers are everywhere" in a century of Chinese movies. Fatherhood as ancestral lineage was particularly important in early-twentieth-century cinema, as we saw with *Tomboy* in chapter 4. Modern notions of society and the state challenged Confucian law, with its complex rules that supported patriarchal imperial power. The concepts relating to father and son and to ruler and subject—filiality and loyalty—were vertical power relationships that applied to family and state, respectively. Filiality (to parents) had primacy over loyalty (to the ruler). In the early twentieth century, there was a dual discursive reversal—from old to young within the family and from family to ruler within the state, that is, from filiality to state loyalty.[16] Twentieth-century Chinese film reflects this shift. It involved overthrowing established imperial notions of legitimate governance in order to establish a modern nation-state in which subjects become citizens. Familial, state, and cosmic law, which had ideally formed a unified ethical order of things, now fragmented.[17] As the old order under the Qing emperor unraveled, the father/ancestor in a patrilineal society became a central and controversial issue in cinematic representations of social justice. One of China's first box office hits, *Orphan Rescues Grandfather* (1923), dramatizes the social conflict early on in film history. It is a simple melodrama, so in one sense the moral issues are quite clear. The modern-educated grandson is the hero who saves his grandfather. Yet the film also diegetically reinstates the old Confucian order after its actual institutional collapse with the end of the imperial system in 1911.

In *Orphan Rescues Grandfather,* the wealthy Yang Shouchang mistakenly believes his daughter-in-law to be unchaste after his son dies, and she is expelled from his house. She lives in poverty and bears a grandson, Yupu, who goes to a school for the poor funded by the grandfather. The unidentified grandson saves his grandfather from murder by his villainous nephew who, on his deathbed, finally confesses that he falsely slandered the daughter-in-law to claim her inheritance. Yupu's true identity as the grandson is now recognized. Yang gives his daughter-in-law half his money and she gives half this inheritance to schooling for the poor. The happy ending is a literal melodrama of recognition, of grand family reunion, and of continued transformation of China. In this story, Yupu is considered an orphan until reunited with the patriarchal family. His mother's existence is irrelevant.

Orphan is primarily about lineage. The character *zu* in the Chinese title for the film (*Gu'er Jiu Zu Ji*) means "ancestor."[18] The family crisis is set up through the opening scenes, beginning with a pastoral shot of swans swimming in the pond, followed by images of villains in the family garden, and then the death of the father when he falls from his horse. "Family serenity is suddenly gone."[19] The grandfather redeems himself by setting up a school for the poor, unknowingly educating his own grandson. The happy ending is not a return to the old order. Mother and grandson reinstate a different family and a new generation, but it is still patriarchal, a recognition of the dead son as the legitimate father. In this sense, *Orphan* translates complex issues surrounding Chinese modernity into family narrative, readily understandable to Chinese audiences. The Confucian ancestor is threatened but still powerful. The father does not save his son; in fact, his death triggers the plot. Instead, the grandson saves his grandfather, suggesting that modernity, through an education system for the poor, is valid precisely because it maintains the old patriarchal system. Besides, the grandfather set up the school. It is patriarchy alone that legitimizes misprized virtue in the film. At the end of *Orphan,* the grandfather cries out: "Good daughter-in-law. Good child!" They become his heirs, perpetuating his lineage.

Hence, premodern concepts did not disappear from modern Chinese cultures, the imaginary, the cinema, or politics in the early twentieth century. These concepts still operate, albeit in new ways, in the late twentieth century. Thus, the death of the father is a cause for the son-narrator's nostalgia in Zhang Yimou's *The Road Home* (1999) and an ambivalent mourning for the passing of the socialist father and socialist state with China's "open door" policy in 1978. Allen Fong's *Father and Son* (1981), discussed in chapter 4, offers a different type of nostalgia for a past era in Hong Kong. It too has a son-narrator. Whereas the son in *The Road Home* is looking back from within China, the son in *Father and Son* flies into Hong Kong from America. The nostalgia records the son's dual displacement in terms of time and place: a lost time of past intimacy and sacrificial love, only now acknowledged by the son from Hong Kong as a place where East and West merge. In colonial Hong Kong's quest for identity, there is a belated recognition of the richness of its local traditions despite the father's powerlessness during his life, which mirrors Hong Kong's own powerlessness in the negotiations between Britain and China over the return of Hong Kong. The films of Taiwan director Lee Hsing, discussed in chapter 4, allegedly promote such traditional family values as filiality but in fact depict the hollowness of paternity itself, which awaits recognition from the young. As we said, paternal powerlessness suggests a wider reading that includes the dislocation of the Nationalists in exile in Taiwan and their inability to hold mainland China. Ang Lee's *Wedding Banquet,* discussed in chapter 7, accepts and fulfills the father's desire for a grandson even as it allows the son to get on with his own life beside his gay lover in America. Jackie Chan, discussed later in this chapter, plays with the father and son relationship by subverting filiality in rites-of-passage plots that end up affirming both the role of the "father" and the masculine autonomy of the son. In short, the hierarchy and obedience so central to the codes of filiality and loyalty are acknowledged in these films, either explicitly or implicitly. But the codes are not stable. Their substance is depicted as increasingly empty, or to be reinvented again and again to correspond to new national and non-national Chinese social structures.

Brotherhood in Chinese film, in contrast to filiality and loyalty, is nominally egalitarian. Another of Kwan's sequences in *Yang + Yin: Gender in the Chinese Cinema* is called "Looking for father, finding older brother"—that is, finding male friendship or sexual love as a relationship that replaces the father. Like filiality and loyalty, brotherly relations in traditional law are hierarchical, revolving around older and younger brothers. However, brotherhood is also a customary and romantic code of friendship, heroism, and honor (but not kinship). The famous martial arts director of the 1960s, Chang Cheh, evokes the code as central to his reinvention of masculine machismo in the Chinese cinema. He says:

> When I began making films I wanted to do something new. So I tried to see some old traditions in a fresh way. The traditional Chinese hero has no truck with women. He is much more concerned with his male friends. The classical archetype [of the hero] is the novel, *The Three Kingdoms.* Its heroes are the blood brothers Liu, Guan, and Zhang. They are the epitome of what I wanted to show in my films.[20]

Kam Louie analyzes the complex relationships embodied in brotherhood in *The Three Kingdoms,* writing that the Chinese title—*Sanguo Yanyi*—could be translated literally as *"The Three Kingdoms* as an Explication of *Yi,"* or "brotherhood." The sworn brotherhood between the three heroes—Liu, Guan, and Zhang—involves loyalty, emotion, sexuality, and male exclusivity. It is nominally egalitarian and so compatible with the legal insistence on equality in Western-style modernity. The code is therefore primarily one of martial masculinity that Chang Cheh and his disciple John Woo translate into high-energy action movies. Chang's focus is the male body and the sword as phallus. Woo's is male bonding, male chivalry, and the gun as phallus. A feature of Woo's male protagonists is that they act as doubles, merging as very bloody "brothers" until, in *Face/Off,* they quite literally become each other.

The codes, masculinity, and the national are discussed in the rest of this chapter in relation to films of Jackie Chan, John Woo, and Zhang Yimou. In the section on Jackie Chan's films, we suggest that *Drunken Master* and *Drunken Master II* are about the liminal state of adolescence that mirrors the liminal status of Hong Kong as a colony that constantly asserts its right to semiautonomous identity. The Hollywood movie *Rush Hour* translates Chan's adolescent persona into that of a cop but he still asserts his role as a Hong Kong outsider who once again saves the day for representatives of the great powers, China and America. Conversely, in the section on John Woo's *The Killer,* nobody is able to save the innocent in society. This film on Hong Kong brotherhood among gangsters and cops depicts a vanishing world of honor within a violent and lawless society. Law as justice is absent. Even codes of honor within the underworld are fast disappearing. The final shoot-out between the "brothers," cops, and triads in a church prefigures the end of British colonial rule in Hong Kong as well as the death of the hero. The church burns and a statue of the Madonna explodes into a vision of hellfire. The final section explores Zhang Yimou's ambivalent attitudes to patriarchy and the state in *The Story of Qiu Ju* and *Hero.* In both films, an ultimate albeit problematic lawgiver defines the nation through state legal codes. In both films, state law conflicts with various individuals' sense of social justice. In both, the state wins.

Saving the Father

Jackie Chan's films, such as *Drunken Master* and *Rush Hour,* do not search for a Hong Kong identity; they *earn* it, they *assert* it, they repeatedly display Hong Kong's right to semiautonomous existence within national and transnational spaces because its people may be careless of state authority and legal institutions, but they repeatedly save them onscreen. This right to exist is constantly renegotiated and always explicitly acknowledged by the "father," the community, or the state in the final scenes of his movies.

Chan's trademark persona is the reluctant hero who eventually saves the day for friends, family, local and national community. Local narratives frequently pay homage to broader national and international settings in both a cultural and political sense, such as saving Chinese antiquities from smugglers at the start of both *Drunken Master II* and *Rush Hour.* There is always a happy ending, played out through a suite of extraordinary combat scenes that climax in the victory for good and the defeat of evil. The final combat is therefore the trial as climax, a legal prototype that avenges villainy, brings moral resolution, purges the social order, and affirms the status of particular national leaders. The "father" is always Chinese—blood father, martial arts master, police chief, or representative of the People's Republic—and he is saved again and again in each film. The villains in both films are not just evil; they are corrupt representatives of the British colonial government who collude with local Chinese criminals to exploit China's riches and its people. Their downfall reestablishes national pride and the Chinese moral order.

Jackie Chan's onscreen masculinity is frequently analyzed in terms of global—predominantly Hollywood—adult representations. He is an unlikely hero; his persona relies on the body in action rather than the body as *machismo*. Mark Gallagher describes his masculinity as feminized, self-mocking, and submissive in a vehicle he made his own: *kung fu* comedy. He writes:

> Comedy often places Chan in submissive, masochistic positions, destabilizing his characters' control over the films' humor, if not their action.... [His] films rely on comic treatments of escape and flight, feminizing his characters while reinscribing his antagonists as caricatures of "serious" masculinity.[21]

We suggest that these features of Jackie Chan's masculinity are not feminine but adolescent. They dramatize all the risks, trauma, and fantasy of male adolescence—adventure, a passing curiosity about girls, humiliations, and trials before the onscreen representatives of "serious masculinity," especially the "father." Stephen Teo aptly calls Chan's early persona "the *kung fu* kid."[22] This is his trademark style.

The style was developed in his early films, where Chan negotiates between his adolescent search for a separate male identity while simultaneously constrained by a family that demands submission to the father. His characters often occupy a liminal, preadult space in which he must constantly prove his manhood. He negotiates between filiality, loyalty, and a desire for personal autonomy and recognition. His later films, in which he often plays a cop, shift the same modus operandi from father to an older male authority figure, such as the colonial police chief in the *Police Story* trilogy or the PRC consul in *Rush Hour*, and he wins despite numerous setbacks. In his Hong Kong films, filiality and loyalty merge through extraordinary combat scenes in which the law eventually defeats the lawless. In his Hollywood films, he represents Hong Kong as an outsider who also must prove his autonomy before "serious" representatives of such "serious" states as the People's Republic and the United States. The struggle for recognition and identity is a physical battle; it is inscribed onto Jackie Chan's own body—he always wins but it hurts! The now-famous sequences of stunts-gone-wrong at the end of his movies bring the real pain of attaining masculine autonomy home to the audience.

Jackie Chan's early onscreen masculinity is not everyday adolescence. In one of the first films that made him a star, *Drunken Master* (1978), he plays a youthful version of the iconic male hero of countless Cantonese martial arts movies from the 1940s—the straight-laced Wong Fei-hung (1847–1924), played by a mature Kwan Tak-hing. The idea came from Chan's first success in an earlier film, *Snake in the Eagle's Shadow* (1978). Chan played the disciple to his martial arts master as a father and son relationship, full of heart and a shared sense of mischief. It was a hit with local audiences. The producer then turned to the Wong Fei-hung legend. He said: "[Wong] had always been so serious. I wondered what he was like *before* he became this Chinese superhero. Maybe he was just another naughty boy!"[23]

The result was the *kung fu* comedy classic, *Drunken Master*. The Wong Fei-hung background gave the film a cultural lineage that places it beyond "the historical vacuum" that Ng Ho believes puts *kung fu* comedy on a par with comic books—"[the characters] have no past or future, only the present."[24] Local Cantonese audiences were steeped in Wong Fei-hung stories, and there is now a museum featuring his exploits in Guangdong. Local audiences brought this knowledge and context to Chan's characterization of Wong as "a naughty boy" on his way to "serious masculinity" and legendary status.[25] At the same time, Yuen Woping created a new form of onscreen fighting by linking Northern-style fighting (out of Beijing opera) with fist or hand-to-hand combat forms: *kung fu* combat.[26]

Bey Logan lists *Drunken Master* as one of "Jackie's ten best bash-em-ups."[27] Audiences of all ages loved it, perhaps because it delivered a benign

FIGURE 6.1 Kwan Tak-hing (*right*) plays Wong Fei-hung in films of the 1950s.

FIGURE 6.2 Jackie Chan plays Wong Fei-hung in *Drunken Master* (1978).

view of adolescence, a new phenomenon in Chinese societies. The Chinese "discovery" of childhood predates that of the West in a Confucian framework that merged childhood, adolescence, and youth.[28] The phenomenon of adolescence is the result of a material shift from feudalism to capitalism within Chinese societies in the twentieth century, and it encapsulates issues of alienation, sexual behavior, social control, consumerism, and economic transformation. Hong Kong was liberated from Confucian constraints as it moved toward commodity capitalism through its status as a British colony. It was therefore the first Chinese society to exhibit the strains of adolescence. In Jackie Chan's early films as in modernizing Chinese societies, there is a fear *for* adolescents, with their Western-style rebellion and individualism, balanced by a fear *of* adolescents as a threat to the moral fabric of Chinese society. But there is no sexual behavior, let alone misbehavior, in his films. Indeed, Chan renders adolescence fun and painful but ultimately tamed because, as we said, there is always a happy ending for everyone except out-and-out villains. At the same time, Chan's adolescent persona reflects Hong Kong's vitality, creativity, and wondrous derring-do as well as its subnational status.

At the age of forty, Jackie Chan returned to the young Wong Fei-hung in another of "Jackie's ten best," *Drunken Master II*. The film replicated his earlier success. Steve Fore also considers it one of his best movies of the 1990s, and it certainly showcases Jackie Chan's style. As Fore comments,

---

DRUNKEN MASTER II (ZUIQUAN 2)

DIRECTOR, LAU KAR-LEUNG

Golden Harvest, 1994

SYNOPSIS

The story begins with a young Wong Fei-hung breaking customs law at a train station. He hides his father's ginseng root in a foreigner's luggage and, upon retrieval, mistakenly picks up a priceless imperial seal in an identical box. The seal is the emblem of Chinese power, stolen by foreigners from the British consulate. This leads to a series of adventures and fights, all involving disobedience to his father, who eventually throws him out of the house. In the end, he defeats the smugglers' top fighter through drunken boxing—strictly forbidden by his father—in a showdown in a metal foundry run by British consulate officials who exploit and then murder the workers. This is a melodrama, ending with public recognition of the young Wong's bravery in saving national treasures, in a family reunion, but with a farcical closure, suggesting father and son will have ongoing conflict.

---

however, it does not have the cross-cultural currency of his other films. This may be due to the play around the cultural concepts of filiality and, to a lesser extent, loyalty in the film. These codes resonate with local and diasporic audiences but not necessarily with Westerners.[29]

The plot is adolescent fantasy. It begins with breaking the law and getting away with it. The story ends with public recognition of the young hero, Wong Fei-hung. In the meantime, he suffers serious humiliations, such as being displayed bound and naked high up in the town square. So the plot, like many martial arts plots, centers on personal, family, and cultural vengeance. Ng Ho describes the hero in *kung fu* comedies as follows:

> [He] is conventionally a bright but hopelessly lazy kid who lacks both the staying power needed for martial arts training and respect for his *sifu* (master). (He may indeed try to cheat his *sifu*.) Often, after suffering a defeat, he will muster the perseverance to train in martial arts more seriously, and will eventually reach the point where he surpasses the skills of his *sifu*.[30]

In *Drunken Master II*, the father is the master. The format is a rites-of-passage plot. It fulfills the criteria of the *kung fu* comedy genre, as outlined above by Ng Ho. Characterization comes early in the plot and is usually the love-hate model between father and son or master and disciple. In *Drunken Master II*, this love-hate relationship and mixture of defiance and submission comes across in the father's constant reprimands on the train early on, repeated to his wife when he suspects her of playing mahjong despite his prohibition. Thus mother and son covertly conspire against the father and cheat him in many comic episodes. Another criterion is that the arch-villain is the second most important character. In this movie, it is the father in the first half and other villains in the second. Finally, there is a mandatory suite of action sequences, which display the skill, bravery, and righteousness of the *kung fu* kid to the adult world.

Gallagher analyzes Chan's bodily distortions as carnivalesque in this movie. We suggest that the entire movie is carnivalesque in the Bakhtinian sense as its comedy relies on "two worlds": the official world of serious masculinity and the transgressive world of adolescence.[31] The carnivalesque in this movie gives license to mock the world of adolescence as well as the official world of Confucian propriety, whether it is the mother's gambling, the father's pomposity, the arrogance of the British, or the powerlessness of the Chinese state to guard its own workers and heritage from thugs and smugglers. The young Wong restores order at the local level and retrieves national treasures. He operates at the level of the cultural, not political, nation.

Wong's transgressions are primarily against the father's authority. The carnivalesque aspects are demonstrated in one particular scene in *Drunken Master II* that is one of Chan's all-time favorites.[32] The shots alternate between Wong fighting the villains and the onlookers, led by his anarchic mother (played by Anita Mui). She eggs him on to retrieve a stolen necklace that she has just pawned to repay gambling debts (unknown to her husband), and Wong moves into a three-part fight sequence after one of the thieves hits her in the face. In the first part he fights the villains in the marketplace, retrieving the necklace. In the second, his mother orders him to fight using drunken-boxing techniques. When she throws him a bottle of wine, he says, "Dad won't let me drink." She answers, "I will." She throws him more wine and he shifts into a surreal and drunken rhythm, part drinking and part fighting. At the same time, he chants his martial moves as a series of wondrous names, such as "Uncle Tsao Cleaning Whiskers at the Brook" and "Drinking Removes Myriad Woes." Villains fly through the air, thump to the ground, and finally run away. In the third part, his father arrives and the young Wong, still drunk, turns and fights him too, chanting "Gods on Birthday Celebrations." His father puts his son in a stranglehold. We see the moment of recognition in a series of point-of-view close-ups aligned to Wong. An image of Wong's contorted face cuts to a close-up of his father's angry face, shot from above, ordering him to stop fighting. The camera cuts to a close-up of Wong, who says, "Father," and then to the father's face again, which floats from upside down to upright as Wong turns to face him. Wong's mother addresses the watching crowd, saying ironically, "What a picture of love between father and son!" Mother and son are taken home in disgrace.

This scene alone is cinematic carnivalesque. It has all the attributes that Patrick Fuery lists in terms of carnival as inversion of the social order. There is certainly "excess": drinking, fighting, and public drunkenness. The "dream-like sequences that accept another law" are physical acts as Chan begins a graceful and wildly funny sequence of drunken combat poses until the rude awakening to his father's presence. The "social disruption" is, among many other things, fighting in the public square in broad daylight. The scene is comic in terms of the combat itself as well as the relationship between father, mother, and son. It is a riotous adolescent fantasy rather than a dark journey. "The distorted but historically recognizable time period" is Wong Fei-hung's youth played as a "naughty boy." This scene inverts the Wong legend, the social order, father-son hierarchies, and public proprieties. At the same time, it acknowledges and exaggerates adolescent desire to confront the father when the young Wong hits him publicly. Finally, the "liminal space" that is essential to the carnivalesque is adolescence itself, a space that crosses the social orders applicable to childhood and adulthood. The young Wong creates his own space through subversion of the notion of filiality itself, mocking and yet affirming its vitality.[33] As is well known, the historical Wong was a seriously masculine figure and movie legend, symbolizing male virtue to family and public alike.

In his early movies, Jackie Chan played precocious young heroes and became the first Chinese "adolescent" superstar. He revisits the formula years later in *Drunken Master II* and it still works. As we said, adolescence is a modern construct, born of such fundamental social changes as industrialization, prolonged education, late marriage, and earlier puberty. It is generally seen as a time of identity formation and risk-taking in the transition from childhood to adulthood.[34] In *Drunken Master II*, Chan negotiates the transition through the treacherous waters of filiality in modern times. The code is recast as part of a modern social order in which law, justice, and morality merge. Yet at the same time, the film also traffics in the deepest fantasies of adolescent masculinity and transgression against the social order.

Kung fu, like adolescence, is a liminal space between swords and guns, in a Hong Kong caught between tradition and modernity, and between British colonialism and Chinese rule. In this sense, Jackie Chan's adolescent negotiations from childhood to adulthood in his films reflect Hong Kong's political reality in terms of its own limited sovereignty and subnational space. There are no laws of adolescence; it is a protected but dependent state. Siu Leung Li sees Hong Kong's *kung fu* imaginary as representing a heroic masculinity, albeit in a daredevil and self-negating mode. He writes that its attraction lies in its subversion of other forms of Chinese "unitary national imagination"[35] and, we would add, unitary laws and custom. In this sense, Jackie Chan's *"kung fu kid"* personifies Hong Kong's subversive and ongoing desire for at least partial autonomy and belonging while parodying the Chinese family-nation he seeks to join. He represents Hong Kong as a dynamic entity. He also represents cultural China more broadly through the Cantonese hero who always saves the day, Wong Fei-hung.

Rush Hour is Chan's first commercially successful Hollywood film. Made just after the 1997 Hong Kong handover to China, Chan represents Hong Kong *within* the PRC to America. Like *Drunken Master II,* the villain, Commander Thomas Griffin, is British but, in this case, at the highest level of government within Hong Kong. Griffin still thinks he owns China's heritage and riches. In the end, the unwanted cops save the formal state representatives of the PRC and the United States by rescuing Han's daughter. In the final combat scene they also save the antiquities on display in the Chinese Exhibition Hall and the $70 million ransom to boot. Loyalty replaces filiality as the primary code in this film.

While working for the greater national good (in a political and diplomatic sense), both Lee and Carter clearly represent local constituencies. Lee is initially unwanted by Carter, the LAPD, or the FBI. He successively proves himself to each and to the consul. Carter as a fast-talking, rap-loving, risk-taking, girl-chasing black detective also proves himself in turn to Lee, the LAPD, and the FBI, which he has always wanted to join.[36] In a final sequence, the FBI approaches Carter and offers him a job. "Shove it up your ass," he says, "I'm LAPD." The final shot is of Lee and Carter on the plane to Hong Kong. Carter is on holiday; Lee is going home. In Chan's films, home is Hong Kong.

RUSH HOUR

DIRECTOR, DAN RATNER
New Line Cinema, 1998

SYNOPSIS

Han is leaving Hong Kong for Los Angeles (L.A.) as Consul for the People's Republic. At his farewell, he hands over Detective Inspector Lee (Jackie Chan) as a "gift" to Commander Thomas Griffin, a British representative in Hong Kong. Lee has just saved money and priceless antiques from Juntao, a notorious crime lord, in a shootout in Hong Kong harbor. Juntao moves to L.A. and kidnaps Han's 11-year-old daughter. Consul Han calls in Lee to work with the FBI. The FBI does not want Lee around and assigns him to a black rookie LAPD cop, Carter, who is not wanted by the LAPD chief because he is a loner. Lee and Carter eventually save the consul's daughter, after an initial foul-up that disgraces Lee. It turns out that Juntao is working for Griffin, who originally stole the collection of priceless Chinese antiquities on exhibition in L.A. and now wants a ransom as compensation.

As Kam Louie notes, this is a buddy film and "the teaming of a Chinese and a black as mismatched buddies is revolutionary."[37] Lee and Carter act as counterfoil and double. Their fathers were both policemen before they died on duty. Their introductory scenes show them both on the job, catching criminals who nevertheless get away. They are both streetwise cops, at home in their own urban underbellies. They both represent ethnic minorities and an intrusive or despised local law enforcement agency—the Hong Kong police and the LAPD—to others while representing China and America to each other. They both succeed. While the FBI claims it has "the best agents in the world," it fails. Carter is the smart-alecky black upstart who kills the Chinese crime lord Juntao. Chan's earlier adolescent persona has given way to that of an outsider, respected in his own territory, who eventually earns the same respect in America. Chan fights numerous armed FBI agents to get into Han's fortified L.A. consulate. And he kills the corrupt Englishman, Griffin. As Lee and Carter become personally closer on the job, national and local symbols begin to merge, as institutions, action, and props. In one scene, Carter and Chan display their skills to the same rhythmic music: black rap bravado alternating with Chinese *kung fu* kick-butt. At the climax, Carter utilizes a giant red Chinese banner to catch Lee as he falls from high up in the atrium of the Exhibition Hall after killing Griffin. Together, they are as international as the crime syndicate that threatens Sino-American relations.[38] Together, they both succeed spectacularly.

Romancing the Brother

Hong Kong director Stanley Tong said that John Woo's films are saturated with traditional codes that once governed Chinese culture:

> In Chinese culture there are four things, four qualities that everyone must know—*zhong* is loyalty, *xiao* [filiality] is being loyal to your parents, *ren* [compassion, pity] is being good to people in general, forgiving them when they are trying to harm you; and *yi* [brotherhood] which means when you are a friend you are willing to give your life for your friend. John Woo's movies contain these elements with which most people identify.[39]

But these codes are fading, perverted, or absent by the end of *The Killer*. The loyalty demanded by Johnny Weng of his disposable hitmen, for instance, is a perversion of the Confucian and underworld codes. So while the familiar elements in *The Killer* locate the film within mythic codes of the Chinese cultural nation, the codes themselves are fast disappearing. This disappearance has been directly linked to Hong Kong's historical situation

THE KILLER (DIEXUE SHUANG XIONG)

DIRECTOR, JOHN WOO

Golden Princess, 1989

SYNOPSIS

John,* an assassin played by Chow Yun-fat, accepts a contract in a church. While carrying out the contract, John shoots and blinds a nightclub singer, Jenny, whom he subsequently befriends and falls in love with. In a different part of the city, Inspector Lee (played by Danny Lee) causes an innocent woman to die of a heart attack when he shoots a gangster on a crowded trolley bus. John accepts one more contract to kill crime boss Tony Weng so he can earn money to pay for a corneal transplant operation overseas for Jenny. After the second kill, Lee pursues John to an island where they confront each other over the hospital bed of a young girl wounded in an island shoot-out between John and his triad contractors. John is betrayed and Lee is taken off the case by his superiors; isolated, the two become friends and men of honor. The climax is a fantastic shoot-out in the church. John is fatally shot and Lee revenges him by killing the new triad boss Johnny Weng, already in the custody of other police officers.

*Note that the English versions have different names for John.

in the 1980s and 1990s. Julian Stringer suggests that Woo conflates two paradigms of Western masculinity in this movie, rejecting the "hard bodies" of Hollywood tradition for a combination of "doing and suffering heroes," excessive action, and melodramatic tears. He argues that the combination reflects the uncertain politics of Hong Kong and its return to China, citing Chiao Hsiung-ping's opinion that the "guns-in-the-face stand-offs" express "China's deadlocked disunity over the last forty years."[40] This observation certainly seems to apply to the gangster-movie boom, with its frenetic violence, at the time. In 1989, the year of *The Killer* and the June 4th Tiananmen Square massacre in China, 100 of the 250 films produced in Hong Kong were gangster movies.[41]

John Woo was surprised at reactions to the extreme violence in *The Killer*. A rise in the numbers of people joining Hong Kong triads in the 1980s accompanied the romanticization of Hong Kong's underworld in films of the 1980s. Woo said that all he intended in his films was to glorify the hero. However, his next film, *Bullet in the Head* (1990), was made without a hero because, he said, "I think I care too much about romanticism."[42] Woo's depiction of Hong Kong is therefore very different from that of Jackie Chan. In Chan's films, good and evil are clearly defined, and law and order are always reestablished at the end. His characters simultaneously affirm Hong Kong's separate identity and its dependence on the wider cultural or political Chinese nation. John Woo's gangster films, in contrast, portray Hong Kong as a bloody world unto itself. His films blur the line between heroes and villains and depict an unending war in Hong Kong's urban spaces and outlying islands.

Kenneth Hall describes John Woo as "a director who genuinely believes in the hero figure as the standard-bearer of honor, integrity, and ethical values."[43] These values are primarily those of brotherhood, enshrined in his hero series of gangster films that began with *A Better Tomorrow 1* and *2* (1986 and 1988), *The Killer* (1989), and *Hardboiled* (1992).[44] Of the hero films, *The Killer*—set in Hong Kong's underworld—is the best known in the West and considered one of Woo's most poetic ballets of blood.

Brotherhood reigns in John Woo's gangster films because there is no father at all, let alone a "father" who commands loyalty and dispenses justice. Cops and criminals fight it out in a brutal world and, in the process, evolve intimate and unlikely friendships that reinvent the code of brotherhood and honor in modern times. Within this scenario, violence between men breeds romance. Romance involves revenge of the "brother." Revenge is a proto-legal system that delivers justice when the law fails, suggesting that the only legitimate system of law and justice in Hong Kong is Chinese custom, not British law. Even then, custom in Woo's film is doomed to fail.

How is the concept of brotherhood developed in *The Killer*? What does this say about law, order, and revenge? And how does brotherhood relate to heroism, honor, and other masculine codes as well as to Hong Kong toward the end of the twentieth century?

John Woo commonly uses the doppelgänger or double to reinforce his focus on heroic brotherhood in his films. The Chinese title of *The Killer* is

FIGURE 6.3 Chow Yun-fat (*right*) in *A Better Tomorrow 1* (1986).

(COURTESY HONG KONG FILM ARCHIVE)

Diexue shuang xiong (literally, "two blood-spattered heroes"). The title exemplifies Woo's use of the double, which structures the narrative and reveals the intense personal bond that develops between a hired killer and the policeman who hunts him. At the same time, the doubling defies the clear distinctions of popular melodrama, such as hero and villain, and good and evil. When John is shot in the church, Lee walks toward him, remembering key sentences in flashback from a pivotal scene midway through the movie. In this earlier scene, Lee extracted a bullet from John's arm after a shootout. Smoking together, they talk. John says, "The only person who really knows me turns out to be a cop, and Lee answers, "I believe in justice but no one trusts me." In the final scene that includes this flashback, the triad boss Weng shoots John and, surrounded by police, drops his weapon and raises his arms in surrender. Lee responds according to justice within the code of brotherhood rather than within Western-style legal protocols. He kills Weng in revenge and cradles John in his arms outside the church, surrounded by police with their guns pointing at him. Revenge may be honorable but it is also futile. He is now on the wrong side of the law. Lee cries, "John ... my friend." In terms of law and lawlessness, Lee the cop becomes Lee the killer. The cycle of violence continues.

It is the romance of brotherhood that partly redeems the violence. The hierarchy of male power involved in legal notions of cop and criminal or traditional notions of brotherhood is appropriated as both egalitarian and personal. John dies and Lee murders his killer. Righteousness in the code is traditionally the domain of men and involves submission, both sexual and political, as part of the right to wield power.[45] Sexuality between men is implicit, and the romance is more visual than verbal. John Woo denies any conscious homoeroticism in his films; they are about male bonding, martial chivalry, and inner turmoil.[46] Many commentators see the bullet-removing scene as homoerotic, at least to Western eyes, but Woo himself saw it as romantic rather than sexual, paradoxically adding that, "I just saw them as people who had got beyond the first-date stage."[47] Whatever the reading, brotherhood in Woo's movies is individualized, passionate, and contrary to the rules of collective organizations, such as police or underworld.

Brotherhood is also exclusively male. Stringer comments that *The Killer* does not "challenge or move outside patriarchal relations."[48] As we said, both Louie's analysis of brotherhood in *The Three Kingdoms* and Chang Cheh's invocation of the patriarchal code in films of the 1960s involve male exclusivity. Jenny is crucial to the plot, but she is not included in Lee and John's growing intimacy. She is the innocent bystander caught up in the violence, and she highlights John's sense of justice for the dispossessed—the hallmark of a modern hero. John accepts one last contract as a killer to pay for a corneal transplant so she can see. The friendship between John and

Jenny lacks the passion of Lee and John's intimacy. John befriends her out of guilt and pity. In terms of the emotions that Woo seeks to express, this is compassion and it serves to reinforce John's role as a killer with honor. Indeed, the innocent bystanders injured in the gang warfare are all female. Jenny's blinding is paralleled by Lee's accidental shooting of a woman on a tram as he fires at a criminal early in the film. John and Lee first come together, guns drawn, over the wounded body of a little girl in hospital who has been caught in gang crossfire as the triad boss attempts to eliminate John on an island. John takes her to hospital at the risk of his own life, and Lee begins to see him as more than a killer. A mutual respect is born through John's treatment of women. Looking at a police identikit picture of John, Lee muses: "He doesn't look like a killer, he comes across so calm, he acts like he has a dream, his eyes are so full of passion."

Jenny's blindness symbolizes her exclusion from John and Lee's journey from enmity to passion: the men only have eyes for each other. Their stand-off in her apartment halfway through the movie is a visual representation of their mutual fascination and "one of the greatest black comic moments in movie history."49 It is another pivotal scene in their friendship, lead-ing to solidarity as they fight back-to-back against the triad mob and to the physical intimacy when Lee removes the bullet from John. In the apart-ment scene, Lee has tracked John to Jenny's place where he awaits him inside the doorway. In a shot–reverse-shot series, Lee listens and waits as John moves into the doorway, cutting to a middle shot of the two men, guns at each other's faces. Four more shot–reverse-shot pairs show close-ups of the two men gazing intently into each other's eyes. Jenny enters from the kitchen, calling for John, and the scene reverts again to shots–reverse shots of the two men still looking at each other. The men continue to stare even as Jenny comes over and cuddles John, asking, "Are you with a friend?" The shot–reverse shots continue as Lee answers for John, smiling at him, "We grew up in the same squatter area . . . I'm Butthead, he's Numbnuts."50 Jenny laughs and leaves. The two men circle each other, guns drawn, until John escapes. This sequence, where the men are enshrined in each other's eyes, is remarkable for its tension and tenderness, and its slowness and stillness. It stands out from the frenetic and bloody scenes of carnage, beat-ings, sadism, and shoot-outs that are Woo's trademark style. Jenny's blind-ness means she is denied the autonomy of her own gaze; each man's gaze is fixed on the other.

Brotherhood therefore represents redemption within the violence as well as personal escape from it. It is the only ethical retreat from the absent center of Hong Kong society, beset by lawlessness. But *The Killer* also la-ments the passing of this old code of honor. A subplot reinforces this mes-sage among the underworld. It revolves around John's relationship with an older contract killer, Sidney, who becomes a middleman between triad and hit men when his hand is injured on the job. When the triad boss, Weng, orders John's elimination for being seen during a kill that Sidney arranged in the church, Sidney ends up sacrificing himself for John because "that's what friends are for—right?" This subplot expresses loyalty among killers as all that is left. The John and Sidney relationship mirrors the John and Lee relationship and emphasizes the disappearance of old notions of honor in modern Hong Kong. John laments, "Our world is changing so fast ... perhaps we are too nostalgic," and Sidney replies, "Nostalgia is our saving grace."

As Julian Stringer comments, the male heroes are powerless to control their own fate, just like Hong Kong itself on the eve of 1997. The film records an end of intimacy at a time of great anxiety in Hong Kong over its future.[51] After all, *The Killer* was made in the same year as the Tiananmen Square massacre in 1989, when Hong Kong's future leaders quashed democracy in Beijing.

Given the imminent Hong Kong handover, it is perhaps not surprising that the film literally explodes symbols of the West. The church—where the underworld hits are organized and where the final showdown takes place—and the statue of the Virgin Mary are both Western symbols that came with British colonialism. We have said that the film depicts the end of pity through the marginalization, death, and disfigurement of the female characters. The symbol of pity is the statue of the Virgin Mary in the church. The camera often lingers on her face. When the villains explode the statue with bullets in the final scene, Woo claims it represents the final destruction of all that is good and pure, the end of goodness.[52] Purity, innocence, and the sacred are feminized as passive casualties of street warfare. To the colonizers, the church is a sacred space; to John (and in Woo's own memory) it is a tranquil place.[53] The climax in the church is therefore profane, transfiguring the sacred and serene into a medieval vision of hellfire, brimstone, and bullets—the end of an era and a horrific vision of times to come. Woo's last Hong Kong film, *Hardboiled*, was made in 1992, and it extends Woo's vision of Hong Kong into a "state of endless purgatory rather than a consummation of passion."[54] Not surprisingly, Woo then moved to Hollywood.

Woo's apocalyptic vision of Hong Kong is one of brutal violence, where upright citizens are crime bosses, killers embody honor and social justice, and women are careless casualties of public gunfights. Reading the film in terms of the myth of brotherhood is reminiscent of David Ray Papke's comments on the American reception of Francis Ford Coppola's *Godfather* trilogy: *The Godfather* (1972), *The Godfather Part II* (1974), and *The Godfather Part III* (1990). Coppola offered the Corleone crime family, in the series, as a symbol of the lawlessness and "ruthless and predatory aspects of capitalist America" in order to "challenge the mythic understanding of the United States as a pluralistic society living by the rule of law and serving as a model for the rest of the world." Viewers, however, consistently read the films in terms of the American myths of the family, the self-made man, and the use of authoritarian power as a "moral necessity."[55] Instead of acting as demythologizers, the *Godfather* films reinforce national myths. John Woo in contrast consciously sought to mythologize and glorify heroic brotherhood. Reviewers focus on the romance of brotherhood. Yet the onscreen vision of Hong Kong is of a city beset by extreme lawlessness and graphic violence. Competing regimes of justice—the police backed by the criminal law and the criminal underworld with its fading notions of honor—merge. There is no invocation of a higher authority, an ultimate and legitimate lawgiver. And unlike Jackie Chan's movies, there is no hero even on the right side of the law who successfully intervenes to reestablish the moral order. John, the hitman with a heart, and Lee, the cop, are both killers.

Brotherhood is Woo's personal response to public disorder. It is a bygone code. Perhaps it is the sense of passing that imbues *The Killer* with its frenetic pace, and its sense of nostalgia, passion, and desperation. Woo's breakout Hollywood movie, *Face/Off*, was made in 1997, the year of Hong Kong's return to China. The film, characters, and settings are American, and there are significant changes in the narrative that highlight the violent characterization of Hong Kong in *The Killer*. In *Face/Off*, Woo retains the doubling motif in the characters of Sean Archer, an FBI agent, who hunts a psychopathic terrorist, Castor Troy. Troy kills Archer's son in the opening scenes of the film. Through plastic surgery Archer and Troy's faces are exchanged; Archer is locked away in prison and Troy assumes Archer's life, FBI identity, and even his wife and daughter. Archer escapes and in the final, frenetic, and blasphemous shoot-out—again in a church—Archer kills Troy and reassumes his life, work, and family, including Troy's orphaned son. Woo shifts from the romance of brotherhood to the cult of the good father and husband, who ultimately reasserts law and order in America as a representative of the FBI. Unlike *Rush Hour* with its emphasis on Jackie Chan's Hong Kong identity, Woo's Hollywood shift leads to a national, cultural, and identity shift in his American movies.

Killing the Father

The father in Zhang Yimou's films, like those of Jackie Chan, refers not only to the blood father but also to a range of men in authority who command obedience. In Zhang's "red" trilogy, the father is familial. He may

---

THE STORY OF QIU JU (QIU JU DA GUANSI)

DIRECTOR, ZHANG YIMOU

Sil-Metropole/Beijing Film Academy–Youth Film Studio, 1992

SYNOPSIS

The plot begins offscreen when the village head, Wang Shoutang, assaults Qiu Ju's husband for abusing him by saying that he can only father "hens" (daughters). This begins Qiu Ju's onscreen search for an apology to her husband through increasingly higher levels of the legal system. First, she goes to the head himself. Then she tries mediation. Finally she litigates and appeals through the courts. In the end, however, Wang saves Qiu Ju and her baby during a difficult birth. She has a son and the dispute is personally resolved. Wang is then arrested by the state and jailed, again offscreen, for criminal assault because X-rays show that Qiu Ju's husband's ribs were broken. The end is ambiguous: Qiu Ju has law but not justice.

---

be either the old husband or the old father, and he commonly symbolizes the aging patriarchal leaders of the People's Republic of China. In contrast, there are two "fathers" in *The Story of Qiu Ju:* Qiu Ju's husband (and father of her baby boy) and also the village chief, who is the "social father" of the baby boy in that he saves the baby's life. In *Hero,* the father is political and national. He is the founder of the Chinese dynastic system over two thousand years ago, the first emperor of the Qin dynasty. Killing the father is the Oedipal myth written politically, where the son or subject desires the death of the "father" as a prerequisite for autonomy and a new national order.

The Story of Qiu Ju records Zhang Yimou's shift from mythic themes in the "red" trilogy (*Red Sorghum, Judou,* and *Raise the Red Lantern*) to stories of contemporary China. A central theme in the trilogy is Oedipal: that "fathers" must die for the young son and his family to live in freedom.[56] "Fathers" in these movies are old husbands; young would-be lovers function as the "son" in competition for the young wife. When the son succeeds in *Red Sorghum,* a vibrant society is born of a new, ribald, and heroic father. When the weak adopted son fails because he cannot transgress the filial code in *Judou,* a perverse and deadly society is perpetuated. In the pessimistic, post–Tiananmen Square massacre film, *Raise the Red Lantern,* there is no son to confront the "father," so the old society continues as barren, ritualistic, and mad. Killing the old father to produce a new China in these films was widely read as the necessity to kill old Communist Party leaders to produce a free and vibrant society. Filial submission or transgression led inexorably to familial and hence national rejuvenation or stultification, respectively. Hence, films such as *Judou* were banned for some time in China.

In the "red" trilogy, Zhang confronts a central tenet of Confucian and Communist codes embedded in socialist realist films: the shift from obedience to the actual father (filiality) to obedience to the state and the Party (loyalty). Hanna Boje Nielsen calls this "forceful usurpation of the father's role by the Communist Party ... an emasculation of all Chinese males."[57] *The Story of Qiu Ju* rehabilitated Zhang in the eyes of China's leaders in that he seems to affirm the state's care of even the poorest citizens through its legal institutions. However, Zhang's films have ambiguous endings. We argue that, in terms of the national, the focus in the film shifts from the family to the usurpation of the local leader's role by the state and the emasculation of the community's political and social father as a result.

The story of contemporary fathers therefore takes a different twist in *Qiu Ju*. Zhang's focus is not only on the family; it is also on village and county communities, and on national institutions. The background to the narrative is Wang Shoutang's unfulfilled desire for sons. Wang is the village chief and, as he often points out, he represents state authority at the most local level. All Chinese viewers would know that the production of sons is the prime duty of the Confucian code of filial piety. The plot is triggered when Wang kicks Qiu Ju's husband, Qinglai, in the "family jewels" (or groin). During a dispute over land regulations, Qinglai had insulted Wang by saying that "his lineage had no sons or grandsons, just a nest of hens" (or daughters). Qinglai is thus rendered ineffectual, sexually and legally, so a heavily pregnant Qiu Ju begins a journey on his behalf to receive a public apology. The journey takes her from local to provincial institutions of the law, and from communal, customary relationships (filiality and loyalty) to national, legal relationships (criminality).

Qiu Ju only seeks an apology, a civil remedy. In the end, Wang saves both Qiu Ju and her baby son and so ends the dispute. But he is then sent to prison for assault. Looking through the grid of father and son, *The Story of Qiu Ju* is subversive: it portrays state law as abstract retribution that disempowers its citizens even as it seems to affirm codified law's accessibility to poor and faraway villagers. Customary law through Wang resolves the dispute while codified law reruptures a local community, criminalizes a civil dispute, and ignores the actual parties. Hence Zhang gives a much more nuanced view of tradition and codes such as filiality and loyalty in *Qiu Ju* than in the trilogy itself. As a result, state censors lifted the bans on his previous films.

Zhang Yimou presents a picture of how men should behave by proffering competing national laws (customs and codes) through a double structure: a mutually subversive linear and cyclic narrative structure.[58] A chronological narrative follows Qiu Ju through pregnancy and birth as she seeks a local then legal "apology" from Wang through mediation and then civil remedies. Without telling her, officials shift the charge to a criminal one. When Wang is arrested, the new criminal code seems to work. A visual spatial narrative, based on the journey motif with a signature tune, undercuts this linear story. The spatial narrative consists of ever-widening concentric circles that mirror Qiu Ju's journeys to seek justice. Each journey is episodic, beginning and ending in the village. The personal dispute is also cyclic, beginning and ending in the village when Wang saves the baby boy to his and everyone else's delight (fig. 6.4).

This is the real closure of the dispute, acknowledged in the village reunion for the baby's naming day. But Wang does not make it. The linear and spatial narratives merge. A distant legal representative drives into the village center, arresting the village head offscreen. A familiar and local patriarchy is replaced by an alien, all male, and new patriarchal system, as Qiu Ju herself comments throughout the film. In legal terms, the two systems are alike in the authority of state power. In terms of masculinity, however, the state disempowers its male citizens even as it perpetuates its power through local representatives and generations of sons and subjects. In the process, both social and biological fathers of the unborn son are dispossessed of community.[59]

In different ways, Jackie Chan and John Woo both document the reinvention and disappearance of old codes of masculine power in governing a family, community, and cultural space. Zhang Yimou also laments the passing of traditional notions of duty and pride embodied in both Wang Shoutang and Qiu Ju. Men and women are caught between familiar and personalized codes of behavior from the past and impersonal state legislation that signal the future governance of China.

The final shot of Qiu Ju's face depicts the locals as victims of state injustice. The images leading to this final shot begin with the village reunion at the baby's naming day when Qiu Ju learns of Wang's arrest. She bursts out of the house, out of the courtyard, and up the snow-covered mountain

FIGURE 6.4 Village chief Wang and Qiu Ju in *The Story of Qiu Ju* (1992)

(COURTESY CHINA FILM ARCHIVE)

slope (fig. 6.5a). She runs frantically across the snowbound wilderness toward the road to catch the police car (figs. 6.5b–6.5e). The road is empty; she is too late (fig. 6.5f). The scene ends the film with a close-up of Qiu Ju's anguished face (fig. 6.5g). It is the only full close-up in the entire movie.

Her face freezes in disbelief and distress. It ends a powerful scene that begins with joy and ends with desolation. The sense of isolation challenges the fundamental capacity of black-letter law to govern China's citizens in this film, especially when it absolutely ignores their simplest and most heartfelt desires.

FIGURE 6.5a Qui Ju runs up the mountainside in *The Story of Qiu Ju* (1992).

FIGURES 6.5b–6.5e Qui Ju runs toward the road.

FIGURE 6.5c

FIGURE 6.5d

FIGURE 6.5e

FIGURE 6.5f The road is empty.

FIGURE 6.5g Qui Ju's anguished face

HERO (YINGXIONG)

DIRECTOR, ZHANG YIMOU

Elite Group Enterprise Inc., Beijing New Image Film Group, 2002 (Chinese release) and 2004 (international release)

SYNOPSIS

Hero is a martial arts epic that tells the story of failed assassination attempts on the King of Qin, who subsumed the warring states into the imperial Qin dynasty over two thousand years ago. A lowly Qin magistrate, Nameless (Jet Li), is summoned by the king to recount his alleged defeat of three powerful warrior enemies: Broken Sword (Tony Leung), Flying Snow (Maggie Cheung), and Sky (Donnie Yen). In retelling the story in numerous flashbacks, Nameless is allowed to move closer in proximity to the king, and plans to kill him using his famous "death-from-ten-paces" sword strike. The suspicious king eventually foils this assassination attempt. He beguiles Nameless, whom he now knows comes from the enemy kingdom of Zhao, with the idea of a unified China (*tianxia*). He orders Nameless's execution, according to the laws of Qin.

Ten years later, Zhang Yimou made yet another shift from primarily contemporary melodramas to the martial arts genre with *Hero*. In *Hero* local customary power relationships in a historical setting again compete with state law—and again the unified state wins. Would-be assassins die or give up their swords rather than avenge their families and states by killing the King of Qin. Representations of the law invoke custom (*li*), social and personal justice (*yi*), and positive law (*fa*, meaning Qin dynasty legalism rather than socialist law in this film) as competing ways to run the country. While male warriors sacrifice everything for the political goal of national unification in *Hero*, embodied in the king, they do not sacrifice themselves for these codes. Rather, they choose sacrifice for a principle that promises an end to the people's suffering, as we stated at the beginning of this chapter. Nevertheless, China's leaders endorsed this film, staging its premiere at the Great Hall of the People in Tiananmen Square.

 Hero's main protagonists are the King of Qin and Nameless. The historical king is a byword for brutality in Chinese culture while Nameless is a fictional master swordsman, born in the enemy kingdom of Zhao. Their meeting is one of words, except for the final confrontation. The combat scenes between the other assassins—so essential to action cinema—are played out in glorious flashbacks, leaving the confrontation of king and swordsman as the narrative anchor. Nameless seeks revenge on Zhao's enemy, Qin, by killing the king. Instead, the King of Qin kills Nameless to pursue a united empire but celebrates him in death as a hero. The question nonetheless remains: who is the hero? Jet Li (who plays Nameless) said that Zhang "wanted to explore what kind of person can become a hero within the framework of fighting, politics, romance, and jealousy. Is it the conquering king? The assassins? The killer of the assassins?"[60] Or all of them? And what does this mean in terms of the national?

There are various readings of this narrative in terms of heroism, nation, and power. Individual warriors from enemy states fight the king, but they are ultimately defeated by the principle of a united empire rather than in combat. The film suggests that submission to this principle is in itself heroic. In this sense, the king and all the male assassins are heroic; the sole female assassin is not. However, within the totality of Zhang's work, the king also represents the new, virulent, and patriarchal authority that promises peace and erases the "old" China, represented by warriors of the other warring states. The subject/son's desire to kill the emperor/father ends with the emperor/father's actual slaying of the subject/son. The fictional narrative ends with the historical reality: the King of Qin wins and founds the patriarchal Chinese empire as universe (*tianxia*). Whatever the reading, a united nation requires submission to a leader who symbolizes China. Whatever the reading, the action revolves around the choice *not* to kill the father/ruler.

The empire is forged by might, and so the sword necessarily dominates *Hero* as a sword-fighting martial arts epic. As Xu Haofeng writes, the sword is the fullest representation of masculinity in this genre.[61] It symbolically unites king and assassins through the king's possession of his allegedly dead enemies' swords and of Broken Sword's red calligraphic rendering of *jian* or "sword" behind the king's throne. Nameless confronts the king without a sword; he must steal the king's to kill him. In the end, the king throws his own weapon to Nameless, thereby permitting his own death. But Nameless does not kill the king, because they are both ultimately enlightened as to the nature of swordsmanship, heroism, war, and even China itself. The idea of peace conquers all. Nameless submits to the king, burying his "trivial" loyalty to the doomed kingdom of Zhao for the sake of a unified China, which brings peace to the people. The King of Qin then executes Nameless according to black-letter national laws (*fa*) that he himself promulgated. Throughout his audience with the king, Nameless never has a sword except when he is given the king's—and this one he abandons. In this sense, Nameless is emasculated by actual kingly power, by the military symbols of power, and by the idea of a united China. So is Broken Sword, which is evident even in his name. For the audience, Nameless's assassination is also erased by historical record in that everyone knows that the King of Qin won, unified China, built the Great Wall, and established a range of national reforms, including legal reform. Winning is crucial to masculine display within action cinema; winning is crucial to China's historical record of the Qin as China's first empire.[62]

The opening sequence of *Hero* conveys the actual and symbolic power of the King of Qin. The sequence depicts the arrival of Nameless, escorted over desert land and through misty mountains to a vast and monumental palace. The summons, the martial music, the majestic horse-riding warriors of Qin, the black flags and black armor, the enormous palace with its rows of serried soldiers and officials, and the long shot of the fortified throne all underscore the King of Qin's military might and vast dominions. This power over place and people extends to Nameless. He is strip-searched and bows, small and low in the frame, to the king, who is isolated before the throne. The King of Qin is almost always shot high in the frame, looking down on his subjects. The king rewards Nameless with gold, land, and the proximity of twenty paces from his person as a reward for killing Sky and, later, ten paces for killing Broken Sword and Flying Snow. For the first time in the film, ruler and subject are shown together in the frame. The shot–reverse-shot structures then continue as the king asks Nameless—the most lowly of all Qin officials—how he could defeat such mighty opponents. Nameless answers that he killed them one by one. The narrative then moves into its first flashback, the alleged defeat of Sky.

The audience with the king is interspersed with striking color-coded flashbacks (and even flashbacks within flashbacks) that unravel the intrigues and betrayals among the assassins to kill the King of Qin. The narrative moves through three stages. The first, Nameless's stories of how he killed Sky (in a soft palette of rain-washed grays) and then Snow and Broken Sword (primarily in red), ends with the king's assertion, "Your story is a lie." The king then retells the stories in the second stage, again with flashbacks in blue-green and springtime colors. He ends by saying, "They all sacrificed themselves for one goal—to get you within ten paces of me ... you are the most dangerous assassin of all." Nameless admits he is a citizen of the kingdom of Zhao, Qin's deadly enemy. The third stage, before the drawn-out deadly coda, offers flashbacks showing what really happened: Sky's sacrifice and then Broken Sword's betrayal of his warrior brothers and his lover, Snow, when he finally storms the palace, meets the king, and refuses to kill him. Why? Because of the two Chinese characters that Broken Sword writes in the desert sand with his sword. These characters are *tianxia,* meaning "All Under Heaven" and benignly translated in the English version of *Hero* as "Our Land." *Tianxia* actually means *all* land under heaven and clearly involves the invasion of neighboring states in the interests of unrivaled imperial rule. The king is finally enlightened about the secret of true swordsmanship and true heroism through Broken Sword's calligraphic rendering of the character for *sword*; he articulates the power of the sword that is concealed in Broken Sword's calligraphy. Like Broken Sword, Nameless cannot bring himself to kill the king. Nameless is now executed, dying from a hail of digitally enhanced arrows that that he sees flying toward him in a point-of-view shot, as he stands against the imperial gate (fig. 6.6). Shots of Nameless's departure, execution, and full military funeral are interspersed with shots of the death of Broken Sword and the suicide of his lover and fellow warrior, Flying Snow. Sky gives up his sword in honor of his dead friends. In short, not one of the male assassins uses the sword as a deadly weapon against the king throughout this movie. In terms of masculinity and power, the King of Qin owns the sword.

The film ends with images of the Great Wall bathed in sunlight, prefiguring the glory of a united imperial China. Heroic masculinity is absorbed into the abstract idea of the Chinese nation and its imperial figurehead, the King of Qin. Young warrior males willingly abandon their swords by choice and hence their warrior masculinity for the greater goal. They attain heroic status by their actions.

Thus the film begins and ends with the imagery of the ruler's might and the submission of his enemies. But the assassins choose their fates. The extended flashbacks are triggers for the visually beautiful combat scenes, shot in such exotic locations as Jiuzhaigou's gorgeous lakes and Mongolia's autumn forests. These combat scenes debate the issue: to kill or not to kill. But the core combat—political, psychological, aesthetic, and martial—is between the king and Nameless, Qin ruler and Qin subject.

Zhang Yimou sees the King of Qin as the embodiment of a new China in the past that can be translated into a powerful, peaceful, and united China

FIGURE 6.6 Nameless's execution in the Qin palace in *Hero* (2002/2004)

in the present. He wrote that he wanted to reinvent the martial arts genre, taking it away from the revenge motif.

> I take the genre in a new direction. In my story the goal is the negation of violence. The characters are motivated by their desire to end the war. For real martial arts masters, true heroes, the heart is far more important than the sword.[63]

True heroism lies in three ascending stages of enlightenment about forging a nation that parallel the narrative. In the first stage, the assassins' vengeance rules through a unity of body and mind focused on combat and killing, encapsulated in the saying, "a sword in the hand and a sword in the heart." In the second stage of enlightenment, the heart rules: there is "no sword in the hand but a sword in the heart." Nameless's unarmed audience with the king exemplifies this. In the final and highest stage, visualized in Broken Sword's calligraphy, "there is no sword in the hand and no sword in the heart." Like Broken Sword, Nameless forgoes vengeance for unity and peace. Enlightenment and true heroism are therefore unity and peace—except that the king kills Nameless in the film and goes on to conquer the other six states. In this sense, Zhang Yimou's male heroism is ambiguous, a marriage of Kam Louie's two paradigms of Chinese masculinity—*wen* and *wu,* or cultural attainment and martial valor.

The film is controversial. Some reviewers find the plot thin and the message unpalatable, to say the least. Yao Xiaolei calls *Hero*'s marriage of chivalry (the art of the sword) with the notion of a unified China (*tianxia*) forged through war logically "absurd." The reconstruction of the ruthless King of Qin as the carrier of Chinese culture and the epitome of Chinese heroism is "nonsense," "laughable," and even "sick in the head." The individual, the lowly, and the outcast are powerless before authority. He writes that Zhang turns his back on a century of filmmaking and decades of his own work that depict China's heroic struggle to remold and even defeat patriarchy in the name of ordinary people.[64] Xu Haofeng claims that the king's enlightenment on the nature of peace is unconvincing. It is so thinly portrayed, he writes, that it is like painting a picture where "the ink is spared as if it were gold."[65] J. Hoberman calls the film "a paean to authoritarianism" and a "glorification of ruthless leadership and self-sacrifice on the altar of national greatness."[66]

Others laud *Hero*'s visual beauty, fantastic combat scenes, and commercial success. Zhang Qiu writes that Zhang Yimou strives for global recognition by merging international film form and production standards with "Eastern sensibilities" and Chinese culture, "such as the lute, chess, calligraphy, landscape, drama, the Great Wall" and, of course, sword-fighting lore and national laws.[67] Robert Y. Eng takes issue with Hoberman's review on *Hero* as "a paean to authoritarianism," claiming the film is a complex deconstruction of "the limits of honor, the concept at the heart of *wuxia* [the knight-errant hero in martial arts stories], imperialism and nationalism." He notes that the film ends on a note of mourning, not patriotism.[68] The execution of Nameless exemplifies this mourning and, indeed, the difficulty of pronouncing a precise message for this or any other Zhang Yimou film.

Certainly, *Hero* is a major turning point for Zhang Yimou. It is his first commercial blockbuster. Like many of his films, it has aroused controversy on the film itself and on the nature of China today. There is, however, a boldness in turning to a story of the founding of the Chinese imperial state and attempting to humanize the King of Qin, despite centuries of bad press. There is a visual grandeur and mysticism in the images that represent China, which both king and assassins fight over. There is a symbolic and philosophical aspect to the dissertation on the sword that is rare in martial arts movies. There is a continued exploration of the grand themes of transgression, submission, and national character that thread through all his work. Finally, there is a timeliness about *Hero*, which debates what China means in the twenty-first century in terms of heroism, masculinity, and the nation as *tianxia*.

Zhang Yimou, Jackie Chan, and John Woo all resort to familiar masculine codes to map complex changes across Chinese societies—China's search for unity and power as a modern nation-state and Hong Kong as an autonomous space within the larger British empire or Chinese nation. The richness and longevity of these codes as a cinematic language is astonishing, although they are not translated cross-culturally in the Hollywood films of Chan and Woo. In Chinese films, they operate as a mythic rule by virtue that measures modernity and finds that it often falls short. Characters who operate outside the moral codes, or unsuccessfully within them, are killed (in *Drunken Master II, Rush Hour, The Killer,* and *Hero*) or criminalized (*The Story of Qiu Ju* and *The Killer*). As we said, the arch-villains who die in Chan's two films are British. This is a conventional "othering" of bad foreigners as part of the process of establishing Chinese cultural identity. In the next chapter, we consider how foreigners appear in Chinese cinema under the umbrella of ethnicity, along with the representation of minority nationalities and intra-Han Chinese difference. And, for the most part, we focus on less usual patterns than "othering."

7

Where Do You Draw the Line?

ETHNICITY IN CHINESE CINEMAS

ANG LEE'S breakthrough hit, *The Wedding Banquet* (1993), is usually understood as a gay comedy. In fact, it is crucial that the lead characters' relationship is not only same-gender but also interracial. In case there is any doubt that both race and sexuality could be a problem for Wai-tung's parents, a prospective bride sent from Taiwan by his mother underlines the point. When Wai-tung is forced to reveal his situation to his potential wife, she understands completely: she has only gone along with the charade because, just like him, she dare not tell her parents she has a white boyfriend. Later in the film, by contracting a false marriage with his tenant from Shanghai, Wai-tung presents his parents with a partner of not only appropriate gender but also appropriate ethnicity. She in turn is not only able to give the family a child of the desired gender—it is taken for granted that the baby will be male—but also of the desired ethnicity.

Ethnic identity is usually important to national identity, although they are not the same thing. In recent years, the production of ethnic identity has been widely understood in academic fields including cinema studies and Chinese studies by extrapolating from the binary model of Western self and Oriental Other, elaborated by Edward Said in *Orientalism*. However, Said saw orientalism as a specifically Western discourse, raising questions about its applicability to Chinese discourses on ethnicity. It would be naive to pretend that China's insertion into European-derived modernity has not involved appropriation of Western models and discourses. But in this chapter we focus on cinematic patterns that cannot be accommodated easily by Said's orientalism alone, even though most are structured as Han Chinese perspectives on those marked as ethnically different.[1] On this basis, we argue that to gain an understanding of the range and specificity of ethnic constructions in Chinese cinemas, we need to examine these constructions as products of the interaction between imported understandings of ethnicity and other Chinese patterns (often with deep historical roots) within the particular circumstances of twentieth-century Chinese communities.

First, we note that although foreigners may be constructed as ethnically different, they are not always "othered." Often, a place is found for foreigners within the Chinese collectivity. The "modern" gay relationship of the European and Taiwan American lovers in Ang Lee's *The Wedding Banquet* cuts across ethnic difference at the same time as the Taiwan family's desire for an ethnically appropriate grandson reinforces it. Supporting our analysis of this film with others, we note a pattern of inclusion and accommodation for the "good" foreigner. Given that most "good" film foreigners are also Westerners and that the Chinese experience of modernity has been violently imposed from the West, this pattern may be a revisionist fantasy.

Second, the "minority nationality film" has existed as a production category in the People's Republic almost since its founding. The People's Republic proclaims itself composed of fifty-six nationalities. If the minority nationalities are citizens yet ethnically different, how are they constructed in this category of film? Using as our main examples two films about Tibet—*Serfs* (1963) and *Horse Thief* (1986)—we argue that major differences exist between the pre- and post–Cultural Revolution minority nationality films. The earlier films represent the minority nationalities as backward peoples liberated from feudalism and led toward modernity by their Han "elder brothers." The later films are marked by an absence of the Communist Party on screen and a high degree of exoticism. Yet in both cases, we note that the apparent emphasis on ethnic difference is complicated by fantasies of cross-ethnic identification.

Finally, we look at how difference among the Han Chinese is manifested in the cinema. The animosity of nationalist projects toward acknowledgment of such difference limits onscreen representation to times and places of migration and reconfiguration of political boundaries. These include the aftermath of the establishment of the People's Republic or the reversion of Hong Kong to Chinese rule and the recent tension between the People's Republic and the Republic of China over Taiwan. Yet the tension between the idea of being Han and European concepts of ethnicity means that only rarely does inter-Han difference appear as ethnic. On the other hand, one constant way it has manifested itself since the coming of sound has been in the regulation and practice of which spoken languages are used in the cinema.

Pictures of Ethnicity: Them and Us Beyond Self and Other

Why has ethnicity become such an important and controversial topic in the age of the modern nation-state? Prasenjit Duara notes, "The problem with territorial nationalism is that, while it is the only acceptable expression of sovereignty in the modern world, it is an inadequate basis of identification within the nation-state."[2] He points out that this prompts state leaders to reach for other potential nodes of identity to bind together the population within the borders of the nation-state. Prominent among these nodes is ethnicity. According to Stevan Harrell, scholar of Chinese minority nationalities, "An ethnic group can be defined as a group of people that shares a putative common origin through descent and a putative commonality of cultural features such as language, food, clothing, and customs that distinguish it from other ethnic groups."[3] Although more recent discussions have emphasized that both race and ethnicity are human inventions subject to constant change, Harrell's description represents the most widely and commonly understood definition of ethnicity.[4]

Therefore, circulating signs of ethnicity is one of the main ways cinema helps to construct national identity. The People's Republic of China even has an ethnically marked category of films: filmgoers there are as likely to say they have seen a "minority nationalities film" (*shaoshu minzu pian*) as a "comedy." And, as in Hollywood, almost any Chinese spy film will feature villainous foreign agents so highly stereotyped it is doubtful they could maintain their cover. To understand these and other cinematic patterns we need a broader understanding of how ethnicity is constructed in modern Chinese cultures.

First, there is the question of scope. To date, much of the work on ethnicity in Chinese culture has attended to the minority nationalities in isolation. This will be discussed in more detail in the third section of this chapter. However, our general context of the national and national identity motivates us to adopt a broader tripartite framework for the examination of ethnicity in the Chinese cinema: Chinese-foreign relations, Han Chinese relations with the minority nationalities, and intra-Han relations. We examine each in the sections that follow.

Second, there is the question of the appropriate conceptual framework. In the rest of this section, we review the existing uses of the self-and-Other model in Chinese studies and the general debates about its usefulness as a model for understanding ethnic difference. We argue for taking into account its provenance in the Chinese context; although China's participation in that European-derived mode known as modernity requires the adoption of self and other binarisms, the preexistence and survival in transformed modern modes of alternative ideas about ethnic difference suggests it may not be monolithic.

Particularly important in Harrell's description of ethnicity is the phrase, "that distinguish it from other ethnic groups." For, as the examples of the "minority nationalities" film and the spy film indicate, what is at stake in

the display of ethnically marked signifiers "such as language, food, clothing, and customs" is not only the establishment of a sense of "us" but also a
sense of "them." This drawing of a line between an ethnic "us" and "them"
can be harnessed to the project of the nation-state. In English-language
academia, by far the most commonly circulated trope used to describe this
binary construction of ethnic difference is "othering," a term closely associated with Edward Said's watershed work, *Orientalism*.[5]

For Said, "orientalism" refers not to particular nineteenth-century scholarly and artistic schools, but to a far broader discourse.[6] Using Foucault's
idea of the episteme, or era defined by shared ideas, he sees this discourse
as a deep and "latent" structure determining almost all knowledge production in the West pertaining to the non-West. Furthermore, he traces orientalism back to ancient Greek examples and suggests that it continues to operate today.[7] Far from being a disinterested scholarly activity, this discourse
is, Said believes, one of the drivers of imperialism. Operating with scant
regard for what actually happens in the societies it purports to describe,
orientalism constructs the "Orient" as an object to be apprehended by the
Western subject. This Orient is often feminized, infantilized, silenced, and
made mysterious or ineffable, as in Said's example of Flaubert's "romantic" description of the Egyptian courtesan Kuchuk Hanem, given relatively
early in Said's book.[8] In this way, one of the main functions of orientalism
is to produce the West in contrast to this Oriental Other.

As Bart Moore-Gilbert puts it, "Even among those who are essentially
hostile to Said, like John MacKenzie or Aijaz Ahmad, *Orientalism* is recognized as a seminal text."[9] In recent years, its range of influence has extended to the study of China in at least three ways. First, since Said's book
was introduced in the People's Republic in the early 1990s, its terminology
has been appropriated as part of the neo-nationalist critique of not only
Western depictions of China but also those Chinese texts believed to indulge Western tastes for the exotic.[10] Here, Said's clear East-West divide
confirms and extends the Maoist line that China is only ever to be seen as
a victim of imperialism.

Inside the People's Republic, the theory of orientalism has rarely if ever
been applied to characterize Chinese discourses about various "Others."
Outside, however, it is increasingly deployed for just such purposes, as for
example in the analysis of discourses on the minority nationalities. Most
English-language scholarship took an empiricist approach until recently,
accepting the existence of the minority nationalities as given and focusing
on sociological comparisons either to the Han Chinese majority or among
the minority nationalities.[11] Increasingly, however, scholarship on the minority nationalities has also examined the construction and maintenance
of these ethnic categories, both in state and popular discourses in the Peo-

ple's Republic. Said's orientalism provides a crucial foundation for many of these essays.[12] The third use of Said's orientalism is in analyses of (mostly mainland) Chinese discourses representing the foreign.[13]

The appropriation of Said within the People's Republic is direct. Both the other instances modify Said's original work. As Louisa Schein puts it in her discussion of what she calls "internal orientalism" in the People's Republic, Said's original division of the world into the East and the West constitutes a "bifurcated mapping." This repeats the very structures Said complains of, reducing the East to a mute object and foreclosing upon any possibility that structures similar in many ways to orientalism itself might also originate within the so-called "Orient."[14]

The examples above, where Han China is positioned as the self in discourses similar to orientalism itself about both minority nationalities and Western "Others," challenge those assumptions. They both acknowledge Chinese agency and undermine claims that China is uniquely free of racial discrimination, such as those made by Premier Zhou Enlai in 1955 and repeated more recently by Party General Secretary Zhao Ziyang in 1988.[15] At the same time, it is important to emphasize that they do not deny that China was and is also positioned as the object of Western orientalisms.

Other critiques of Said's universalizing tendency are more fundamental, suggesting a need to do more than just extend the range of examples to which the model can be applied. Of the problems pointed out, one in particular interests us here. By totalizing orientalism, Said forecloses not only on the possibility that the "Orient" might orientalize but also that relationships different from "othering" might exist across lines of cultural and ethnic difference. Dennis Porter argues that "counter-hegemonic writings or an alternative canon may exist within the Western tradition," and that contrary to Said's assertions that orientalism operates separately from the Orient, there may also be "a textual dialogue between Western and non-Western cultures." Lisa Lowe has placed greater emphasis on the historical and national specificity of different forms of orientalism. And Mary Louise Pratt's work on travel writing analyzes it not as fantasy or projection but as the product of "contact zones" producing "transculturation," leading her to attend to a variety of relationships ranging from scientific distance to sentimental narratives about interracial marriage.[16]

None of this work denies or diminishes the unequal power relations that structure colonial relations and discourse, nor do they suggest that other structures are necessarily more positive. However, in a remark that sums up their direction, Robert Young argues against the "remorseless Hegelian dialectalization" of the "othering" trope. He goes on to argue "that for an understanding of the historical specificity of the discourse of colonialism, we need to acknowledge that other forms of racial distinction have worked simultaneously alongside this model." In support, he cites Deleuze and Guattari's direct attack in *A Thousand Plateaus* on the understanding of Western racism as operating on a self-and-Other model of binary exclusion and their argument for the use of a norm and deviance model with grades of variation.[17]

If Said understands orientalism as a Western construct, it is necessary to ask if other models for understanding cultural and ethnic difference operate in China. For even if quasi-orientalist concepts may be common as a result of what Lydia Liu terms "translingual practices" of appropriation, there is no reason to assume they have supplanted preexisting models *tout court*. Indeed, as Liu insists, appropriated concepts are necessarily made sense of on preexisting discursive horizons, creating locally specific meanings and practices.[18] We shall explore exactly what some of those preexisting models are in the following sections. But the relevance of Liu's insight is clear even in the existing work on ethnicity in contemporary China that draws on Said, for this work often includes reference to phenomena that exceed Said's framework.

For example, Louisa Schein's examination of how Han-dominated discourses and practices in post-Mao China other the Miao nationality also acknowledges that Miao who have moved to the cities often engage in the reification of their own traditions.[19] Similarly, Ralph Litzinger notes that Yao nationality elites have cooperated in the production of essentialized constructions of Yao identity in their effort to recover from the changes pressed upon them during the Maoist era.[20] Stevan Harrell's conceptual framework of "civilizing projects" for understanding relationships between Han Chinese and peripheral others is similar to Said's self-and-Other model in terms of power balance, but crucially different in that "as an interaction between peoples, a civilizing project requires two sets of actors."[21] Chen Xiaomei's discussion of "occidentalism" attends to phenomena that do not simply reverse Said's orientalism but appropriate selectively from the West for local use.[22]

With these considerations in mind, to grasp the historical and local specificity of Chinese cinematic constructions of ethnic difference, it may be most productive at this point to move the spotlight away from the self-and-Other model. Therefore, although we acknowledge that many examples of "othering" can be found in Chinese cinema, we focus on constructions of ethnic difference in Chinese cinema that diverge from this model. Our argument is not that these representations escape the self-and-Other model in an absolute sense, but that they are the syncretic and performative productions of the intersection of the self-and-Other model with other local discourses of cultural and ethnic difference.

THE WEDDING BANQUET (XIYAN)

DIRECTED BY ANG LEE

Central Motion Picture Corporation, Good Machine, 1993

SYNOPSIS

Taiwan migrant landlord Wai-tung lives happily in New York with his Anglo lover Simon, interrupted only by his parents' efforts to find him a bride. Simon suggests a marriage of convenience to Wei-wei, a tenant from Shanghai in need of a green card. But the best plans go awry when Wai-tung's parents, the Gaos, visit and an old friend insists on throwing a lavish wedding banquet. On the wedding night, Wei-wei "liberates" Wai-tung and gets pregnant. His parents' departure is delayed by Mr. Gao's stroke, which provokes Wai-tung to come out to his mother. She makes him swear never to tell his father. However, Mr. Gao reveals to Simon that he has figured it out, but swears him to secrecy, too. Asked why he has perpetuated this charade, the old man says, "Otherwise, how would I have got my grandson?"

Accommodating Foreigners: Cherishing Men from Afar

Despite wide-ranging commentary, the ethnic dimension of Ang Lee's international hit comedy *The Wedding Banquet* has been largely overlooked in favor of sexuality. *The Wedding Banquet* may be the first mainstream Taiwan film to portray homosexuality sympathetically, so this is understandable. On the rare occasions when ethnicity is discussed, the focus is on how Western spectators might interpret the film or how it represents ethnic issues within American gay communities, where European and Asian men attracted to each other are often disparaged as "rice queens" and "potato queens," respectively.[23] The importance of ethnicity to the family drama at the center of the film is comparatively neglected.[24]

However, despite Simon's problematic ethnic difference, *The Wedding Banquet* does not make him an incommensurable Other to be expelled and extinguished. Instead, we see the story from his point of view as much as anyone else's, and the plot accommodates him in the Gao family structure. Both elements have their origins in a common strategy of dealing with the arrival of a foreigner by inclusion rather than exclusion. In regard to perspective, Ang Lee's film revives the conventions of the family melodrama, a format largely absent from Taiwan movie screens in recent years. Unlike Hollywood family melodrama, which focuses on the travails of an individual family member and encourages audience identification with her or him, here the family group functions as collective protagonist. Efforts are made to resolve tensions within the group by enabling mutual empathy both between the characters and for the audience, drawing a line around the group to maintain it rather than between the individual self and the Other. Although this helps to explain the operations of the group, it does not explain how the foreigner or outsider gains access. Two factors are crucial. First, a suitable role must be found for them to take up, and they must be willing to take up this role and therefore submit to the group order. Second, they must have something to contribute to the group. This approach to dealing with the foreigner by inclusion has older precedents—for example, in the so-called "tribute system"—and can also be seen in other Chinese films that represent "good" foreigners, such as *Dr. Bethune* and *Black Cannon Incident.*

If the tensions between family members in the Chinese melodrama are overdetermined by an ideology of inclusion, how is this manifested in cinematic and narrative conventions? Two features of *The Wedding Banquet* stand out. First, when the narrative does draw attention to difference, rather than leading to othering it is the starting point for empathy. For example, although Simon could be a sexual and ethnic Other from the perspective of the Gaos and middle-class heterosexual Taiwan audiences, the film works against this. New York gay lifestyles may be unfamiliar, but Simon and Wai-tung are represented in a manner designed to assuage prejudice rather than inflame it. Simon is in the medical profession, dedicated to helping others. He and Wai-tung maintain what appears to be the gay equivalent of a monogamous, middle-class household. Pink triangles and black leather jackets do appear, but in the admirable context of AIDS education and fund-raising. If anything, as commentators have pointed out, it is the Chinese wedding rituals that are made to appear exotic, especially when director Ang Lee appears in a cameo commenting to incredulous Caucasian wedding guests that, "You're witnessing the results of five thousand years of sexual repression."[25] However, even this comic remark suggests not so much othering as a way for Western audiences to place the seemingly exotic in the familiar framework of sexual liberalization as part of modernization.

Second, it follows from this inclusive strategy that no one character's perspective predominates. The film opens with Wai-tung working out while listening to an audiotape letter from his mother, so it begins from his worldview, with his mother's voice functioning almost as superego. However, by the end of the film, only Simon, Mr. Gao, and the audience understand the whole picture, and Mr. Gao appears in control of this distribution of knowledge. When Wai-tung comes out to his mother, she forbids him from telling his father for fear of provoking another stroke. Although Mr. Gao later reveals to Simon that he understands English and knows what is going on, he forbids Simon from telling the others. Presumably, he worries that discovering he is less traditional than thought may dampen their enthusiasm for presenting him with the desired grandson.

In her extensive feminist critique of *The Wedding Banquet*, Cynthia Liu argues that the film is "reasserting the patriarch as the privileged point of identification."[26] It is true that he is the character that we know least well at the beginning and get to know better as the film progresses. But although this enables empathy for him, does this necessarily override empathy for the others, also often based on insight into their private moments? The film ends at the airport where the newly constituted family of the Gaos, Wai-tung, Wei-wei, Simon, and the fetus in Wei-wei's womb gathers to look at the wedding photos before seeing the Gaos off. As Mr. Gao arrives at the metal detector and raises his arms to allow an inspection, the frame freezes. How should we interpret this? As a gesture of triumph, or of surrender? And whose perspective is this? Are we focused on Mr. Gao to better appreciate his feelings, or as a representation of how his wife sees him, or of the perspective of those gathered to farewell them? If the film has successfully enabled us to understand the different positions of all the members of the Gao family group, the answer can only be "all of the above."

However, although *Wedding Banquet* enables us to empathize with all the main characters, it would be a mistake to see this social order as egalitarian or free. In this regard, Cynthia Liu is quite right to note that men's interests predominate, and that the whole narrative is driven by a determination to satisfy the demands of the Confucian patriarchal order represented by Mr. Gao and symbolized by the grandson. The narrative may trace give-and-take on all sides, but weaker participants and in particular women have to give up more. Wei-wei needs her green card and gives up independence

FIGURE 7.1 Saying good-bye at the airport in *The Wedding Banquet* (1993).

(COURTESY CENTRAL MOTION PICTURE CORPORATION)

and any realistic hope of sexual fulfillment to get it. Wai-tung's mother is completely dependent on his father and exists only to assist him.

If inclusion is understood as a strategy for maintaining an existing order, it may help to examine a comparable system for dealing with foreigners—the so-called "tribute system." In his study of the Macartney Embassy of 1793, *Cherishing Men from Afar,* James Hevia describes the usual understanding of this system developed by sinologists:

> China developed early in its history a unique method of dealing with foreign powers, one that required the acknowledgment of the supremacy of China's "Son of Heaven" (*Tianzi*) as superior to all other rulers in the world. Foreign princes expressed their acceptance of this proposition in two "symbolic" ways, by presenting ritual tribute (*gong*) and performing the "full" *koutou,* kneeling three times, each time bowing their head to the ground thrice.... This system defined Chinese attitudes and practices in foreign relations from virtually the dawn of Chinese civilization until the confrontation with the West in the nineteenth century.[27]

Hevia's study questions the assumed rigidity and timelessness of the system, emphasizing historical specificity and strategic malleability, and also the assumption that the Qing dynasty system consisted of "empty" or meaningless rituals obstructing apprehension of "reality." These assumptions produce a position complicit with that of the Western powers. Instead, Hevia argues for understanding the encounter as one between two different imperial orders in which each used the conduct of the encounter to assert its cosmology, its reality, and its power. Where someone was seated, whether the emperor got up, what gifts were exchanged, and so on were all part of a process that signified where each side was attempting to place the other in its order. Cooperation determined whether friendly relations could be established.

From this perspective, the various "rituals" of the Gao family's wedding banquet represent less their refusal to see the "reality" of their son's gay identity and more a struggle over which reality will prevail. Hevia's analysis of Qing relations with Inner Asian rulers and Tibetan lamas indicates a high degree of flexibility in their efforts to achieve their basic aims.[28] Similarly, the Gaos are flexible in their efforts to get their grandson. They visit New York when their son does not bring his bride back home, as would be more customary. Similarly, they work to accommodate Simon. This is made relatively straightforward by the existence of the "best man" role in American wedding ritual. However, as Liu points out, within the Chinese family structure his role is more like that of a concubine, or unofficial second wife. He has made an effort to learn Chinese, cooks, looks after Mr.

Gao during his recovery from his stroke, and so on. Wei-wei has public recognition, especially once pregnant with the grandson. However, when Mr. Gao gives Simon a red packet of money during the same encounter in which he reveals his English abilities, Simon's place within the family structure is privately acknowledged, as might be the case for a son's lover unsuitable to become a bride.[29]

Simon's willingness to cooperate, unlike the British diplomats who notoriously refused to kowtow to the Chinese emperor,[30] helps to make him a good foreigner, even if he himself is not knowingly doing this. The Gaos also implicitly accede to their son's lifestyle in New York so long as they get their grandson, so this is not a one-way street. This draws attention to a second factor required of a good foreigner: Simon must have something the Gaos want. What he has is a call on their son's loyalty that rivals their own. Without his cooperation, it is doubtful if the grandson would arrive. Indeed, it is Simon who suggests the marriage of convenience in the first place. In this sense, Wai-tung himself and by extension the grandson become the "tribute" that Simon offers up to Mr. Gao in exchange for a place within the Gao family.

Of course, not all Chinese films with positive representations of foreigners are family melodramas like *The Wedding Banquet*. But the strategy of accommodation is common to many narratives of positive encounters with foreigners in Chinese cinema. Two examples from the People's Republic are *Black Cannon Incident* (1986) and *Dr. Bethune* (1963). In both cases the foreigners have modern technology and skills to offer. (In a sense, Simon's

FIGURE 7.2 Simon gets the red packet from Mr. Gao in *The Wedding Banquet* (1993).

compromise also offers a way for the Gaos to accommodate contemporary conceptions of sexuality in the Confucian family system.) The German engineer Hans in *Black Cannon Incident* has equipment and knowledge about its installation and operation, and Dr. Bethune has medical skill. Equally important, both foreigners are willing to work within the Chinese systems pertaining in each film. Dr. Bethune is motivated by internationalist support for the Communist order.[31] Hans, on the other hand, is a more interesting case. On the one hand, he faces a Chinese Communist bureaucracy deeply suspicious of foreigners, especially those from capitalist lands, and prone to treat him as an Other. On the other hand, he and the Chinese engineer and translator he works most closely with, Zhao Shuxin, share a professional code that enables him to take up a place as this man's colleague. For example, when his Chinese counterpart demonstrates an error in the German calculations, Hans admits this readily and apologizes. This makes it possible for at least one Chinese, Zhao, to cherish this man from afar.[32]

The Minority Nationalities Films: From (Br)otherhood to (Alie)nation

The suspicion directed toward Hans in *Black Cannon Incident* reminds us that the inclusive strategy of drawing the line of belonging around good foreigners is complemented by an exclusive strategy of drawing a line between Chinese and other foreigners. The European-derived system of nation-states pressed upon the "Middle Kingdom" by the Western powers and adopted by China's own modernizers encourages such an approach; as Benedict Anderson points out, the territorial nation-state is defined by borders rather than allegiance to a monarch, throne, or other central point.[33] However, no such option to include the "good" and exclude the "bad" exists for non-Han ethnic groups living within the territory of the new nation-state of the People's Republic. The appearance of the term "minority nationalities" and the production category "minority nationality films" (*shaoshu minzu pian*) is a symptom of the effort to stabilize the tension between ethnic difference and national identity posed by the presence of non-Han peoples.

Before the nation-state system, all non-Han people were barbarians (*yi*) of one sort or another, differentiated not by territory but hierarchically in terms of their cultural and racial degree of difference from the Han Chinese. As Frank Dikötter puts it, "The *shengfan*, literally 'raw barbarians,' were considered savage and resisting. The *shufan*, or 'cooked barbarians,' were tame and submissive."[34] With the transition to the nation-state system, non-Han people outside became foreigners (*waiguoren*, "people from outside countries") and those inside the People's Republic became "minority nationalities" (*shaoshu minzu*). In the 1950s, Chinese anthropologists went into the contact zones to distinguish minority nationalities; they used four Stalinist criteria: common language, territory, economic life, and culture.[35] This was accompanied by the development of different policies, laws, and rights for the different nationalities.[36] This process can be understood as performative, negotiating older ideas of ethnic difference and hierarchy and newer ideas of egalitarian national citizenship to produce the concept of the minority nationalities.[37]

The category of "minority nationality films" (*shaoshu minzu pian*) was developed after 1949 as a supplementary discourse promoting this new syncretic thinking about ethnic difference to the population at large. Before the 1949 revolution, minority nationalities appeared relatively rarely in Chinese films and were not concentrated in any single production category.[38] After 1949, minority nationality films became a regular production category, constituting 6 percent of overall output between 1949 and 1986.[39] In an essay on the seventeen years following 1949, Li Yiming notes that the emphasis on political education in these films leads to consistent omission of the "feudal remnants" of religion and legend from most films. Important exceptions include such popular hits as *Five Golden Flowers* (1959), *Third Sister Liu* (1960), and *Ashima* (1964), the sources for all of which were nonetheless subject to revision.[40]

The negotiation of older and newer concepts of ethnic identity manifests itself in the minority nationalities film in a number of ways. First, as Paul Clark notes in the earliest significant article on these films in English, a combination of stable visual signifiers (such as costumes and dances) and

---

SERFS (NONGNU)

DIRECTOR, LI JUN

August First Film Studio, 1963

Written by Huang Zongjiang

SYNOPSIS

Jampa comes from a family of serfs. When he is small, the serf owner kills his parents, and in his teens he is given to the young master as a "human horse." In response, he becomes mute. After the People's Liberation Army enters Tibet in 1951, he deliberately throws the young master off. A PLA officer saves Jampa from a beating and lets him ride his own horse. The young master has Jampa dragged behind a horse as punishment. Jampa flees, but is recaptured. The young master takes part in the 1959 rebellion against the Chinese. When it fails he flees, forcing Jampa to carry him again. Jampa throws him again, and the PLA saves him again in the nick of time. Jampa rushes back to the temple to reveal the cache of arms hidden there. When the serfs are finally liberated, Jampa recovers the ability to speak.

narrative traits produces the collective identity of each nationality. Here, identity seems to be understood in a manner characteristic of modernity as essential; it is given, ahistorical, and shared by all. Clark also distinguishes two subcategories of minority nationality film. One focuses on the peoples of subtropical southwestern China, representing them as happy, colorful, and fond of singing and dancing, whereas the second focuses on the peoples of the northwestern deserts and highlands, representing them as fierce fighters.[41] These two types seem to extend older distinctions between "cooked" and "raw" barbarians.

Furthermore, although the constitution of the People's Republic conforms to a modern concept of national citizenship by specifying that all fifty-six nationalities are equal, the narratives in the minority nationality films suggest the legacy of older thinking where China was the center of civilization bestowing largess on its supplicants. In these films, this pattern is reconfigured as the "civilizing project" of the Chinese Communist Party, justified by anthropological measures that placed different nationalities along a teleological line of development.[42] In the case of *Serfs*, widely regarded in the People's Republic as the acme of pre–Cultural Revolution minority nationality films,[43] the first part of the film displays old Tibet as a cruel and exploitative feudal theocracy. Then the Communist Party appears literally as the cavalry over the horizon to liberate the serfs. Not only do they prevent the serf master from riding Jampa as a "human horse" (fig. 7.3). By also placing Jampa on one of their own horses, they signify how superior, egalitarian, and more civilized they are (figs. 7.4a–7.4f). Repetition of this rescue implies that the Tibetan serfs could not liberate themselves without the Chinese Communist Party.[44]

This pattern of simultaneous Han Chinese and socialist self-styled benevolence is common during this period. Yet the self-and-Other relation-

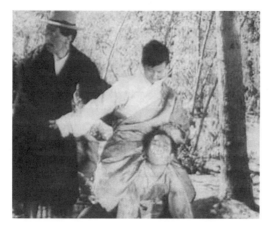

FIGURE 7.3 The young master rides Jampa in *Serfs* (1963).

FIGURE 7.4a The PLA offers Jampa a horse to ride home after they have healed his wounds in *Serfs* (1963).

FIGURE 7.4b Jampa kneels to let the PLA officer mount.

FIGURE 7.4c The PLA officer is shocked ...

FIGURE 7.4d ... and goes to help Jampa up.

FIGURE 7.4e He offers Jampa the reins.

FIGURE 7.4f Jampa finally understands.

ship it implies is complicated by the frequent use of the brotherhood metaphor to express this relationship. This patriarchal image constructs the nation as one family, and it is hierarchical, for there is never any doubt about who is little brother or big brother.[45] Furthermore, while these films mark physical signifiers of ethnic difference such as clothing, they also construct sameness in other ways. Most notably, the narrative pattern of class-based exploitation and liberation by the Chinese Communist Party in *Serfs* and other minority nationality films is also found in Chinese socialist

---

HORSE THIEF (DAOMA ZEI)

DIRECTOR, TIAN ZHUANGZHUANG
Xi'an Film Studio, 1986

Written by Zhang Rui

SYNOPSIS

Although he is a horse thief, Norbu is devout, spending the proceeds of his crimes on sacred objects to protect his son Tashi. Nonetheless, his son sickens and dies, and Norbu and wife Dolma are banished because of his crimes. They go on a pilgrimage and she becomes pregnant again. The tribe's sheep die and they move on. Norbu follows the tribe, performing taboo ritual functions in his efforts to atone. However, only his wife and son are allowed to return to the tribe, and Norbu himself goes to his death.

---

films in general. As Li Yiming points out, from the first minority nationality film, *Victory of the Mongolian People* (1950), on, these films follow the pattern set by the "model work" *The White-haired Girl* (1950) in substituting class identity for other nodes of identity, including ethnic identity. Frequently, a hidden class enemy is unearthed to consolidate this shift, such as the head lama in *Serfs*.[46] By placing the exploited members of minority nationalities in the same narrative position as liberated workers, peasants, and soldiers, class overrides ethnicity as the common characteristic constituting the "people" of the People's Republic, while the metaphor of more "advanced" or "backward" development accounts for continued difference and hierarchy.

The production of "minority nationality films" is ongoing and was the subject of a 1996 conference.[47] At first sight, Tian Zhuangzhuang's 1986 film about Tibet, *Horse Thief,* seems similar to *Serfs*. Both begin with cultural and landscape iconography that would appear exotic to Han audiences. *Serfs* has right-to-left long-shot pans across treeless landscapes above the clouds, accompanied by sonorous blasts from long *ragdung* trumpet horns. The final pan brings us to a close-up of lamas in distinctive robes and hats blowing the horns. It then moves to a sequence showing serfs carrying huge sacks of grain, which they deliver to the lamasery as tribute. *Horse Thief* opens with close-ups of lamas chanting as they play *drilbu* handbells alternating with long shots of prayer flags. Vultures gather near and circle above the flags. The sound track consists of synthesizer music, some imitating the kind of horn blasts that open *Serfs*. Eventually, it becomes clear that this is one of the famous "sky burials," where vultures eat the body and take the soul up to the heavens.[48]

FIGURE 7.5 The sky burial in *Horse Thief* (1986)

However, beyond a common Han perspective and construction of exotic ethnic others, there are important differences. *Serfs* opens with a prologue-scrolling title, read out by a male narrator and giving the People's Republic line on prerevolutionary Tibet, but *Horse Thief* only has a title with the date, "1923." And while unforgiving laws, material poverty, and total religious belief characterize both Norbu and Jampa's lives, the Chinese Communist Party does not ride to the rescue in *Horse Thief*. Indeed, the Han Chinese in general are entirely absent. Furthermore, *Horse Thief* pays great attention to local religious and cultural rituals, which would have been seen previously as indulging superstition.

Leaving out the Communist Party and including ritual, seminudity, relaxed sexual customs, and even religion has been a widely noted feature of recent minority nationality films. Zhang Wei, who writes with a concern for realist representation, categorizes these recent tendencies as excess, distortion, and novelty seeking. He also notes the tendency of contemporary filmmakers to eschew modernization among the minority nationalities in favor of more colorful "primitive customs."[49] In the case of popular films, this can be accounted for by the change in the structure of the Chinese film industry. The state-funded system that operated without interruption until

FIGURE 7.6 Religious observance in *Horse Thief* (1986)

the 1980s classified films according to "theme" or "topic" (*timu*), referring
to the political line that they illustrated. After the rollback of state subsidies
in the 1980s, the "theme" system of classification was gradually replaced
with that of "genres" (*leixing*), which correspond to marketing categories
and audience appeal.[50] Although both the term *minority nationality films*
and the Han perspective on the minority nationalities continue,[51] the shift
from pedagogy to commerce is clear in the new surge of "genre" minority
nationality films that appeared in the mid- to late 1980s,[52] many of which
display fantasies of savagery and sexuality (and savage sexuality) for Han
metropolitan consumption.[53]

However, *Horse Thief* does not fit this market-driven explanation: it only
sold two prints in China.[54] Furthermore, the film frustrates pleasure in its
documentary-like presentation at length and without any voice-over explanation of rituals and practices that could otherwise easily be sensational-
ized. Rather than the titillation of otherness packaged for easy consumption, the result seems to have produced the effect of an encounter with
radical alterity in which the audience felt excluded and at a loss.[55] Director
Tian Zhuangzhuang speaks approvingly of one Han audience member
who planned to visit Tibet "at his own expense" to learn more after being

confronted by *Horse Thief.*[56] The film also won praise for the "authenticity" of its attention to local detail and use of local actors and locations.[57]

Dru C. Gladney has pointed out that this display of the rugged and "natural" lifestyle of the Tibetans (and the Mongols in Tian's previous film, *On the Hunting Ground,* 1985) is romanticized in implicit comparison to the effete and overcivilized Chinese.[58] However, he also notes later in the same article that the film can function as a metaphorical discourse for the Cultural Revolution through its "tension between individual victimization and group survival," not to mention the tragic consequences of blind faith.[59] This makes *Horse Thief* a paradoxical text, simultaneously admiring Tibet as an Other lost to Han modernity and fearing it as a savage metaphor for self.[60]

This paradoxical simultaneous identification and othering constitutes a structure of self-critical alienation. This is distinct from both the negotiation of othering and identification through the metaphor of brotherhood in earlier minority nationality films and the pleasurable consumption of otherness undisturbed by self-criticism in more commercial recent films. It is by no means unique to *Horse Thief.* For example, another widely discussed minority nationality film from this period, Zhang Nuanxin's *Sacrificed Youth* (1985), is about the experiences of a Han girl "sent down" to the Dai nationality area during the Cultural Revolution. First there is identification. Hu Ke notes that unlike the old minority nationality films, the Han

FIGURE 7.7 The Han Chinese heroine adopts Dai ways in *Sacrificed Youth* (1985)

(COURTESY CHINA FILM ARCHIVE)

girl is not the liberator but the one who is educated by the encounter, and it is not the Dai who seek to follow the Han but the girl who is drawn to their culture; "the Han are not always advanced, rational, or civilized."[61] But then there is also othering. Esther Yau, Zhang Yingjin, Dru C. Gladney, and Stephanie Donald have all noted that the recruitment of the Dai to a Han self-critique still exoticizes them and appropriates them as objects for Han use.[62] Combined, this constitutes the same structure of alienation found in *Horse Thief*.

This structure of alienation also underpins the "primitive passions" Rey Chow has noted in other so-called Fifth Generation films of this period and characterized, significantly from the perspective of this chapter, as "auto-ethnography."[63] Chow traces this not only in the fascination of Fifth Generation filmmakers for remote places, classes, and times but also in earlier Chinese twentieth-century culture, and she connects it to the colonial experience of radical disjuncture upon forced and sudden entry into modernity. In the late 1980s, after the institution of the "open door" policy and the end of some thirty years of socialist isolation, the voluntary reencounter with the West may have combined with the end of the Cultural Revolution and concomitant loss of faith in socialism to produce a similar shock of the new. Given that the new was also foreign, perhaps it is not surprising that the ethnic difference inherent to a minority nationality film like *Horse Thief* was also an appropriate site for the construction of one of the most striking examples of this self-critical alienation.

The cinema not only of the People's Republic, but also that of Taiwan, features ethnic minorities. Before the arrival of the Han Chinese, Malayo-Polynesian tribes populated Taiwan.[64] Their descendants are known as aboriginals (*tuzhuren*) or, more colloquially, as mountain people (*shandiren*), following their retreat upcountry in the face of Chinese settlement.[65] This history and geography gives them a different symbolic status from the minority nationalities on the mainland, encountered mostly on the borderlands as Chinese settlement spread. In films, Taiwan aboriginals are often symbols of Taiwan itself. This was true in the Japanese occupation period; the most famous film shot on Taiwan then is probably *Sayon's Bell* (1943), which eulogizes the enthusiasm of aboriginals for the Imperial Army.[66] The first Mandarin Chinese-language film completed on the island, *The Alishan Uprising* (1949), focused on a famous revolt by aboriginals.[67] However, just as in the mainland, most cinematic representations of the Taiwan aboriginals have been made by non-aboriginals, and only recently have aboriginals engaged in filmmaking themselves.[68]

Clearly, there is important further research to be done on this topic, in order to discover whether there are also patterns exceeding the self-and-Other model at work here as there are in the mainland Chinese "minority nationality" film. However, for our final section, we turn to a third pattern that cannot be accommodated by a self-and-Other model. If the Han are "self," how are we to account for differences among the Han concerning the various factors of language, putative common origin, and so on that constitute ethnic identity?

Regionality and Ethnicity: Differences Among the Han

Difference among the Han Chinese themselves has been prominent in times of territorial and political reorganization, with concomitant population flows. The early 1990s, preceding Hong Kong's reversion to Chinese rule and following the end of martial law on Taiwan, was just such a period. Inter-Han differences and tensions appeared in many films, including *City of Sadness* (1989), discussed in chapter 2. Mainlanders started appearing prominently in Hong Kong films as criminals who had smuggled themselves across the border—and this continues to be true. However, to show that the recent period is not exceptional, we focus on another time of upheaval, the years following the Communist Revolution of 1949. We argue that although inter-Han difference does appear in film, its appearance is relatively rare and is almost never constructed as ethnic difference rather than local color. This is partly because of the hostility of nationalist governments to anything that could encourage separatism, and partly because, as discussed below, being Han challenges European definitions of ethnicity. Although narrative representation of inter-Han difference may be rare, a more consistent manifestation can be found in the negotiation of spoken language in Chinese cinemas since the coming of sound.

The modern concept of an ethnicity as a people sharing common cultural features and descent came to prominence in the transition to nation-states in Europe. As Anderson points out, because older state formations such as religious communities and dynastic realms were defined by allegiance, commonalities among the peoples they ruled were not important. But with a nation-state, the unity of a people was an important reason for drawing the borders defining the territory of the state.[69] This unity correlates to the idea of ethnicity. However, until the recent adoption of the term *zuqun*, there was no Chinese translation for "ethnicity," and the most commonly used substitute has been the term *minzu*, meaning a nation in the sense of a people.[70] Maybe one reason for this is the relative elasticity of the category of Han, which is often understood to be a Confucian cultural identity able to absorb outsiders who subscribe to it.[71] Even Patricia Ebrey, who has argued for the importance of genealogy rather culture alone in the definition of being Han, notes that the Han have absorbed numerous outside groups, for whom constructing a suitable genealogy becomes part of the process of becoming Han.[72] A second reason might be the survival of numerous local differences among the Han, which results in a strong sense of local identity within Han identity.

Although the last two centuries have seen numerous divisions of the territory of the Chinese empire and despite strong local cultures that could easily be seen as ethnic,[73] mostly these have not been accompanied by the appearance of separate ethnic identity.[74] The notable recent exception to this has been the strong emergence of the Taiwan independence movement, which is grounded in ethnic difference,[75] but whether film has promoted this line is discussed in chapter 2 in regard to *City of Sadness*. In the twentieth century, those engaged in Chinese nationalist projects worked hard to contain inter-Han differences, and so film's susceptibility to state control has mostly limited acknowledgment of inter-Han differences to signs of local color. But in times of upheaval, and especially in Taiwan and Hong Kong where local identities are not only distinct but linked to territorial boundaries, such differences do make their way into film narratives.

In the late forties, for instance, the Communist Revolution triggered flight to both Hong Kong and Taiwan and their isolation from the mainland. The Kuomintang had only resumed rule of Taiwan four years before, after fifty years of Japanese colonial rule during which the local population had been encouraged to see themselves as loyal subjects of the Japanese emperor.[76] The tragic result of the tensions between the local Taiwanese (*Taiwanren*) and "the people from outside the province" (*waishengren*) is the subject of *City of Sadness*. However, although martial law suppressed public discussion of the February 28th Incident for forty years, during which the government denied the *Taiwanren-waishengren* divide,[77] there was no pretense in the Taiwan cinema of the fifties and sixties that communal differences did not exist. Instead, narratives were produced that emphasized common Chinese identity and good relations despite these differences.

Bai Ke's 1956 *Descendants of the Yellow Emperor* is the earliest surviving Taiwan film. It opens with a long shot of a schoolyard, with the flag of the Republic of China flying and a portrait of Chiang Kai-shek. The children sing that they are all descendants of the Yellow Emperor and the people of one country.[78] However, inside the classroom, a teacher asks a local boy whose descendant he is, to which he replies, "I am my grandfather's descendant." The rest of the film ensures that both he and the audience gain a correct understanding of their true heritage, complete with careful discussion of how grandfather's forefathers came from mainland China. In 1958, Lee Hsing, who went on to become the prime exponent of healthy realism in the 1960s (discussed in chapter 4), made his debut film, *Brother Wang and Brother Liu Tour Taiwan*. Having grown up in Shanghai, Lee himself was a *waishengren,* and as the son of a Kuomintang official, he was strongly nationalist.[79] Yet this box office hit (which inspired a string of sequels) featured a Laurel and Hardy–style pair of local Taiwanese comedians and was addressed to local Taiwanese audiences.[80] In this film, one is a weighty shoeshine man and the other the puny rider of a large and cumbersome rickshaw tricycle. A lottery win elevates them from poverty and they tour the island to celebrate. Numerous comic incidents follow, but in the process not only the characters but also the audience, regardless of where they were from, got a chance to see sights composing what was now the existing territory of the Republic of China and their new common home.

In 1962, Lee Hsing also made a romantic comedy called *Both Sides Are Happy,* which followed the formula of misunderstandings between the older generations of a *waisheng* and a Taiwanese family undercut by romance between the younger generations.[81] This was based on the 1961 Hong Kong hit, *The Greatest Civil War on Earth.*[82] There, the influx of refugees from the mainland had also resulted in films dealing with communal tensions. Without the imperative optimism of martial law found in Taiwan, Hong Kong films did not always have a happy ending. In particular, in the years just after 1949, nostalgia for the mainland was particularly apparent in films produced by those who had fled from Shanghai. As Stephen Teo notes in regard to one company's productions, "while they were shot in Hong Kong, the films' characters and setting were usually specified as Shanghai, avoiding any reference to Hong Kong."[83] And if Hong Kong did appear, it was not in a favorable light. For example, Zhu Shilin's 1952 film *The Show Must Go On* is about a traveling acrobatic troupe that struggles to survive by performing nightclub acts in Hong Kong after the establishment of the People's Republic. When the troupe leader's daughter is asked to perform in diaphanous outfits, they walk out. But then they are sued for breach of contract and face harassment from gangsters when they perform in public spaces. However, here again, although inter-Han difference appears, the film represents it not as ethnic but as due to the impact of "imperialist" culture in Hong Kong (as the opening title puts it). At the end of the film, the troupe returns to start a new life in the mainland.

A more consistent site where inter-Han difference manifests itself in the cinema is to be found not in the narratives, but in language use. Common language is one of the attributes Stevan Harrell gives in his definition of ethnicity cited at the beginning of this chapter, and Anderson emphasizes the production of a standardized national language in the formation of many modern nation-states.[84] Yet the very nature of Chinese languages challenges European-derived ideas of ethnicity. Written Chinese is pictographic; there is no connection between the written form and the spoken forms of the language. As a result, there is one written form—Chinese characters—but there are numerous spoken forms. These spoken forms are not mere variations but are in fact mutually unintelligible, yet the written form enables communication across the boundaries of speech. Furthermore, while the different spoken languages support local identities, the use of written characters simultaneously contributes to a larger sense of community. Should this local identity be regarded as regional or as ethnic? Are these spoken forms "dialects," as they are usually designated, or "languages"? Is there something about being Han that does not fit the European idea of ethnic—and national—identity?

However, despite such difficulties of fit, Anderson notes that in the nineteenth century the independent nation-state had become a model that "imposed certain 'standards,'" including the idea of a unified national language.[85] Chinese embarked on the project of constructing a Chinese nation-state made various language-reform efforts, most of them directed toward the production and promotion of a national language.[86] In the cinema, this only became an issue with the arrival of sound films. One of the most important censorship acts of the 1930s was the ban on films in any spoken language other than Mandarin, because "in the eyes of the central government, local dialect was a factor supporting regional separatism."[87] According to Stephen Teo, this prompted filmmakers based in Canton to move to Hong Kong and make the city the base for Cantonese-language film production from then on.[88] Because Hong Kong was not a national polity, language used in films was not an issue for its British rulers, and the cycles of Mandarin-language and Cantonese-language films produced there were largely market-driven.

In contrast, because the Communists shared the Kuomintang's project to construct China as a nation-state with an integrated national culture, the Mandarin monopoly was maintained after the Communist takeover in 1949. Only very recently, with the relaxation of central control and increased determination by the marketplace, have there been a few exceptions to this rule. They include Tian Zhuangzhuang's *On the Hunting Ground* and *Horse Thief*, originally made in Mongolian and Tibetan, respectively (but dubbed into Mandarin for release within China), and Zhang Yimou's *The Story of Qiu Ju* (1992), made in the local dialect as part of the film's documentary-style realism.

On Taiwan, however, the Kuomintang faced a practical obstacle to continuing its insistence on Mandarin. During fifty years of Japanese colonial occupation, Japanese had been the "national language" residents were encouraged to learn.[89] As a result, the local population the KMT encountered upon the island's reversion to Chinese rule in 1945 spoke either Japanese or the Minnanhua version of Hokkienese also known as Taiwanese (*taiyu*), but little or no Mandarin at all. Many of the Kuomintang and their follow-ers who came to Taiwan spoke neither Japanese nor Taiwanese. The result-ing communication problems created tension between the Kuomintang's desire to promote Mandarin as the national language and its eagerness to communicate with the islanders and promote Chinese identity, as opposed to the Japanese identity promoted by the island's former rulers.

On the one hand, the evidence from surviving films indicates that they were happy to see their message get across in either Mandarin or Taiwan-ese. For example, *Descendants of the Yellow Emperor* is in Mandarin, *Brother Wang and Brother Liu Tour Taiwan* is in Taiwanese, and *Both Sides Are Happy* is a relatively rare example from that time of a film made in both languages (and realistically representing mutual incomprehension).

On the other hand, the Kuomintang steadily pursued policies promot-ing Mandarin as the national language. Outside the cinema, these included policies intended to ensure acquisition of Mandarin by the island's major-ity Taiwanese-speaking population, such as the insistence that all educa-tion as well as radio and television broadcasts be in Mandarin.[90] In the cinema, no ban was ever placed on the production of films in Taiwanese, and there were large waves of Taiwanese-language films in the late fifties and sixties. However, during this period, the film industry was divided be-tween government-owned and -financed studios and private corporations. The government studios mostly produced Mandarin-language films. The Taiwanese-language cinema had to be purely privately funded, and as a re-sult was relatively undercapitalized. In addition to the limitations imposed by lack of capital and limited overseas markets for Taiwanese-language films, the government added further disincentives for the production of Taiwanese-language films by limiting awards, prizes, and other monetary incentives to Mandarin-language films.[91]

However, the decline of Kuomintang central control and the eventual end of martial law has not resulted in the rebirth of the Taiwanese-language cinema. Instead, one of the hallmarks of the Taiwan New Cinema's real-ism since its beginnings in the early 1980s has been the use of multiple spoken languages in film in a manner duplicating what might be heard in a real-life scene in Taiwan (or elsewhere in China, for that matter). Hou Hsiao Hsien's films are particularly famous for this, and *City of Sadness* features Mandarin, Taiwanese, Shanghainese, Hakka, and Japanese. It is almost certain that there is no audience in the world that can understand it without reading the subtitles, but that any Chinese audience could un-derstand it by reading the same subtitles regardless of the differences be-tween their spoken languages. The one country whose language policies have further complicated this situation is Singapore. Although the Chinese are the largest ethnic group by far, English is the national first language. As a result of many years of emphasis on English, perhaps a considerable number of ethnically Chinese Singaporeans might have trouble with the Chinese character subtitles. This leads us to the Chinese diaspora and back to Chinese cinema in the intersection of the national and the transnational, which is the topic of our final chapter.

8

The National in the Transnational

IN CHAPTER 1, we noted that the idea of "national cinemas" has given way to "transnational film studies." However, instead of following the rush to abandon the national altogether, we asked what happens to the national in transnational film studies. We called for the final abandonment of the old national cinemas model, which assumed nation-states were stable and coherent and that films expressed singular national identity. We suggested its place be taken by a problematic or set of questions around "cinema and the national." And we have tried to explore how that problematic plays out through Chinese cinemas in the other chapters of this book.

However, our exploration would not be complete without a return to the terrain of the transnational itself. In this chapter, we show that the common opposition between the national and the transnational is false. Even in times of relatively restricted exchange, national film industries have never been hermetically sealed enterprises. Exposure to transnational cinematic flow has effects on filmmakers' work, and imports and exports shape national industries. Just before embarking on the production of China's first Hollywood-style blockbuster, *Hero* (also discussed in chapter 6), Zhang Yimou commented: "The market for films in many countries was not good in 1998. But the commercial Hollywood films made a lot of money. Hollywood is still number one in the film business. All filmmakers should be very clear about that."[1] *Hero* (2002) was not only a deliberate appropriation of Hollywood models aimed at the global market but also a return to one of the oldest foundation myths for the country—the story of Qin Shi Huangdi, the first emperor to unite China and the builder of the Great Wall. In these circumstances, we need to ask—both in terms of imagery and industry—where and what is the national in the transnational?

To explore this question for Chinese cinemas, we look at some examples of what Anna Tsing calls "transnational projects." Tsing uses the term

"transnational project" in her discussion of the debates around globalization. Like some of the other authors we cited in the introduction, Tsing
criticizes those who write about "globalization" as though it were a force of
nature. She argues that there is no single thing called "globalization," but
only many historically and geographically specific "transnational projects"
that forge connections across national borders.[2]

The particular transnational projects we have chosen complicate existing
impressions of transnational Chinese cinema. Sheldon Lu has pointed out
that attention to "transnational Chinese cinema" has followed the greater
communication between the three Chinese filmmaking territories of Hong
Kong, Taiwan, and the People's Republic of China after the People's Republic ended its isolation in the late seventies.[3] This has also become the
era when Chinese films have become regular award-winners on the international film festival circuit and the most significant non-Western films in
European and American movie theaters. Therefore, the tone of the discussion has been divided between an uncritical celebration of ethnic national
pride and a critique of "selling out" to foreigners. Both tendencies are based
on a model of separate and competitive nation-states that is too simple for
a world of transnational connection.

The transnational projects we examine here all complicate the existing
debates in various ways. First, they challenge the image of "transnational
Chinese cinema" as necessarily new, export-oriented, and formed in opposition to national cinema. Furthermore, they all indicate that if successful
participation in the transnational is to be understood as a form of resistance
to the history of imperialism, resistance needs to be rethought. It is not, as
is commonly believed, the same as simple rejection or refusal of the foreign.
Instead, it is often the attainment of agency through a kind of transaction
within the transnational. Certain things are given up and other things are
appropriated from outside in order to transform the local within the transnational. In other words, disempowerment is resisted but a price is paid.

To investigate this further, it seems appropriate to begin and end with
Bruce Lee, China's first global film star, whose image continues to circulate
as part of a global cinematic vocabulary. First, we examine Bruce Lee's own
international success in countering the image of China and the Chinese
man as the "sick man of Asia." The Bruce Lee phenomenon reminds us
that the transnational export success of Chinese cinema dates back to earlier than 1985. Furthermore, the visual iconography of Bruce Lee's remas-
culinization of the Chinese image is produced through the appropriation of
elements of Hollywood American masculinity. In the process, established
models of Chinese masculinity are transformed.

Second, we focus on the film trade. Here, the transnational is not confined to the much-touted Chinese export phenomenon. It also includes

both imports and the piracy business. As Sheldon Lu has pointed out, because cinema arrived in China as an import, Chinese cinema has always been transnational.[4] Here, we focus on the two decades since 1985, when there has been a flood of Hollywood imports into the People's Republic, Hong Kong, and Taiwan, creating fears for the survival of the film industry in each territory. Piracy has sometimes been seen as one way of "talking back" to power. This form of resistance may appeal to local consumers, but we argue that its harm to local film industries may be greater than its power to irritate Hollywood. A different mode of resistance is the development of a local blockbuster discourse. Just as Bruce Lee's appropriations from Hollywood revitalized Chinese masculinity, the first mainland Chinese blockbuster—Zhang Yimou's *Hero*—revitalized the local industry on the mainland.

Finally, we look at the new Singapore film industry and its first transnational success, *Forever Fever* (1998), in which the image of Bruce Lee again plays an important role. This new Singapore film industry challenges the idea of an opposition between the transnational and the national, first because it originates within the transnational economy. The Singaporean government has encouraged it as a high value-added economic sector of the information economy appropriate to Singapore's new place in the transnational trading order. Furthermore, the national imagery of Singapore that it produces differs according to three different industrial modes—the local popular cinema, the modernist festival cinema, and the international commercial art cinema. These three modes, with their specific relations to the national, operate not only in Singapore but also in the cinemas of much of the rest of the world, constituting three places for the national in the transnational. But whether and how they constitute resistance is much harder to determine.

Bruce Lee: Patriotic Masculinity, Transnational Appeal

In Europe and America, 1980s art cinema successes gave Chinese film the highest profile among non-Western cinemas. Trade has a special place in China's experience of imperialism. As we noted in chapter 2, films about modern Chinese national history usually begin with the wound of forced opium imports. Therefore, export is often understood as resistance to imperialism. However, the transnationalization of Chinese cinema by export began earlier. Apart from early exports to the diaspora, probably the first Chinese cinema star to attain international fame was Bruce Lee. Lee revitalized the international image of Chinese masculinity and became an icon for the triumph of the underdog.

THE WAY OF THE DRAGON (A.K.A. THE RETURN OF THE DRAGON) *(MENGLONG GUOJIANG)*

WRITTEN AND DIRECTED BY BRUCE LEE

Golden Harvest, 1972

SYNOPSIS

Tang Lung (Bruce Lee) arrives in Rome from the Hong Kong New Territories to help his female cousin. She is being pressured to sell her restaurant to the Mafia, and Tang's uncle thinks she should give in. However, Tang trains the waiters in martial arts and stands up to the Mafia. The Mafia boss hires the best Japanese and European martial artists to fight Tang, but Tang easily finishes them off. The final showdown is with the American martial artist Colt (Chuck Norris) in Rome's famous Coliseum. After Colt's defeat, it is revealed that Tang's uncle was in cahoots with the Mafia. Tang returns to Hong Kong, leaving his cousin to run her business in peace.

Iconic images of bare-chested Bruce continue to appear on T-shirts, book covers, DVD covers, and fan Web pages. Stripped to the waist, lean muscles taut with fury, and poised to pounce, Lee created a new international image of Chinese manhood as powerful and worthy of emulation, no longer the "sick man of Asia." His deployment of his body as a weapon to win international and interracial competitions has been variously celebrated as the triumph of the Chinese, Asian, or Third World underdog. However, less attention has been paid to Lee's transformation of Chinese masculinity itself. At the same time that Lee represents Chinese resistance to the West—often literally in his fight scenes—his new Chinese masculinity is grounded in appropriation of and therefore submission to some of the values of modern American masculinity.

Bruce Lee's breakthrough as the first Chinese global star was based on only four features he made as an adult before his untimely death. In the Lee legend, this achievement is narrated as a triumph of the underdog and a struggle against racism.[5] Born in the United States in 1940, Lee grew up in Hong Kong, where he was a child star in the 1950s. He returned to the United States and graduated from the University of Washington in Seattle with a B.A. in philosophy. After some success on American television, he lost the role of Caine in the *Kung Fu* series to Caucasian actor David Carradine.[6] American martial arts star Chuck Norris is reported to have commented sarcastically, "Carradine's as good at martial arts as I am at acting."[7] Returning to Hong Kong, Lee debuted as an adult in features in 1971 with *The Big Boss*.[8] He followed this in 1972 with *Fist of Fury*. Both films set new box office records, enabling Lee to establish his own production company and write and direct *The Way of the Dragon*. In 1973 he made *Enter the Dragon* for Warner Bros. At this high point, he died of a mysterious brain seizure. A fifth film, *The Game of Death,* completed later by splicing scenes he had already shot with new footage using stand-ins, was released in 1978.

Like his biography, each film is also a variation on the "triumph of the underdog" theme. In *The Big Boss,* Lee is a Chinese migrant working at a factory run by a Chinese boss in Thailand. The film ends with him arrested after killing the drug smuggling boss. Set almost entirely in the Chinese community, *The Big Boss* is focused mostly on class. On the other hand, *Fist of Fury* is his most evidently nationalistic work. Set in semicolonized Shanghai in 1908, it is based on a true event—the death of the founder of the Jingwu martial arts school. Lee plays a student who pursues bloody revenge against the Japanese assassins. The film ends on a freeze frame of Lee in mid-leap as we hear his characteristic angry shriek and the hail of police gunfire. As Tony Rayns points out, *The Way of the Dragon* combines the migrant worker theme from *The Big Boss* with the contest or tournament theme from *Fist of Fury.*[9] The box office success of all these films led to Warner Bros.'s international distribution of *Enter the Dragon.* Playing off the popularity of the James Bond series, Lee takes on the familiar role of an international police agent combating a wealthy evildoer.

The wide range of ethnic and national affiliations in this small body of work hardly constitutes an artist's oeuvre that inscribes a consistent signature. As a result, audiences and commentators emphasize different aspects of different films to support the particular underdog they see Lee as representing.[10] There are four main patterns: Lee as Hong Kong;[11] Lee as

FIGURE 8.1 Bruce Lee in *The Big Boss* (1971)

(COURTESY HONG KONG FILM ARCHIVE)

cultural and/or diasporic China;[12] Lee as Third World anti-imperialist (despite working for MI-5 in *Enter the Dragon*);[13] and Lee as Asian American champion.[14]

Most commentators make no connection between the "triumph of the underdog" narrative and the masculinity Lee deploys. Jachinson Chan is an exception, placing Lee as a breakthrough in the representation of Asian American men, who had appeared feminized in figures such as Fu Manchu and Charlie Chan. However, even for Chan, masculinity only exists in the singular. As discussed in chapter 6, Kam Louie's 2002 study of Chinese masculinity enables a different understanding. He details two long-standing masculinities, both valorized in Chinese culture. *Wen*, or refined masculinity, is symbolized by Confucius and the gentleman scholar. It emphasizes cultural rather than physical prowess. Highly attractive to women, the *wen* man may dally but in the end must abandon erotic pleasure to fulfill his ethical obligations. *Wu*, or martial masculinity, is symbolized by the fighters who inhabit the mythical spaces of the *jianghu* ("rivers and lakes") outside civil society. These heroes emphasize physical strength and skill. Except when drunk, they eschew women completely. Their primary commitments are to their blood brothers, as discussed in chapter 6. In neither case is the male body eroticized, and the fighter's body signifies his martial prowess only.[15]

Louie notes that, "The Bruce Lee screen persona has all three characteristics of loyalty, righteousness, and mateship to justify him as a *wu* hero." He adds that, "Like the *wu* heroes in traditional narratives ... the Bruce Lee characters do not romance ... beauties like a *wen* scholar would do: he always attends to his social obligations first."[16] Jachinson Chan, apparently unaware of the *wu* codes, interprets Lee's behavior within the conventions of American masculinity only. For him, Lee disappointingly "perpetuates the asexual role that Western culture has constructed for Asian men and does not spend the night with the Asian female character—something that would be unthinkable in a James Bond film."[17] But behavior that would represent masculine achievement within American codes would signal failure within *wu* masculinity. (These tensions continue to dog Chinese male martial arts stars trying to cross over into the international market, as indicated by both Jackie Chan and Jet Li's awkward negotiation of sexuality.)

Louie treats neither of the two Chinese masculinities as static. International success constitutes the Bruce Lee phenomenon as "a reassertion of a Chinese *wu* masculinity in the international arena." But he also notes that "the world dominance of American media means that the Western masculine ideals ... are becoming more and more commonly accepted in China," and that Lee's display of his body along with gossip about his alleged offscreen womanizing breaks with the old *wu* masculinity because it "exudes much sexuality." Therefore, Lee represents not just a reassertion of *wu* masculinity but also a modification "to suit the new hybrid culture of the diaspora Chinese."[18]

However, Louie may understate Lee's departure from the established *wu* model. First, the display of the eroticized body is a startling break with almost all other martial arts stars. The occasional display of the male hero's body was initiated in Hong Kong director Chang Cheh's films in the 1960s. The heroes of earlier Hong Kong action films appeared not just clothed but usually enveloped in loose outfits that completely downplayed the body. Bruce Lee made the display of his torso a personal trademark. Although self-display may have been novel in the martial arts genre, the fit body as a mark of modernization has a long history in the Chinese cinema. As early as the 1930s, Li Lili appeared in bathing costumes and gymnastics outfits in *Queen of Sports* (1934), and male stars appeared stripped to the waist as road workers building a highway to help the army get to the front and fight the Japanese in *Big Road* (1934). Bruce Lee's own hybridization of Chinese *wu* masculinity and American masculinity can be read with this larger history in mind. In this context, it appears closely tied to the various nationalist and anticolonial interpretations of the "triumph of the underdog" narratives in his films: Lee asserts Chinese/Asian/Third World reempowerment through his assertion of neo-*wu* masculinity.

Furthermore, within a dynamic Chinese context, Lee also symbolizes choosing *wu* over *wen* masculinity to carry out this mission. This is a significant shift. As Kam Louie points out, in premodern China *wu* was not generally as highly valued as the more refined *wen*, which stresses submission to order and rule through ethics over the disruptive aggression and force associated with *wu*. *Way of the Dragon* also deviates from the older codes, with Lee's modern and transnational neo-*wu* masculinity appropriating from American codes. Usually, the legal and ethical breaches that *wu* violence constitutes must be eliminated, even if they are used to restore order. This is why Lee is arrested at the end of *The Big Boss* and even shot by the Chinese foreign-settlement police at the end of *Fist of Fury*. However, in *Way of the Dragon*, Lee simply bids good-bye to his young cousin, returning to Hong Kong and leaving her to run her restaurant in peace. This is equivalent to the cliché of the cowboy who rides off into the sunset, regretfully leaving the young widow after saving her life and homestead. By *Enter the Dragon*, Lee has appropriated the American masculinity codes of the gunfighter film and the Bond movie even more fully, as he is hired by MI-5 specially to take on the evil Han.

There is another way in which Lee's neo-*wu* masculinity appropriates from American masculinity. The moment at which he can no longer turn the other cheek is also often when the shirt literally comes off and he bares his muscular upper body. The response of women characters signifies that this is not just a display of weaponry but also an erotic moment. But it is not only women that are attracted to Lee's stripped torso. His body is appropriated for queer viewing pleasure, not only in the critical literature but also in the films themselves.[19]

In *The Way of the Dragon*, Wei Ping'ao reprises the role of the traitorous translator from *Fist of Fury*. In the earlier film, he worked for the Japanese karate school that assassinated the Jingwu master. This time he works for the Italian gangsters. In *Fist of Fury*, he already embodied the physically weak and fawning "sick man of Asia." But in *The Way of the Dragon*, what was just a certain lack of masculinity becomes fully-fledged effeminate homosexuality. Not only does he flounce around in a variety of Elton John–style seventies outfits, but also he makes no effort to hide his attraction to Lee's character. At the end of an attempt to browbeat the restaurant owner, Wei literally bumps into Lee on his way out. Annoyed at first, his tone changes when he steps back and gets a better look at Lee. Reaching down between Lee's legs to where Lee's cloth belt is dangling, Wei picks it up and tucks into his waistband. "Watch where you're going," he tells Lee sweetly. The symbolic possibilities of the belt action leave little doubt that Wei hopes Lee might be going his way.

The eroticization of the male hero under the queer gaze of Wei Ping'ao's character further reveals the degree to which Lee's neo-*wu* masculinity is hybridized with and positioned within globalized American masculinity. Homophobia and its attendant anxieties are an integral component of the globalized American masculinity that features display of the eroticized as well as martial male body. The ultimate goal of this model of masculinity is to win the approving acknowledgment of other men. This homosocial aim can also tip all too easily into homosexuality if respect and admiration

FIGURE 8.2 Belt action in *The Way of the Dragon* (1972)

become the foundation for desire, and therefore the boundary line between the two must be rigorously policed.[20]

As Robin Wood has pointed out, the action movie can be understood as a site where these tensions are worked out. Under this symbolic umbrella, violence between men displaces and transforms the threat of desire, expelling it with the same force as the punches landed on the opponent.[21] Bruce Lee's neo-*wu* masculinity carries the full force of this homophobic structure. However, it is further complicated and specified by the politics of imperialism and anti-imperialism. As is often noted, there is usually a racial hierarchy among Lee's opponents. Taking on other Chinese or even Japanese is an easy beginning. The ultimate test is often a Caucasian opponent, like the Russian champion employed by the Japanese in *Fist of Fury,* or the Chuck Norris character employed by the gangsters in *The Way of the Dragon.*

In addition, there is a marked difference in the way Lee treats his different opponents in some of his films. Whereas other Asian fighters are crushed with contempt, Caucasian opponents are taken seriously. In the Coliseum scene in which Lee takes on and defeats Norris toward the end of *The Way of the Dragon,* Norris is even treated with respect. Cheng Yu points out that Lee eschews "his usual tactics of shrieking, grimacing, or sneering at his opponent."[22] Tony Rayns writes, "the entire sequence is predicated on the fighters' mutual respect for each other's art.... [Lee] kills him *in a spirit of reverence.* After the killing, he drapes the dead man's tunic and black belt over the body, and kneels beside it in silence."[23]

Furthermore, the loving homosociality of the Coliseum scene contrasts with the fate of the Wei Ping'ao characters. Absolutely despised, they do not even have the status of a true opponent and do not even make the bottommost rung on the hierarchy of Lee's adversaries in discussions by other writers. In *Fist of Fury,* Lee's first revenge killings are the two henchmen—one Chinese and one Japanese—who assassinated his teacher. They are dispatched with a series of furious and unrestrained blows to the stomach, and are found hanging from a lamppost the next day. Wei Ping'ao's traitorous translator is next. But where an actual fight scene is used to dispatch the assassins, he does not even merit this. Lee disguises himself as a rickshaw driver whom Wei hires one night. Taking him down a blind alley, Lee lifts the rickshaw by the shafts with Wei in it, tossing it to its destruction. His aim is to get Wei to confess who ordered the assassination. Gutless and without loyalty even to his foreign masters, Wei quickly tells all. But when Lee turns, Wei grabs a brick to bludgeon him. Lee turns back in fury, but the film does not even consider it worth showing us the actual crushing of this insect-like figure; an immediate cut to the next morning reveals Wei's body hanging from a lamppost. In *The Way of the Dragon,* Lee does not even deign to lay a finger on his homosexual suitor. Rather, after the Coliseum scene, when the Wei Ping'ao character runs up to Uncle Tang to tell him the bad news, his Italian boss at the same time drives up and shoots him before he can speak. In other words, he is treated as an afterthought.

The contrast between Lee's loving killing of Chuck Norris in the Coliseum and the treatment of Wei's characters as vermin is thought-provoking. Could it be that in the cosmos of Lee's neo-*wu* masculinity, the slender body that used to signify the refined *wen* scholar now signifies effeminacy and even "the sick man of Asia"? Where *wen* refinement was combined with education to signify wisdom and the superior power of the cerebral over the merely muscular, along with a sure command of ethics, in the neo-*wu* cosmos it is bundled together with spinelessness and disloyalty to signify not only failed Chinese masculinity but even the "fag" or "pansy."

A particular exchange and translation mechanism is at work here. Lee reinvigorates *wu* by appropriating elements of modern American masculinity; agency is produced in exchange for jettisoning various aspects of earlier Chinese masculinities. In this way, the Lee persona's trajectory resembles the classic production of the subject (or self) through a process of subjection, whereby one is acknowledged and given agency in return for subjecting oneself to a higher law. In the process the "fag" is produced as the hated part of the self that is to be repressed and symbolically expelled. However, in the case of Bruce Lee, the intersection of coloniality and masculinity in the production of neo-*wu* masculinity further marks this despised "fag" or "pansy" as Chinese, and the model to be admired and emulated as white. Here an irony emerges in Bruce Lee's otherwise completely un-ironic persona: while appearing to overcome all odds and defeat the imperialist, Lee in fact achieves this goal by subscribing to the other's larger value system.

Pirates and Blockbusters: Resistance Through Trade?

Bruce Lee's appropriation of—and submission to—some of the values of American masculinity in his revitalization of Chinese masculinity tempers the triumphant rhetoric of his anti-imperialist fight scenes. Many commentators have also raised questions about the export success story of recent Chinese cinema. They worry that Chinese filmmakers pander to Western audiences and that Western audiences and scholars appropriate and distort Chinese films for Orientalist and neo-imperialist ends.[24] We argue that these complexities produce ambivalence necessitating rethinking resistance in a transnational environment. Is it a meaningful concept anymore? How has it changed?

Chinese cinema's export successes have not occurred in isolation. Rather, they have been part of the increasing integration of Chinese-language cinemas into a transnational film economy dominated by Hollywood. The dismantling of protectionist trade barriers in the name of free trade has not only facilitated exports. In this section, we focus on two other comparatively neglected phenomena. First, Hollywood imports have flooded the market in each territory. Second, the "Greater China" area composed of Taiwan, Hong Kong, and mainland China has become the epicenter of global video piracy. Some scholars have found an ironic "talking back" to Hollywood in piracy. However, we note that for the Chinese film industries, this has only added to the prevailing gloom. In contrast, it is through the apparent submission to Hollywood's values in the development of a local "blockbuster"—Zhang Yimou's Hero—that the mainland Chinese film industry has overcome the domestic box office record set by Titanic (1997). With these examples in mind, we argue that resistance under transnational conditions needs to be understood not as rejection, but through ambivalent metaphors of exchange ranging from theft, poaching, and appropriation, to paying a price.

Any thorough analysis of the changing fortunes in the Chinese film export and import trade would have to treat Hong Kong, Taiwan, and mainland China separately and include consideration of locally specific conditions. However, the decline in local film production has been marked in all three Chinese territories. And as local production drops, Hollywood's share of the box office goes up. Hong Kong is a free trade port. But in the other two territories, there is a further correlation with entry to the World Trade Organization (WTO) and the dismantling of trade barriers.

At the beginning of the new millennium, the People's Republic of China was producing about one hundred films annually, of which only 10 to 20 percent were profitable. This is part of a general pattern of decline since the late 1980s, with annual box office receipts dropping from 2.4 billion yuan (approximately US$290 million) to 810 million yuan (approximately US$90 million) and over 70 percent of cinemas closing.[25] In the 1980s, annual output was between 150 and 200 films.[26]

As local film production has fallen, Hollywood imports have risen. Before 1995, the film trade remained a monopoly of the government-owned China Film Export and Import Corporation (hereafter, China Film). Furthermore, China Film could not set up "box-office-split" deals acquiring rights on imported films in return for a percentage of the box office. China Film had to use foreign exchange from exports to buy rights, and its earnings did not meet Hollywood's high prices for leading films. In 1992 the flat fee figure was only between $30,000 and $50,000.[27] After 1995, China Film was permitted to do box office splits on ten films a year.[28] These ten films have taken over at least 60 percent of the local market, with off-the-record sources putting the figure as high as 85 percent. Conditions for China's accession to the WTO in 2001 have only increased the pressure of imports on local producers, with the number of box-office-split imports being doubled to twenty films a year.[29]

The Taiwan film industry has seen an even more extreme reversal of fortune. Annual feature film production on the island has been uneven since its beginnings in 1949, but it has often been well over 100, and even reached 189 in 1968. However, although Taiwan films have become consistent prizewinners at festivals in the 1990s, output has slipped to thirty films or less per year.[30] Furthermore, as Taiwan film production has dropped, the box office has been taken over by Hollywood. In 1994, American films took 85.25 percent of the box office, and local films took only 2.05 percent. Hong Kong films took most of the remainder.[31] Before the 1990s, Hollywood films had rarely taken more than 50 percent. By 1999 the decline had gone further, with only fourteen Taiwan-produced films released in Taipei, and "foreign" films (not including Hong Kong films and therefore mostly from Hollywood) taking 96.7 percent of the city's box office.

The parallels between Taiwan and the People's Republic go further. As Ti Wei points out in regard to Taiwan, "Hollywood's victory correlates to the retreat of state regulation."[32] Import quotas, print quotas, and screen-time quotas introduced in the 1950s were steadily reduced in response to pressure from the United States. Taiwan's entry into the WTO on January 1, 2002, led to the complete deletion of all such measures.[33]

The tendencies described for both the People's Republic and Taiwan have been part of a worldwide trend. Hollywood's share of the global box office has risen steadily as it has lobbied successfully for the breaking down of protectionist measures. Only those countries like France and South Korea, which have challenged the "level playing field" justification of free trade and continue to support their film industries, have been able to resist.[34] For many years, Hong Kong's film industry prided itself on its ability to fend off Hollywood's challenge and dominate its local box office without the aid of quotas and other such measures. However, from the late 1990s on, even this bastion of Chinese cinema began to see a drop-off in output, by 25 percent between 2002 and 2003 alone, for example.[35] Even in 2002, the output of 126 features was only just over half of the 1993 figure of 242, and ticket sales had dropped correspondingly.[36] Again, this correlated to Hollywood's increasing share of the box office, exceeding 50 percent for the first time in the mid-1990s. American pressure for removal of trade barriers did not apply in Hong Kong's free trade environment. However, Wang Shujen sums up a combination of local factors that help to explain the turnaround in the fortunes of the local industry: "economic crisis in

Asia in 1997 and 1998, the turnover of Hong Kong to the mainland and the ensuing exodus of Hong Kong film talents to Hollywood and elsewhere, falling production standards and heavy reliance on formulaic genres, mass-produced low-budget films, infrastructural problems of distribution and exhibition, and optical disk piracy."[37]

Video piracy is the third side of China's transnational film trade. Ironically, it has been facilitated by the same breaking down of political and trade barriers that has enabled the connections between Taiwan, Hong Kong, and the People's Republic of China, as well as their integration into the international capitalist economy. In her study of piracy, Wang Shujen notes that resource complementarity has driven the general development of a "Greater China Economic Circle": "China, with its cheap and abundant labor base, its rich and sizable land, and its billion-plus untapped consumer market, becomes an attractive investment site. Given its free port and financial center status ... Hong Kong ... not only provides management know-how, capital, and financial services but also serves as a natural link between the mainland and Taiwan.... Taiwan offers capital and expertise in high-tech manufacturing and enterprise management."[38] In the rest of her study, Wang details how the same resource complementarity has also made the Greater China Economic Circle the global center of video piracy.

There is no question that thriving piracy is not an intended outcome of the free trade movement. Therefore, it is not surprising that piracy is often understood as a blow against First World—and specifically American—imperialism. When the Taiwan government moved against piracy following accession to the WTO on January 1, 2002, it provoked protests in the name of resisting American imperialism. The protesters chose May 4 to stage their demonstration—the anniversary of the famous (May Fourth) 1919 protests against imperialism.[39] Wang Shujen comments that with the adoption of VCD technology for piracy, "the state, local manufacturers, and consumers collude to resist and redefine globalization and standardization."[40]

The steady output of statistics from Hollywood claiming to document the losses caused by piracy may well encourage the perception of piracy as resistance to imperialism. But the damage to Hollywood is a fleabite on an elephant compared to the damage done to local film industries. Almost any new Hong Kong, Taiwan, or mainland Chinese film is pirated on release. As a result, generating revenue in the local market is so compromised that some producers even pirate their own work.[41] Yet this collateral damage, which turns pirates into cannibals, receives little attention in discussions on the topic.

To understand why the damage to local industries is omitted from so much discussion, we need to examine the idea of "resistance" itself. As

Tony Bennett notes, "Although used extensively, the concept of resistance has received relatively little sustained theoretical attention.... Whether in physics, industry, or political theory, resistance is usually described as a defensive reaction of one force or body against another in conditions where the force or body that resists is regarded as existing separately from the force or body it resists."[42] Such a framework, in which the two bodies are understood as separate and only one can be the aggressor and the other the resister, is also the conceptual framework of the international order of nation-states that grounds the classical discourse on imperialism. This framework does not allow for the possibility that the body resisting is also aggressing against itself.

Furthermore, the fundamental presumption of the transnational is that the clear separation between nation-states no longer exists. This challenges the premises of the classical idea of resistance. This may seem like a recent phenomenon. However, there is good reason to question whether the old international order of nation-states was ever truly outside this transnational situation. The very idea of the nation-state is one that has been appropriated from the outside and under duress by countries like China in a process of treaty signing and negotiation. This process then instates them as collective agencies in what is already a larger transnational order. It may only be the rhetoric of national sovereignty that claims separation.

What are the implications of this for the idea of resistance? If there is no separation—and therefore a total repulsion and rejection of the aggressor is impossible because the aggressor and the aggressed already overlap—does this mean that there is no resistance? Or do we need to rethink the idea of resistance itself? If the separation implied in sovereignty was a rhetorical production only but there is also contestation of power among nation-states, it seems that we do need to rethink resistance. Here it may be helpful to remember Foucault's recasting of power. Instead of thinking of power as something that one person or body has and exerts on another, Foucault insists that power is produced and exercised in a relationship between two or more persons or bodies, and is exerted in both directions, although to varying degrees. This suggests that to achieve power—i.e., to be able to act upon another—is by definition to submit to the order that establishes the relationship.[43]

With this understanding in mind, resistance is better understood as a negotiation or process of contested transaction rather than a simple refusal. Even refusal can be seen as one form of this contested transaction, insofar as it is a response to an engagement. For a nation-state to close itself off, as Maoist China did, it needs to be engaged first. And to achieve the ability to withdraw, the Maoist state also appropriated various elements from other nation-states, such as Stalinist socialism in one country. What defines resistance within this reconceptualization is the effort to achieve agency of some sort.

Bruce Lee's revitalization of *wu* masculinity by appropriating and grafting on elements from Hollywood masculinity is another example of this resistance as negotiation. But in that case it leads not to withdrawal but to entry through film exports and achievement of agency within the existing "Western" international order. This can be seen in the narrative of *Enter the Dragon,* for example, where Lee is hired by MI-5 because of his martial skills, and in the process is also able to achieve the revenge he originally wanted to gain for his sister. This was also Lee's first film made for a Hollywood studio (Warner Bros.).

Video piracy is another kind of resistance as negotiation. On the one hand, as the high seas metaphor suggests, it is not a withdrawal or self-isolation. But on the other hand, rather than submitting to achieve agency it does so by subverting the technological standards, government policies, and international trading agreements of the Western-dominated liberal capitalist order at the same time as it relies on the technologies and trading patterns established by that order.

Piracy, as we have noted, may produce a benefit for Chinese consumers—most of whom would lack access to authentic products at the prices companies want to charge—and for those who produce the pirate goods and market them. However, pirates are not patriotic: they pirate local films as readily as Hollywood ones, and by destroying the domestic market do far greater damage to Chinese film industries than to foreign ones.

However, our second case study in this section on imports as part of the Chinese film world's engagement with the transnational also provides the only example so far where the local Chinese film industry has been able to counter the wave of imports. This is the idea and practice of the blockbuster in mainland China. In China today, *dapian* or "big film" most frequently appears coupled with *Meiguo* or "America" in the phrase "the American big film." It is the closest Chinese equivalent to "blockbuster" and is used in Chinese-language discussions of Hollywood blockbusters.

Sustained contact with blockbusters only began with the box-office-split deals in 1995. This is when the first cluster of articles using the term "big film" is to be found. Many of them indicate that this is a new term because they explain it, placing great emphasis on budgets.[44] Many writers also carried out comparisons. "At the moment, a thirty million *renminbi* budget [under US$4 million] counts as a 'big film' in China. Actually, in America that would be a 'little film,' " writes Zhang Baiqing, a point echoed by many others. Zhang notes this represents a tenfold increase on the most expensive 1980s films, that some budgets are even higher, and that the increase has been spurred by a desire to emulate Hollywood blockbusters following their Chinese success. However, Zhang's article is also predicated on the financial impossibility of direct emulation, implying that Chinese block-busters are necessarily different from American blockbusters.[45]

Unsurprisingly, given the history of the opium wars, there was discomfort about the 1995 decision to admit ten films per year on a box office split, as there was in 2001 about feared impact of entry to the WTO on the local film industry.[46] As discussed in chapter 2, Xie Jin's *The Opium War* (1997) assumed its audience was fully aware of the debate around the Western rhetoric of free trade versus the Chinese response of fair trade. In a brief essay on the film, leading scholar and filmmaker Zheng Dongtian underlined the analogy, however inexact, with the American forcing open of the Chinese market for the contemporary "opium" of Hollywood entertainment. Hence his conclusion that after considering the history of the opium wars, the word "blockbuster" does not roll off the tongue as lightly as it used to.[47]

In these initial critical responses, then, we can see a great desire to resist Hollywood by refusing it. Indeed, the coining of the term "big film" (*dapian*) for foreign imports is itself a mark of this, because it draws a line between Hollywood blockbusters and a local Chinese lineage of epic films. Before the American "big film," there was the local "giant film" (*jupian*). Sometimes, "giant film" has been used to translate "blockbuster."[48] But usually "giant film" implies something different and local. The earliest references to the "giant film" we have traced so far are from 1988 and refer to Ding Yinnan's revolutionary historical bio-pic, *Dr. Sun Yatsen* (1986). However, familiar use of the term suggests it was already well established. All commentaries note *Dr. Sun Yatsen* had a high budget, spectacular scenes with large casts, and a seriousness of purpose.[49] In the following years, there was a cycle of such films, all referred to as "giant films." Examples include *The Birth of New China* (1989), *The Kunlun Column* (1988), *Mao Zedong and His Son* (1991), *The Decisive Engagement* (1991), and *Zhou Enlai* (1991). This sets up a conceptual distinction between the "giant film" (or "epic") and the "big film" (or "blockbuster"). Blockbusters are, by implication, less serious and lacking in pedagogical purpose. "Giant films" follow what the government refers to as the "main melody" (*zhuxuanlu*), meaning the prioritization of pedagogy, whereas the emphasis on entertainment in "big films" places them outside this category.

However, this rhetorical operation to keep the foreign blockbuster and the Chinese epic clearly distinguished did not last very long. Xie Jin's 1997 *Opium War* is clearly a historical epic. Also, as analyzed in chapter 2, the events it relates are crucial precursors to revolutionary history. At 100 million *renminbi*, it also had the largest Chinese budget at the time of its production and spectacular scenes with casts of thousands, if not special effects.[50] However, in local criticism, *The Opium War* is referred to not as a "giant film" but as a "big film" or blockbuster. This suggests a watershed moment where the line between the giant film and the big film begins to blur. The film was a local box office success, although it is unclear to what extent it was aided by government-sponsored ticket buying.

However, this success was eclipsed very rapidly in 1998, when *Titanic* was released in China as one of that year's "ten big films" and went on to set an all-time box office record for the People's Republic of US$38.6 million.[51] As Jonathan Noble has argued, because *Titanic* was distributed by the state-owned monopoly distributor China Film Corporation, its triumph provides a prime example of "how processes involving both the *commercialization of official discourse* and the *officialization of commercial practices* are informing the culture industry in China today."[52] Noble notes government rhetoric claimed this transnational "marketization" (*shichanghua*) aimed to stimulate competition and enable Chinese participation in the global economy. From this perspective, Zhang Yimou's *Hero* is the proof of the pudding.

We have already analyzed *Hero*'s controversial narrative in chapter 6. However, for many Chinese commentators its box office success was at least as significant as the film itself. The film was made on a budget of over US$30 million and brought in about that amount at the Chinese box office. However, it was seen by more people than saw *Titanic*.[53] Soon after, it was also exhibited successfully almost everywhere else (except the United States, where it hadn't opened yet), grossing over US$100 million, including US$32 million in Japan, a new record for an Asian film in that market.[54] When it was finally released in the United States in 2004, it opened at the top of the box office charts and added an extra US$53 million to the total.[55] Hu Ke of the China Film Art Research "believes that the success of *Hero* is evidence that the Chinese film industry is more than capable of facing up to the challenges brought about by membership in the WTO."[56]

If *Hero* enabled the Chinese cinema to move to become a producer as well as consumer of popular international cinema, then this is another example of resistance as the achievement of agency through appropriation and submission, like Bruce Lee's revitalization of Chinese masculinity. Xie Jin's *Opium War* marked the point where the rhetorical divide between the "epic film" and the "big film" disappeared, but *Hero* marks the total absorption of the "epic film" into the blockbuster model and China's first local blockbuster fully modeled on the contemporary Hollywood blockbuster. As Steve Neale has demonstrated, within Hollywood itself the idea of the blockbuster has a history during which the term has denoted different types of films and industry practices.[57] However, *Hero* has many of the characteristics associated with the contemporary Hollywood blockbuster.

First, as already noted, it had an enormous budget, and that money is visible on the screen as costumes, huge casts, and so forth. All of its major stars are internationally known: Tony Leung, Maggie Cheung, and Jet Li from Hong Kong, and Zhang Ziyi fresh from her triumph in Ang Lee's *Crouching Tiger, Hidden Dragon*. This facilitated the global reach of the film, which contemporary Hollywood blockbusters are also designed to achieve. The contemporary Hollywood blockbuster has specialized in action-centered films that were previously considered B genres, rather than the earlier more middle- to highbrow literary adaptations like *Gone with the Wind*. Similarly, if Xie Jin's *Opium War* was a highbrow historical drama, *Hero* is a martial arts action film. Finally, in terms of textual characteristics, as with most contemporary Hollywood blockbusters, not only is there a grand display of spending, but there is also a heavy reliance on very visible special effects.

The appropriation of the contemporary Hollywood blockbuster mode with *Hero* also extended to finances and marketing. Most notably, Miramax was reported to have paid the very high price of US$20 million for North American and European rights. But within China, the film's soundtrack and VCD/DVD distribution rights were also reportedly presold for US$7.2 million, another record figure.[58] As a result, Zhang Yimou was able to express satisfaction because "we'd recovered our costs before the movie was premiered."[59] Furthermore, just as with the major Hollywood blockbusters, the enormous amount of publicity enabled a vast series of ancillary products to be sold. For *Hero*, these included a documentary for television, a book version, a cartoon version, and even a series of postage stamps.[60]

Finally, the adoption of the contemporary Hollywood blockbuster model extended to a massive concern with the prevention of piracy in order to protect the massive investment in the film. *Hero* seems to have been much more successful in this regard than any other recent Chinese film. During the premiere of the film in Shenzhen, "Viewers could not take bags, cell phones, or watches into the theatre, and eyeglasses were checked for hidden micro-camcorders.... There was one security guard for every three members of the audience." Illegal Web sites were vigorously blocked.[61] At this point, two different modes of Chinese resistance within transnationalism came into conflict: the parasitic mode of piracy and the "if you can't beat 'em, join 'em" mode of the Chinese blockbuster. How this struggle will play out remains to be seen.

Although *Hero* marks a new departure for Zhang Yimou in many ways, in one important aspect it continues a pattern that he pioneered for People's Republic Chinese cinema. Like so many of his previous films, *Hero* tells a Chinese story for potential global consumption. In the early 1990s, this inscription of the national in the transnational was forced upon Zhang, when strict censorship after the Tiananmen Square massacre made it impossible for him to reach his Chinese audience. Today, it is levered by the integration of the Chinese film industry into the global film market. And ironically, it is by borrowing the techniques and models of the international film industry—Hollywood—that Zhang is able to regain the Chinese audience otherwise lost to domestic films.

Zhang Yimou's experience further demonstrates that the way the national is imagined in a film is not a natural expression of a national cultural essence for a preexisting national audience. Instead, both the audience itself and the way the national appears are conditioned by economic and industrial structures that—maybe now more than ever—are likely to be simultaneously national and transnational. It is this sense of the simultaneously national and transnational that we examine further here by looking at what may be the newest Chinese cinema, the reborn cinema of Singapore.

Singapore Stories: Transnational Cinematic Modes and National Images

Because of Singapore's free trade economy, the small domestic box office, and the local dominance of Hollywood, this new national film industry has been structured by its place within the transnational film economy from the beginning. Much the same could be said for Singapore itself, a new nation founded in 1965 and defining itself culturally and building itself economically in distinction from its past as part of British Malaya and most recently Malaysia. Ah Hock, the struggling grocery clerk protagonist of the retro-chic film *Forever Fever* (1998), seems to embody a national everyman in the 1970s. The distinguishing characteristic of Ah Hock—and by implication Singapore—is that he is a transnational and transcultural mimic. At the beginning of the film, Ah Hock is revealed to be a Bruce Lee addict, practicing *kung fu* in the supermarket aisles. When he gets home, he mimics Lee directly when watching *The Way of the Dragon* on television. As Ah Hock mirrors Lee's moves on the television, the film invokes a scene where Lee himself practices in front of the mirror. But as the film title suggests, Bruce Lee is soon superseded by John Travolta and the lure of the disco beat. That Ah Hock's story of self-discovery by mimicking others is a metaphor for Singapore's own scramble to maturity is made explicit in the film's opening intertitle: "In 1965, after 146 years of British rule, Singapore became an independent country. East Meets West in Singapore, where English is the official language and chopsticks the official utensil. In search of an identity, this young country finally found its feet when disco came to town ... " This is truly a case of the national formed in rather than against the transnational.

In addition to further analysis of *Forever Fever*, in this final section we also consider how the national appears in Singapore films according to their place within the film industry. We find three patterns. First, there are films that are limited to a local population by virtue of the high level of specific local knowledge required. These films are necessarily mass market and therefore working- and lower-middle-class films, because only they can find a large enough local box office to be economically viable. Second, there are low-budget, modernist films that are artistically avant-garde and socially and politically critical. These films circulate on the international festival circuit and are aimed at an educated elite. Finally, there is a group of films made with an international crossover market in mind—the new international commercial art cinema. We pay particular attention to *Forever Fever* to show how Singapore is commodified to appeal simultaneously to global and local audiences. All three modes enable Singaporean agency in the transnational through the production of national self-images, but whether they can be considered "resistant" (and to what) is more open to question.

Initially, we must acknowledge that to call the Singapore film industry either "Chinese" or "new" is not without complications. First, Singapore is not officially a Chinese nation-state, but a multiethnic state with four national languages: Malay, Mandarin Chinese, Tamil, and English. Nonetheless, three-quarters of the population are Chinese and Chinese culture is a powerful component of every Singaporean film. Singaporean film today is predominantly, but not exclusively, about Chinese stories. Second, today's Singaporean film industry is often referred to as "revived" rather than "new." However, both Singapore and the Singapore film industry today are so different from what came before that maybe the old film industry should be considered completely separately.

Filmmaking in Singapore began in the 1930s, when Loke Wan Tho's Cathay Organization began producing films, followed by the Shaw Brothers. The industry experienced a so-called "golden age" in the 1950s and early 1960s, when it was producing between fifteen and twenty films a year. Then it dwindled down to nothing in the 1970s, after which there was no consistent feature film production again until the mid-1990s. Although the producers in the earlier period were Chinese, the films were not. At that time, films made in Singapore were exclusively Malay and intended for an audience across the Malay Peninsula. Furthermore, until 1965, Singapore was simply a city on the Malay Peninsula, first in the British colony of Malaya, and after 1957 in the independent nation of Malaysia (an episode simply omitted in the opening intertitle of *Forever Fever*). Singapore only separated from Malaysia in 1965 and became an independent nation-state. The bad blood resulting from that event helped to spell the end of the early film industry in Singapore, as major Malay filmmakers moved to Kuala Lumpur.[62] In other words, although earlier filmmaking is part of the heritage of the city, it is more difficult to claim it as the heritage of the Singaporean nation-state,[63] and it is certainly not the largely Chinese cinema produced in Singapore today. Furthermore, while the early cinema could be claimed as a Malay "national cinema," it is only the new Singapore film industry that could be seen as a "Singapore national cinema."

However, the eventual appearance of the new Singapore film industry in the mid-1990s cannot simply be attributed to notions found in the old national cinemas approach, such as a maturing sense of national identity or a growing pressure for its cinematic expression. Rather, it must also be located in relation to structural transformation. This national film industry has been born and developed—like Singapore itself—within a transnational economy and with the support of national government policies. It seems that in its first decades the authoritarian Singapore government was not particularly perturbed by the absence of a national film industry. Indeed, a history of strict censorship indicates wariness of popular media.[64]

The country started out using its low-cost labor to assemble electronics goods. But per capita annual income rose from S$2,825 (US$1,653) in 1970 to S$21,657 (US$12,675) in 1990. In these circumstances, the government turned to high value-added industries that depended on specialized expertise.[65] In 1987 a committee of the city-state's Economic Development Board cited the anticipated exodus of Hong Kong filmmakers prior to 1997 as a reason for establishing an infrastructure for a local film industry.[66] Money was poured into education, studios, and postproduction facilities.[67] Even censorship rules and other bureaucratic restrictions were relaxed, as "part of the increasing attempts to situate Singapore as a regional center on the information highway."[68] In the mid-nineties, one or two feature films appeared every year from 1994, and annual production reached around ten by the beginning of the new millennium.

Perhaps the Singapore government's earlier wariness of film was not unwarranted, because the great bulk of new Singapore films do not represent the tidy town paradise the government likes to promote. (However, even this plays to the government's advantage, as it can suggest liberalization and tolerance.) Three patterns can be discerned in the new cinema. Chua Beng Huat has noted and analyzed two of these discourses. We add a third pattern, and also correlate all three to different structural positions in the transnational film industry to produce three modes.

In his writing on the new Singapore cinema, Chua Beng Huat has contrasted Jack Neo's films to those of Eric Khoo.[69] Both are pioneering figures who have found different kinds of success in the new Singapore cinema.

Neo is a television comedian known for his character Granny Liang.[70] He has capitalized on his local popularity by writing and directing a series of extremely successful films that express the frustrations of ordinary Singaporeans in comedy format. For example, his first hit, *Money No Enough*, was released in 1998 in the wake of the 1997 Asian economic crisis, and focused on the tribulations of three middle-aged men trying to get by in difficult times. It grossed S$5.84 million at the local box office, making it the third most successful film of all time after *Titanic* and *The Lost World: Jurassic Park*.[71]

Eric Khoo also focuses on the darker side of Singapore life, but not through mainstream comedy. Khoo was discovered as a local director of short films by the Singapore International Film Festival.[72] His first feature, *Mee Pok Man* (1995), depicts the desire of a noodle seller for a local sex worker. When she is killed in an accident, he takes her body home, and the film enters the territory of necrophilia.

Chua contrasts Neo and Khoo through a comparison of two other films—Neo's *I Not Stupid* (2001) and Khoo's *12 Storeys* (1997), in which Neo also has an acting role. *I Not Stupid* takes on Singapore's high-pressure education system by focusing on boys who are literally not making the grade. Khoo's *12 Storeys* puns on "story" and "storey" to look at the lives of inhabitants in one of the HDB (Housing Development Board) government housing blocks where the vast majority of Singaporeans live. Chua's comparison is enabled by a shared suicide subplot in both films. Unable to do well no matter how hard he tries and fearing his mother's reaction, one of the boys in *I Not Stupid* sets out to throw himself off an HDB block. In *12 Storeys*, a geeky young loner does throw himself off the HDB block where the film is set.

Chua points out that not only is the boy saved in *I Not Stupid*, but also the reasons for his depression are thoroughly communicated to the audience. In contrast, the suicide in *12 Storeys* is a "random happening," symptomatic of Khoo's "cold and objective, perhaps analytic lens, distant and unsympathetic to those who have fallen out of the 'success net.' "[73] In contrast, Neo's films are more empathetic and produced from within what is sometimes referred to as the "HDB heartland" culture. But as Chua also notes, whereas Khoo sustains his critical eye to the end, Neo, with his need for a happy ending, "can be said to have appropriated himself into a version of the 'success' myth."[74]

The distinctions Chua draws between Neo and Khoo correspond to the classic critical distinction between the popular catharsis of lowbrow commercial cinema and the critical modernism of highbrow art cinema. This in turn corresponds to different distribution and exhibition networks, which shape the films that get produced for them. Neo's films circulate primarily on the Singapore mainstream commercial market. They do not travel far. Khoo is much more of a festival filmmaker, which takes his films around the world but not to wide audiences. These economic factors correlate closely to the kind of Singapore that appears in their films.

First, Neo's films are packed full of local knowledge that makes them appealing to Singapore locals, but may make it hard for them to travel. Titles like *I No Stupid* and *Money No Enough* are in the local "Singlish," and Hokkienese dominates the dialogue. As Chua Beng Huat points out, both of these moves are a gesture of defiance against the government's preference for Standard English and Mandarin Chinese. Hokkienese is the dominant Chinese language in Singapore, especially among ordinary people as opposed to the elite. These ordinary people are also far more likely to speak Singlish than Standard English.[75] This is another instance of the complex politics of language and identity discussed in chapter 7, but this time extending to class as well as ethnicity. But in relation to film economics, these and other "local" characteristics are necessary for any film whose primary audience is Singaporean; they help it to appeal to a wide enough proportion of the city-state's limited population to become commercially viable. A film made in Standard English and/or Mandarin would have much more limited appeal. The ironic result of this is that the local characteristics that are therefore most likely to appear in Singapore films for Singapore audiences produce a national mirror image for Singapore's citizens, but one that is defined against the idealized images promoted by the government.

Furthermore, the very local Singapore characteristics that help to make Neo's films so popular with the HDB heartland also limit their ability to travel outside Singapore. To continue with the language example, much of the comedy in the films comes from Hokkienese puns, which even the majority of Chinese audiences elsewhere are unlikely to grasp. In contrast, although Eric Khoo's films may have many local elements, these are less incomprehensible to the international festival audience. Indeed, most international film festivals publicize the national origins of the films they show, creating a cinematic equivalent of the international food courts found in shopping malls.[76] In this context, the title of a film like *Mee Pok Man* intrigues with the promise of an exotic local specialty, which the foreign festival audience soon finds out refers to noodles that are indeed a Singapore dish. The theme of necrophilia also fits into the long festival tradition of pushing boundaries on sex and violence, at the same time as it limits its appeal to wider audiences, as does its bleak tone.

The popular mainstream and critical modernist festival films produce Singaporean national imageries that are not only different from the government's but also different from each other. However, it seems that both modes produce national images of Singapore that are recognizable (if not always acceptable) to many Singaporeans. There is, however, a third mode that has a more complex and ambivalent relationship to the local population. This mode produces films designed for the international commercial art cinema, including its local outlets in Singapore.

The distinction between the film festival circuit and the commercial art cinema is not absolute. However, it has been growing over the last decade or so. In the post–World War II era when film festivals were being founded around the world, a separate art cinema circuit developed in some countries to handle local demand for some of the mostly foreign films that were being shown in festivals only. More recently, however, the number of film festivals has grown. For the less commercial films on the festival circuit, that means demand is satiated entirely by the festivals. On the other hand, the existence of the art cinema circuit has led to more films being produced specifically with that outlet in mind. This in turn has led to the commercialization of the art cinema and adoption of the distribution and exhibition practices of the mainstream. Put simply, this could be called the "miramaximization" of the art cinema, after the company that has pioneered many of these developments.

Zhang Yimou's early 1990s films such as *Judou* and *Raise the Red Lantern* are prime examples of this international commercial art cinema. They were funded from outside China with foreign art cinema audiences in mind. The particular censorship circumstances of the post-Tiananmen period cut these films off from their local audiences. However, generally speaking, films circulated on the international art cinema circuit aim to appeal to both international and domestic audiences. Furthermore, the "international food court" principle of identifying films by nation applies to the international commercial art cinema just as it does to the film festival circuit. This encourages the makers of these films to try to find characteristically national imagery that is recognizable and acceptable to both local and international audiences, as well as being pleasurable and easily digested by as wide an audience as possible.

The first Singapore effort at making films for the international art cinema circuit was *Bugis Street* (1995). The film had a Hong Kong director, Yon Fan. It also featured an emerging Hollywood star, Hiep Thi Le, who had just appeared in Oliver Stone's *Heaven and Earth* (1993). Both these features were presumably intended to give the film greater international appeal as well as a regional "Asian" character. The film's setting was also presumably intended to work in this way. Bugis Street in the 1960s, when the film is set, was an internationally as well as locally known landmark. However, this may have been a mistake. For, if *Mee Pok Man* showed the seamy side of present-day Singapore, Bugis Street (both the film and the locale) represents a past that many Singaporeans may prefer to forget and many foreigners might find of rather particular appeal only. For, as the film reveals, *Bugis Street* was known for its local transvestite sex workers catering to foreign sailors who came to shore in Singapore. As a metaphor for the early stages of Singapore's development and its dependent relationship with Western capitalism, Bugis Street does not paint a pretty picture from the ultrarespectable perspective of middle-class Singapore today. Possibly, the filmmakers were trying to capitalize on another recent commercial international art cinema hit, the Australian film *The Adventures of Priscilla, Queen of the Desert* (1994). Certainly, it aimed for the same glam comedy feel. However, the film was not well received in Singapore,[77] and internationally it was largely confined to the gay and lesbian film festival circuit.[78]

The first Singapore film to break through internationally and the most successful to date also had a retro-chic appeal. This was *Forever Fever*, which was bought by Miramax for a reported US$4.5 million and distributed in the United States under the title *That's the Way I Like It*. The film also pursued what are sometimes called "international standards" in its production. Jack Neo's films may have Singlish titles, but Hokkienese dominates the dialogue. In contrast, *Forever Fever* features both Hokkienese and English—giving the film local authenticity and a Singapore flavor internationally—but favors the more easily understood Singlish over Hokkienese. Furthermore, instead of damaging the image of local authenticity by employing a foreign director as *Bugis Street* did, the writer and director was a local theater figure, Glen Goei, who had also had plenty of international professional experience. Foreign expertise was employed in less visible roles. Sound mixing was done in Australia. The cinematographer was Brian Breheny, known for his work on what seems to have been an important contemporary model for the commercial international art cinema, *The Adventures of Priscilla, Queen of the Desert*.[79]

FOREVER FEVER (A.K.A. *THAT'S THE WAY I LIKE IT*)

WRITTEN AND DIRECTED BY GLEN GOEI

Chinarunn Pictures and Tiger Tiger Productions, 1998

SYNOPSIS

In 1978, grocery clerk Ah Hock lives with his parents, his sister, and his medical student brother, Ah Beng. His parents adore successful Ah Beng. Ah Hock fantasizes about being Bruce Lee and buying a motorcycle. When he learns there is a cash prize, he enters a disco-dancing competition. During dance classes, he is drawn to childhood friend Mei, but she already has a rich boyfriend. Things do not look good for Ah Hock, but then he goes to see *Saturday Night Fever* and gets some personal tutoring from John Travolta.

Furthermore, opening the film by showing Ah Hock to be a Bruce Lee fan is also an astute move, enabling international audiences to relate to a distinctively Singaporean character through the common reference point of a global star. Lee is also an appropriate ideal for Ah Hock, because Ah Hock is portrayed very much as the underdog in these opening scenes. Like so many other Singapore films, the lead character of *Forever Fever* is someone overlooked by the Singapore economic miracle. His brother, Ah Beng, studying to be a doctor, is the success story in the family. Ah Hock is treated by his parents as an embarrassment. In the early scenes of the film, he comes home from working at the store. There, he has been humiliated by the manager and customers, including one rich young playboy who later crushes Ah Hock's bicycle with his red MG sports car and turns out to be Ah Hock's rival in love. However, his parents make him and his sister wait for Ah Beng to come home before the meal is served. Not only does Ah Hock himself mimic Bruce Lee, but the film mimics elements of the typical Bruce Lee film with this underdog narrative

However, the primary text to be mimicked is of course *Saturday Night Fever* and John Travolta. No matter that Ah Hock only sees *Saturday Night Fever* because the Lee film he meant to see has finished, or that even then he attends against his will, protesting that dance films are for "*ah-kua*" (queers). Soon, he is fascinated by Travolta. And instead of repeating Bruce Lee's "grasshopper"-style aphorisms, he finds himself following the instructions of his Indian disco dance teacher. This guru's words of wisdom include, "The more you dance, the more you romance" and "The more you shake it, the more you'll make it." Furthermore, in this hour of need, it is "John Travolta" who steps down from the silver screen to advise Ah Hock not only how to dress but also what to wear, and how to talk to girls. Correspondingly, the film itself mimics *Saturday Night Fever*'s plot, with Ah Hock's participation in the dance competition, and also its look and style, with seventies fashion and disco music pulsating from beginning to end.

However, it would be wrong to consider *Forever Fever* as simply an unthinking celebration of the abandonment of Chinese anti-imperialist cultural nationalism (Bruce Lee) and capitulation to American consumerist imperialism (Travolta). For Bruce Lee makes a comeback toward the end of the film. After he has won the dance competition, Ah Hock is set upon by his wealthy rival and a gang of thugs. As he lies on the ground writhing in pain, he remembers Bruce. Standing up, for a few moments Ah Hock becomes Bruce Lee again, recovering his mastery of the kicks, jumps, and screams he needs to flatten the bad guys. In fact, the film has already indicated that for Ah Hock, there is no East-West conflict. Even when he is having trouble learning to disco dance earlier in the film, it is Bruce Lee's maxim "Don't think, feel" that enables him to overcome his inhibitions.

FIGURE 8.3a In *Forever Fever* (1998), Ah Hock practices his *kung fu* at work …

FIGURE 8.3b … mimics Bruce Lee on the television at home …

FIGURE 8.3c … and catches disco fever on the dance floor.

This double mimicry of Lee and Travolta is an ingenious metaphorical structure in *Forever Fever*. First, because Bruce Lee and John Travolta are globally recognized, it enables audiences from everywhere to enter the world of the film with relative ease. Furthermore, it effectively suggests both Singapore's lineage and its survival tactic in the transnational capitalist order of appropriating whatever works. This mimicry becomes a process of hybrid identity-construction both for Ah Hock and, by inference, for the new nation-state of Singapore itself, empowering and enabling within the transnational flows of liberal capitalism. In this way, Ah Hock, Singapore—and Singapore's filmmakers—achieve agency.

However, does this process constitute resistance? Homi Bhabha has argued in his famous essay on colonialism and mimicry that although colonial mimicry demonstrates a certain submission to the colonial order, its inherent ambivalence can simultaneously constitute resistance. The colonial order encourages the colonized to aspire to be like the colonizer. But it rests upon the requirement that this aspiration never quite be realized—the colonial mimic will always be "not quite white." Resistance starts when, as a result of following the imperative to mimic, the colonized demands the things the colonizer would deny her or him, such as political sovereignty, for example.[80]

With Bhabha's essay in mind, it is tempting to declare the arrival of the latest Chinese film industry an act of mimicry as resistance, along with the export achievements of other Chinese cinemas in the last few years. However, whether this is true may not be easily determined. First, is there any evidence in the new global capitalist order today that the old Western imperialist powers or their transnational corporate inheritors are trying to block these achievements? Some might argue that the production and maintenance of a small export and local cinema at the same time that the mass market is decisively occupied by Hollywood constitutes a fig leaf covering up a more complete (neo)colonization. But even this argument is difficult to sustain once it is understood that these achievements make some formerly colonized achieve agency as players within the new transnational order, and that this order may be driven by corporations at least as much as by states. In the case of filmmakers, this manifests itself in transnational investment, talent, and markets that cut across nation-states.

Second, can the vectors of power be reduced only to the binary pair of former colonizer and colonized? Almost all the new Singapore films that have been successful at the box office, including those discussed here, do not present a particularly glamorous image of the city or one that conforms to the government's hopes. Ah Hock imitates Bruce Lee, but his enemies in *Forever Fever* are not foreign imperialists or foreigners at all. Instead, his primary rival is a class enemy and representative of the local Singapore elite. This shift seems to sum up the new national in the transnational. Bruce Lee himself deployed the rhetoric of resistance as rejection of the foreign, but produced this image as a global commodity. In contrast, in the world of Ah Hock, the transnational is no longer the old Western imperialist order but instead one in which—as symbolized by Bruce Lee's global circulation—Chinese already participate. His primary concern is not to reject it but to figure out how he can join it.

Chronology

Unless stated, entries refer to mainland China.

DATE	GENERAL HISTORY	CINEMA HISTORY
221–207 b.c.	The Qin dynasty unifies China, establishing the imperial system that ends in 1911.	Many films such as *Hero* retell the story of the unification of China under the First Emperor of Qin. (See chapter 6.)
1840–42 & 1856–1860	The Opium Wars 1 and 2: Britain enforces cession of Hong Kong "in perpetuity" (1842) and of Kowloon Peninsula (1860) until 1997, beginning a carve-up of the Chinese Qing empire by Western powers.	Films on the Opium Wars are a favorite topic for nationalist filmmakers. (See chapter 2.)
1885	Taiwan is made a province of the Qing empire.	
1895	Taiwan is ceded to Japan "in perpetuity" when Japan wins the Sino-Japanese war.	
1896		August 11 is the date of the first recorded film screening in Shanghai, by a foreign projectionist who shows Lumière films.
1900	The Boxer Rebellion, led by Christian-influenced rebels against the Manchu Qing dynasty, is suppressed by foreign powers, who then extract heavy indemnities from China.	
1903		China enters the film industry when Lin Zhushan brings a projector and films to Peking.

DATE	GENERAL HISTORY	CINEMA HISTORY
1905	Abolition of the imperial examination system. Sun Yat-sen forms the Alliance Society, precursor to the Kuomintang (KMT) Nationalist Party.	China's first film is produced in Beijing: the opera film, *Dingjun Mountain.* (See chapter 3.)
1909		Hong Kong produces its first films: the opera films, *Right a Wrong with Earthenware Dish* and *Stealing a Roasted Duck.* (See chapter 3.)
1911	The 1911 Revolution overthrows the Qing dynasty (1644–1911) and establishes the Republic of China (ROC) under the Kuomintang (KMT).	
1913		The first independent screenplay is filmed in Shanghai: *The Difficult Couple.* World War I disrupts supplies of film stock.
1916	The death of Yuan Shikai, president of ROC, leads to a loss of central authority and to the warlord era.	Zhang Shichuan establishes the first Chinese-owned film production company when film stocks are renewed.
1919	The May Fourth movement to modernize and revitalize China is launched to protest the Versailles Treaty, which gives Shandong Province to Japan. This heralds a modern, cultural renaissance based on the rejection of local "feudal" traditions and the appropriation of Western culture into Chinese culture.	
1921	The Chinese Communist Party (CCP) is established.	The first feature-length film is produced: *Yan Ruisheng.* Its success stimulates imitators.
1923	Sun Yat-sen and Chiang Kai-shek's KMT Nationalists establish links with Moscow, leading to a series of united front operations with the CCP.	Zhang Shichuan's film, *Orphan Rescues Grandfather,* is a box office hit that stimulates the Chinese film industry. (See chapter 6.)
1925	Death of Sun Yat-sen.	Martial arts films, costume films, and romances dominate the film industry. Almost none has survived. (See chapter 3.)
1927	Chiang Kai-shek seizes Shanghai and massacres the Communists. The united front between the KMT and CCP ends.	Soviet documentarist Bliokh films Chiang's massacre of the Chinese Communists.
1928	The warlord era ends with establishment of the KMT Nationalist government, led by Chiang Kai-shek.	

DATE	GENERAL HISTORY	CINEMA HISTORY
1929		The KMT introduce film censorship (see chapter 3).
1930	Urban revolts led by the Communists are a failure, which lays the foundation for Mao Zedong's later rural-based leadership.	Luo Mingyou sets up the Lianhua Studio, which becomes committed to the production of less commercial, more high-minded films. It also becomes the center for leftist film production. (See chapter 5.)
1931	Japan annexes Manchuria.	Mingxing Company premieres the first sound film, featuring opera: *Sing-Song Girl Red Peony*. (See chapter 3.) The League of Left-wing Dramatists is established, including filmmakers affiliated to the CCP. Martial arts films are banned as "feudal" and "realist" dramas about the sufferings of ordinary Chinese fill the screens. (See chapters 3, 4, and 5.)
1932	On the pretext of anti-Communist demonstrations, the Japanese bomb Shanghai. The Communists declare war on the Japanese, but the KMT government prefers appeasement.	Temporary disruption of the Shanghai-based film industry by the bombing, as depicted in *Center Stage*. (See chapter 5.)
1933	Further Japanese territorial encroachments in the north.	A large numbers of leftist films begin to appear, including *Little Toys* and *Spring Silkworms*. (See chapter 5.) The first Cantonese-language film is made in Shanghai: the Cantonese opera, *White Gold Dragon*. (See chapter 3.)
1934	The Communists under Mao begin the Long March to escape KMT leader Chiang Kai-shek's efforts to eliminate them.	Major leftist films are produced, including *The New Woman, The Goddess*, and *Big Road*. (See chapter 5.)
1935	The Long March ends in the guerrilla base of Yan'an. Mao Zedong takes control of the CCP and begins to assert independence from the Russian-dominated international socialist organization, Comintern.	The leftist film *Song of the Fishermen* wins China's first international film award at the Moscow Film Festival. Icon of the age and film star Ruan Lingyu commits suicide. (See chapter 5.)
1936	The Xi'an Incident. The warload Zhang Xueliang imprisons Chiang Kai-shek, effectively forcing him to focus his energies less on destroying the Communists and more on the Japanese.	*Tomboy*, a conservative, cross-dressing romance from Shanghai, is a box office hit. (See chapter 4.)

DATE	GENERAL HISTORY	CINEMA HISTORY
1937	China's Anti-Japanese War of Resistance begins. Japan takes over Shanghai, and at the end of the year carries out the Nanjing Massacre.	The leftist film *Street Angel* is made in Shanghai just before the Japanese takeover (see chapter 4). Chinese filmmakers disperse. Some follow the Nationalist government upriver to Wuhan and then Chongqing. Some flee to Hong Kong. Some join the Communists in Yan'an. Some stay on the "orphan island" of the foreign concession in Shanghai, and some work with the Japanese.
1938	The Nationalists set up government in Chongqing in the southwest.	Filmmakers with the KMT start producing patriotic war films.
1939	World War II begins in Europe.	Joris Ivens gives the Communist 8th Route Army its first 35mm camera. The first documentaries from the Communist mountain stronghold of Yan'an follow.
		The Japanese set up a film industry in Manchuria and take over the Shanghai film industry.
1941	Hong Kong falls to the Japanese.	
	America enters the war in the wake of the Japanese attack on Pearl Harbor.	
1942	Mao's *Talks on Literature and Art at the Yan'an [Yenan] Forum* set cultural policy for the Communists, based on the idea of the subordination of art to politics. (See chapter 3.)	
1943		Filmmakers in Shanghai work with the Japanese to make the Opium War film *Eternal Fame*. (See chapter 2.)
1945	End of WWII and the Anti-Japanese War of Resistance. Taiwan is returned to China; Hong Kong is returned to Britain.	
1946	Civil War between the KMT and the CCP begins. By 1946, 90% of Japanese settlers are expelled from Taiwan.	Progressive filmmakers return to Shanghai, take over Lianhua again, and determine to resist the KMT, later setting up the new Kunlun Studio as their base of operations.

DATE	GENERAL HISTORY	CINEMA HISTORY
1947	The Russians retreat from Manchuria, allowing the Communists to take it over and shift their attack to the north. In Taiwan, the KMT suppresses the February 28 rebellion against KMT rule. (See chapter 2.)	The Communists set up Northeast Film Studio at Xingshan. The war and class war epic, *A Spring River Flows East*, is made in Shanghai.
1948		China's first color film, *Remorse at Death*, incorporates Beijing opera. (See chapter 3.) *Spring in a Small Town* signals the end of an era in mainland China. (See chapter 4.)
1949	The People's Republic of China (PRC) is established in October under Chairman Mao Zedong. Land reform is enforced throughout China. Chiang Kai-shek and the KMT retreat to Taiwan, with Taipei as the "provisional" capital of the ROC.	Northeast Film Studio moves to Changchun and work begins on its first feature: *Bridge*. The Taiwan film industry is based around documentary filmmakers who retreat to Taiwan with the KMT. The first in a series of over 80 Wong Fei-hung films is made in Hong Kong. (See chapter 6.)
1950	Beginning of the Korean War. China invades Tibet.	Remaining American films are withdrawn from circulation. Northeast Film Studio produces *The White-haired Girl*, an opera film about land reform. (See chapter 3.) In Hong Kong, Bruce Lee debuts in *The Kid*. (See chapter 4.)
1951	Crackdown against counter-revolutionaries in the PRC. Tibet is annexed as an autonomous region of the PRC.	Campaign against the film, *The Life of Wu Xun*. (See chapter 3.)
1953	Launch of the first 5-year plan. End of the Korean War.	Complete nationalization of the film industry achieved, and efforts made to extend film distribution beyond the major cities using mobile projection teams.
1954	Chinese leaders announce that liberation of Taiwan is official policy.	

DATE	GENERAL HISTORY	CINEMA HISTORY
1956	Hungarian Uprising against Russian puppet government.	In the PRC, the Hundred Flowers Campaign, a liberalization in literature and the arts, results in production of satirical film comedies and articles criticizing previous films for their un-popularity at the box office. Beijing Film Studio produces *New Year's Sacrifice* (see chapter 4).
		The first Taiwanese-language film is made in Taiwan: the *gezaixi* opera film, *Xue Pinggui and Wang Baochuan* (see chapter 3). Taiwanese-language cinema takes off (see chapter 7).
		Descendents of the Yellow Emperor is made, the earliest surviving Taiwan film (see chapter 7).
1957	The Anti-Rightist Campaign is launched to check the "excesses" of the Hundred Flowers. Many prominent intellectual and cultural figures are condemned.	Satires are banned in the People's Republic and succeeded by Maoist orthodoxy.
1958	Sino-Soviet split, precipitated by Khruschev's "revisionist" Anti-Stalin stance. The Great Leap Forward is launched with the aim of forcing rapid modernization by sheer human effort.	Soviet socialist realism is replaced by the Chinese combination of "revolutionary realism and revolutionary romanticism" as the model in all the arts, including filmmaking. (See chapter 3.)
1959	The Great Leap Forward continues.	Film production is also increased massively, including *Song of Youth* (see chapter 5) and large numbers of revolutionary documentaries.
1960–61	The excesses of the Great Leap Forward lead to famine and then a reduction in Mao's power.	Relaxation of Maoist line in literature and art leads to the replacement of pure proletarian heroes with more ambiguous "middle characters." (See chapter 5.)
1963	Jiang Qing (Mme Mao) advances "reform" of the theater, gradually replacing classical productions with revolutionary operas. (See chapter 3.)	The Chinese minority nationalities film *Serfs* on Tibet is released (see chapter 7). The Shaw Brothers (HK) opera film, *Love Eterne*, becomes one of China's best-loved films outside the mainland (see chapter 3). Healthy realism is launched in Taiwan (see chapter 4).
1965	In the PRC, press discussion of "capitalist roaders" and the need to resort to force mark the beginnings of Mao's efforts to reassert power.	In Taiwan, healthy realism produces two box office hits: *Oyster Girl* and *Beautiful Duckling* (1965). (See chapter 4.)

DATE	GENERAL HISTORY	CINEMA HISTORY
1966	The Cultural Revolution (1966–1976) is launched in the PRC.	Feature film production ceases in the PRC, and the film industry becomes a particular target for Mao's wife and former starlet Jiang Qing. Many industry figures are "sent down" to the countryside or imprisoned. Many die or commit suicide.
1968	The People's Liberation Army (PLA) restores order after factional fighting among Mao's Red Guards has reached dangerous levels. Deng Xiaoping is expelled from the Party.	
1970		Feature-length production recommences with films that record stage productions of Jiang Qing's revolutionary operas, such as *Taking Tiger Mountain by Strategy* (1970) and *Azalea Mountain* (1974). (See Chapter 3.)
1971	Lin Biao, head of the PLA and Mao's successor, is eliminated in a plane "accident." The PRC becomes the legitimate representative of China at the UN; Taiwan is expelled.	Bruce Lee's *The Big Boss* becomes number one at the Hong Kong box office. (See chapter 8.)
1972	American President Nixon visits China.	
1973	PRC Premier Zhou Enlai engineers the return of Deng Xiaoping.	Although highly controlled, regular feature-film production recommences. Bruce Lee, Asia's first international superstar, dies suddenly in Hong Kong. (See chapter 8.)
1975	KMT leader Chiang Kai-shek dies in Taiwan and is succeeded by his son, Chiang Ching-kuo.	Taiwan's martial arts movie *A Touch of Zen* wins an international award at Cannes (see chapter 3).
1976	Zhou Enlai dies in January. Mao dies in September. The Gang of Four (including Jiang Qing) falls in October. Hua Guofeng takes over from Mao.	Film production falls again, but rapidly returns to pre–Cultural Revolution levels.
1978	Deng Xiaoping emerges as prime leader after 3rd Plenum of 11th CCP Central Committee. Democracy Wall starts up. President Carter "de-recognizes" the ROC to establish diplomatic ties with the PRC.	Cultural relaxation leads to criticism of the Cultural Revolution in many films. The Beijing Film Academy reopens and takes in a new class of filmmakers, later to be known as the "Fifth Generation." Jackie Chan's *Drunken Master* is number two at the Hong Kong box office. (See Chapter 6.)

DATE	GENERAL HISTORY	CINEMA HISTORY
1979	After the rehabilitation of various pre–Cultural Revolution figures at the beginning of the year, the Party cracks down on liberalization, closing down Democracy Wall in December.	Films like *Troubled Laughter* lead the way in the filmic translation of "the four modernizations" with zooms, multiple flashbacks, and other techniques hitherto rare. Hong Kong's New Wave cinema takes off, with such films as *The Butterfly Murders* and *The Secret*.
1980	Zhao Ziyang replaces Hua Guofeng as premier. The trial of the Gang of Four (including Jiang Qing) is held in Beijing, inaugurating a new system of socialist law. (See chapter 6.)	*The Legend of Tianyun Mountain* extends criticism to the Anti-Rightist Campaign of 1958. Gangster films take off in Hong Kong. (See chapter 6.)
1981		*Bitter Love* (1980) is banned. Film experimentation slows. Hong Kong's New Wave continues with Allen Fong's maiden feature, *Father and Son*. (See chapter 6.)
1982	People's Republic leader Deng Xiaoping puts forward the concept of "one country, two systems." Britain and China begin talks on Hong Kong's future.	The Fifth Generation graduates from the Beijing Film Academy. The New Taiwan Cinema movement (1982–1986) is established.
1983	Anti-"spiritual pollution" campaign.	Various "violent" or "vulgar" films are banned. Wu Tianming becomes head of Xi'an Film Studio and pursues a policy of subsidizing experimental work such as *Horse Thief* (see chapter 7) with ruthlessly commercial films, which later makes the studio a haven for the Fifth Generation and a box office challenge to Shanghai Film Studio.
1984	The "responsibility system" devolves power in the PRC. A market economy is tried in the cities and countryside. Britain and China sign the Joint Declaration on Hong Kong, stating that China will resume sovereignty on July 1, 1997.	Two Fifth Generation films are produced: *One and Eight* and *Yellow Earth*. *One and Eight* is banned from export. (See chapter 2.)
1985		*Yellow Earth* is ignored in China, but it is a success overseas, first in Hong Kong in 1985 and then on the international festival circuit. It launches China's New Wave. (See chapters 2 and 4.)

DATE	GENERAL HISTORY	CINEMA HISTORY
1986		Xi'an Film Studio produces *Horse Thief* on the Tibetan nationality minority. (See chapter 7.)
1987	Taiwan lifts martial law, imposed after the February 28 Incident of 1947.	
1988	Runaway inflation promotes dissatisfaction among the urban workforce in the People's Republic. ROC President Chiang Ching-kuo dies and is succeeded by Lee Teng-hui.	*Red Sorghum* wins the Golden Bear at Berlin and is the first Fifth Generation film to be a major hit at home. (See chapter 5.)
1989	Students demanding democracy in the People's Republic are joined by dissatisfied urban workers. The army responds with the Tiananmen Square massacre and martial law. A million people protest the massacre in Hong Kong.	Wu Tianming (head of the Xi'an Film Studio) and Chen Kaige (director of *Yellow Earth*) are in the United States at the time and remain abroad. Tian Zhuangzhuang (director of *Horse Thief*) returns and joins other colleagues still in China. Zhang Yimou makes *Judou*, which is banned in China but later nominated for an Oscar (see chapter 5). The Taiwan film *City of Sadness* (about the February 28 Incident, 1947) wins the Golden Lion at Venice (see chapter 2). Hong Kong's gangster film *The Killer* becomes an international hit (see chapter 6).
1990	Martial law is lifted in the People's Republic. Beijing promulgates the Basic Law of the Hong Kong Special Administrative Region (SAR) of the PRC.	
1991		*Raise the Red Lantern* (1990) by Zhang Yimou is banned in China but wins numerous overseas awards. (See chapter 5.)
1992	Deng Xiaoping goes on a southern tour to relaunch his economic programs and promote the market economy. Christopher Patten becomes the last governor of Hong Kong.	The ban on Zhang Yimou's films is lifted with the release of *The Story of Qiu Ju* (see chapter 6). *Center Stage*, linking 1930s Shanghai film and contemporary Hong Kong film, is made in Hong Kong (see chapter 5).
1993	Jiang Zemin becomes president of China.	*Wedding Banquet* leads to international prestige for Taiwan director Ang Lee (see chapter 7).
1996	Lee Teng-hui wins Taiwan's first popular presidential election.	

DATE	GENERAL HISTORY	CINEMA HISTORY
1997	Deng Xiaoping dies. Hong Kong returns to China under Chief Executive Tung Chee-hwa.	Xie Jin's *The Opium War* marks the return of Hong Kong to China in 1997. (See chapter 2.)
1998		*Forever Fever* is the first Singaporean film to break into the international market. (See chapter 8.)
1999	Macau returns to China, after 400 years of occupation by Portugal.	
2000	The KMT loses Taiwan's general election. Chen Shui-bian becomes Taiwan's first non-KMT president.	*In the Mood for Love* (Hong Kong) wins numerous awards, including at Cannes and HKFA. (See chapter 2.)
2001	China joins the World Trade Organization.	*Crouching Tiger, Hidden Dragon* wins four Oscars. (See chapter 6.)
2002		*Hero* is premiered at the Great Hall of the People and becomes China's biggest ever blockbuster. (See chapters 6 and 8.)
2003	Hu Jintao becomes president of China. In October, China launches its first man into space in the rocket *Shenzhou 5*.	
2005		Celebrations of the centenary of Chinese cinema are held around the world.

Notes

1. Introduction: Cinema and the National

1. In the light of the tensions between the People's Republic of China and those favoring Taiwan independence, the term "Chinese-language film" has been used to sidestep the possibility of seeming to endorse or having to oppose the "one China" claims of the People's Republic. However, not all the Chinese films we examine in this book are in Chinese. Therefore, we have continued to use the term *Chinese,* but in a cultural sense that recognizes its different facets and does not imply affiliation to any nation-state on our part.

2. Steve Fore has analyzed Chan's career trajectory and transformation at length in "Jackie Chan and the Cultural Dynamics of Global Entertainment" and "Life Imitates Entertainment: Home and Dislocation in the Films of Jackie Chan."

3. Bob the moo, "Awful dubbing, awful acting but good action."

4. Prasenjit Duara argues that Hegel's remark that the British defeat of China was necessary implies two things: first, only territorial nations can participate in the world system, and second, these territorial nations assumed the freedom to destroy other polities, such as tribal systems and empires. Duara, "The Regime of Authenticity: Timelessness, Gender, and National History in Modern China," 289.

5. Mitsuhiro Yoshimoto, "The Difficulty of Being Radical: The Discipline of Film Studies and the Postcolonial World Order," 338.

6. *Republic of China Yearbook 1991–92,* 141. Thank you to Bruce Jacobs for this citation.

7. Sheldon Hsiao-peng Lu, "Historical Introduction: Chinese Cinemas (1896–1996) and Transnational Film Studies," in Lu, ed., *Transnational Chinese Cinemas: Identity, Nationhood, Gender,* 1.

8. Lu, "Historical Introduction," 25.

9. Mohammed A. Bamyeh, "Transnationalism," 1.

10. Masao Miyoshi, "A Borderless World? From Colonialism to Transnationalism and the Decline of the Nation-State," 86–87.

11. See, for example, Ulf Hannerz, *Transnational Connections: Culture, People, Places,* 6; and Prasenjit Duara, "Transnationalism and the Predicament of Sovereignty: China 1900–1945," 1030.

12. Edward Said, *Orientalism*; Samuel Huntington, "The Clash of Civilizations?"; Stephen Uhalley Jr., " 'Greater China': The Contest of a Term"; Tu Wei-ming, "Cultural China: The Periphery as the Center."

13. Benedict Anderson, *Imagined Communities: Reflections on the Origin and Spread of Nationalism.*

14. Michael Walsh, "National Cinema, National Imaginary," p. 6.

15. Anderson, *Imagined Communities*, 20–28.

16. Michael Hardt and Antonio Negri, *Empire.*

17. Homi K. Bhabha, "DissemiNation: Time, Narrative, and the Margins of the Modern Nation," in Bhabha, ed., *Nation and Narration*, 297.

18. Ann Anagnost, *National Past-Times: Narrative, Representation, and Power in Modern China*, 2.

19. Judith Butler, *Excitable Speech: A Politics of the Performative.* On drag, see Judith Butler, *Gender Trouble: Feminism and the Subversion of Identity.*

20. Tsung-I Dow, "The Confucian Concept of a Nation and Its Historical Practice."

21. All these factors are mentioned and the third is particularly emphasized in Andrew Higson, "The Concept of National Cinema."

22. Yingjin Zhang, *Chinese National Cinema.* As we accept the importance of this approach but do not follow it here, we believe Zhang's work can be an important complement to our own.

23. Walsh, "National Cinema, National Imaginary."

24. Yingjin Zhang, *Screening China: Critical Interventions, Cinematic Reconfigurations, and the Transnational Imaginary in Contemporary Chinese Cinema.*

25. Rey Chow, "Introduction: On Chineseness as a Theoretical Problem," 4–5.

26. Yeh Yueh-Yu, "Defining Chineseness"; and Yeh Yueh-Yu and Abe Mark Nornes, "Introduction" to *Narrating National Sadness* (1998).

27. Chow, "Introduction: On Chineseness," 9–10. See also Stephanie Donald, "Women Reading Chinese Films: Between Orientalism and Silence."

2. Time and the National: History, Historiology, Haunting

1. Mao dates the end of feudal society and the emergence of semifeudal, semicolonial China to the Opium War of 1840 in *The Chinese Revolution and the Chinese Communist Party.*

2. Robert A. Rosenstone, "The Historical Film: Looking at the Past in a Postliterate Age," 54.

3. Andrew H. Plaks, "Towards a Critical Theory of Chinese Narrative," in Plaks, ed., *Chinese Narrative: Critical and Theoretical Essays*, 312.

4. Traditional and modern examples are official historiography in biographical form (*jizhuanti*), historical biography (*zhuan*), unauthorized or fictional biography (*waizhuan*), tales of marvels (*chuanqi*) and the historical novel (*Shuihuzhuan* or *Water Margin*). Also see Plaks, "Towards a Critical Theory," 318–19. For further analysis of the relationship between fiction and historiography, see Sheldon Hsiao-peng Lu, *From Historicity to Fictionality: The Chinese Poetics of Narrative.*

5. Dai Jinhua, *A handbook of film theory and criticism* (in Chinese), 169.

6. Duara, "The Regime of Authenticity," 289. Partha Chatterjee has traced the same defensive logic in the Indian move from Puranic to nationalist historiography in chapters 4 and 5 of *The Nation and its Fragments: Colonial and Postcolonial Histories.*

7. Maureen Robertson, "Periodization in the Arts and Patterns of Change in Traditional Chinese Literary History," 11.

8. Reinhart Koselleck's *Futures Past: On the Semantics of Historical Time* argues the same was true of European history before the modern mode came to dominate.

9. Q. Edward Wang, *Inventing China Through History: The May Fourth Approach to Historiography*, 3.

10. Benedict Anderson, *Imagined Communities: Reflections on the Origin and Spread of Nationalism*, 19, cited in Homi K. Bhabha, "Introduction: Narrating the Nation," in Bhabha, ed., *Nation and Narration*, 1. This is misquoted in Bhabha, with "nations" appearing as "nation states," but this may be a more precise way of stating the point.

11. Chow, "Introduction: On Chineseness," 4–5.

12. Ann Anagnost, "Making History Speak," in *National Past-times*, 17–44.

13. Chen Da, "A call to national consciousness: on seeing the film, *The Opium War*" (in Chinese), 14. In both quotations, the original Chinese term used for "nation" (*minzu*) specifically designates the national people rather than the nation-state.

14. Sigmund Freud, "Analysis of a Phobia in a Five-Year-Old Boy ('Little Hans')."

15. Jacques Lacan, "The Mirror Stage as Formative of the Function of the I."

16. Laura Mulvey draws on Freud's *Three Essays on Sexuality* to make the classic statement in film studies of this thesis in "Visual Pleasure and Narrative Cinema." For further discussion, see ch. 4 (this volume).

17. Prasenjit Duara, *Rescuing History from the Nation: Questioning Narratives of Modern China*, 4.

18. Cheng Jihua et al., "The 'Orphan Island' film movement and the occupation regime's monopoly over the cinema," in *The history of the development of the Chinese cinema* (in Chinese), vol. 2:117.

19. David Desser, "From the Opium War to the Pacific War: Japanese Propaganda Films of World War II." See also Washitani Hana, "*The Opium War* and the Cinema Wars: A Hollywood in the Greater East Asian Co-Prosperity Sphere."

20. This scholarship is covered in the latest (and most thoroughly researched) intervention into the debate: Poshek Fu, "The Struggle to Entertain: The Politics of Occupation Cinema, 1941–1945," in *Between Shanghai and Hong Kong: The Politics of Chinese Cinemas*, 93–132.

21. Freda Freiberg, "*China Nights* (Japan, 1940): The Sustaining Romance of Japan at War."

22. Rebecca E. Karl, "The Burdens of History: *Lin Zexu* (1959) and *The Opium War* (1997)," 236.

23. The literature on this topic forms a vast and contested debate, but foundational writings on the how cinematic rhetoric may position spectators includes Jean-Pierre Oudart, "The System of the Suture," and Mulvey, "Visual Pleasure and Narrative Cinema."

24. The standard analysis of the classical cinema's primary features remains David Bordwell, "The Classical Hollywood Style," in David Bordwell, Janet Staiger, and Kristin

Thompson, eds., *The Classical Hollywood Cinema: Film Style and Mode of Production to 1960*, 1–84.

25. Ron Suskind, "A Plunge into the Present," 89. The title's consignment of those living outside Western culture to the past repeats the refusal—also typical of this modern and colonial mode—of "coeval" coexistence. See Johannes Fabian, *Time and the Other: How Anthropology Makes Its Object*. Philip Rosen traces the critique of modern historical thinking and its intimate connection to colonialism to Claude Lévi-Strauss's attack on Jean-Paul Sartre in *The Savage Mind* in *Change Mummified: Cinema, Historicity, Theory*, xiii. For a lively direct account of the cultural and historical specificity of understandings of time, see Anthony Aveni, *Empires of Time: Calendars, Clocks, and Cultures*.

26. Trinh T. Minh-ha, "Truth and Fact: Story and History," in *Woman, Native, Other: Writing Postcoloniality and Feminism*, 119–21.

27. Vivian Sobchak, "Introduction: History Happens," in Sobchak, ed., *The Persistence of History: Cinema, Television, and the Modern Event*, 4.

28. Ann Curthoys and John Docker, "Is History Fiction?"

29. Plaks, "Towards a Critical Theory," 314.

30. Lionel Gossman, "History and Literature: Reproduction or Signification," 5, cited in Curthoys and Docker, "Is History Fiction?" 14.

31. Nicholas B. Dirks, "History as a Sign of the Modern," 25.

32. Wang, *Inventing China Through History*, 14.

33. Of course, settler nation-states, such as the United States of America or Australia, must acknowledge their newness. But for them, previously existing monarchies are not the competing polities, but rather those of prior inhabitants.

34. Johannes Fabian, "Time and Movement in Popular Culture," in *Moments of Freedom: Anthropology and Popular Culture*, 88.

35. For further discussion of the changes at this time, see Chris Berry, "Market Forces: China's 'Fifth Generation' Faces the Bottom Line," in Berry, ed., *Perspectives on Chinese Cinema*.

36. Zhang Xudong discusses the films in these terms in *Chinese Modernism in the Era of Reforms*.

37. Yomi Braester, *Witness Against History: Literature, Film, and Public Discourse in Twentieth-Century China*.

38. Crucially for the survival of the film, China's conservative censors would be among those least likely to perceive this metaphorical possibility. Furthermore, given that even perceiving such a possibility would breach a fundamental assumption of Chinese revolutionary discourse, it is unlikely that they would admit to perceiving it.

39. This experience is detailed in Ni Zhen, *Memoirs from the Beijing Film Academy: The Origins of China's Fifth Generation Filmmakers*.

40. Fifth Generation films are not the only mainland examples of critical historiology. Chris Berry discusses the sharing of memories of postrevolutionary suffering in the films of the late 1970s in *Postsocialist Cinema in Post-Mao China: The Cultural Revolution After the Cultural Revolution*.

41. Chen Kuan-Hsing discusses other films that recover subaltern memory from both sides of Taiwan's divide between locals and "mainlanders" in "Why is 'Great Reconciliation'

Im/possible? De-Cold War/decolonization, or modernity and its tears." Also in abbreviated form in Chris Berry and Feii Lu, eds., *Island on the Edge: Taiwan New Cinema and After*.

42. The reorientation and democratization of Taiwan since the late 1980s has changed this situation. What was New Park near the Presidential Palace has been renamed Peace Park and is home to a memorial to the victims of the February 28 Incident. See Fran Martin, *Situating Sexualities: Queer Representation in Taiwanese Fiction, Film, and Public Culture*, 74–78.

43. The reaction is discussed in Robert Chi, "Getting It on Film: Representing and Understanding History in *A City of Sadness*." Chi gives the box office statistics on p. 47. A primary example of the critique of the film available in English is Liao Ping-hui, "Passing and Re-articulation of Identity: Memory, Trauma, and Cinema."

44. David Bordwell, *Ozu and the Poetics of Cinema*, 120–42.

45. On Mizoguchi's long takes, see Donald Kirihara, *Patterns of Time: Mizoguchi and the 1930s*, 125–29.

46. Abe Mark Nornes and Yeh Yueh-yu, "Behind City of Sadness," 1994.

47. Nick Browne, "Hou Hsiao-hsien's *Puppetmaster*: The Poetics of Landscape."

48. Esther C. M. Yau, "*Yellow Earth*: Western Analysis and a Non-Western Text."

49. Rey Chow, "Silent Is the Ancient Plain: Music, Filmmaking, and the Concept of Social Change in the New Chinese Cinema," in *Primitive Passions: Visuality, Sexuality, Ethnography, and Contemporary Chinese Cinema*, 79–107.

50. Françoise Proust, *L'Histoire á Contretemps*.

51. Benedict Anderson, *The Spectre of Comparisons*. See also Pheng Cheah, *Spectral Modernity: Passages of Freedom from Kant to Postcolonial Literatures of Liberation*.

52. Kim Soyoung and Chris Berry, " 'Suri Suri Masuri': The Magic of the Korean Horror Film: A Conversation," 53.

53. Bliss Cua Lim, "Spectral Times: The Ghost Film as Historical Allegory," 289, 292.

54. Ackbar Abbas, *Hong Kong: Culture and the Politics of Disappearance*, 39–44; Rey Chow, "A Souvenir of Love," in *Ethics After Idealism: Theory—Culture—Ethnicity—Reading*, 133–48; Audrey Yue, "Preposterous Horror: On *Rouge, A Chinese Ghost Story*, and Nostalgia."

55. Feii Lu, "Another Cinema: *Darkness and Light*," in Chris Berry and Feii Lu.

56. Abbas, *Hong Kong*, 24.

57. Tony Rayns, "The Innovators, 1990–2000: Charisma Express," 36.

58. Lim, "Spectral Times," 54.

59. Tony Rayns, "Poet of Time," 12–14.

60. For an explanation of "step-printing" and "smudge-motion," see Janice Tong, "*Chungking Express*: Time and Its Dislocation," in Chris Berry, ed., *Chinese Films in Focus: 25 New Takes*, 50.

61. David Bordwell, *Planet Hong Kong: Popular Cinema and the Art of Entertainment*, 274.

62. Bordwell, *Planet Hong Kong*, 280.

63. Two extended examples of allegorical readings of Wong's films are Lisa Odham Stokes and Michael Hoover, *City on Fire: Hong Kong Cinema*, and Curtis Tsui, "Subjective Culture and History: The Ethnographic Cinema of Wong Kar-wai."

64. Jeremy Tambling, *Wong Kar-wai's "Happy Together*," 15.

65. Stephen Teo suggests this "restraint" is "ennobling" and "poignant," constituting "a touching reminder of the didactic tradition in Chinese melodrama" ("Wong Kar-wai's *In the Mood for Love:* Like a Ritual in Transfigured Time").

66. Bordwell, *Planet Hong Kong,* 266.

67. Teo, "Wong Kar-wai's *In the Mood for Love*"; Audrey Yue, "*In the Mood for Love:* Intersections of Hong Kong Modernity," in Berry, ed., *Chinese Films in Focus.*

68. Ewa Mazierska and Laura Rascaroli, "Trapped in the Present: Time in the Films of Wong Kar-wai," 2.

69. Mazierska and Rascaroli, "Trapped in the Present," 4.

70. Tong, "*Chungking Express,*" 49–50.

3. Operatic Modes: Opera Film, Martial Arts, and Cultural Nationalism

1. Wade Major, " 'Tiger' Time," 31.

2. David Bordwell, for example, comments, "Hong Kong filmmakers, probably drawing from indigenous Chinese traditions of theatre and martial arts, have developed a rhythmic conception of expressive movement." The rhythm is in fact central to the operatic mode across all Chinese cinemas. Bordwell, "Transcultural Spaces: Toward a Poetics of Chinese Film," 13.

3. Luo Yijun, "A preliminary discussion of national style in film" (in Chinese), 268–69.

4. Geremie Barmé, "Persistence de la tradition au 'royaume des ombres,' " 113.

5. Lu Hongshi, "Evaluations of Ren Qingtai and first Chinese films" (in Chinese), 86.

6. Sek Kei, "Thoughts on Chinese Opera and the Cantonese Opera Film," 16.

7. Stephen Teo, *Hong Kong Cinema,* 111. While the statements by both Teo and Sek Kei (note above) refer to Cantonese opera film and Hong Kong martial arts, they apply more generally to the transformation of twentieth-century art and literature, as recognized in Mao Zedong's famous "Talks at the Yan'an [Yenan] Forum on Literature and Art" (1942), for example. For the distinction between cultural and political nationalism, see Anthony D. Smith, *National Identity,* and John Hutchinson, "Re-interpreting Cultural Nationalism," 392–407.

8. Paul Pickowicz, *Marxist Literary Thought in China: The Influence of Chü Ch'iu-pai [Qu Qiubai],* 99.

9. For example, Teo, *Hong Kong Cinema.* See references to discussions of Hong Kong martial arts films later in this chapter and throughout the other chapters.

10. Tom Gunning, "Early American Cinema," 255.

11. Thomas Elsaesser, "General Introduction," 1.

12. Tom Gunning, "The Cinema of Attractions," 58–59.

13. Li Suyuan and Hu Jubin, *Chinese Silent Film History,* 39.

14. Zhong Dafeng, Zhen Zhang, and Yingjin Zhang, "From *Wenmingxi* [Civilized Play] to *Yingxi* [Shadowplay]," 53; Chen Xihe, "Shadowplay," 192–204. Chen calls for "an archaeological" comparative study of Chinese film aesthetics.

15. Li Suyuan, "About film theories in early China" (in Chinese), 25.

16. Bai Jingshen, "Throw Away the Walking Stick of Drama," 5–9.

17. Li, "About film theories in early China" (in Chinese), 22. Li analyses three categories of terms used to denote early film. One of these, the northern word "electric shadows" (*dianying*), is the term used today.

18. Cheng, *The history of the development of Chinese cinema* (in Chinese), 2:8–9n4.

19. Li, "About film theories in early China" (in Chinese), 22.

20. The films are *Dingjun Mountain*, Beijing (1905), and *Right a Wrong with Earthenware Dish* and *Stealing a Roasted Duck*, Hong Kong (1909).

21. The first Cantonese film was of Cantonese opera, *White Gold Dragon* (1933), made in Shanghai; it broke all box office records in Hong Kong and Guangdong (Teo, *Hong Kong Cinema*, 40). For a history of Taiwanese-language films, see Oral Cinema History Unit, *The era of Taiwanese-language films* (in Chinese).

22. Luo, "A preliminary discussion" (in Chinese), 273–74.

23. Gunning, "Early American Cinema," 263.

24. Verina Glaessner, *Kung fu: Cinema of Vengeance*, 7–14.

25. Lu, "Evaluations" (in Chinese), 86.

26. Ibid., and Barmé, "Persistence de la tradition au 'royaume des ombres,'" 114.

27. Hu Ke, "Hong Kong Cinema in the Chinese Mainland (1949–1979)," 16.

28. Teo, *Hong Kong Cinema*, 77–78.

29. Rick Lyman, "Watching Movies with Ang Lee."

30. Lin Nien-tung, "Some Problems in the Study of Cantonese Films of the 1950s," 32.

31. Sek Kei, "Li Hanxiang," 93.

32. Wu Hao, "The Legend and Films of Huang Fei-hong," 101. See also Hector Rodriguez, "Hong Kong Popular Culture as an Interpretative Arena: The Huang Feihong Film Series," 6. For a Peking opera–Hong Kong martial arts family tree, see Bey Logan, *Hong Kong Action Cinema*, 11.

33. Stephen Teo, "Only the Valiant: King Hu and His *Cinema Opera*," 19–24. See also Mary Farquhar, "*A Touch of Zen*: Action in Martial Arts Movies," 167–74.

34. Yamada Hirokazu and Koyo Udagawa, "King Hu's Last Interview," 75."

35. The PRC government supported this genre in the 1950s and 1960s. See Yingjin Zhang and Zhiwei Xiao, *Encyclopaedia of Chinese Film*, 167.

36. For example, *Sing-Song Girl Red Peony* (1931) and *Two Stage Sisters* (1964).

37. See Ben Xu, "*Farewell My Concubine* and Its Nativist Critics," 155–70.

38. Elsaesser, "General Introduction," 4.

39. Lu, "Evaluations" (in Chinese), 82. Lu corrects many factual errors, including miscalling him "Ren Fengtai."

40. Ibid., 83.

41. Charles Musser, "The Nickelodeon Era Begins," 257.

42. Lu Hsun, *A Brief History of Chinese Fiction*, 320.

43. Colin Mackerras, *Chinese Drama*, 71.

44. For information on these films, see Li and Hu, *Chinese Silent Film History*, 18–19, and the Chinese original, *Zhongguo wusheng dianying shi*, 15–16.

45. Mackerras, *Chinese Drama*, 67.

46. Wu Zuguang, Huang Zuolin, and Mei Shaowu, *Peking Opera and Mei Lanfang*, 8–9.

47. Hong Shi, "The first film tide—On Chinese commercial movies in the period of silent film" (in Chinese), 6.

48. Mackerras, *Chinese Drama*, 71.

49. Lu, "Evaluations" (in Chinese), 83.

50. Huang Zuolin, "Mei Lanfang, Stanislavsky, Brecht," 114. See also Gina Marchetti, "*Two Stage Sisters*," 103, for a discussion of Brecht and Chinese opera, especially Brecht's understanding of Chinese opera as "alienating" and the actors' "awareness of being watched," core features of a cinema of attractions.

51. Li and Hu, *Chinese Silent Film History*, 18.

52. For more discussion see Li and Hu, *Chinese Silent Film History*, 245–49, and Zhang Zhen, "Bodies in the Air: Magic of Science and the Fate of the Early 'Martial Arts' Film in China," 43–60.

53. Chen, "Shadowplay," 196–97.

54. Qu cited in Pickowicz, *Marxist Literary Thought in China*, 109, 163–64, 175. The title of this section, a proletarian cinema of attractions, is adapted from Qu Qiubai's call for a "proletarian May Fourth."

55. Mao, "Yenan Forum on Literature and Art," 82.

56. David Holm, *Art and Ideology in Revolutionary China*, 312–13, 332.

57. Zhang Gang, "Reminiscences of the drama movement in 'Luyi' before and after the Yan'an Forum on Literature and Art" (in Chinese), 11, cited in Holm, *Art and Ideology in Revolutionary China*, 322.

58. Zhang, "Reminiscences of the drama movement" (in Chinese), 11–12, cited in Holm, *Art and Ideology in Revolutionary China*, 322.

59. James Belden, *China Shakes the World*, 210–11, quoted in Lois Wheeler Snow, *China on Stage: An American Actress in the People's Republic*, 202.

60. Chinese Filmmakers Association, *A discussion of Chinese minority films* (in Chinese), 177.

61. Lee Haiyan, "On *The White-haired Girl*: class and sexual politics in the national narrative" (in Chinese), 110–18.

62. Zhou Weizhi, "On the film *The White-haired Girl*" (in Chinese), 18.

63. Ibid., 15. Note that black-and-white characterization is a feature of a cinema of attractions. See Gunning, "The Cinema of Attractions," 59.

64. Zhai Jiannong, "Ups and downs of new model opera films" (in Chinese), 40.

65. *Peking Review* 17.4 (January 25, 1974): 12, quoted in Colin Mackerras, *The Chinese Theatre in Modern Times*, 209–210. See also Lowell Dittmer, "Radical Ideology and Chinese Political Culture," 126–51.

66. See Shao Zhou, "Sun Yu and the film *The Life of Wu Xun*" (in Chinese), 96.

67. Richard Curt Kraus, *Pianos and Politics in China: Middle-Class Ambitions and the Struggle Over Western Music*, 133–39.

68. Zhai, "Ups and downs of new model opera films" (in Chinese), 41.

69. Barmé, "Persistence de la tradition au 'royaume des ombres,'" 119–20.

70. Dai Jinhua, "Xia Yan's *Problems of Screenwriting*," 75–84.

71. Dai, "Xia Yan's *Problems of Screenwriting*," 81.

72. Ibid., 80.

73. Bordwell, *Planet Hong Kong*, 163–64.

74. Barmé, comments to Farquhar (July 2000).

75. Luo, "A preliminary discussion" (in Chinese), 268–69.

76. Craig S. Smith, "*Hero* Soars and Its Director Thanks *Crouching Tiger*."

77. Ang Lee, "Foreword," in Linda Sunshine, ed., *Crouching Tiger, Hidden Dragon: A Portrait of the Ang Lee Film*, 7.

78. Huang Ren, *Lamenting Taiwanese-language films* (in Chinese), 23.

79. Zeng Yongyi, *Development and changes in Taiwan's gezaixi* (in Chinese), 51–53.

80. Ye Longyan, *Spring flowers and dreams of dew*, in Huang, *Lamenting Taiwanese-language films* (in Chinese), 68.

81. Li Xiangxiu, *The Lost Kingdom—the Gongle Opera Troupe.*

82. Ye, *Spring flowers and dreams of dew*, 68, in Huang, *Lamenting Taiwanese-language films* (in Chinese), 231.

83. Miriam Hansen, *Babel and Babylon: Spectatorship in American Silent Film*, 24.

84. Bai in Ye, *Spring flowers and dreams of dew*, in Huang, *Lamenting Taiwanese-language films* (in Chinese), 68.

85. Sunshine, ed., *Crouching Tiger, Hidden Dragon* (dust jacket).

86. Stephen Chan, "Figures of Hope and the Filmic Imaginary of Jianghu in Contemporary Hong Kong Cinema," 489.

87. Ang Lee, "Foreword," 7.

88. Ibid.

89. Stephen Teo, "Love and Swords: The Dialectics of Martial Arts Romance."

90. Lyman, "Watching Movies with Ang Lee," 2, 6.

91. For an account of various readings, see Felicia Chan, "*Crouching Tiger, Hidden Dragon*," 56–64.

92. Craig S. Smith, "*Hero* Soars and Its Director Thanks *Crouching Tiger*."

93. Ian Whitney, "*Hero*."

94. J. Hoberman, "Review of *Hero*."

95. Craig S. Smith, "*Hero* Soars and Its Director Thanks *Crouching Tiger*."

96. Tim Edensor, *National Identity, Popular Culture, and Everyday Life*, 29.

97. Henry Chu, "Beijing—Crouching tiger, hidden who?"

4. Realist Modes: Melodrama, Modernity, and Home

1. Julia Hallam with Margaret Marshment, *Realism and Popular Cinema*, 122.

2. Linda Williams, *Playing the Race Card: Melodramas of Black and White from Uncle Tom to O. J. Simpson*, 44.

3. Yin Hong and Ling Yan, "Foreword" (in English), *A history of Chinese cinema, 1949–2000* (in Chinese), n.p.

4. Hallam with Marchment, *Realism and Popular Cinema*, x. They claim that realism is the "dominant form of representation" in Western culture and explore its diversity through realist "moments."

5. Ginette Vincendeau, "Melodramatic Realism: On Some French Women's Films in the 1930s," 51–65.

6. Chang Hsiao-hung, quoted in Fran Martin, "*Vive L'Amour*: Eloquent Emptiness," 126.

7. Peter Brooks, *The Melodramatic Imagination: Balzac, Henry James, Melodrama, and the Mode of Excess*, 56–80.

8. Ted Huters, "Ideologies of Realism in Modern China: The Hard Imperatives of Imported Theory," 161.

9. Gillian Beer, *Darwin's Plots: Evolutionary Narrative in Darwin, George Eliot, and Nineteenth-Century Fiction*, 145.

10. Zheng Zhengqiu, "How to walk on the road ahead," in Tan Chunfa, "An appreciation of *Twin Sisters:* mistress and maid from the same family" (in Chinese), 36.

11. Stephen Teo, "Hong Kong's New Wave in Retrospect," 17–23.

12. The term is not equivalent to the English word. Raymond Williams suggests that the difficulty with the English term, *realism,* lies partly in the complex disputes in art and philosophy and partly in the intricate history of the related words *real* and *reality.* The Chinese inherited some of these Western difficulties when they appropriated realism as an aesthetic: *xianshizhuyi.* The everyday word for "real" is different: "zhen." Like Chinese political rhetoric, the Chinese usage of *xianshi* emphasizes modernity as desire and modernization (*xiandaihua*) as process: changing present reality (however perceived) into a better future reality (however imagined). Williams, *Keywords,* 216.

13. See Hallam with Marshment, *Realism and Popular Cinema,* 190–96, 149–50, and 32, for discussions on social realism, critical realism, and socialist realism, respectively.

14. Huters, "Ideologies of Realism in Modern China," 160–61. See also Marston Anderson, *The Limits of Realism: Chinese Fiction in the Revolutionary Period.*

15. Susan Hayward, *Key Concepts in Cinema Studies,* 141–43.

16. Law Wai-ming, "A Time for Tears," 23.

17. Leung Noong-kong, "The Long Goodbye to the China Factor," 72.

18. Law "A Time for Tears," 23.

19. John Hutchinson, "Myth Against Myth: The Nation as Ethnic Overlay," 109–123.

20. Raymond Williams, *Culture and Society, 1780–1950,* 48.

21. Jaroslav Průšek, *The Lyrical and the Epic: Studies of Modern Chinese Literature,* 2. For a detailed discussion of debates around romanticism in the interwar period, see Mary Farquhar, *Children's Literature in China: From Lu Xun to Mao Zedong,* 91–142.

22. Ma Junxiang, "The nationalist creation of modern Chinese cinema" (in Chinese), 114–18; Linda Ehrlich and Ma Ning, "College Course File: East Asian Cinema," 63–64.

23. Christopher Williams, "After the Classic, the Classical, and Ideology: The Differences of Realism," 282. See also Geoffrey Nowell-Smith, "Minnelli and Melodrama," 74, and Hallam with Marshment, *Realism and Popular Cinema,* 18–22.

24. Brooks, *The Melodramatic Imagination,* 108. See also Thomas Elsaesser, "Tales of Sound and Fury: Observations on the Family Melodrama," 49, and L. Williams, *Playing the Race Card.*

25. Brooks, *The Melodramatic Imagination,* 155.

26. Mulvey, "It Will Be a Magnificent Obsession: The Melodrama's Role in the Development of Contemporary Film Criticism," 121.

27. Elsaesser, "Tales of Sound and Fury," 68n3. For a discussion of scholarship on Chinese cinema and melodrama, see Zhang, *Screening China,* 61–63. See also Wimal Dissanayake, ed., *Melodrama and Asian Cinema*; Ma Ning, "Symbolic Representation and Symbolic Violence: Chinese Family Melodrama of the Early 1980s," 32–49; Ying Xiong, "'The dazzling dusk of classical writing: Xie Jin's world of family values" (in Chinese),

46–59; Paul Pickowicz, "The 'May Fourth' Tradition of Chinese Cinema," 295–326; Nick Browne, "Society and Subjectivity: On the Political Economy of Chinese Melodrama," 40–56 and 295–326; Steve Fore, "Tales of Recombinant Femininity," 57–70; and Jerome Silbergeld, *China into Film*, 188–233. For a discussion of the "Xie Jin model," see Zhu Dake, "The Drawback of Xie Jin's model"; Li Jie, "Xie Jin's Era Should End," 14–148, and Silbergeld, *China into Film*, 204–233.

28. Zhong, Zhen, and Zhang, "From *Wenmingxi* (Civilized Play) to *Yingxi* (Shadowplay)," 46–64.

29. Li Suyuan, "The narrative model of Chinese early cinemas" (in Chinese), 28–34. He writes: "*Datuanyuan* closures are an aesthetic representation of the ideology of 'fullness' [expressed in *tuan* and *yuan*], reflecting Chinese hope and desire for happiness. Therefore these closures romanticize real life, painting it with light. They also bring a pleasurable warmth that consoles and satisfies audience emotions" (29).

30. Ma, "Symbolic Representation and Symbolic Violence," 82.

31. Law Kar, "Archetypes and Variations: Observations on Six Cantonese Films," 15. The lineage has shifting subcategories. An early example is *Orphan Rescues Grandfather* (1923), a box office success that inaugurated Chinese family melodrama as popular film form (see ch. 6). This was then called "a social film" (*shehuipian*). According to Li Suyuan and Hu Jubin in *Chinese Silent Film History*, 128, the "social film" then gave rise to various subgenres that are categorized by content: the family lineage–children's education film (*yichan he jiaoyu wenti*), women's film (*funü wenti*), and ethical film (*lunlipian*), with a focus on family ethics (*jiating lunlipian*). An example of the family ethics film is *Mother's Happiness* (*Ersun fu*, dir. Shi Dongshan, 1926). The title is ironic: a mother sacrifices her life for her children, who abandon her until literally reunited in tears on her deathbed. In retrospect, all of these so-called subgenres are arguably a single genre and mode: melodrama with its tears, coincidences, virtuous victims, and family reunions (or *datuanyuan*). For a further discussion of melodrama as genre, see Chris Berry, "*Wedding Banquet:* A Family (Melodrama) Affair," 183–90.

32. Law, "Archetypes and Variations," 15.

33. See Daniel Gerould, "Melodrama and Revolution," 185, for a general discussion on melodrama and revolution. He argues that the focus on victims means that "evil" may be transferred from the personal to the "social and existential level." See also Elsaesser, "Tales of Sound and Fury," 64.

34. Raymond Williams, *Marxism and Literature*, 112–13.

35. Elsaesser, "Tales of Sound and Fury," 68*n*1.

36. Yi Dai, "The theory of realist cinema" (in Chinese), 6–7.

37. Mu Weifang, "*Tomboy*" (in Chinese), 832; originally published in *Minbao* 7 (June 1936).

38. Feng Min, "*Street Angel* and neo-realism" (in Chinese), 95–100.

39. Ma Ning, "The Textual and Critical Difference of Being Radical: Reconstructing Chinese Leftist Films of the 1930s," 22–31.

40. Mu Yun, "A wan feeling—seeing *Spring in a Small Town*" (in Chinese), 272.

41. See Li Cheuk-to, "*Spring in a Small Town:* Mastery and Restraint," 59–64.

42. Ying, "The dazzling dusk of classical writing" (in Chinese), 13–14. For a discussion of poetry and painting in Fei Mu's films and his rejection of film as drama, see Li Shaobai, "A forerunner of modern Chinese film: on the historical significance of Fei Mu's *Spring*

in a Small Town, parts 1 and 2" (in Chinese), 73–78 and 34–42, respectively. See also the special edition on Fei Mu in *Dangdai Dianying* 80 (1997): 9.

43. Dudley Andrew, "Sound in France: The Origins of a Native School," 62–63. See also Andrew, "Poetic Realism," 115–19.

44. Vincendeau, "Melodramatic Realism," 52.

45. Mu, "*Tomboy*" (in Chinese), 832.

46. Ibid., 833.

47. Cheng Jihua et al., eds., *The history of the development of Chinese cinema* (in Chinese), vol. 2:495.

48. Mu, "*Tomboy*" (in Chinese), 832.

49. Gao Feng, "*Tomboy* and other matters" (in Chinese), 834.

50. Peter Brooks, "Melodrama, Body, Revolution," 11.

51. Lu Xun, "Preface to *Call to Arms*," 34–35.

52. Ma , "The Nationalist creation of modern Chinese cinema," (in Chinese), 114–18.

53. Ma, "The Textual and Critical Difference of Being Radical," 22–31.

54. Chen Mo, "On Fei Mu's films" (in Chinese), 39.

55. Li, "A forerunner of modern Chinese film, part 2" (in Chinese), 77–78.

56. For examples and a discussion of walls in Lu Xun's writing, see Farquhar, *Children's Literature in China,* 53. For examples of the continuing use of Lu Xun's metaphor in post-Mao culture, see Geremie Barmé and John Minford, "Walls," in *Seeds of Fire: Chinese Voices of Conscience,* 1–62.

57. Li, *Spring in a Small Town:* Mastery and Restraint," 64.

58. Elsaesser, "Tales of Sound and Fury," 62.

59. Nowell-Smith, "Minnelli and Melodrama," 73.

60. Ashish Rajadhyaksha, "Realism, Modernism, and Post-colonial Theory," 415.

61. Brooks, *The Melodramatic Imagination,* 13, 15.

62. Farquhar, *Children's Literature in China,* 30.

63. Wang Yunman, "Director Lee Hsing's aesthetic point of view" (in Chinese), 13.

64. Lu Feii, *Taiwan cinema: politics, economics, aesthetics* (in Chinese), 103–104.

65. For more discussion on the distinction between *xieshi* and *xieyi* in Chinese animation, see Mary Farquhar, "Monks and Monkeys: A Study of 'National Style' in Chinese Animation," 14–19.

66. Lee, quoted in Huang Ren, *In the footsteps of a filmmaker: Lee Hsing's films over fifty years* (in Chinese), 133.

67. Lu, *Taiwan cinema* (in Chinese), 104–106.

68. Martin, "*Vive L'Amour:* Eloquent Emptiness," 176.

69. Law Kar, "An Overview of Hong Kong's New Wave Cinema," 50. See also Law Kar, "Hong Kong New Wave: Modernization Amid Global/Local Counter Cultures," 47.

70. Zhang, *Screening China,* 276–87. See also Teo, "Hong Kong's New Wave in Retrospect," 17–23.

71. Martin, "*Vive L'Amour:* Eloquent Emptiness," 173–82.

72. Law, "Hong Kong New Wave," 47.

73. Teo, *Hong Kong Cinema,* 71. Teo is talking here of *The Orphan* and, by extension, the other early films in the cycle. See also Stephen Teo, "The Father-Son Cycle: A Critique of Thematic Continuity in Cantonese Cinema," 42–47.

74. L. Williams, *Playing the Race Card*, 59.

75. Fruit Chan's Hong Kong trilogy: *Made in Hong Kong* (1997), *The Longest Summer* (1998), and *Little Cheung* (1999). See Bryan Chang, "Hollywood Hong Kong: Fruit Chan's Heaven and Hell," 86–88.

76. Ni Zhen, "After *Yellow Earth*" (in Chinese), 196. The film script and full commentary are available in English in Bonnie S. McDougall, *The Yellow Earth: A Film by Chen Kaige, with a Complete Translation of the Filmscript*. English essays solely on the film include Yau, "*Yellow Earth:* Western Analysis and a Non-Western Text," 62–79, and Chow, "Silent Is the Ancient Plain," 79–107.

77. Yang Ping, "A Director Who Is Trying to Change the Audience," 127.

78. Dai Jinhua, "Severed Bridge: The Art of the Son's Generation," 23–24.

79. For more on the historical project, see Helen Leung, "*Yellow Earth:* Hesitant Apprenticeship and Bitter Agency," 192.

80. Hallam with Marshment, *Realism and Popular Cinema*, 80.

81. "*Yellow Earth:* full production script" (in Chinese), 92–93. Gu Qing tells the family why songs are crucial to the revolution: "When our soldiers hear songs about why wives and daughters are beaten, why workers and peasants want revolution, they cross the river to fight the Japanese devils and [Chinese] landlords, unafraid of blood and death. Even Chairman Mao and General Zhu love folksongs.... Our Chairman Mao wants all China's poor to eat millet without the chaff" (142).

82. Ni, "After *Yellow Earth*" (in Chinese), 197.

83. Barmé and Minford, *Seeds of Fire*, 265.

84. David Bordwell, "The Art Cinema as a Mode of Film Practice," 56–64.

85. Mary Farquhar, "The Hidden Gender in *Yellow Earth*," 154–64. For a detailed discussion of the aesthetics of *Yellow Earth* (cinematography, color, and composition), see Chris Berry and Mary Farquhar, "Post-socialist Strategies: An Analysis of *Yellow Earth* and *Black Cannon Incident*," in Ehrlich and Desser, *Cinematic Landscapes*, 84–100.

86. "*Yellow Earth:* full production script" (in Chinese), 194.

87. Ibid., 148–49.

88. Chen Kaige, "A film of hope" (in Chinese), 2.

89. Arjun Appadurai, *Modernity at Large: Cultural Dimensions of Globalization*, 4.

5. How Should a Chinese Woman Look? Woman and Nation

1. Nira Yuval-Davis, *Gender and Nation*, 1. See also Anne McClintock, *Imperial Leather: Race, Gender, and Sexuality in the Colonial Context*, 353–58.

2. Yuval-Davis, *Gender and Nation*, 45. See also Madhu Dubey, "The True 'Lie' of the Nation: Fanon and Feminism."

3. Chatterjee, *The Nation and Its Fragments*. See esp. chs. 6 and 7.

4. See, for example, Roland B. Tolentino, "*Inangbayan*, the Mother-Nation, in Lino Brocka's *Bayan Ko: Kapit Sa Patalim* and *Orapronobis*," and Rosie Thomas, "Sanctity and Scandal: The Mythologization of Mother India."

5. This is not to suggest that mothers and mothering are not important in Chinese culture. For analyses that pursue this line of inquiry further, see Sally Taylor Lieberman, *The Mother and Narrative Politics in Modern China.* An additional area worthy of further detailed study in its own right is the connection between mother-daughter lineages and diaspora (as opposed to the patriarchal lineage usually associated with the nation-state) in films such as Wayne Wang's 1993 *Joy Luck Club* and Ann Hui's 1990 *Song of the Exile.* These were both made around the same time as *Center Stage,* which we discuss in detail later as another film that also invokes a different lineage from the patriarchal nation-state. There, too, the family link between Ruan Lingyu, her mother, and her daughter is also emphasized.

6. Shuqin Cui, *Women Through the Lens: Gender and Nation in a Century of Chinese Cinema.*

7. Maggie Humm, *Feminism and Film,* 16–17, 25.

8. Mulvey, "Visual Pleasure and Narrative Cinema."

9. Mary Ann Doane, "Film and Masquerade: Theorizing the Female Spectator"; Elizabeth Cowie, "Fantasia"; Kaja Silverman, *The Acoustic Mirror: The Female Voice in Psychoanalysis.*

10. Kaja Silverman, *Male Subjectivity at the Margins.*

11. Jacqueline Bobo, *Black Women as Cultural Readers*; Richard Dyer, *Now You See It: Studies on Lesbian and Gay Film.*

12. D. N. Rodowick, *The Difficulty of Difference: Psychoanalysis, Sexual Difference, and Film Theory.*

13. Chris Berry, "Sexual Difference and the Viewing Subject in *Li Shuangshuang* and *The In-Laws,*" in Berry, ed., *Perspectives on Chinese Cinema,* 30–39. For further discussion see also Berry, *Postsocialist Cinema in Postsocialist China.*

14. Ma Junxiang, "Revolutionary womanhood and the problem of the 'Gaze' in *Shanghai Girl*" (in Chinese).

15. Ma, "Revolutionary womanhood" (in Chinese), 18.

16. Sang Hu, "The Ascendancy of China's Women Directors," 9.

17. Dai Jinhua, "Invisible Women: Contemporary Chinese Cinema and Women's Film."

18. Key examples of this work include Judith Stacey, *Patriarchy and Socialist Revolution in China*; Marjory Wolf, *Revolution Postponed: Women in Contemporary China*; and Kay Ann Johnson, *Women, the Family, and Peasant Revolution in China.*

19. Meng Yue, "Female Images and National Myth," 125–29.

20. Lydia H. Liu, "The Female Tradition in Modern Chinese Literature: Negotiating Feminisms across East/West Boundaries," 24.

21. Tani E. Barlow, "Theorizing Woman: *Funü, Guojia, Jiating.*" See also Tani E. Barlow, "Politics and Protocols of *Funü:* (Un)Making National Woman."

22. Eric Hobsbawm and Terence Ranger, ed., *The Invention of Tradition.*

23. Elisabeth Croll cites an analysis of the *Biographies of Women (Lie Nü Zhuan)* that lists nineteen examples of benevolence, nineteen of chastity, eighteen of widow chastity, eighteen of widow virtue, eighteen negative examples, sixteen of maternal excellence, and sixteen of docile constancy in Elisabeth Croll, *Changing Identities of Chinese Women: Rhetoric, Experience, and Self-Perception in Twentieth-Century China,* 14. She also discuss-

es the cult of domesticity under the New Life Movement, in Elisabeth Croll, *Feminism and Socialism in China*, 160.

24. *Mulan* (1998), directed by Barry Cook and Tony Bancroft, 87 min. See also Chris Berry, "Disney's *Mulan*, Disney's Feminism: Universal Appeal and Mutually Assured Destruction," and Joseph M. Chan, "Disneyfying and Globalizing the Chinese Legend Mulan: A Study in Transculturation," on how Disney produces an American version of a Chinese national legend.

25. Louise Edwards, "Domesticating the Woman Warrior: Comparisons with *Jinghua yuan*," in *Men and Women in Qing China: Gender in "The Red Chamber Dream*," 87.

26. Joseph R. Allen, "Dressing and Undressing the Chinese Woman Warrior."

27. Rey Chow, *Primitive Passions*.

28. Allen, "Dressing and Undressing," 355.

29. Hung Chang-Tai notes that portrayals of women warriors like Mulan reached unprecedented numbers during the War of Resistance Against Japan (1937–1945) in "Female Symbols of Resistance in Chinese Wartime Spoken Drama," 169–70.

30. Chris Berry, "China's New 'Women's Cinema,'"; E. Ann Kaplan, "Problematising Cross-Cultural Analysis: The Case of Women in the Recent Chinese Cinema"; Hu Ying, "Beyond the Glow of the Red Lantern; Or, What Does It Mean to Talk about Women's Cinema in China?"; and Cui, Women Through the Lens, 171–238.

31. For further details see Xie Fang, *On and off-screen* (in Chinese).

32. Mao Zedong, "Talks at the Yan'an Conference on Literature and Art," in Bonnie S. McDougall, *Mao Zedong's "Talks at the Yan'an Conference on Literature and Art": A Translation of the 1943 Text with Commentary*, 65.

33. Susan Rubin Suleiman, *Authoritarian Fictions: The Ideological Novel as a Literary Genre*, 64–100.

34. Translation drawn from the English subtitles. The full Chinese postproduction script of the film by Lin Gu, Xu Jin, and Xie Jin can be found in Meng Tao, ed., *Two Stage Sisters: from treatment to film* (in Chinese), 149–268. An analysis of the film as revolutionary cinema can be found in Marchetti, "*Two Stage Sisters*."

35. Both the preproduction script by original novelist Yang Mo and the postproduction script by directors Cui Wei and Chen Huaikai can be found in Yang Mo et al., *Song of Youth: from novel to film* (in Chinese), 1–96, 97–236.

36. Dai Jinhua, "*Song of Youth*: a re-reading from a historical perspective" (in Chinese), in *Handbook of film theory and criticism*, 215.

37. Meng, "Female Images," 125–29.

38. Antonia Finnane notes this tendency in "What Should Chinese Women Wear? A National Problem," 18–23. It has also been frequently commented upon by Chinese women writing since the end of the Cultural Revolution. For example, see the remarks of woman film director Zhang Nuanxin in Chris Berry's interview with her in *Camera Obscura*, 23. And in the review of a book of interviews with Chinese women by Meng Xiaoyuan, Professor Dai Jinhua of Beijing University compares the difficulties women face in public space to those of Hua Mulan: "The dilemma is that women have to play the traditional role of men. They have to stifle their female identity and 'disguise' themselves as men to fulfill their social value." Ou Shuyi, "In the Minds of Women."

39. Glamorization and the class backgrounds of the characters are just two of the elements in these films that would place them at the Shanghai end of the Shanghai-Yan'an spectrum Paul Clark proposes to describe the range of postrevolutionary films from relatively moderate to hard-line Maoist. These were also reasons that led to many attacks from the left on all of Xie Fang's films. Paul Clark, *Chinese Cinema: Culture and Politics Since 1949*, 25–34.

40. For an earlier discussion of gender and the pedagogical engagement of the spectator in postrevolutionary cinema, see Berry, "Sexual Difference and the Viewing Subject," 30–39.

41. For photos, biographies, articles from the 1930s, tributes and other materials concerning Ruan Lingyu, see Cheng Jihua, ed., *Ruan Lingyu* (in Chinese).

42. Luo Mingyou, "Some respectful suggestions to fellow members of the profession concerning the question of the revival of Chinese cinema" (in Chinese), cited in Li Suyuan and Hu Jubin, *A History of Chinese Silent Film* (in Chinese), 198. On the foundation of Lianhua, see Li and Hu, *A History of Chinese Silent Film*, 198–205; Pang Laikwan, *Building a New China in Cinema: The Chinese Left-Wing Cinema Movement, 1932–1937*, 24–25.

43. Li and Hu, *A History of Chinese Silent Film*, 302–307.

44. Wang Zhimin, *Fundamentals of modern film aesthetics* (in Chinese), 294.

45. Pang Laikwan discusses Ruan Lingyu at length in her chapter, "Women's Stories On-Screen versus Off-Screen" (*Building a New China in Cinema*, 113–32). Although there are overlaps with our analysis, she does devote more attention to Ruan's role on- and off-screen as a mother than we do here.

46. Kristine Harris, "*The New Woman* Incident: Cinema, Scandal, and Spectacle in 1935 Shanghai," 279.

47. William Rothman, "*The Goddess:* Reflections on Melodrama East and West," 66–67.

48. Finnane, "What Should Chinese Women Wear?" 18–20.

49. Rey Chow, *Woman and Chinese Modernity: The Politics of Reading Between West and East*, 107–113, 139–56.

50. Harris, "*The New Woman* Incident," 280.

51. Ibid., 282.

52. On the concept of the star image, see Richard Dyer, *Stars*.

53. For an analysis of Gong Li's appeal and star image, see Bérénice Reynaud, "Gong Li and the Glamour of the Chinese Star."

54. Harris, *The New Woman* Incident," 279.

55. Chris Berry, "The Sublimative Text: Sex and Revolution in Big Road."

56. Ma, "Revolutionary motherhood" (in Chinese), 24–25.

57. Wang Yuejin, "*Red Sorghum:* Mixing Memory and Desire."

58. Esther C. M. Yau, "Cultural and Economic Dislocations: Filmic Phantasies of Chinese Women in the 1980s."

59. Wang Yichuan, *The end of the Zhang Yimou myth: aesthetic and cultural perspectives on Zhang Yimou's cinema* (in Chinese), and Zhang Yiwu, "Zhang Yimou in the context of global postcoloniality" (in Chinese).

60. Hu Ying, "Beyond the Glow of the Red Lantern."

61. Chow, *Primitive Passions*, 166–68, 170; Mary Ann Farquhar, "Oedipality in *Red Sorghum* and *Judou*," 73; Jenny Kwok Wah Lau, "*Judou:* A Hermeneutical Reading of Cross-cultural Cinema," 2–10.

62. Chow, *Primitive Passions*, 167–72.

63. On the intellectual and cultural character of the pre-1989 Tiananmen Democracy movement period, see Wang Jing, *High Culture Fever: Politics, Aesthetics, and Ideology in Deng's
China* and Zhang Xudong, *Chinese Modernism in the Era of Reforms.*

64. Audrey Ing-Sun Yue, "Pre-Post 1997: Postcolonial Hong Kong Cinema, 1984–1997,"
158–59.

65. Biographical information about Maggie Cheung can be found on any number of Web
sites. The number of her films is derived from the listings at the Internet Movie Database (*see* http://imdb.com).

66. The classic text on star and star image remains Richard Dyer's *Stars.*

67. Anne T. Ciecko and Sheldon H. Lu, "The Heroic Trio: Anita Mui, Maggie Cheung, Michelle Yeoh—Self-Reflexivity and the Globalization of the Hong Kong Action Heroine."

68. For example, Zeng Jingchao invokes the long-standing interpretation of Ruan's tragedy
as China's tragedy, concluding that despite the intense commercialism of Hong Kong,
Stanley Kwan has made "a Chinese film that Chinese people need not be ashamed of."
Zeng Jingchao, "*Center Stage*" (in Chinese), 38.

69. Many of the writings that focus on the film's eye-catching deconstructive techniques fall
into this category. Wang Zhimin examines them as formal technique (*Fundamentals in
modern film aesthetics* [in Chinese], 290–99). Robert Ru-Shou Chen argues they articulate a tension between a modernist epistemological drive to discover the truth about
Ruan and a postmodernist ontological questioning of what the truth about history is
("Interpreting *Center Stage*" in *Empire of films: another kind of gaze: research on film culture*
[in Chinese], 180–87). Cui Shuqin argues the tension is between a feminist promotion
of the female autonomous subject and a postmodernist undermining of the very idea of
the autonomous subject (*Women Through the Lens*, 30–50). For Brett Farmer, the uncanny redramatizations recall Freud's mystic writing pad and lead to the kind of questions
about cinema's relation to modernity and memory we have also considered in chapter
2 ("*Mémoire en Abîme:* Remembering (through) *Center Stage*"). The deconstructive elements are more present in the original 167-minute version of *Center Stage*, also known
as *The Actress.* However, the producers cut this version and a negative of the original no
longer survives (Bérénice Reynaud, "Re: *Chinese Cinema-Digest*—Number 628"). Nonetheless, it circulates on video, and the discussion here is based on the original version.

70. Leung Ping-Kwan, "Problematizing National Cinema: Hong Kong Cinema in Search of
Its Cultural Identity," 39.

71. Yue, "Pre-Post 1997," 162–63.

72. Wang Yiman, "Screening the Past, Re-centering the Stage."

73. The standard history of the People's Republic, *The history of the development of Chinese
cinema* (in Chinese), by Cheng Jihua et al., is the key work in which 1930s Shanghai
cinema is claimed for the People's Republic. Ironically, this claim was repudiated from
the left during the Cultural Revolution and landed Cheng Jihua in trouble. Part of his
response after the Cultural Revolution was to edit his 1985 book on Ruan Lingyu.

74. Julian Stringer, "*Centre Stage:* Reconstructing the Bio-Pic," 30, 39.

75. Stringer, " *Centre Stage*," 39.

76. Michael G. Chang, "The Good, the Bad, and the Beautiful: Movie Actresses and Public
Discourse in Shanghai, 1920s—1930s." In the same volume, Andrew D. Field examines

how singing and dancing hostesses took the place of the courtesan, and the moral pan-
ics generated around them ("Selling Souls in Sin City: Shanghai Singing and Dancing
Hostesses in Print, Film, and Politics, 1920–1949"). Editor Zhang Yingjin considers
representations of female sex workers, citing a range of models including symbolic representations of both backward and modern China ("Prostitution and Urban Imagination: Negotiating the Public and the Private in Chinese Films of the 1930s," in Zhang,
ed., *Cinema and Urban Culture in Shanghai, 1922–1943*, 160–80).

77. Abbas, *Hong Kong.*
78. Cui, *Women Through the Lens,* 34–36.
79. Stringer, "*Centre Stage,*" 37–39.
80. Ibid., 38.
81. For an account of this period, including Mui's difficulties, see David Lague, "Triads Hit
the Screen."
82. Bérénice Reynaud, "Icon of Modernity."
83. In Teo, *Hong Kong Cinema,* 29–40.
84. Ibid., 29, 38.
85. Ibid., 34.
86. Carlos Rojas, "Specular Failure and Spectral Returns in Two Films with Maggie Cheung
(and One Without)."
87. Olivia Khoo, "'Anagrammatical Translations': Latex Performance and Asian Femininity
Unbounded in Olivier Assayas's *Irma Vep,*" 387.
88. Khoo, "'Anagrammatical Translations,'" 389; Ken Gelder, *Reading the Vampire,* 123.
89. Audrey Yue, "Migration-as-Transition: Pre-Post 1997 Hong Kong Culture in Clara Law's
Autumn Moon."
90. Olivia Khoo seems to favor the former interpretation, Cui Shuqin the latter.

6. How Should Chinese Men Act?

1. Han Meng, "Leaders Ponder a Return to Society's Roots to Stop the Rot."
2. Chow, *Primitive Passions,* 168.
3. "An Interview with Zhang Yimou," no pagination.
4. Law and film emerged out of the law and literature movement in the 1980s, signaling a
shift from elite literature into popular culture. For an overview, chronology, and select bibliography, see Stefan Machura and Peter Robson, "Law and Film: An Introduction," 1–8.
5. Kwai-cheung Lo, "Transnationalization of the Local in Hong Kong Cinema of the
1990s," 263. See also Lo, "Double Negations: Hong Kong Cultural Identity in Hollywood's Transnational Representations," 472–79.
6. Patrick Fuery, *New Developments in Film Theory,* 109–111, 183.
7. Anthony D. Smith calls the historical link between past and present "the myths and
memories of nation." In a seminal body of work, Smith argues that modernist approaches to nation and nationalism fail to "accord any weight to the pre-existing cultures
and ethnic ties of the nations that emerged in the modern epoch ... myths, memories,
traditions, and symbols of ethnic heritage." These traditions are reconstituted as national identities in each generation through potent myths and symbols. Smith calls this

approach "ethnosymbolism," finding continuities and change in national identities. See Smith, *Myths and Memories of Nation*, 9. Filmmakers' use of the myths and legends surrounding assassination attempts of the ruthless Qin ruler are a case in point. Recent examples are *Hero* and Chen Kaige's *The Emperor and the Assassin* (1998). They retell the "immemorial past" of empire building just as stories of the Opium War discussed in chapter 2 variously retell of China's humiliating past in modern nation-building.

8. China has a rich legal tradition. Modern Chinese states and territories encompass the gamut of modern legal families: civil law on German-Japanese models in the Republic of China on the mainland before 1949 and in Taiwan, English common law with some customary family law in colonial Hong Kong, and socialist law in the People's Republic of China.

9. David A. Black, *Law in Film: Resonance and Representation*, 2, 13 (emphasis added).

10. Joseph Needham, *Science and Civilization in China* 2:544.

11. John Hoffman, *Gender and Sovereignty: Feminism, the State, and International Relations*, 9.

12. Yuval-Davis, *Gender and Nation*, 7–8. See also Tim Edensor, *National Identity, Popular Culture, and Everyday Life*, 9 and 10, for the importance of looking at popular culture, such as film, to account for the dynamic and contested relationship between culture and national identity.

13. Yvonne Tasker, *Spectacular Bodies: Gender, Genre, and the Action Cinema*, 8.

14. Kam Louie, *Theorizing Chinese Masculinity: Society and Gender in China*, 2.

15. *Yang + Yin: Gender in Chinese Cinema* (1997, dir. Stanley Kwan), and Louie, *Theorizing Chinese Masculinity*, 4–5.

16. This is the male, reformist discourse in early-twentieth-century China, exemplified by the famous writer Lu Xun. For a full discussion of fathers, sons, and the modernization of China in Lu Xun's work, see Farquhar, *Children's Literature in China*, 41–89.

17. For a discussion of traditional legal terms, see Needham, *Science and Civilization in China* 2:518–83. For a discussion of filial piety, see Bodde and Morris, *Law in Imperial China*, 41–43.

18. Cheng, *The history of the development of Chinese cinema* (in Chinese), 60–61.

19. Li Shaobai and Hong Shi, "An introduction and evaluation of China's first group of feature films" (in Chinese), 85–86.

20. *Yang+Yin: Gender in the Chinese Cinema.* (1997).

21. Mark Gallagher, "Masculinity in Translation: Jackie Chan's Transcultural Star Text," 25 and 31.

22. Teo, *Hong Kong Cinema*, 123.

23. Ng See Yuan, quoted in Logan, *Hong Kong Action Cinema*, 63.

24. Ng Ho, "Kung-fu Comedies: Tradition, Structure, Character," 42.

25. For background on the Wong Fei-hung films and their circulation, see Teo, *Hong Kong Cinema*, 169–73, and Rodriguez, "Hong Kong Popular Culture as an Interpretive Arena," 1–24.

26. Sek Kei, "The Development of Martial Arts in Hong Kong Cinema," 28.

27. Logan, *Hong Kong Action Cinema*, 60.

28. Anne Behnke Kinney, ed., *Chinese Views on Childhood*; Farquhar, *Children's Literature in China*; and Ann Barrott-Wicks, ed., *Children in Chinese Art*.

29. Fore, "Life Imitates Entertainment," 136.

30. Ng, "Kung-fu Comedies," 42.

31. Mikhail Bakhtin, *Rabelais and His World*, 6.

32. Chen Long [Jackie Chan], *I am Jackie Chan* (in Chinese), 555–56.

33. Fuery, *New Developments in Film Theory*, 115–23.

34. See Borge Bakken, *The Exemplary Society: Human Improvement, Social Control, and the Dangers of Modernity in China*.

35. Li, "Kung Fu: Negotiating Nationalism and Modernity," 515.

36. For a discussion of Chan's American roles as underdog, see Gina Marchetti, "Jackie Chan and the Black Connection," 137–58.

37. Louie, *Theorizing Chinese Masculinity*, 153.

38. Sheldon Lu comments: "The persona of Jackie Chan, in the role of a Hong Kong cop, is the new quintessential Hong Kong traveler and citizen with a fluid, transnational, cross-cultural identity." Lu, "Hong Kong Diaspora Film and Transnational TV Drama: From Homecoming to Exile to Flexible Citizenship," 142.

39. Christopher Heard, *Ten Thousand Bullets: The Cinematic Journey of John Woo*, 50.

40. Julian Stringer, "Your Tender Smiles Give Me Strength: Paradigms of Masculinity in John Woo's *A Better Tomorrow* and *The Killer*," 34.

41. Ryan, "Blood, Brothers, and Hong Kong Gangster Movies: Pop Culture Commentary on 'One China,'" 65.

42. Woo, quoted in Heard, *Ten Thousand Bullets*, 73.

43. Kenneth Hall, *John Woo: The Films*, 2.

44. See Law Kar, "Comparing John Woo's 'Hero Series' with Ringo Lam's 'Wind and Cloud Series'" (in Chinese), 59–63.

45. Louie, *Theorizing Chinese Masculinity*, 25–41. For a Western take on the laws and practices of amity as exclusively male, see Peter Goodrich, "Laws of Friendship," 23–52.

46. *Yang+Yin: Gender in the Chinese Cinema* (1997).

47. Ibid. Such scenes as the bullet-removing scene are, according to Kwan, typically Chinese and outside mainstream Hollywood.

48. Stringer, "Your Tender Smiles Give Me Strength," 27.

49. Richard Meyers, *Inside Kung-fu Magazine*, quoted in Heard, *Ten Thousand Bullets*, 69.

50. Hall talks of the impossibility of translating these two childhood nicknames, variously rendered as in the text or as "Mickey Mouse" and "Dumbo." Hall, *John Woo*, 215n28.

51. Stringer, "Your Tender Smiles Give Me Strength," 39, 40.

52. Logan, *Hong Kong Action Cinema*, 121.

53. Heard, *Ten Thousand Bullets*, 67–68.

54. Barbara Scharres, quoted in Heard, *Ten Thousand Bullets*, 103.

55. David Ray Papke, "Myth and Meaning: Francis Ford Coppola and the Popular Response to the *Godfather* Trilogy," 1, 6, 8.

56. Farquhar, "Oedipality in *Red Sorghum* and *Judou*," 60–86.

57. Hanna Boje Nielsen, "The Three Father Figures in Tian Zhuangzhuang's Film *The Blue Kite*: The Emasculation of Males by the Communist Party" 83.

58. Zha Jianying, *China Pop*, 74.

59. An earlier version of this argument about *The Story of Qiu Ju* has been published in Mary Farquhar, "Silver Screen," in Jane Orton et al., *Bridges to Chinese: Internet/CD Postgraduate Course*.

60. Jet Li, quoted in Robert Y. Eng, " Is *Hero* a Paean to Authoritarianism?"

61. Xu Haofeng, "Zhang Yimou's *Hero*" (in Chinese), 7.

62. Tasker, *Spectacular Bodies*, 105.

63. Stephen Short and Susan Jakes, "Making of a Hero."

64. Yao Xiaolei, "Classic constructions and reconstructions: *xia, tianxia,* and heroism in art—speaking from Zhang Yimou's *Hero*" (in Chinese), 46–48, 49–51.

65. Xu, "Zhang Yimou's *Hero*" (in Chinese), 8.

66. Hoberman, "Review of *Hero*."

67. Zhang Qiu, "*Hero:* Zhang Yimou's turning point" (in Chinese), 7.

68. Eng, "Is *Hero* a Paean to Authoritarianism?"

7. Where Do You Draw the Line? Ethnicity in Chinese Cinemas

1. The Han constitute the ethnic group commonly referred to as Chinese. However, the People's Republic of China has numerous other "minority nationalities," hence the distinction.

2. Duara, "Transnationalism and the Predicament of Sovereignty," 1032.

3. Stevan Harrell, "Introduction," in Melissa J. Brown, ed., *Negotiating Ethnicities in China and Taiwan*, 2. The term *ethnicity* is a notoriously slippery one, prone to many different definitions and overlapping both race and culture.

4. For an introduction to the topic, see Marcus Banks, *Ethnicity: Anthropological Constructions.*

5. Edward Said, *Orientalism.* Although Said does state on the first page of his book that for the West, the Orient is "one of its deepest and most recurring images of the Other," Freud and Lacan get no explicit recognition as a source of his work. Foucault and Gramsci are credited more heavily. Nonetheless, it seems clear that Said's idea of the Orient as a discursive projection of all that the West is not is at least implicitly informed by concepts of subjectivity grounded in the idea of constructing the self by constructing others.

6. For a critique of Said that tries to reanchor the term "orientalism" in these nineteenth-century movements, see John M. MacKenzie, *Orientalism: History, Theory, and the Arts.*

7. Said, *Orientalism*, cites the *Iliad* on page 56 and closes with a chapter entitled "The Latest Phase," 284–328.

8. Said, *Orientalism*, 5–6.

9. Bart Moore-Gilbert, "Edward Said: *Orientalism* and Beyond," in *Postcolonial Theory: Contexts, Practices, Politics,* 35.

10. The finger has been pointed most strongly at Zhang Yimou. For further discussion, see the section on Gong Li in chapter 5. On the career of Said's postcolonialism in the People's Republic, see Tang Xiaobing, "Orientalism and the Question of Universality: The Language of Contemporary Chinese Literary Theory"; Ben Xu, " 'From Modernity to Chineseness': The Rise of Nativist Cultural Theory in Post-1989 China"; and Henry Y. H. Zhao, "Post-Isms and Chinese New Conservatism."

11. A synthesis of this work is Colin Mackerras, *China's Minority Cultures: Identities and Integration Since 1912.*

12. A key example would be Dru C. Gladney, "Representing Nationality in China: Refiguring Majority/Minority Identities." The very title of Ralph Litzinger's *Other Chinas: The Yao and the Politics of National Belonging* attests to the importance of the discourse of the "Other" in this field of study. Articles devoted specifically to Chinese films that draw on the theory of orientalism are attended to in the third section of this chapter.

13. See, for example, Chen Xiaomei, *Occidentalism: A Theory of Counter-Discourse in Post-Mao China*; Louisa Schein, "The Consumption of Color and the Politics of White Skin in Post-Mao China"; and Geremie R. Barmé, "To Screw Foreigners Is Patriotic," in *In the Red: On Contemporary Chinese Culture*, 255–80.

14. Louisa Schein, *Minority Rules: The Miao and the Feminine in China's Cultural Politics*, 103.

15. Zhou Enlai cited in Barry Sautman, "Anti-Black Racism in Post-Mao China," 436; Zhao Ziyang cited in Barry Sautman, "Racial Nationalism and China's External Behavior," 80. In addition to these official claims, academics in both China and the West have made similar arguments, as Gregory Eliyu Guldin points out in his review of Stevan Harrell's *Cultural Encounters on China's Ethnic Frontiers*.

16. Dennis Porter, "*Orientalism* and Its Problems," 181; Lisa Lowe, *Critical Terrains: French and British Orientalisms*; Mary Louise Pratt, *Imperial Eyes: Travel Writing and Transculturation*. Numerous other works could be cited.

17. Robert J. C. Young, *Colonial Desire: Hybridity in Theory, Culture, and Race*, 179–81. A second problem often raised by critics is whether Said believes there is a "real" orient knowable only to authentic "Orientals," or whether he believes all knowledge is situated and constructed.

18. Lydia H. Liu, "Translingual Practice: The Discourse of Individualism Between China and the West."

19. Louisa Schein, "Gender and Internal Orientalism in China," 85.

20. Ralph A. Litzinger, "Memory Work: Reconstituting the Ethnic in Post-Mao China."

21. Stevan Harrell, "Introduction: Civilizing Projects and the Reaction to Them," in Harrell, ed., *Cultural Encounters on China's Ethnic Frontiers*, 4.

22. Chen Xiaomei, *Occidentalism*.

23. On the responses of "Western" audiences, see Sheng-mei Ma, "Ang Lee's Domestic Tragicomedy: Immigrant Nostalgia, Exotic/Ethnic Tour, Global Market." On the film's challenge to stereotypes of "rice queens" and "potato queens," see Cynthia W. Liu, "'To Love, Honor, and Dismay': Subverting the Feminine in Ang Lee's Trilogy of Resuscitated Patriarchs." On both, see Gina Marchetti, "*The Wedding Banquet*: Global Chinese Cinema and Asian American Experience."

24. This dimension of the film is only touched upon in passing. Two reviews mention the Gaos' hope that their son will marry "a nice Chinese girl": Jem Axelron, "*The Wedding Banquet*," and Roger Ebert, "*The Wedding Banquet*." One Taiwan article focused on gay issues also notes the interracial dimension of the film; Lin Yihua, "Delight and emptiness: feelings after seeing *The Wedding Banquet*" (in Chinese). It is not mentioned at all in any of the other reviews and press articles we have sourced: Geoff Andrew, "East Is Wed"; David Ansen, "Straightening Up the House"; David Armstrong, "Something Old, Something New"; Bai Ning, "Broadminded and fair: Ang Lee discusses *The Wedding Banquet*" (in Chinese); Nancy Blaine, "New York Story: Tale of Taiwan Immigrants Is a Fine Feast"; Georgia Brown, "Three's Company"; Laurence Chua, "Queer Wind

from Asia"; Richard Corliss, "All in the Families"; David Denby, "Family Ties"; Derek Elley, "*Hsi Yen (The Wedding Banquet)*"; Edward Guthmann, "'Datebook': Wedded Mess: Gay Man's Marriage to Pacify Taiwanese Parents Begets Laughs"; Stephen Holden, "*The Wedding Banquet*"; Andrew Horn, "*The Wedding Banquet*"; Ann Hornaday, "A Director's Trip from Salad Days to a 'Banquet'"; Li Youxin, "Two faces of Taiwanese gay cinema: *Rebels of the Neon God* and *The Wedding Banquet*" (in Chinese); Li Youxin, "Ang Lee, Winston Chao, and Mitchell Lichtenstein answer questions: the press conference for *The Wedding Banquet*" (in Chinese); Ling Wen, "The political implications behind the poignant humor" (in Chinese); Lu Deng, "*The Wedding Banquet*'s purely commercial flavor" (in Chinese), 112–13; David Noh, "*The Wedding Banquet*"; Patrick Pacheco, "Cultural Provocateur: In 'The Wedding Banquet' Ang Lee Stirs Up Custom"; Tony Rayns, "5000 Years Plus One: *The Wedding Banquet*"; Tony Rayns, "*Xiyan (The Wedding Banquet)*"; Dale Reynolds, "Marry Me a Little"; Michele Shapiro, "Wedding-Bell Blues"; Doris Toumarkine, "Giving Good 'Banquet'"; Kenneth Turan, "Marriage of Convenience Yields a Full 'Banquet'"; Wang Wenhua, "*The Wedding Banquet* in the United States" (in Chinese); and Jeff Yang, "Out of Asia." It is also not noted in the entries describing the film in the catalogs for the 1993 Berlin, Hong Kong, Melbourne, Montreal, Munich, San Sebastian, Sydney, and Warsaw film festivals.

25. Ma, "Ang Lee's Domestic Tragicomedy"; Cynthia W. Liu, "'To Love, Honor, and Dismay'"; and Marchetti, "*The Wedding Banquet.*"

26. Cynthia W. Liu, "'To Love, Honor, and Dismay,'" 2.

27. James L. Hevia, *Cherishing Men from Afar: Qing Guest Ritual and the Macartney Embassy of 1793*, 9. Hevia refers readers to John Y. Fairbank and S. Y. Teng, "On the Ch'ing Tributary System," for the "original" formulation.

28. Hevia, "A Multitude of Lords," in *Cherishing Men from Afar*, 29–56.

29. Cynthia W. Liu, "'To Love, Honor, and Dismay'" 27, 40. Bai Ning, "Broadminded and fair" (in Chinese), 42, describes the film as featuring "one husband and two wives." On the differences between wives and concubines, see Rubie S. Watson, "Wives, Concubines, and Maids: Servitude and Kinship in the Hong Kong Region, 1900–1940." In fact, there is room for further analysis of how *Wedding Banquet* plays on established roles like these. For example, the only socially acceptable reason for taking a concubine into the family is the failure of the first wife to produce a son, and so in this regard Wei-wei is more like the concubine. Also, although Simon is feminized within the household metaphor, within the tribute system metaphor he is the representative of the foreign patriarch Mr. Gao must deal with, as is implicitly recognized by their shared secret.

30. For a discussion of this controversy and its reception in Europe and American, see Hevia, *Cherishing Men from Afar*, 232–37.

31. For the script of *Dr. Bethune*, see Zhang Junxiang and Zhao Ta, "*Dr. Bethune*" (in Chinese), 409–508.

32. For the script, see Huang Jianxin et al., *Black Cannon Incident: from novel to film* (in Chinese).

33. Anderson, *Imagined Communities*, 20–28.

34. Frank Dikötter, *The Discourse of Race in Modern China*, 9. According to Dikötter, at this time there was no meaningful distinction between culture and race in the modern sense (2–3).

35. Thomas Heberer, *China and Its National Minorities: Autonomy or Assimilation?* 30–39.

36. Arienne M. Dwyer, "The Texture of Tongues: Languages and Power in China," in William Safran, ed., *Nationalism and Ethnoregional Identities in China*, 68–85.

37. The idea of identity as performatively produced rather than given is developed by Judith Butler in *Gender Trouble: Feminism and the Subversion of Identity*.

38. Paul Clark, "Ethnic Minorities in Chinese Films: Cinema and the Exotic," 17.

39. Zhang Wei, "My opinion on minority nationality films" (in Chinese), 51. In the tables printed in Gao Honghu et al., eds., *Chinese minority nationality films* (in Chinese), 193 films are listed for the 1949–1995 period.

40. Li Yiming, "Cultural perspective and themes in the minority nationality films of the 'Seventeen Years'" in Gao Honghu et al., eds., *Chinese minority nationality films* (in Chinese), 172–73. Paul Clark argues that the initial appeal of minority nationality films lay in their ability to include the exotic, romance, dance, and other generally colorful elements lacking from politically dourer mainstream films; he understands this as a substitution for elements common in the sophisticated and westernized Shanghai milieu of pre-1949 films (Clark, "Ethnic Minorities in Chinese Films," 20). For further information on the folkloric origins and various transformations of the "Third Sister Liu" story, see Lydia H. Liu, "The Metamorphosis of a Song Immortal: Understanding Official Popular Culture in Twentieth-Century China."

41. Clark, "Ethnic Minorities in Chinese Films," 15–21.

42. Harrell, "Introduction," in Harrell, ed., *Cultural Encounters on China's Ethnic Frontiers*. On scaling based on mode of production, see 22–23.

43. Li Yiming, "Cultural perspective and themes" (in Chinese), 180.

44. Both the pre- and postproduction scripts of *Serfs* can be found in Huang Zongjiang et al., *Serfs: from script to screen* (in Chinese).

45. Harrell, "Introduction," in Harrell, ed., *Cultural Encounters on China's Ethnic Frontiers*, 14.

46. Li Yiming, "Cultural perspective and themes" (in Chinese), 175–78.

47. Gao Honghu et al., eds., *Chinese minority nationality films* (in Chinese), collects the papers given at the conference.

48. For an account which emphasizes different similarities between *Serfs* and the films of the late 1980s, see Ying Xiong, "*Serfs*: narrative tension" (in Chinese). This article emphasizes form, and this rather than the more politically sensitive topic of ethnicity attracted most attention on *Horse Thief*'s release in China; see Xia Hong, "The Debate Over *Horse Thief*."

49. Zhang Wei, "My opinion on minority nationality films" (in Chinese), 51–52.

50. For further discussion of these terms, see Chris Berry, "A Turn for the Better? Genre and Gender in *Girl from Hunan* and Other Recent Mainland Chinese Films." On the shifts in the economic structure of the film industry in the 1980s, see Chris Berry, "Market Forces: China's 'Fifth Generation' Faces the Bottom Line," in Berry, ed., *Perspectives on Chinese Cinema*, 114–40.

51. Li Yiming, "Cultural perspectives and themes" (in Chinese), 174, notes that lack of trained minority nationality filmmakers meant Han filmmakers produced all the early films. However, studios have been established in outlying regions (such as the Tianshan Film Studio in the Chinese central Asian province of Xinjiang), and minority nation-

alities directors (such as Guang Chunlan, who works at Tianshan), have been trained. Guang's own narrative of her Beijing upbringing and training, along with the question of who approves and funds Tianshan's films and their intended audiences, indicates that ethnic provenance of the films is a complex issue; Guang Chunlan, "Representing the exciting and colorful nationality lifestyles: on the making of fourteen nationality films" (in Chinese), in Gao Honghu et al., eds., *Chinese minority nationality films*, 10–24. This volume includes accounts from numerous other minority nationality filmmakers.

52. In 1984 there were twelve minority nationality films; in 1985, eleven; in 1986, fourteen; and in 1987, nineteen. Zhao Shi, "Turn of the century: in search of a development strategy for minority nationality films," in Gao Honghu et al., eds, *Chinese minority nationality films* (in Chinese), 3.

53. Dru C. Gladney surveys contemporary "oriental orientalism" as a broad cultural phenomenon in "Representing Nationality in China."

54. In-person interview by Chris Berry with Wu Xiaojin, deputy director of planning and research, China Film Corporation, February 15, 1988, at China Film Corporation's offices.

55. On the notorious lack of audience for the film in mainland China and the director's equally notorious response, see Yang Ping, "A Director Who Is Trying to Change the Audience," 127–30.

56. Ibid., 129.

57. See, for example, Peggy Hsiung-Ping Chiao, "Tian Zhuangzhuang and *Horse Thief*," in Chiao, ed., *Li Lianying Da Taijian* (in Chinese), 193–98; and Chris Berry, "Race (*Minzu*): Chinese Film and the Politics of Nationalism."

58. Dru C. Gladney, "Tian Zhuangzhuang, the Fifth Generation, and Minorities Film in China," 169. This essay is reworked in Gladney's new book, *Dislocating China: Reflections on Muslims, Minorities, and Other Subaltern Subjects*, which we regret appeared too late for us to take into account when writing this chapter.

59. Gladney, "Tian Zhuangzhuang, the Fifth Generation, and Minorities Film in China," 172.

60. Readers familiar with psychoanalytic theory will note this structure parallels psychoanalytic understandings of the construction of the coherent subject through a process of repressions, which are then simultaneously mourned as lost and feared as threatening to return.

61. Hu Ke, "The relationship between the minority nationalities and the Han in the cinema," in Gao Honghu et al., eds., *Chinese minority nationality films* (in Chinese), 210.

62. Zhang Yingjin, "From 'Minority Film' to 'Minority Discourse': Questions of Nationhood and Ethnicity in Chinese Cinema," in Sheldon Hsiao-peng Lu, ed., *Transnational Chinese Cinemas: Identity, Nationhood, Gender*; Gladney, "Representing Nationality in China"; Esther C. M. Yau, "Is China the End of Hermeneutics? Or, Political and Cultural Usage of Non-Han Women in Mainland Chinese Films"; and Donald, "Women Reading Chinese Films." This critique also applies to *Horse Thief*'s treatment of the Tibetans, as some of these authors note.

63. Chow, *Primitive Passions*, 38.

64. Simon Long, *Taiwan: China's Last Frontier*, 3–4. Long points out that the origins of these peoples have been disputed according to the needs of different political regimes.

65. On the continuing impact of the Han on the aborigine demographics and their political mobilization, see Chiu Yen Liang (Fred), "From the Politics of Identity to an Alternative Cultural Politics: On Taiwan Primordial Inhabitants' A-systemic Movement."

66. Robert Ru-Shou Chen discusses both the notorious Japanese film *Sayon's Bell* (1943), about the supposedly willing self-sacrifice of Taiwan aboriginals for the Japanese Imperial Army, and more recently representations such as *Song of Orchid Island*, in two essays in his book *Empire of Films:* "The colonial circumstances of *Sayon's Bell*" (in Chinese) and "Cultural studies and aboriginals: from *Song of Orchid Island* to the Orchid Island point of view" (in Chinese), 214–21, 222–39.

67. Feii Lu, *Taiwan cinema: politics, economics, aesthetics, 1949–1994* (in Chinese), 23–28.

68. For further Chinese-language discussion of *Sayon's Bell*, the response of Taiwan aboriginals to its screenings on the island in 1994, and Taiwanese aboriginal filmmaking, see the special section in *Film appreciation (Dianying Xinshang)*, 12.3 (1994): 15–64 (in Chinese).

69. Anderson, *Imagined Communities*, 20–28.

70. For a discussion of the range of definitions of "ethnicity" and the problems of applying them in a Chinese context, see Huang Shu-min, Chen Chung-min, and Chuang Ying-chang, "Introduction: Problems of Ethnicity in the Chinese Cultural Context," in Chen, Chuang, and Huang, eds., *Ethnicity in Taiwan: Social, Historical and Cultural Perspectives*, 3–22. They note that the terms "dialect or speech groups," "ethnic or subethnic groups," and "regional or provincial groups" have all been coined to designate these local groupings in the Chinese context (15).

71. For a study of becoming Han in process, see Jean Berlie, *Sinisation*. A history of such a process is traced for the area from which the long-term Chinese on Taiwan migrated in Huang Shu-min, "Customs and Culture," in Y. M. Yeung and David K.Y. Chu, eds., *Fujian: A Coastal Province in Transition and Transformation*, 508–527.

72. Patricia Ebrey, "Surnames and Han Chinese Identity," in Melissa J. Brown, ed., *Negotiating Ethnicities in China and Taiwan*, 24.

73. Guldin notes "the similarity of these processes [producing the identities of minority nationalities] with those impinging on Han regional and local identities, such as those of the Cantonese and Hakka" (review, Stevan Harrell, ed., *Cultural Encounters on China's Ethnic Frontiers*, 370).

74. Decentralization and geographically uneven development in recent years has produced a literature about the phenomenon, including the question of the strains this might be producing on the fabric of the nation. What is notably missing among the phenomena studied in this literature is the appearance of localized ethnic identities that might provide a foundation for alternative nation-states. See, for example, Hans Hendrischke and Feng Chongyi, eds., *The Political Economy of China's Provinces: Comparative and Competitive Advantage*; Si-ming Li and Wing-shing Tang, eds., *China's Regions, Polity, and Economy: A Study of Spatial Transformation in the Post-Reform Era*; David Shambaugh, ed., *Is China Unstable? Assessing the Factors*; and David S. G. Goodman and Gerald Segal, eds., *China Deconstructs: Politics, Trade, and Regionalism*. Perhaps this lack of alternative ethnic identities is one reason behind the title of John Fitzgerald's essay in the latter volume: " 'Reports of My Death Have Been Greatly Exaggerated': The History of the Death of China," 21–58.

75. Chang Mau-kuei makes this argument in "Toward an Understanding of the *Sheng-chi Wen-ti* in Taiwan: Focusing on Changes after Political Liberalization," in Chen Chung-min, Chuang Ying-chang, and Huang Shu-min, eds., *Ethnicity in Taiwan*, pp. 93–150.

76. Long, *Taiwan: China's Last Frontier*, 28–29.

77. Chang Mau-kuei, "Toward an Understanding of the *Sheng-chi Wen-ti* in Taiwan," 99, 103.

78. This film appears to support Ebrey's point about the importance of genealogy rather than culture alone in defining Han identity.

79. Cai Hongsheng, "The master of Taiwan native film—Lee Hsing," in *Taiwan and Hong Kong films and film stars* (in Chinese), 94–6.

80. Feii Lu, *Taiwan cinema* (in Chinese), 117. The film was made when the Taiwanese-language cinema was in its first boom and Lee was trying to get a break, so he probably had less control than with his later films.

81. Another well-known example would be Bai Ke's 1962 film, *Love at Longshan Temple*. In *Both Sides Are Happy*, the heads of the two families are a Tokyo-trained Western medicine doctor and a Chinese-medicine doctor from the mainland. As neighbors they fight for clients, but when the mainland wife consults her husband's rivals about an ailment, the Taiwanese wife says she herself believes in Chinese medicine. In *Love at Longshan Temple* there is also more than romance undermining disputes between the families: it transpires that the local Taiwanese suitor for the lead female character is in fact the long-lost brother of his mainland rival, a situation with obvious metaphorical meanings.

82. Feii Lu, *Taiwan cinema* (in Chinese), 104.

83. Teo, *Hong Kong Cinema*, 12. See also Leung Noong-kong, "The Changing Power Relationship Between China and Hongkong: An Examination of the Concept of 'Home' and Its Function in Hongkong Movies in the 40's and 50's."

84. Anderson, *Imagined Communities*, 66–79. Anderson quotes Johann von Herder's late-eighteenth-century declaration of language as the cornerstone of national identity; "Denn *jedes* Volk ist Volk; es hat seine National Bildung wie *seine* Sprache." He judiciously notes that this declaration was made "in blithe disregard of some obvious extra-European facts" (6).

85. Anderson, *Imagined Communities*, 78.

86. Wang Hui gives an account of the complex cultural politics of language reform in the late nineteenth and early twentieth centuries in "Local Forms, Vernacular Dialects, and the War of Resistance Against Japan: The 'National Forms' Debates."

87. Xiao Zhiwei, "Constructing a New National Culture: Film Censorship and the Issues of Cantonese Dialect, Superstition, and Sex in the Nanjing Decade," in Zhang Yingjin, ed., *Cinema and Urban Culture in Shanghai*, 184.

88. Teo, *Hong Kong Cinema*, 6.

89. This aspect of Japanese colonialism on Taiwan is represented poignantly in Wu Nien-jen's 1994 film, *A Borrowed Life*, about the continuing loyalty to Japan felt by some older islanders. The film's Chinese title, *Duo-sang*, is a Chinese rendering of the lead character's Japanese-style name, "Duo-San." For further discussion, see Darrell William Davis, "Borrowing Postcolonial: *Dou San* and the Memory Mine."

90. Alan M. Wachman, *Taiwan: National Identity and Democratization*, 107–109.

91. Feii Lu, *Taiwan cinema* (in Chinese), 110.

8. The National in the Transnational

1. Ben Moger-Williams and Wu Runmei, "The Art of Compromise: An Interview with Film Director Zhang Yimou."

2. Anna Tsing, "The Global Situation."

3. Sheldon Lu, "Historical Introduction," 8–9.

4. Ibid., 4.

5. There are numerous books and Web sites devoted to Lee. For this essay, we have drawn on John R. Little, *Bruce Lee: A Warrior's Journey*. Written with the cooperation of Lee's widow, it glosses over the rumors that he died in the bed of a Taiwanese actress. Earlier biographies include Bruce Thomas, *Bruce Lee: Fighting Spirit*; Linda Lee, *The Bruce Lee Story*; and Robert Clouse, *Bruce Lee: The Biography*.

6. On the *Kung Fu* television series (as well as Lee's actual appearance in *The Green Hornet* TV series), see Darrell Y. Hamamoto, *Monitored Peril: Asian Americans and the Politics of TV Representation*, 59–63, and Sheng-mei Ma, *The Deathly Embrace: Orientalism and Asian American Identity*, 60–61.

7. Richard Meyers, Amy Harlib, and Karen Palmer, *From Bruce Lee to the Ninjas: Martial Arts Movies*, 221, cited in Meaghan Morris, "Learning from Bruce Lee: Pedagogy and Political Correctness in Martial Arts Cinema," 183.

8. Lee's first three films had different English titles in the United States. *The Big Boss* is better known there as *Fists of Fury*. *Fist of Fury* is known as *The Chinese Connection*. And *The Way of the Dragon* is known as *The Return of the Dragon*.

9. Tony Rayns, "Bruce Lee and Other Stories," 28.

10. Formalist appreciation of the fighting style by First World critics is also common. However, noting Lee's Caucasian opponents in *Fist of Fury* and *Way of the Dragon*, Stephen Teo is rightly suspicious of this approach in "True Way of the Dragon: *The Films of Bruce Lee*," 70.

11. Kwai-cheung Lo, "Muscles and Subjectivity: A Short History of the Masculine Body in Hong Kong Popular Culture."

12. Yingchi Chu, *Hong Kong Cinema: Coloniser, Motherland, and Self*, 38; Stephen Teo, "Bruce Lee: Narcissus and the Little Dragon," in *Hong Kong Cinema: The Extra Dimensions*, 110–114.

13. Vijay Prashad, "Bruce Lee and the Anti-imperialism of Kung Fu: A Polycultural Adventure."

14. Jachinson Chan, *Chinese American Masculinities: From Fu Manchu to Bruce Lee*, 75; Sheng-mei Ma, *The Deathly Embrace*, 54–55. Other writers further complicate the picture by emphasizing class issues: Chiao Hsiung-Ping, "Bruce Lee: His Influence on the Evolution of the Kung Fu Genre"; David Desser, "The Kung Fu Craze: Hong Kong Cinema's First American Reception," in Poshek Fu and David Desser, eds., *The Cinema of Hong Kong: History, Arts, Identity*; Verina Glaessner, "The Dance of Death: Bruce Lee," in *Kung Fu: Cinema of Vengeance*, 83–96; and Stuart M. Kaminsky, "Kung Fu as Ghetto Myth."

15. Louie, *Theorizing Chinese Masculinity*, 1–22 ff.

16. Ibid., 145, 147.

17. Jachinson Chan, *Chinese American Masculinities*, 89.

18. Louie, *Theorizing Chinese Masculinity*, 148, 13, 147–48. No doubt, Lee's Caucasian wife also complicated the conventional picture.

19. An example of the queer appreciation of Lee is Tony Rayns, "Bruce Lee: Narcissism and Nationalism." Teo, "True Way of the Dragon: The Films of Bruce Lee," is an example of the controversy it has provoked.

20. Eve Kosofsky Sedgwick, *Between Men: English Literature and Male Homosocial Desire*.

21. Robin Wood, "Two Films by Martin Scorsese," in *Hollywood from Vietnam to Reagan*, 245–69.

22. Cheng Yu, "Anatomy of a Legend," 25.

23. Rayns, "Bruce Lee: Narcissism and Nationalism," 112.

24. Prime examples include Dai Jinhua, "Postcolonialism and the Chinese Cinema of the Nineties"; Wang Yichuan, *The End of the Zhang Yimou Myth* (in Chinese); Zhang Yingjin, *Screening China*; and Zhang Yiwu, "Zhang Yimou in the context of global post-coloniality" (in Chinese).

25. Mark O'Neill, "Film-makers Jittery as Hollywood Comes Calling."

26. More precise figures can be obtained by consulting the *China Film Yearbook* series (in Chinese).

27. Stanley Rosen, "'The Wolf at the Door?': Hollywood and the Film Market in China from 1994–2000."

28. Wang Zhiqiang, "1995 market summary for film imports" (in Chinese).

29. Wang Shujen, *Framing Piracy: Globalization and Film Distribution in Greater China*, 65.

30. For figures on numbers of Taiwan-produced films submitted for censorship since 1949, see tables 1a and 1b in Feii Lu, *Taiwan cinema: politics, economics, aesthetics* (in Chinese), n.p.

31. Table 22f in Feii Lu, *Taiwan cinema* (in Chinese), n.p.

32. Ti Wei, "Reassessing New Taiwanese Cinema: From Local to Global," 34.

33. For a detailed account, see Wang Shujen, *Framing Piracy*, 106–114.

34. Toby Miller, Nitin Govil, John McMurria, and Richard Maxwell, *Global Hollywood*, 3–10.

35. Liz Shackleton, "Hong Kong—The Sequel Means Business."

36. Mary Kwong, "HK Movie World's Fortunes Take a Tumble."

37. Wang Shujen, *Framing Piracy*, 169. There have, of course, been repeated efforts to counter this. In 2003, Hong Kong and Beijing announced a "Closer Economic Partnership Arrangement," which, among other things, facilitates cooperation between the film industries of Hong Kong and the mainland. Whether this will turn things around for either industry remains to be seen.

38. Wang Shujen, *Framing Piracy*, 44.

39. Ibid., 162.

40. Ibid., 50.

41. Ibid., 139.

42. Tony Bennett, *Culture: A Reformer's Science*, 167, 169.

43. Michel Foucault, *Power/Knowledge*, 142.

44. Ni Zhen, "*Titanic* sums up a century of cinema" (in Chinese).

45. Zhang Baiqing, "Chinese blockbusters need to get it together" (in Chinese), 14.

46. Stanley Rosen, "'The Wolf at the Door?'."

47. Zheng Dongtian, "What's big about the "big film"?—a memo on reading *The Opium War*" (in Chinese).

48. Wang Rui, "Hollywood films and the Hollywood phenomenon" (in Chinese), 79.

49. Zhou Xiangwen, "Discussing Ding Yinnan on the basis of *Dr. Sun Yatsen*" (in Chinese); Ding Yinnan et al., "Film roundtable: on the epic film, *Dr. Sun Yatsen*" (in Chinese); Jin Xiang, "On the music in *Dr. Sun Yatsen*" (in Chinese).

50. Zhang Baiqing, "Chinese blockbusters need to get it together" (in Chinese), 14.

51. "*Hero* Becomes China's Top-Grossing Film, to Open in the U.S. Later this Year."

52. Jonathan Noble, "*Titanic* in China: Transnational Capitalism as Official Ideology?" 170 (emphasis in the original).

53. Michael Patrick and Zhang Yilei, "Beijing."

54. Leonard Klady, "Alien: The Unkindest Cuts."

55. Michael Bodey, "Holding Out for a Hero."

56. "New Start for Film Industry."

57. Steve Neale, "Hollywood Blockbusters: Historical Dimensions," in Julian Stringer, ed., *Movie Blockbusters*, 47–60.

58. "*Hero:* Box Office Savior." There are variations in the dollar figures quoted by different sources.

59. Zhang Yimou, quoted in "New Start for Film Industry."

60. "*Hero:* Box Office Savior."

61. Ibid.

62. Jan Uhde and Yvonne Ng Uhde, *Latent Images: Film in Singapore.*

63. For example, Uhde and Ng Uhde detail the dispute over whether Malaysia or Singapore could claim early filmmaker P. Ramlee that followed a Ramlee retrospective at the 1999 Singapore International Film Festival (*Latent Images*, 12).

64. Given the absence of a local industry at the time of writing, David Birch devotes much of his 1996 essay on film policy in Singapore to detailing its notorious censorship regime: "Film and Cinema in Singapore: Cultural Policy as Control," in Albert Moran, ed., *Film Policy: International, National, and Regional Perspectives*, 185–211.

65. Gary Rodan, "Class Transformations and Political Tensions in Singapore's Development," in Richard Robison and David S. G. Goodman, eds., *The New Rich in Asia: Mobile Phones, McDonalds, and Middle-Class Revolution*, 19–45.

66. Cited in Uhde and Ng Uhde, *Latent Images*, 61.

67. For details, see Uhde and Ng Uhde, *Latent Images*, 59–80, and Birch, "Film and Cinema in Singapore," 187–89. For government policy and funding initiatives, see the Web site of the Singapore Film Commission: *see* www.sfc.org.sg.

68. Birch, "Film and Cinema in Singapore," 191.

69. Chua Beng Huat with Yeo Wei Wei, "Cinematic Critique from the Margins and the Mainstream," in Chua Beng Huat, *Life Is Not Complete Without Shopping: Consumption Culture in Singapore*, 177–89.

70. Although not directed by Neo, a successful 1999 movie was built around the character. Uhde and Ng Uhde, *Latent Images*, 135–38.

71. *See* www.sfc.org.sg/statistics/statistic_top5.shtm (accessed June 20, 2004).

72. Uhde and Ng Uhde interview Khoo (*Latent Images*, 121–25).

73. Chua, "Cinematic Critique," 184, 188.

74. Ibid., 188.

75. Chua Beng Huat, "Taiwan's Future/Singapore's Past: Hokkien Films in Between," in Chua, *Life Is Not Complete Without Shopping*, 160–62.

76. Bill Nichols, "Discovering Form, Inferring Meaning: New Cinemas and the Film Festival Circuit," 16–26.

77. For further discussion of the film and its poor critical reception in Singapore compared to *Mee Pok Man*, see Chris Berry, "The Scenic Route versus the Information Superhighway."

78. Uhde and Ng Uhde, *Latent Images*, 111.

79. Ibid., 127–30.

80. Homi K. Bhabha, "Of Mimicry and Man: The Ambivalence of Colonial Discourse," in *The Location of Culture*, 85–92.

European-language Bibliography

Abbas, Ackbar. *Hong Kong: Culture and the Politics of Disappearance*. Minneapolis: University of Minnesota Press, 1997.

Allen, Joseph R. "Dressing and Undressing the Chinese Woman Warrior." *Positions* 4.2 (1996): 343–80.

Anagnost, Ann. *National Past-Times: Narrative, Representation, and Power in Modern China*. Durham: Duke University Press, 1997.

Anderson, Benedict. *Imagined Communities: Reflections on the Origin and Spread of Nationalism* (1983). Rev. ed. London: Verso, 1991.

———. *The Spectre of Comparisons*. London: Verso, 1998.

Anderson, Marston. *The Limits of Realism: Chinese Fiction in the Revolutionary Period*. Berkeley: University of California Press, 1990.

Andrew, Dudley. "Poetic Realism. " In Bandy, ed., *Rediscovering French Film*, 115–19.

———. "Sound in France: The Origins of a Native School." In Bandy, ed., *Rediscovering French Film*, 57–65.

Andrew, Geoff. "East Is Wed." *Time Out* (September 22, 1993).

Ansen, David. "Straightening Up the House." *Newsweek* (August 16, 1993).

Appadurai, Arjun. *Modernity at Large: Cultural Dimensions of Globalization*. Minneapolis: University of Minnesota Press, 1996.

Armstrong, David. "Something Old, Something New." *San Francisco Examiner*, August 4, 1993, B1, B7.

Aveni. Anthony. *Empires of Time: Calendars, Clocks, and Cultures*. New York: Basic Books, 1989.

Axelron, Jem. "*The Wedding Banquet*." *Box Office* (September 1993).

Bai Jingshen. "Throw Away the Walking Stick of Drama." In George S. Semsel, Xia Hong, and Hou Jianping, eds., *Chinese Film Theory*, 5–9.

Bakhtin, Mikhail. *Rabelais and His World*. Translated by Helen Iswolsky. Cambridge and London: MIT Press, 1986.

Bakken, Borge. *The Exemplary Society: Human Improvement, Social Control, and the Dangers of Modernity in China*. Oxford: Oxford University Press, 2000.

Bamyeh, Mohammed A. "Transnationalism." *Current Sociology* 41.3 (1993): 1–95.

Bandy, Mary Lea, ed. *Rediscovering French Film.* Boston: Little, Brown, 1983.

Banks, Marcus. *Ethnicity: Anthropological Constructions.* New York: Routledge, 1996.

Barlow, Tani E. "Politics and Protocols of *Funü:* (Un)Making National Woman." In Christina K. Gilmartin, Gail Hershatter, Lisa Rofel, and Tyrene White, eds., *Engendering China: Women, Culture, and the State,* 339–59. Cambridge: Harvard University Press, 1994.

——. "Theorizing Woman: *Funü, Guojia, Jiating.*" In Angela Zito and Tani E. Barlow, eds., *Body, Subject, and Power in China,* 253–90. Chicago: University of Chicago Press, 1994.

Barmé, Geremie R. *In the Red: On Contemporary Chinese Culture.* New York: Columbia University Press, 1999.

——. "Persistence de la tradition au 'royaume des ombres', Quelques notes visant à contribuer à une approche nouvelle du cinéma chinoise." In Marie-Claire Quiquemelle, ed., *Le Cinéma Chinois,* 113–27. Paris: Centre Georges Pompidou, 1985.

Barmé Geremie and John Minford. *Seeds of Fire: Chinese Voices of Conscience.* New York: Noonday Press, 1989.

Barrott-Wicks, Ann, ed. *Children in Chinese Art.* Honolulu: University of Hawaii Press, 2002.

Beer, Gillian. *Darwin's Plots: Evolutionary Narrative in Darwin, George Eliot, and Nineteenth-Century Fiction.* London and Boston: Ark, 1985.

Bennett, Tony. *Culture: A Reformer's Science.* Sydney: Allen and Unwin, 1998.

Berlie, Jean. *Sinisation.* Paris: Éditions Guy Trédaniel, 1998.

Berry, Chris. "China's New 'Women's Cinema.'" *Camera Obscura* 18 (1989): 8–19.

——. "Disney's *Mulan,* Disney's Feminism: Universal Appeal and Mutually Assured Destruction." *TAASA Review: The Journal of the Asian Arts Society of Australia* 9.1 (2000): 6–7.

——. "Interview with Zhang Nuanxin." *Camera Obscura* 18 (1989): 20–25.

——. *Postsocialist Cinema in Post-Mao China: The Cultural Revolution After the Cultural Revolution.* New York: Routledge, 2004.

——. "Race (*Minzu*): Chinese Film and the Politics of Nationalism." *Cinema Journal* 31.2 (1992): 45–58.

——. "The Scenic Route versus the Information Superhighway." In Phyllis G. L. Chew and Anneliese Kramer-Dahl, eds., *Reading Culture: Textual Practices in Singapore,* 201–216. Singapore: Times Academic Press, 1999.

——. "The Sublimative Text: Sex and Revolution in Big Road." *East-West Film Journal* 2.2 (1988): 66–86.

——. "A Turn for the Better? Genre and Gender in *Girl from Hunan* and Other Recent Mainland Chinese Films." *Post Script* 14.1–2 (1994–1995): 82–103.

——. " *Wedding Banquet:* A Family (Melodrama) Affair." In Berry, ed., *Chinese Films in Focus,* 183—190.

Berry, Chris, ed. *Chinese Films in Focus: 25 New Takes.* London: British Film Institute, 2003.

——. *Perspectives on Chinese Cinema.* London: British Film Institute, 1991.

Berry, Chris and Feii Lu, eds. *Island on the Edge: Taiwan New Cinema and After.* Hong Kong: Hong Kong University Press, 2005.

Berry, Chris and Mary Farquhar, "Post-socialist Strategies: An Analysis of *Yellow Earth* and *Black Cannon Incident.*" In Linda Ehrlich and David Desser, *Cinematic Landscapes,* 84–100. Austin: University of Texas Press, 1996.

Bhabha, Homi K. "DissemiNation: Time, Narrative, and the Margins of the Modern State." In Bhabha, ed., *Nation and Narration,* 139–70.

——. "Introduction: Narrating the Nation." In Bhabha, ed., *Nation and Narration*, 1–7.

——. *The Location of Culture*. London: Routledge, 1994.

Bhabha, Homi K., ed. *Nation and Narration*. London: Routledge, 1990.

Birch, David."Film and Cinema in Singapore: Cultural Policy as Control." In Albert Moran, ed., *Film Policy: International, National, and Regional Perspectives*, 185–211. London: Routledge, 1996.

Black, David A. *Law in Film: Resonance and Representation*. Urbana: University of Illinois Press, 1999.

Blaine, Nancy. "New York Story: Tale of Taiwan Immigrants Is a Fine Feast." *L.A. Village View,* August 6–12, 1993.

Bob the moo. "Awful dubbing, awful acting but good action" January 28, 2004 (*see* www.imdb.com/title/tt0113326/usercomments) (accessed November 5, 2004).

Bobo, Jacqueline. *Black Women as Cultural Readers*. New York: Columbia University Press, 1995.

Bodde, Derk and Clarence Morris, *Law in Imperial China: Exemplified by 190 Ch'ing Dynasty Cases*. Philadelphia: University of Pennsylvania Press, 1973.

Bodey, Michael. "Holding Out for a Hero." November 4, 2004; *see* http://entertainment.news.com.au/common/story_page/0,4459,11282918%255E10431%255E%255Enbv,00.html (accessed November 25, 2004).

Bordwell, David. "The Art Cinema as a Mode of Film Practice." *Film Criticism* 4.1 (Fall 1979): 56–64.

——. *Ozu and the Poetics of Cinema*. Princeton: Princeton University Press, 1988.

——. *Planet Hong Kong: Popular Cinema and the Art of Entertainment*. Cambridge: Harvard University Press, 2000.

——. "Transcultural Spaces: Toward a Poetics of Chinese Film." *Post Script* 20.2–3 (Winter, Spring, Summer 2001): 9–24.

Bordwell, David, Janet Staiger, and Kristin Thompson, eds. *The Classical Hollywood Cinema: Film Style and Mode of Production to 1960*. London: Routledge and Kegan Paul, 1985.

Braester, Yomi. *Witness Against History: Literature, Film, and Public Discourse in Twentieth-Century China*. Stanford: Stanford University Press, 2003.

Bratton, Jacky, Jim Cook, and Christine Gledhill, eds. *Melodrama: Stage, Picture, Screen*. London: British Film Institute, 1994.

Brooks, Peter. "Melodrama, Body, Revolution." In Bratton, Cook and Gledhill, eds., *Melodrama*, 11–24.

——. *The Melodramatic Imagination: Balzac, Henry James, Melodrama, and the Mode of Excess*. New Haven: Yale University Press, 1976.

Brown, Georgia. "Three's Company." *Village Voice,* August 10, 1993, 49.

Brown, Melissa J., ed. *Negotiating Ethnicities in China and Taiwan*. Berkeley: Institute of East Asian Studies, University of California, Berkeley, 1996.

Browne, Nick. "Hou Hsiao-hsien's *Puppetmaster:* The Poetics of Landscape." *Asian Cinema* 8.1 (1996): 28–38. In Berry and Lu, eds., *Island on the Edge*, 79–88.

——. "Society and Subjectivity: On the Political Economy of Chinese Melodrama." In Browne, Pickowicz, Sobchak, and Yau, eds., *New Chinese Cinemas*, 40–56.

Browne, Nick, Paul G. Pickowicz, Vivian Sobchak, and Esther Yau, eds. *New Chinese Cinemas: Form, Identities, Politics*. New York: Cambridge University Press, 1994.

Butler, Judith. *Excitable Speech: A Politics of the Performative.* New York: Routledge, 1997.

——. *Gender Trouble: Feminism and the Subversion of Identity.* New York: Routledge, 1990.

Chan, Felicia. "*Crouching Tiger, Hidden Dragon:* Cultural Migrancy and Transation." In Berry, ed., *Chinese Films in Focus,* 56–64.

Chan, Jachinson. *Chinese American Masculinities: From Fu Manchu to Bruce Lee.* New York: Routledge, 2001.

Chan, Joseph M. "Disneyfying and Globalizing the Chinese Legend Mulan: A Study in Transculturation." In *In Search of Boundaries: Communication, Nation-States, and Cultural Identities,* 225–48. Westport, Conn.: Greenwood, 2002.

Chan, Stephen Ching-kiu. "Figures of Hope and the Filmic Imaginary of Jianghu in Contemporary Hong Kong Cinema." *Cultural Studies* 15.3–4 (2001): 486–514.

Chang, Bryan. "Hollywood Hong Kong: Fruit Chan's Heaven and Hell." In Bono Lee, ed., *Hong Kong Panorama, HKIFF 2001–2002,* 86–88. Hong Kong: Hong Kong Arts Development Council, 2002.

Chang, Michael G. "The Good, the Bad, and the Beautiful: Movie Actresses and Public Discourse in Shanghai, 1920s—1930s." In Zhang Yingjin, ed., *Cinema and Urban Culture in Shanghai,* 128–59.

Chatterjee, Partha. *The Nation and Its Fragments: Colonial and Postcolonial Histories.* Princeton: Princeton University Press, 1993.

Cheah, Pheng. *Spectral Nationality: Passages of Freedom from Kant to Postcolonial Literatures of Liberation.* New York: Columbia University Press, 2003.

Chen Chung-min, Chuang Ying-chang, and Huang Shu-min, eds. *Ethnicity in Taiwan: Social, Historical, and Cultural Perspectives.* Taipei: Institute of Ethnology, Academia Sinica, 1994.

Chen Kuan-Hsing. "Why is 'Great Reconciliation' Im/possible? De-Cold War/decolonization, or modernity and its tears." *Inter-Asia Cultural Studies* 3.1&2 (2002): 77–99 and 233–51. In abbreviated form in Berry and Lu, eds., *Island on the Edge,* 39–54.

Chen Xiaomei. *Occidentalism: A Theory of Counter-Discourse in Post-Mao China.* Oxford: Oxford University Press, 1995.

Chen Xihe. "Shadowplay: Chinese Film Aesthetics and Their Philosophical and Cultural Fundamentals." In George S. Semsel, Xia Hong, and Hou Jianping, eds., *Chinese Film Theory,* 192–204.

Cheng, Yu. "Anatomy of a Legend." In Li Cheuk-to, ed., *A Study of Hong Kong Cinema in the Seventies,* 18–25. Hong Kong: Urban Council, 1984.

Chi, Robert. "Getting It on Film: Representing and Understanding History in *A City of Sadness.*" *Tamkang Review* 29.4 (1999): 47–84.

Chiao Hsiung-Ping. "Bruce Lee: His Influence on the Evolution of the Kung Fu Genre." *Journal of Popular Film and Television* 9.1 (1984): 30–42.

Chiu Yen Liang (Fred). "From the Politics of Identity to an Alternative Cultural Politics: On Taiwan Primordial Inhabitants' A-systemic Movement," in Rob Wilson and Arif Dirlik, eds., *Asia/Pacific as Space of Cultural Production,* 120–44. Durham: Duke University Press, 1995.

Chow, Rey. *Ethics After Idealism: Theory—Culture—Ethnicity—Reading.* Bloomington: Indiana University Press, 1998.

——. "Introduction: On Chineseness as a Theoretical Problem." *Boundary 2* 25.3 (1998): 1–24.

——. *Primitive Passions: Visuality, Sexuality, Ethnography, and Contemporary Chinese Cinema.* New York: Columbia University Press, 1995.

——. "Silent Is the Ancient Plain: Music, Filmmaking, and the Concept of Social Change in the New Chinese Cinema." In Chow, *Primitive Passions,* 79–107.

——. *Woman and Chinese Modernity: The Politics of Reading Between West and East.* Minneapolis: University of Minnesota, 1991.

Chu, Henry. "Beijing—Crouching tiger, hidden who?" *Los Angeles Times,* January 19, 2001, A1.

Chu, Yingchi. *Hong Kong Cinema: Coloniser, Motherland, and Self.* London: Routledge Curzon, 2003.

Chua Beng Huat. *Life Is Not Complete Without Shopping: Consumption Culture in Singapore.* Singapore: Singapore University Press, 2003.

Chua, Laurence. "Queer Wind from Asia." *The Nation* (July 5, 1993).

Ciecko, Anne T. and Sheldon H. Lu. "The Heroic Trio: Anita Mui, Maggie Cheung, Michelle Yeho—Self-Reflexivity and the Globalization of the Hong Kong Action Heroine." *Post Script* 19.1 (1999): 70–86.

Clark, Paul. *Chinese Cinema: Culture and Politics Since 1949.* Cambridge: Cambridge University Press, 1987.

——. "Ethnic Minorities in Chinese Films: Cinema and the Exotic." *East-West Film Journal* 1.2 (1987): 4–21.

Clouse, Robert. *Bruce Lee: The Biography.* Burbank: Unique, 1988.

Corliss, Richard. "All in the Families." *Time* (September 13, 1993): 68–9.

Cowie. Elizabeth. "Fantasia." *m/f* 9 (1984): 71–104.

Croll, Elisabeth. *Changing Identities of Chinese Women: Rhetoric, Experience, and Self-Perception in Twentieth-Century China.* Atlantic Highlands, N.J.: Zed Books, 1995.

——. *Feminism and Socialism in China.* London: Routledge and Kegan Paul, 1978.

Cui, Shuqin. *Women Through the Lens: Gender and Nation in a Century of Chinese Cinema.* Honolulu: University of Hawaii Press, 2003.

Curthoys, Ann and John Docker. "Is History Fiction?" *The UTS Review* 2.1 (1996): 18–37.

Dai Jinhua. "Imagined Nostalgia." In T. H. Chen, Arif Dirlik, and Xudong Zhang, eds., *Postmodernism and China,* 205–221. Durham: Duke University Press, 2000.

——. "Invisible Women: Contemporary Chinese Cinema and Women's Film." *Positions* 3.1 (1995): 255–80.

——. "Postcolonialism and the Chinese Cinema of the Nineties." Trans. Harry H. Kuoshu. In Jing Wang and Tani E. Barlow, eds., *Cinema and Desire: Feminist Marxism and Cultural Politics in the Work of Dai Jinhua,* 49–70. London: Verso, 2002.

——. "Severed Bridge: The Art of the Son's Generation." In Jing Wang and Tani E. Barlow, eds., *Cinema and Desire: Feminist Marxism and Cultural Politics in the Work of Dai Jinhua,* 13–48. London: Verso, 2002.

——. "Xia Yan's *Problems of Screenwriting*." In George S. Semsel, Xia Hong, and Hou Jianping, eds., *Chinese Film Theory,* 75–84.

Davis, Darrell William. "Borrowing Postcolonial: *Dou San* and the Memory Mine." *Post Script* 20.2–3 (2001): 94–114.

Denby, David. "Family Ties." *New York* (August 30, 1993): 136.

Denvir, John, ed. *Legal Reelism: Movies as Legal Texts.* Urbana: University of Illinois Press, 1996.

Desser, David. "From the Opium War to the Pacific War: Japanese Propaganda Films of World War II." *Film History* 7.1 (1995): 32–48.

——. "The Kung Fu Craze: Hong Kong Cinema's First American Reception." In Poshek Fu and David Desser, eds., *The Cinema of Hong Kong: History, Arts, Identity,* 19–43. Cambridge: Cambridge University Press, 2000.

Dikötter, Frank. *The Discourse of Race in Modern China.* London: Hurst, 1992.

Dirks, Nicholas B. "History as a Sign of the Modern." *Public Culture* 2.2 (1990): 25–33.

Dissanyake, Wimal, ed. *Melodrama and Asian Cinema.* Cambridge and New York: Cambridge University Press, 1993.

Dittmer, Lowell. "Radical Ideology and Chinese Political Culture: An Analysis of Revolutionary *Yangbanxi.*" In Richard Wilson, Sidney Greenblatt, and Amy Wilson, eds., *Moral Behavior in Chinese Society,* 126–51. Hong Kong: Oxford University Press, 1981.

Doane, Mary Ann. "Film and Masquerade: Theorizing the Female Spectator." *Screen* 23.3–4 (1982): 74–87.

Donald, Stephanie "Women Reading Chinese Films: Between Orientalism and Silence." *Screen* 36.4 (1995): 325–40.

Dow, Tsung-I. "The Confucian Concept of a Nation and Its Historical Practice." *Asian Profile* 10.4 (1982): 347–61.

Duara, Prasenjit. "The Regime of Authenticity: Timelessness, Gender, and National History in Modern China." *History and Theory* 37.3 (1998): 287–99.

——. *Rescuing History from the Nation: Questioning Narratives of Modern China.* Chicago: University of Chicago Press, 1995.

——. "Transnationalism and the Predicament of Sovereignty: China 1900–1945." *American Historical Review* 102.4 (1997): 1030–51.

Dubey, Madhu. "The True 'Lie' of the Nation: Fanon and Feminism." *Differences* 10.2 (1993): 1–29.

Dwyer, Arienne M. "The Texture of Tongues: Languages and Power in China." In William Safran, ed., *Nationalism and Ethnoregional Identities in China,* 68–85. London: Frank Cass, 1998.

Dyer, Richard. *Now You See It: Studies on Lesbian and Gay Film.* London: Routledge, 1990.

——. *Stars.* London: British Film Institute, 1982.

Ebert, Roger. "The Wedding Banquet." *Beverly Hills Courier,* August 27, 1993, 16.

Edensor, Tim. *National Identity, Popular Culture, and Everyday Life.* Oxford and New York: Berg, 2002.

Edwards, Louise. *Men and Women in Qing China: Gender in "The Red Chamber Dream."* Leiden: E. J. Brill, 1994.

Elley, Derek. "*Hsi Yen (The Wedding Banquet).*" *Variety,* March 1, 1993.

Elsaesser, Thomas. "General Introduction: Early Cinema from Linear History to Mass Media Archaeology." In Thomas Elsaesser, with Adam Barker, eds., *Early Cinema: Space—Frame—Narrative,* 11–30. London: British Film Institute, 1990.

——. "Tales of Sound and Fury: Observations on the Family Melodrama." In Gledhill, ed., *Home Is Where the Heart Is,* 43–69.

Eng, Robert Y. "Is *Hero* a Paean to Authoritarianism?" (August 25, 2004). *See* mclc@lists.acs. ohio-state.edu (accessed November 27, 2004).

Ehrlich, Linda and Ma Ning. "College Course File: East Asian Cinema." *Journal of Film and Video* 42.2 (1990): 53–70.

Fabian, Johannes. *Moments of Freedom: Anthropology and Popular Culture.* Charlottesville: University of Virginia Press, 1998.

——. *Time and the Other: How Anthropology Makes Its Object.* New York: Columbia University Press, 1983.

Fairbank, John Y. and S. Y. Teng. "On the Ch'ing Tributary System." *Harvard Journal of Asiatic Studies* 6.2 (1941): 135–246.

Farmer, Brett. "*Mémoire en Abîme:* Remembering (through) *Centre Stage.*" *Intersections* 4 (2000); *see* wwwsshe.murdoch.edu.au/intersections/issue4/centre_review.html (accessed September 22, 2000).

Farquhar, Mary. *Children's Literature in China: From Lu Xun to Mao Zedong.* New York: M E Sharpe, 1999.

——. "The Hidden Gender in *Yellow Earth.*" *Screen* 33.2 (Summer 1992): 154–64.

——. "Monks and Monkeys: A Study of 'National Style' in Chinese Animation." *Animation Journal* 1.2 (1993): 14–19.

——. "Oedipality in *Red Sorghum* and *Judou.*" *Cinemas* 3.2–3 (1993): 60–86.

——. "Silver Screen." In Jane Orton et al., *Bridges to Chinese: Internet/CD Postgraduate Course.* Melbourne: University of Melbourne, 1999.

——. "*A Touch of Zen:* Action in Martial Arts Movies." In Berry, ed., *Chinese Films in Focus,* 167–74.

Field, Andrew D. "Selling Souls in Sin City: Shanghai Singing and Dancing Hostesses in Print, Film, and Politics, 1920–1949." In Zhang Yingjin, ed., *Cinema and Urban Culture in Shanghai,* 99–127.

Finnane, Antonia. "What Should Chinese Women Wear? A National Problem." In Antonia Finnane and Anne McLaren, eds., *Dress, Sex, and Text in Chinese Culture,* 20–23. Clayton, Australia: Monash Asia Institute, 1999.

Fore, Steve. "Jackie Chan and the Cultural Dynamics of Global Entertainment." In Sheldon Hsiao-peng Lu, ed., *Transnational Chinese Cinemas,* 239–62.

——. "Life Imitates Entertainment: Home and Dislocation in the Films of Jackie Chan." In Esther C. M. Yau, ed., *At Full Speed,* 122–37.

——. "Tales of Recombinant Femininity: *The Reincarnation of Golden Lotus,* the *Chin Ping Mei,* and the Politics of Melodrama in Hong Kong," *Journal of Film and Video* 45.4 (1993): 57–70.

Foucault, Michel. *Power/Knowledge.* New York: Pantheon, 1972.

Freiberg, Freda. "*China Nights* (Japan, 1940): The Sustaining Romance of Japan at War." In John Whiteclay Chambers II and David Culbert, eds., *World War II, Film, and History,* 31–46. New York: Oxford University Press, 1996.

Freud, Sigmund. "Analysis of a Phobia in a Five-Year-Old Boy ('Little Hans')" (1909). In *The Pelican Freud Library,* vol. 8, *Case Histories I, "Dora" and "Little Hans,"* 167–305. Harmondsworth: Penguin Books, 1977.

Fu, Poshek. *Between Shanghai and Hong Kong: The Politics of Chinese Cinemas.* Stanford: Stanford University Press, 2003.

Fuery, Patrick. *New Developments in Film Theory*. New York: St. Martin's, 2000.

Gallagher, Mark. "Masculinity in Translation: Jackie Chan's Transcultural Star Text." *Velvet Light Trap* 39 (Spring 1997): 23–41.

Gateward, Frances, ed. *Zhang Yimou: Interviews*. Jackson: University Press of Mississippi, 2001.

Gelder, Ken. *Reading the Vampire*. London: Routledge, 1994.

Gerould, Daniel. "Melodrama and Revolution. " In Bratton, Cook, and Gledhill, eds., *Melodrama*, 185–98.

Gladney, Dru C. *Dislocating China: Reflections on Muslims, Minorities, and Other Subaltern Subjects*. Chicago: University of Chicago Press, 2004.

——. "Representing Nationality in China: Refiguring Majority/Minority Identities." *The Journal of Asian Studies* 53.1 (1994): 92–123

——. "Tian Zhuangzhuang, the Fifth Generation, and Minorities Film in China." *Public Culture* 8.1 (1995): 161–75.

Glaessner, Verina. *Kung Fu: Cinema of Vengeance*. New York: Bounty, 1974; London: Lorrimer, 1974.

Gledhill, Christine, ed. *Home Is Where the Heart Is: Studies in Melodrama and the Woman's Film*. London: British Film Institute (BFI), 1987.

Goodman, David S.G. and Gerald Segal, eds. *China Deconstructs: Politics, Trade, and Regionalism*. London: Routledge, 1994.

Goodrich, Peter. "Laws of Friendship." *Law and Literature* 15.1 (2003): 23–52.

Gossman, Lionel. "History and Literature: Reproduction or Signification." In Robert H. Canary and Henry Kozicki, eds., *The Writing of History: Literary Form and Historical Understanding*, 3–40. Madison: University of Wisconsin Press, 1978.

Guldin, Gregory Eliyu. "Review: Stevan Harrell, *Cultural Encounters on China's Ethnic Frontiers.*" *Journal of Asian and African Studies* 33.4 (1998): 369–70.

Gunning, Tom. "The Cinema of Attractions: Early Film, Its Spectator and the Avant-Garde." In Elsaesser with Barker, eds., *Early Cinema*, 56–62.

——. "Early American Cinema." In John Hill and Pamela Church Gibson, eds., *The Oxford Guide to Film Studies*, 255–71. Oxford: Oxford University Press, 1998.

Guthmann, Edward. "'Datebook': Wedded Mess: Gay Man's Marriage to Pacify Taiwanese Parents Begets Laughs." *San Francisco Chronicle*, August 1, 1993, 23.

Hall, Kenneth. *John Woo: The Films*. Jefferson, N.C., and London: McFarland, 1992.

Hallam, Julia, with Margaret Marshment. *Realism and Popular Cinema*. Manchester and New York: Manchester University Press, 2000.

Hamamoto, Darrell Y. *Monitored Peril: Asian Americans and the Politics of TV Representation*. Minneapolis: University of Minnesota Press, 1994.

Han Meng. "Leaders Ponder a Return to Society's Roots to Stop the Rot." *South China Morning Post*, December 6, 2004. See mclc@lists.acs.ohio-state.edu ("Bringing Back Confucius") (accessed December 9, 2004).

Hannerz, Ulf. *Transnational Connections: Culture, People, Places*. London: Routledge, 1996.

Hansen, Miriam. *Babel and Babylon: Spectatorship in American Silent Film*. Cambridge: Harvard University Press, 1991.

Hardt, Michael and Antonio Negri. *Empire*. Cambridge: Harvard University Press, 2001.

Harrell, Stevan, ed. *Cultural Encounters on China's Ethnic Frontiers*. Seattle: University of Washington Press, 1995.

Harris, Kristine. "*The New Woman* Incident: Cinema, Scandal, and Spectacle in 1935 Shanghai." In Sheldon Hsiao-peng Lu, ed., *Transnational Chinese Cinemas*, 277–302.

Hayward, Susan. *Key Concepts in Cinema Studies*. London and New York, Routledge, 1996.

Heard, Christopher. *Ten Thousand Bullets: The Cinematic Journey of John Woo*. Los Angeles: Lone Eagle, 2000.

Heberer, Thomas. *China and Its National Minorities: Autonomy or Assimilation?* Armonk, N.Y.: M. E. Sharpe, 1989.

Hendrischke, Hans and Feng Chongyi, eds. *The Political Economy of China's Provinces: Comparative and Competitive Advantage*. London: Routledge, 1999.

"Hero: Box Office Savior." *Zhongguo Wang*, January 14, 2003; *see* www.china.org.cn/english/BAT/53523.html (accessed June 19, 2004).

"*Hero* Becomes China's Top-Grossing Film, to Open in the U.S. Later this Year." *Banana Cafe* (2003); *see* www.bananacafe.ca/0303/fr-ent-2a-0303/html (accessed June 19, 2004).

Hevia, James L. *Cherishing Men from Afar: Qing Guest Ritual and the Macartney Embassy of 1793*. Durham: Duke University Press, 1995.

Higson, Andrew. "The Concept of National Cinema." *Screen* 30.4 (1989): 36–46.

Hoberman, J. "Review of *Hero*." *Village Voice*, August 23, 2004. *See* www.villagevoice.com/issues/0434/hoberman2.php in mclc@lists.acs.ohio-state.edu (accessed August 27, 2004).

Hobsbawm, Eric and Terence Ranger, eds. *The Invention of Tradition*. Cambridge: Cambridge University Press, 1983.

Hoffman, John. *Gender and Sovereignty: Feminism, the State, and International Relations*. Houndsmill, Eng., and New York: Palgrave, 2001.

Holden, Stephen. "*The Wedding Banquet*." *New York Times*, August 4, 1993, C18.

Holm, David. *Art and Ideology in Revolutionary China*. Oxford: Clarendon Press, 1991.

Hong Kong Movie Database. *See* http://hkmdb.com.

Horn, Andrew "*The Wedding Banquet*." *Screen International* (March 5, 1993): 22.

Hornaday, Ann. "A Director's Trip from Salad Days to a 'Banquet.'" *New York Times*, August 1, 1993.

Hu Ke. "Hong Kong Cinema in the Chinese Mainland (1949–1979)." In Law Kar, ed., *Hong Kong Cinema Retrospective*, 18–25.

Hu Ying. "Beyond the Glow of the Red Lantern; Or, What Does It Mean to Talk about Women's Cinema in China?" In Diana Robin and Ira Jaffe, eds., *Redirecting the Gaze: Gender, Theory, and Cinema in the Third World*, 257–82. Albany: State University of New York Press, 1999.

Huang Zuolin, "Mei Lanfang, Stanislavsky, Brecht," In Wu Zuguang, Huang Zuolin, and Mei Shaown, eds., *Peking Opea and Mei Lanfang*. Beijing: New World Press, 1981.

Humm, Maggie. *Feminism and Film*. Edinburgh: Edinburgh University Press, 1997.

Hung Chang-Tai. "Female Symbols of Resistance in Chinese Wartime Spoken Drama." *Modern China* 15.2 (1989): 149–77.

Huntington, Samuel. "The Clash of Civilizations?" *Foreign Affairs* 72.3 (1993): 22–49.

Hutchinson, John. "Myth Against Myth: The Nation as Ethnic Overlay." *Nations and Nationalism* 10.1–2 (2004): 109–123.

——. "Re-interpreting Cultural Nationalism." *Australian Journal of Politics and History* 45. 3 (1999): 392–407.

Huters, Ted. "Ideologies of Realism in Modern China: The Hard Imperatives of Imported Theory." Kang Liu and Xiaobing Tang, eds., *Politics, Ideology, and Literary Discourse in Modern China*, 147–73. Durham: Duke University Press, 1993.

"An Interview with Zhang Yimou." ERA brochure on *Raise the Red Lantern*. No author, date, or pagination. Translated from an interview, *Esquire* magazine (Chinese version, 1991).

Johnson, Kay Ann. *Women, the Family, and Peasant Revolution in China*. Chicago: University of Chicago Press, 1983.

Kaminsky, Stuart M. "Kung Fu as Ghetto Myth." In Michael T. Marsden and John G. Nachbar, eds., *Movies as Artifacts: Cultural Critiques of Popular Film*, 137–45. Chicago: Nelson-Hall, 1982.

Kaplan, E. Ann. "Problematising Cross-Cultural Analysis: The Case of Women in the Recent Chinese Cinema." In Berry, ed., *Perspectives on Chinese Cinema*, 141–55.

Karl, Rebecca E. "The Burdens of History: Lin Zexu (1959) and The Opium War (1997)." In Zhang Xudong, ed., *Whither China? Intellectual Politics in Contemporary China*, 229–62. Durham: Duke University Press, 2001.

Khoo, Olivia. " 'Anagrammatical Translations': Latex Performance and Asian Femininity Unbounded in Olivier Assayas's *Irma Vep*." *Continuum: Journal of Media and Cultural Studies* 13.3 (1999): 383–93.

Kim Soyoung and Chris Berry. " 'Suri Suri Masuri': The Magic of the Korean Horror Film: A Conversation." *Postcolonial Studies* 3.1 (2000): 53–60.

Kinney, Anne Behnke, ed. *Chinese Views on Childhood*. Honolulu: University of Hawaii Press, 1995.

Kirihara, Donald. *Patterns of Time: Mizoguchi and the 1930s*. Madison: University of Wisconsin Press, 1992.

Klady, Leonard. "Alien: The Unkindest Cuts." *Movie City News* 6 (November 2003); *see* www.moviecitynews.com/columnists/klady/2003/gb_031106.html (accessed June 19, 2004).

Koselleck, Reinhart. *Futures Past: On the Semantics of Historical Time*. Cambridge: MIT Press, 1985.

Kraus, Richard Curt. *Pianos and Politics in China: Middle-Class Ambitions and the Struggle Over Western Music*. New York and Oxford: Oxford University Press, 1989.

Kwong, Mary. "HK Movie World's Fortunes Take a Tumble." *Straits Times*, September 19, 2002; *see* http://straitstimes.asia1.com.sg/asia/story/0,1870,144163,00.html (accessed September 19, 2002).

Lacan, Jacques. "The Mirror Stage as Formative of the Function of the I." In *Écrits: A Selection*, 1–7. New York: Norton, 1977.

Lague, David. "Triads Hit the Screen." *Australian Magazine* (October 31–November 1, 1992): 48–53.

Lau Shing-Hon, ed. *A Study of the Hong Kong Martial Arts Film: The 4th Hong Kong International Film Festival, April 3–18, 1980, City Hall*. Hong Kong: Urban Council, 1980.

Lau, Jenny Kwok Wah. "*Judou*: A Hermeneutical Reading of Cross-Cultural Cinema." *Film Quarterly*, 45.2 (1991–92): 2–10.

Law, Kar. "Archetypes and Variations: Observations on Six Cantonese Films." In Li Cheuk-to, ed., *Cantonese Melodrama, 1950–1969*, 15–20.

——. "Hong Kong New Wave: Modernization Amid Global/Local Counter Cultures." In Law Kar, ed., *Hong Kong New Wave,* 44–50.

——. "An Overview of Hong Kong's New Wave Cinema." In Esther C. M. Yau, ed., *At Full Speed,* 31–52.

Law Kar, ed. *Hong Kong Cinema Retrospective: Border Crossings in Hong Kong Cinema.* Hong Kong: Leisure and Culture Services Department, 2000.

——. *Hong Kong New Wave: Twenty Years After.* Hong Kong: Provisional Urban Council of Hong Kong, 1999.

——. *Transcending the Times: King Hu and Eileen Chang.* Hong Kong: The Provisional Urban Council of Hong Kong, 1998.

Law Wai-ming. "A Time for Tears." In Li Cheuk-to, ed., *Cantonese Melodrama, 1950–1969,* 23–25.

Lee, Ang. "Foreword." In Sunshine, ed., *Crouching Tiger, Hidden Dragon,* 7.

Lee, Leo Ou-fan. *Shanghai Modern: The Flowering of a New Urban Culture in China, 1930–1945.* Cambridge: Harvard University Press, 1999.

Lee, Linda. *The Bruce Lee Story.* Santa Clarita Calif.: Ohara, 1989.

Lent, John A., ed. *Asian Popular Culture.* San Francisco: Westview Press, 1995.

Leung, Helen Hok-Sze. "*Yellow Earth:* Hesitant Apprenticeship and Bitter Agency." In Berry, ed., *Chinese Films in Focus,* 191–97.

Leung Noong-kong. "The Changing Power Relationship Between China and Hongkong: An Examination of the Concept of 'Home' and Its Function in Hongkong Movies in the 40's and 50's." In Li Cheuk-to, ed. *The 12th Hong Kong International Film Festival: Changes in Hong Kong Society Through Cinema,* 25–28. Hong Kong: Urban Council, 1988.

——. "The Long Goodbye to the China Factor." In Li Cheuk-to, ed. *The China Factor in Hong Kong Cinema,* 71–76.

Leung, Ping-Kwan. "Problematizing National Cinema: Hong Kong Cinema in Search of Its Cultural Identity." *River City* 16.1 (1996): 23–40.

Li Cheuk-to, "*Spring in a Small Town,* Mastery and Restraint." *Cinemaya* 49 (2000): 59–64.

Li Cheuk-to, ed. *Cantonese Opera Film Retrospective.* Hong Kong: Urban Council, 1987.

——. *Cantonese Melodrama, 1950–1969.* Hong Kong: Urban Council of Hong Kong, 1986.

——. *The China Factor in Hong Kong Cinema.* Hong Kong: Urban Council, 1990.

Li Jie. "Xie Jin's Era Should End." In George S. Semsel, Xia Hong, and Hou Jianping, eds., *Chinese Film Theory,* 147–48.

Li , Si-ming and Wing-shing Tang, eds. *China's Regions, Polity, and Economy: A Study of Spatial Transformation in the Post-Reform Era.* Hong Kong: Chinese University Press, 2000.

Li Siu Leung. "Kung Fu: Negotiating Nationalism and Modernity." *Cultural Studies* 15.3–4 (2001): 529–36.

Li Suyuan and Hu Jubin. *Chinese Silent Film History.* Trans. Wang Rui, Huang Wei, Hu Jubin, Wang Jingjing, Zhen Zhong, Shan Wanli, and Li Xun. Beijing: China Film Press, 1997.

Liao Ping-hui. "Passing and Re-articulation of Identity: Memory, Trauma, and Cinema." *Tamkang Review* 29.4 (1999): 85–114.

Lieberman, Sally Taylor. *The Mother and Narrative Politics in Modern China.* Charlottesville: University Press of Virginia, 1998.

Lim, Bliss Cua. "Spectral Times: The Ghost Film as Historical Allegory." *Positions: East Asia Cultural Critique* 9.2 (2001): 287–329.

Lin Nien-tung. "Some Problems in the Study of Cantonese Films of the 1950s." In Lin Nien-tung, ed., *Cantonese Cinema Retrospective (1950–1959)*, 28–33.

Lin Nien-tung, ed., *Hong Kong Cinema Survey (1946–1968)*. Hong Kong: Urban Council, 1979.

——. *Cantonese Cinema Retrospective (1950–1959)*. Hong Kong: Urban Council, 1978.

Little, John R. *Bruce Lee: A Warrior's Journey*. Chicago: Contemporary Books, 2001.

Litzinger, Ralph. "Memory Work: Reconstituting the Ethnic in Post-Mao China." *Cultural Anthropology* 13.2 (1998): 224–55.

——. *Other Chinas: The Yao and the Politics of National Belonging*. Durham: Duke University Press, 2000.

Liu, Cynthia W. " 'To Love, Honor, and Dismay': Subverting the Feminine in Ang Lee's Trilogy of Resuscitated Patriarchs." *Hitting Critical Mass: A Journal of Asian American Cultural Criticism* 3.1 (1995): 37–40.

Liu, Lydia H. "The Female Tradition in Modern Chinese Literature: Negotiating Feminisms Across East/West Boundaries." *Genders* 12 (1991): 22–44.

——. "The Metamorphosis of a Song Immortal: Understanding Official Popular Culture in Twentieth-Century China." In Judith Zeitlin and Lydia Liu, eds., *Writing and Materiality in China*, 553–603. Cambridge: Harvard University Press, 2003.

——. "Translingual Practice: The Discourse of Individualism Between China and the West." *Positions* 1.1 (1993): 160–93.

Lo, Kwai-cheung. "Double Negations: Hong Kong Cultural Identity in Hollywood's Transnational Representations." *Cultural Studies* 15.3–4 (2001): 472–79.

——. "Muscles and Subjectivity: A Short History of the Masculine Body in Hong Kong Popular Culture." *Camera Obscura* 39 (1996): 105–126.

——. "Transnationalization of the Local in Hong Kong Cinema of the 1990s." In Esther C. M. Yau, ed., *At Full Speed*, 261–76.

Logan, Bey. *Hong Kong Action Cinema*. London: Titan Books, 1995.

Long, Simon. *Taiwan: China's Last Frontier*. London: Macmillan, 1991.

Louie, Kam. *Theorizing Chinese Masculinity: Society and Gender in China*. New York: Cambridge University Press, 2002.

Lowe, Lisa. *Critical Terrains: French and British Orientalisms*. Ithaca: Cornell University Press, 1991.

Lu Feii. "Another Cinema: Darkness and Light." In Berry and Lu, eds., *Island on the Edge*, 137–48.

Lu Hsun [Lu Xun]. *A Brief History of Chinese Fiction*. Trans.Yang Hsien-I and Gladys Yang. Peking: Foreign Languages Press, 1976.

Lu, Sheldon H[siao-ping]. *From Historicity to Fictionality: The Chinese Poetics of Narrative*. Stanford: Stanford University Press, 1994.

——. "Historical Introduction: Chinese Cinemas (1896–1996) and Transnational Film Studies," in Lu, ed., *Transnational Chinese Cinemas*, 1–25.

——. "Hong Kong Diaspora Film and Transnational TV Drama: From Homecoming to Exile to Flexible Citizenship." *Post Script* 20.2–3 (2001): 137–46.

Lu, Sheldon, ed.. *Transnational Chinese Cinemas: Identity, Nationhood, Gender*. Honolulu: University of Hawaii Press, 1997.

Lu Xun. "Preface to Call to Arms." In *Lu Xun: Selected Works, Vol. 1*, trans. Yang Xianyi and Gladys Yang, 33–38. Beijing: Foreign Languages Press, 1980.

Lyman, Rick. "Watching Movies with Ang Lee," *New York Times,* March 9, 2001; *see* www.nytimes.com?2001/03/09WATC.html (accessed March 14, 2001).

Ma Ning. "Culture and Politics in Chinese Film Melodrama [Manuscript]: Traditional Sacred, Moral Economy, and the Xie Jin Mode." Ph.D diss., Monash University, 1992.

——. "Spatiality and Subjectivity in Xie Jin's Film Melodrama of the New Period." In Browne, Pickowicz, Sobchak, and Yau, eds., *New Chinese Cinemas,* 15–39.

——. "Symbolic Representation and Symbolic Violence: Chinese Family Melodrama of the Early 1980s." *East-West Film Journal* 4.1 (December 1989): 32–49.

——. "The Textual and Critical Difference of Being Radical: Reconstructing Chinese Leftist Films of the 1930s." *Wide Angle* 11.2: 22–31.

Ma, Sheng-mei. "Ang Lee's Domestic Tragicomedy: Immigrant Nostalgia, Exotic/Ethnic Tour, Global Market." *Journal of Popular Culture* 30.1 (1996): 197–99.

——. *The Deathly Embrace: Orientalism and Asian American Identity.* Minneapolis: University of Minnesota Press, 2000.

Machura, Stefan and Peter Robson. "Law and Film: An Introduction." *Journal of Law and Society* 28.1 (2001): 1–8.

MacKenzie, John M. *Orientalism: History, Theory, and the Arts.* Manchester: Manchester University Press, 1995.

Mackerras, Colin. *China's Minority Cultures: Identities and Integration Since 1912.* New York: St. Martin's, 1995.

—— . *Chinese Drama: A Historical Survey.* Beijing: New World Press, 1990.

——. *The Chinese Theatre in Modern Times: From 1840 to the Present Day.* London: Thames and Hudson, 1975.

Major, Wade. " 'Tiger' Time: Director Ang Lee and Actress Michelle Yeoh Discuss Their Breakthrough Martial Arts Epic *Crouching Tiger, Hidden Dragon* from Sony Classics." *Boxoffice* (December 2000): 30–31.

Mao Tse-tung [Mao Zedong]. *The Chinese Revolution and the Chinese Communist Party.* Peking: Foreign Languages Press, 1960.

——. "Yenan [Yan'an] Forum on Literature and Art" (1942). In Mao Tse-tung, *Selected Works of Mao Tse-tung* 3:69–98. Peking: Foreign Languages Press, 1975

Marchetti, Gina. "Jackie Chan and the Black Connection." In Tinkcom and Villarejo, eds., *Keyframes: Popular Cinema and Cultural Studies,* 137–58.

——. "*Two Stage Sisters:* The Blooming of a Revolutionary Aesthetic." In Sheldon Hsiao-peng Lu, ed., *Transnational Chinese Cinemas,* 59–80; originally published in *Jump Cut* 34 (1989): 89–106.

——. "*The Wedding Banquet:* Global Chinese Cinema and Asian American Experience." In Sandra Liu and Darrell Y. Hamamoto, eds., *Countervisions: Asian-American Film Criticism,* 275–97. Philadelphia: Temple University Press, 2000.

Martin, Fran. *Situating Sexualities: Queer Representation in Taiwanese Fiction, Film, and Public Culture.* Hong Kong: Hong Kong University Press, 2003.

——. "*Vive L'Amour:* Eloquent Emptiness." In Berry, ed., *Chinese Films in Focus,* 175-82.

Mazierska, Ewa and Laura Rascaroli. "Trapped in the Present: Time in the Films of Wong Kar-wai." *Film Criticism* 25.2 (2000–2001): 2–20.

McClintock, Anne. *Imperial Leather: Race, Gender, and Sexuality in the Colonial Context.* New York: Routledge, 1995.

McDougall, Bonnie S. *Mao Zedong's "Talks at the Yan'an [Yenan] Conference on Literature and Art": A Translation of the 1943 Text with Commentary.* The University of Michigan Center for Chinese Studies: Michigan Papers in Chinese Studies no. 39, 1980.

——. *The Yellow Earth: A Film by Chen Kaige, with a Complete Translation of the Filmscript.* Hong Kong: Chinese University Press, 1991.

Meng Yue. "Female Images and National Myth." In Tani Barlow, ed., *Gender Politics in Modern China: Writing and Feminism,* 118–36. Durham: Duke University Press, 1993.

Meyers, Richard, Amy Harlib, and Karen Palmer. *From Bruce Lee to the Ninjas: Martial Arts Movies.* New York: Carol Publishing Group, 1991.

Miller, Toby, Nitin Govil, John McMurria, and Richard Maxwell. *Global Hollywood.* London: British Film Institute, 2001.

Miyoshi, Masao. "A Borderless World? From Colonialism to Transnationalism and the Decline of the Nation-State." In Rob Wilson and Wimal Dissanayake, eds., *Global/Local: Cultural Production and the Transnational Imaginary,* 78–106. Durham: Duke University Press 1996.

Moger-Williams, Ben and Wu Runmei. "The Art of Compromise: An Interview with Film Director Zhang Yimou." *Beijing This Month* 63 (February 1999); *see* http://cbw.com/btm/issue63/16.html (accessed September 27, 2000).

Moore-Gilbert, Bart. *Postcolonial Theory: Contexts, Practices, Politics.* London: Verso, 1997.

Morris, Meaghan. "Learning from Bruce Lee: Pedagogy and Political Correctness in Martial Arts Cinema." In Tinkcom and Villarejo, eds., *Keyframes: Popular Cinema and Cultural Studies,* 171–86.

Mulvey, Laura. "It Will Be a Magnificent Obsession: The Melodrama's Role in the Development of Contemporary Film Criticism." In Bratton, Cook, and Gledhill, eds., *Melodrama,* 121–33.

——. "Visual Pleasure and Narrative Cinema." *Screen* 16.3 (1975): 6–18.

Musser, Charles. "The Nickelodeon Era Begins, Establishing the Framework for Hollywood's Mode of Representation." In Elsaesser with Barker, eds., *Early Cinema,* 56–73.

Neale, Steve. "Hollywood Blockbusters: Historical Dimensions." In Julian Stringer, ed., *Movie Blockbusters,* 47–60. London: Routledge, 2003.

Needham, Joseph. *Science and Civilization in China.* Vols. 1–4. Taipei: Dayuan yinshua chang, 1973.

"New Start for Film Industry." *CRIonline,* 2003; *see* http://web12.cri.com.cn/english/2003/Feb/87224.html (accessed June 19, 2004).

Ng Ho. "Kung-fu Comedies: Tradition, Structure, Character." In Lau Shing-Hon, ed., *A Study of the Hong Kong Martial Arts Film,* 42–46.

Ni Zhen. *Memoirs from the Beijing Film Academy: The Origins of China's Fifth Generation Filmmakers.* Trans. Chris Berry. Durham: Duke University Press, 2002.

Nichols, Bill. "Discovering Form, Inferring Meaning: New Cinemas and the Film Festival Circuit." *Film Quarterly* 47.3 (1994): 16–26.

Nielsen, Hanna Boje. "The Three Fathers in Tian Zhuangzhuang's Film *The Blue Kite:* The Emasculation of Males by the Communist Party." *China Information* 13.4 (1999): 83–96.

Noble, Jonathan. "*Titanic* in China: Transnational Capitalism as Official Ideology?" *Modern Chinese Literature and Culture* 12.1 (2000): 164–98.

Noh, David. "*The Wedding Banquet.*" *Film Journal* (September 1993): 22.

Nornes, Abe Mark and Yeh Yueh-yu. "Behind City of Sadness." 1994. See the CinemaSpace Web site (at http://cinemaspace.berkeley.edu/Papers/CityOfSadness/table.html).

Nowell-Smith, Geoffrey. "Minnelli and Melodrama." In Gledhill, ed., *Home Is Where the Heart Is*, 70–75.

Odham Stokes, Lisa and Michael Hoover. *City on Fire: Hong Kong Cinema*. London: Verso, 1999.

O'Neill, Mark. "Film-makers Jittery as Hollywood Comes Calling." *South China Morning Post*, October 9, 2000.

Ou Shuyi. "In the Minds of Women." *China Daily*, February 11, 2000. *See* www.chinadaily. com.cn/cndydb/2000/02/d8–1book.211.html (accessed April 13, 2001).

Oudart, Jean-Pierre. "The System of the Suture." *Screen* 18.4 (1977–78): 35–47.

Pacheco, Patrick. "Cultural Provocateur: In 'The Wedding Banquet' Ang Lee Stirs Up Custom." *Los Angeles Times*, August 4, 1993, F1, F5, F6.

Pang Laikwan. *Building a New China in Cinema: The Chinese Left-Wing Cinema Movement, 1932–1937*. Lanham, Md.: Rowman and Littlefield, 2002.

Papke, David Ray. "Myth and Meaning: Francis Ford Coppola and the Popular Response to the *Godfather* Trilogy." In Denvir, ed., *Legal Reelism: Movies as Legal Texts*, 1–22.

Patrick, Michael and Zhang Yilei. "Beijing." *Persimmon* (2003); *see* www.persimmon-mag. com/spring2003/city_scan.html (accessed June 19, 2004).

Pheng Cheah, *Spectral Modernity: Passages of Freedom from Kant to Postcolonial Literatures of Liberation*. New York: Columbia University Press, 2003.

Pickowicz, Paul. *Marxist Literary Thought in China: The Influence of Chú Ch'iu-pai [Qu Qiubai]*. Berkeley and London: University of California Press, 1981.

——. "The 'May Fourth' Tradition of Chinese Cinema." In Ellen Widmer and David Der-wei Wang, eds., *From May Fourth to June Fourth: Fiction and Film in Twentieth-Century China*, 295–326. Cambridge: Harvard University Press, 1993.

Plaks, Andrew H. "Towards a Critical Theory of Chinese Narrative." In Plaks, ed., *Chinese Narrative*, 309–52.

Plaks, Andrew H., ed. *Chinese Narrative: Critical and Theoretical Essays*. Princeton: Princeton University Press, 1977.

Porter, Dennis. "*Orientalism* and Its Problems." In Francis Barker et al., *The Politics of Theory*, 179–93. Colchester: University of Essex, 1983.

Prashad, Vijay. "Bruce Lee and the Anti-imperialism of Kung Fu: A Polycultural Adventure." *Positions: East Asia Cultural Critique* 11.1 (2003): 51–90.

Pratt, Mary Louise. *Imperial Eyes: Travel Writing and Transculturation*. New York: Routledge, 1992.

Proust, Françoise. *L'Histoire á Contretemps*. Paris: Les éditions du Cerf, 1994.

Prušek, Jaroslav. *The Lyrical and the Epic: Studies of Modern Chinese Literature*. Bloomington: Indiana University Press, 1980.

Rajadhyaksha, Ashish. "Realism, Modernism, and Post-colonial Theory." In John Hill and Pamela Church Gibson, eds., *The Oxford Guide to Film Studies*, 413–25. Oxford: Oxford University Press, 1998.

Rayns, Tony. "Bruce Lee: Narcissism and Nationalism." In Lau Shing-Hon, ed., *A Study of the Hong Kong Martial Arts Film*, 110–12. Hong Kong: Urban Council, 1980.

——. "Bruce Lee and Other Stories." In Li Cheuk-to, ed., *A Study of Hong Kong Cinema in the Seventies*, 26–29. Hong Kong: Urban Council, 1984.

——. "5000 Years Plus One: *The Wedding Banquet*." *Berlin International Film Festival 1993* catalog.

——. "The Innovators, 1990–2000: Charisma Express." *Sight and Sound* 10.1 (2000): 34–36.

——. "Poet of Time." *Sight and Sound* 5, no.9 (1995): 12–14.

——. "*Xiyan*" (*The Wedding Banquet*)." *Sight and Sound* 3.10 (1993): 56.

Republic of China Yearbook: 1991–92. Taipei: Kwang Hua Publishing, 1991.

Reynolds, Dale. "Marry Me a Little." *Frontiers* (August 13 1993).

Reynaud, Bérénice. "Gong Li and the Glamour of the Chinese Star." *Sight and Sound* 3.8 (1993): 12–15. Republished in Pam Cook and Philip Dodd, eds. *Women and Film: A Sight and Sound Reader*, 21–29. Philadelphia: Temple University Press, 1993.

——. "Icon of Modernity." *Cinemaya* 37 (1997): 32–36.

——. "Re: *Chinese-Cinema-Digest*—Number 628." In Shelley Kraicer, ed., *Chinese-Cinema-Digest* 630 (July 3, 2001). E-mail distribution list (July 3, 2001).

Robertson, Maureen. "Periodization in the Arts and Patterns of Change in Traditional Chinese Literary History." In Susan Bush and Christian Murck, eds., *Theories of the Arts in China*, 3–27. Princeton: Princeton University Press, 1983.

Rodan, Gary. "Class Transformations and Political Tensions in Singapore's Development." In Richard Robison and David S. G. Goodman, eds., *The New Rich in Asia: Mobile Phones, McDonalds, and Middle-Class Revolution*, 19–45. London: Routledge, 1996.

Rodowick, D. N. *The Difficulty of Difference: Psychoanalysis, Sexual Difference, and Film Theory.* London: Routledge, 1991.

Rodriguez, Hector. "Hong Kong Popular Culture as an Interpretative Arena: The Huang Fei-hong Film Series." *Screen* 38.1 (Spring 1997): 1–24.

Rojas, Carlos. "Specular Failure and Spectral Returns in Two Films with Maggie Cheung (and One Without)." *Senses of Cinema* 12 (2000); *see* www.sensesofcinema.com/contents/01/12/cheung.html (accessed July 5, 2001).

Rosen, Philip. *Change Mummified: Cinema, Historicity, Theory.* Minneapolis: University of Minnesota Press, 2001.

Rosen, Stanley. "'The Wolf at the Door'?: Hollywood and the Film Market in China from 1994 to 2000" (n.d.); *see* www.usc.edu/isd/archives/asianfilm/china/wolf.html (accessed March 27, 2001).

Rosenstone, Robert A. "The Historical Film: Looking at the Past in a Postliterate Age." In Marcia Landy, ed., *The Historical Film: History and Memory in the Media*, 50–67. New Brunswick: Rutgers University Press, 2001.

Rothman, William. "*The Goddess*: Reflections on Melodrama East and West." In Wimal Dissanayake, ed., *Melodrama and Asian Cinema*, 59–72. Cambridge: Cambridge University Press, 1993.

Ryan, Barbara. "Blood, Brothers, and Hong Kong Gangster Movies: Pop Culture Commentary on 'One China.'" In Lent, ed., *Asian Popular Culture*, 61–76.

Said, Edward. *Orientalism.* New York: Vintage Books, 1976.

Sang Hu. "The Ascendancy of China's Women Directors." *China Screen* 1 (1986): 9.

Sautman, Barry. "Anti-Black Racism in Post-Mao China." *China Quarterly* 138 (1994): 413–37.

——. "Racial Nationalism and China's External Behavior." *World Affairs* 160.2 (1997): 78–95.

Schein, Louisa. "The Consumption of Color and the Politics of White Skin in Post-Mao China." *Social Text* 41 (1994): 141–64.

——. "Gender and Internal Orientalism in China." *Modern China* 23.1 (1997): 69–98.

——. Minority Rules: The Miao and the Feminine in China's Cultural Politics. Durham: Duke University Press, 2000.

Sedgwick, Eve Kosofsky. *Between Men: English Literature and Male Homosocial Desire*. New York: Columbia University Press, 1985.

Sek Kei. "The Development of Martial Arts in Hong Kong Cinema." In Lau Shing-hon, ed., *A Study of the Hong Kong Martial Arts Film*, 27–38.

——. "Li Hanxiang." In Lin Nien-tung, ed., *Hong Kong Cinema Survey (1946–1968)*, 92–94.

——. "Thoughts on Chinese Opera and the Cantonese Opera Film." In Li Cheuk-to, ed., *Cantonese Opera Film Retrospective*, 14–17.

Semsel, George S., Chen Xihe, and Xia Hong, eds. *Film in Contemporary China: Critical Debates, 1979–1989*. Westport: Praeger, 1993.

Semsel, George S., Xia Hong, and Hou Jianping, eds. *Chinese Film Theory: A Guide to a New Era*. Trans. Hou Jianping, Li Xiaohong, and Fan Yuan. Westport and London: Praeger, 1990.

Shackleton, Liz. "Hong Kong—The Sequel Means Business." February 27, 2003; *see* www.screendaily.com (accessed March 4, 2003).

Shambaugh, David, ed. *Is China Unstable? Assessing the Factors*. Armonk, N.Y.: M. E. Sharpe, 2000.

Shapiro, Michele. "Wedding-Bell Blues." *New York* (August 2, 1993): 19.

Short, Stephen and Susan Jakes, "Making of a Hero," *Timeasiacom* (2001); *see* www.time.com/time/asia/features/hero/story.html (accessed January 18, 2002).

Silbergeld, Jerome. *China into Film: Frames of Reference in Contemporary Chinese Cinema*. London: Reaktion, 1999.

Silverman, Kaja. *The Acoustic Mirror: The Female Voice in Psychoanalysis*. Bloomington: Indiana University Press, 1988.

——. *Male Subjectivity at the Margins*. New York: Routledge, 1992.

Smith, Anthony D. *Myths and Memories of Nation*. Oxford: Oxford University Press, 1999.

——. *National Identity*. Harmondsworth: Penguin, 1991.

Smith, Craig S. "*Hero* Soars and Its Director Thanks *Crouching Tiger*," *New York Times*, February 9, 2004 (*see* www.nytimes.com/2004/09/02.movies/02zhan.html) in MCLC lists (owner-mclc@acs.ohio-state.edu, accessed September 3, 2004).

Snow, Lois Wheeler. *China on Stage: An American Actress in the People's Republic*. New York: Random House, 1972.

Sobchak, Vivian, ed. *The Persistence of History: Cinema, Television, and the Modern Event*. New York: Routledge, 1996.

Stacey, Judith. *Patriarchy and Socialist Revolution in China*. Berkeley: University of California Press, 1983.

Stam, Robert. "Introduction: The Question of Realism." In Robert Stam and Toby Miller, eds., *Film and Theory: An Anthology*, 223–28. Malden, Mass., and Oxford: Blackwell, 2000.

Stringer, Julian. "*Centre Stage*: Reconstructing the Bio-Pic." *Cineaction* 42 (1997): 28–39.

——. "Your Tender Smiles Give Me Strength: Paradigms of Masculinity in John Woo's *A Better Tomorrow* and *The Killer*." *Screen* 38.1 (1997): 25–41.

Suleiman, Susan Rubin. *Authoritarian Fictions: The Ideological Novel as a Literary Genre.* New York: Columbia University Press, 1983.

Sunshine, Linda, ed. *Crouching Tiger, Hidden Dragon: A Portrait of the Ang Lee Film.* New York: New Market Press, 2000.

Suskind, Ron. "A Plunge into the Present." *New York Times Magazine,* December 2, 2001, 84–89.

Tambling, Jeremy. *Wong Kar-wai's "Happy Together."* Hong Kong: Hong Kong University Press, 2003.

Tan Ye. "From the Fifth to the Sixth Generation: An Interview with Zhang Yimou." In Gateward, ed., *Zhang Yimou: Interviews,* 151–65.

Tang Xiaobing. "Orientalism and the Question of Universality: The Language of Contemporary Chinese Literary Theory." *Positions* 1.2 (1993): 389–413.

Tasker, Yvonne. *Spectacular Bodies: Gender, Genre, and the Action Cinema.* London: Routledge, 1993.

Teo, Stephen. "The Father-Son Cycle: A Critique of Thematic Continuity in Cantonese Cinema." In Li Cheuk-to, ed., *Cantonese Melodrama, 1950–1969,* 42–47.

——. *Hong Kong Cinema: The Extra Dimensions.* London: BFI Publishing, 1997.

——. "Hong Kong's New Wave in Retrospect." In Law Kar, ed., *Hong Kong New Wave,* 17–23.

——. "Love and Swords: The Dialectics of Martial Arts Romance." *Senses of Cinema* 11 (December 2000–January 2001); *see* www.sensesofcinema.com/contents/0011/crouching. html (accessed January 9, 2001).

——. "Only the Valiant: King Hu and His *Cinema Opera.*" In Law Kar, ed., *Transcending the Times,* 19–24.

——. "True Way of the Dragon: The Films of Bruce Lee." In Law Kar, ed., *Overseas Chinese Figures in Cinema: The 16th Hong Kong International Film Festival* (April 10, 1992–April 25, 1992), 70–80. Hong Kong: Urban Council, 1992.

——. "Wong Kar-wai's *In the Mood for Love:* Like a Ritual in Transfigured Time." *Senses of Cinema* 1.13 (no date). *See* www.sensesofcinema.com/contents/01/13/mood.html.

Thomas, Bruce. *Bruce Lee: Fighting Spirit.* Berkeley: Frog, 1994.

Thomas, Rosie. "Sanctity and Scandal: The Mythologization of Mother India." *Quarterly Review of Film and Video* 11.3 (1989): 11–30.

Ti Wei. "Reassessing New Taiwanese Cinema: From Local to Global." In Kim Ji-Seok and Jungsuk Thomas Nam, eds., *Taiwanese Cinema, 1982–2002: From New Wave to Independent.* Pusan: Pusan International Film Festival, 2002.

Tinkcom, Matthew and Amy Villarejo, eds. *Keyframes: Popular Cinema and Cultural Studies.* London and New York: Routledge, 2001.

Tolentino, Roland B. "*Inangbayan,* the Mother-Nation, in Lino Brocka's *Bayan Ko: Kapit Sa Patalim* and *Orapronobis.*" *Screen* 37.4 (1996): 368–88.

Tong, Janice. "*Chungking Express:* Time and Its Dislocation." In Berry, ed., *Chinese Films in Focus,* 47–55.

Toumarkine, Doris. "Giving Good 'Banquet.'" *Hollywood Reporter* (June 8, 1993).

Trinh T. Minh-ha. *Woman, Native, Other: Writing Postcoloniality and Feminism.* Bloomington: Indiana University Press, 1989.

Tsing, Anna. "The Global Situation." *Cultural Anthropology* 15.3 (2000): 327–60.

Tsui, Curtis. "Subjective Culture and History: The Ethnographic Cinema of Wong Kar-wai." *Asian Cinema* 7.2 (1995): 93–124.

Tu, Wei-ming. "Cultural China: The Periphery as the Center." *Daedalus* 120.2 (1991): 1–32.

Turan, Kenneth. "Marriage of Convenience Yields a Full 'Banquet.'" *Los Angeles Times*, August 4, 1993, F1, F4.

Uhalley (Jr.), Stephen. "'Greater China': The Contest of a Term." *Positions* 2.2 (1994): 274–93.

Uhde, Jan and Yvonne Ng Uhde. *Latent Images: Film in Singapore*. Singapore: Oxford University Press, 2000.

Vincendeau, Ginette. "Melodramatic Realism: On Some French Women's Films in the 1930s." *Screen* 30.3 (1989): 51–65.

Wachman, Alan M. *Taiwan: National Identity and Democratization*. Armonk, N.Y.: M. E. Sharpe, 1994.

Walsh, Michael. "National Cinema, National Imaginary." *Film History* 8.2 (1996): 5–17.

Wang Hui. "Local Forms, Vernacular Dialects, and the War of Resistance Against Japan: The 'National Forms' Debates." *The UTS Review* 4.1–2 (1998): 25–41, 27–56.

Wang Jing. *High Culture Fever: Politics, Aesthetics, and Ideology in Deng's China*. Berkeley: University of California Press, 1996.

Wang, Q. Edward. *Inventing China Through History: The May Fourth Approach to Historiography*. Albany: State University of New York Press, 2001.

Wang Shujen. *Framing Piracy: Globalization and Film Distribution in Greater China*. Lanham, Md.: Rowman and Littlefield, 2003.

Wang Yiman. "Screening the Past, Re-centering the Stage." Paper presented at the annual meeting of the American Comparative Literature Assocation, University of Colorado, Boulder, April 22, 2001.

Wang Yuejin. "*Red Sorghum*: Mixing Memory and Desire." In Berry, ed., *Perspectives on Chinese Cinema*, 80–103.

Washitani, Hana. "*The Opium War* and the Cinema Wars: A Hollywood in the Greater East Asian Co-Prosperity Sphere." *Inter-Asia Cultural Studies* 4.1 (2003): 63–76.

Watson, Rubie S. "Wives, Concubines, and Maids: Servitude and Kinship in the Hong Kong Region, 1900–1940." In Rubie S. Watson and Patricia Buckley Ebrey, eds., *Marriage and Inequality in Chinese Society*, 231–55. Berkeley: University of California Press, 1991.

Whitney, Ian. "*Hero.*" *Dual Lens* (March 22, 2003); *see* www.duallens.com/index.asp?reviewId = 31503 (accessed May 8, 2004).

Williams, Christopher. "After the Classic, the Classical, and Ideology: The Differences of Realism," *Screen* 35.3 (1994): 275–92.

Williams, Linda. *Playing the Race Card: Melodramas of Black and White from Uncle Tom to O. J. Simpson*. Princeton and Oxford: Princeton University Press, 2001.

Williams, Raymond. *Culture and Society, 1780–1950*. Harmondsworth: Penguin, 1963.

———. *Keywords*. Glasgow: Fontana/Croom Helm, 1976.

———. *Marxism and Literature*. Oxford: Oxford University Press, 1977.

Wolf, Marjory. *Revolution Postponed: Women in Contemporary China*. London: Methuen, 1985.

Wood, Robin. *Hollywood from Vietnam to Reagan*. New York: Columbia University Press, 1986.

Wu Hao. "The Legend and Films of Huang Fei-hong." In Lin Nien-tung, ed., *Cantonese Cinema Retrospective (1950–1959)*, 100–101.

Wu Zuguang, Huang Zuolin, and Mei Shaowu. *Peking Opera and Mei Lanfang*. Beijing: New World Press, 1981.

Xia Hong. "The Debate Over *Horse Thief*." In George S. Semsel, Chen Xihe, and Xia Hong, eds., *Film in Contemporary China*, 39–50.

Xu, Ben. "*Farewell My Concubine* and Its Nativist Critics." *Quarterly Review of Film and Video* 16.2 (1997): 155–70.

——. "'From Modernity to Chineseness': The Rise of Nativist Cultural Theory in Post-1989 China." *Positions* 6.1 (1998): 203–238.

Yamada Hirokazu and Koyo Udagawa. "King Hu's Last Interview." In Law Kar, ed., *Transcending the Times*, 74–78.

Yang, Jeff. "Out of Asia." *Village Voice*, October 12, 1994, 16. Republished in Larry Gross and James D. Wood, eds. *The Columbia Reader on Lesbians and Gay Men in Media, Society, and Politics*, 644–46. New York: Columbia University Press, 1999.

Yang Ping. "A Director Who Is Trying to Change the Audience: A Chat with Young Director Tian Zhuangzhuang." Trans. Chris Berry. In Berry, ed., *Perspectives on Chinese Cinema*, 127–33.

Yau, Esther C. M. "Cultural and Economic Dislocations: Filmic Phantasies of Chinese Women in the 1980s." *Wide Angle* 11.2 (1989): 6–21.

——. "Is China the End of Hermeneutics? Or, Political and Cultural Usage of Non-Han Women in Mainland Chinese Films." *Discourse* 11.2 (1989): 115–38.

——. "*Yellow Earth*: Western Analysis and a Non-Western Text." In Berry, ed., *Perspectives on Chinese Cinema*, 62–79.

Yau, Esther C. M, ed. *At Full Speed: Hong Kong Cinema in a Borderless World*. Minneapolis and London: University of Minnesota Press, 2001

Yeh Yueh-Yu. "Defining Chineseness." *Jump Cut* 42 (1998): 73–76.

Yeh Yueh-yu and Abe Mark Nornes. "Introduction." *Narrating National Sadness: Cinematic Mapping and Hypertextual Dispersion* (University of California, Berkeley, Film Studies Program, 1998). See the *CinemaSpace* Web site (at http://cinemaspace.berkeley.edu/Papers/CityOfSadness/table.html) (accessed August 16, 2001).

Yeung, Y. M. and David K.Y. Chu. eds. *Fujian: A Coastal Province in Transition and Transformation*. Hong Kong: Chinese University Press, 2000.

Yoshimoto, Mitsuhiro. "The Difficulty of Being Radical: The Discipline of Film Studies and the Postcolonial World Order." In Masao Miyoshi and H. D. Harootunian, eds., *Japan in the World*, 338–53. Durham: Duke University Press, 1993.

Young, Robert J. C. *Colonial Desire: Hybridity in Theory, Culture, and Race*. London: Routledge: 1995.

Yue, Audrey Ing-Sun. "*In the Mood for Love*: Intersections of Hong Kong Modernity." In Berry, ed., *Chinese Films in Focus*, 128–36.

——. "Migration-as-Transition: Pre-Post 1997 Hong Kong Culture in Clara Law's *Autumn Moon*." *Intersections* 4 (2000); *see* wwwsshe.murdoch.edu.au/intersections/issue4/yue.html (accessed July 17, 2001).

——."Pre-Post 1997: Postcolonial Hong Kong Cinema, 1984–1997." Ph.D. diss., La Trobe University, 1999.

——. "Preposterous Horror: On *Rouge, A Chinese Ghost Story,* and Nostalgia." In Ken Gelder, ed., *The Horror Reader,* 365–99. New York: Routledge, 2000.

Yuval-Davis, Nira. *Gender and Nation.* London: Sage, 1997.

Zha Jianying. *China Pop.* New York: The New Press, 1994.

Zhang, Yingjin. *Chinese National Cinema.* New York: Routledge, 2004.

——. *Screening China: Critical Interventions, Cinematic Reconfigurations, and the Transnational Imaginary in Contemporary Chinese Cinema.* Ann Arbor: Michigan Monographs in Chinese Studies, 2002.

Zhang, Yingjin, ed., *Cinema and Urban Culture in Shanghai, 1922–1943.* Stanford: Stanford University Press, 1999.

Zhang, Yingjin and Zhiwei Xiao. *Encyclopaedia of Chinese Film.* London and New York: Routledge, 1999.

Zhang Xudong. *Chinese Modernism in the Era of Reforms.* Durham: Duke University Press, 1997.

Zhang Zhen. "Bodies in the Air: Magic of Science and the Fate of the Early 'Martial Arts' Film in China." *Post Script* 20.2–3 (2001): 43–60.

Zhao, Henry Y. H. "Post-Isms and Chinese New Conservatism." *New Literary History* 28.1 (1997): 31–44.

Zhong Dafeng, Zhen Zhang, and Yingjin Zhang. "From *Wenmingxi* [Civilized Play] to *Yingxi* [Shadowplay]: The Foundations of the Shanghai Film Industry in the 1920s." *Asian Cinema* 9.1 (1997): 46–64.

Zhu Dake. "The Drawback of Xie Jin's Model." In George S. Semsel, Xia Hong, and Hou Jianping, eds., *Chinese Film Theory,* 144–46.

Chinese-Language Bibliography

Bai Ning (白宁). "有容乃大, 无欲则刚——李安谈 《喜宴》 [Broadminded and fair: Ang Lee discusses *The Wedding Banquet*]." 香港电影双周刊 374 期 (1993): 42–43.

Cai Hongsheng (蔡洪声). 台港电影与影星 [*Taiwan and Hong Kong films and films stars*]. 北京: 中国文艺出版社, 1992.

Chiao, Peggy Hsiung-Ping (焦雄屏). "田壮壮与 《盗马贼》 [Tian Zhuangzhuang and *Horse Thief*]." 焦雄屏, ed., 李莲英大太监, pp. 193–98. 台北: 万象, 1991.

Chen Da (陈达). "呼唤民族的自觉自省: 观影片 《鸦片战争》 [A call to national consciousness: on seeing the film, *The Opium War*]." 大众电影, 531 期 (1997): 14.

Chen Kaige (陈凯歌). "希望片 [A film of hope]." 中国电影放映公司, ed., 黄土地, p. 2. 北京: 中国电影出版社, 1984.

Chen Mo (陈墨). "费穆电影论 [On Fei Mu's films]." 当代电影 8, 9 期 (1997): 39.

Chen, Robert Ru-Shou (陈儒修). "解构 《阮玲玉》 [Interpreting *Center Stage*]." In 电影帝国: 另一种注视: 电影文化研究, pp. 180–87. 台北: 万象, 1995.

——. 电影帝国: 另一种注视: 电影文化研究 [*Empire of films: another kind of gaze: research on film culture*]. 台北: 万象, 1995.

Cheng Jihua. 阮玲玉 [*Ruan Lingyu*]. 北京: 中国电影出版社, 1985.

Cheng Jihua et al. (程季华). 中国电影发展史, 上下 [*The history of the development of Chinese cinema*, vols. 1 and 2]. 北京: 中国电影出版社, 1981.

Cheng Long [Jackie Chan] (成龙). 我是成龙 [*I am Jackie Chan*]. 台北: 时报文化, 1998.

Chinese Filmmakers Association (中国电影家协会), ed. 论中国少数民族电影 [*A discussion of Chinese minority nationality films*]. 北京: 中国电影出版社, 1997.

Dai Jinhua (戴锦华). 电影理论与批评手册 [*A handbook of film theory and criticism*]. 北京: 科学技术文献出版社, 1993.

——. "《青春之歌》: 历史视域中的重读 [*Song of Youth*: a rereading from a historical perspective]." In 中国理论与批评手册, pp. 199–217. 北京: 科学技术文献出版社, 1993.

Ding Yinnan (丁荫楠) et al. "影片纵横谈: 巨片《孙中山》 [Film roundtable: on the epic film, *Dr. Sun Yatsen*]." 电影艺术 295 期 (1997): 3–18.

Feng Min (封敏). "《马路天使》与新现实主义 [*Street Angel* and neorealism]." 当代电影 32.5 期 (1989): 95–100.

Gao Feng (高風). "《化身姑娘》及其它 [*Tomboy* and other matters]." In Chen Bo (陈播), ed., 三十年代中国电影评论文选, pp. 834–36. 北京: 中国电影出版社, 1993.

Gao Honghu (高鸿鹄) et al., ed. 论中国少数民族电影 [*Chinese minority nationality films*]. 北京: 中国电影出版社, 1997.

Hong Shi (弘石). "第一次浪潮——默片期中国商业电影现象述评 [The first film tide—on Chinese commercial movies in the period of silent film]." 当代电影 65.2 期 (1995): 5–12.

Huang Jianxin (黄建新) et al., 《黑炮事件》: 从小说到电影 [*Black Cannon Incident: from novel to film*]. 北京: 中国电影出版社, 1988.

Huang Ren (黄仁). 行者影迹, 李行电影五十年 [*In the footsteps of a filmmaker: Lee Hsing's films over fifty years*]. 台北: 时报文化出版企业股份有限公司, 1999.

——. 悲情台语片 [*Lamenting Taiwanese-language films*]. 台北: 万象, 1994.

Huang Zongjiang (黄宗江) et al. 农奴: 从剧本到影片 [*Serfs: from script to screen*]. 北京: 中国电影出版社: 1965.

Jin Xiang (金湘). "评影片《孙中山》的音乐 [On the music in *Dr. Sun Yatsen*]." 电影艺术 184 期 (1987): 42–43.

Law Kar (罗卡). "风云出英雄: 吴宇森《英雄系列》与林岭东《风云系列》之比较 [Comparing John Woo's 'Hero Series' with Ringo Lam's 'Wind and Cloud Series']." 当代电影 78.5 期 (1997): 59–63.

Lee Haiyan (李海燕). "话说《白毛女》——民族叙事中的阶级与性别政治 [On *The White-haired Girl*—class and sexual politics in the national narrative]." 二十一世纪 52.4 期 (1999): 110–18.

Li Shaobai (李少白). "中国现代电影的前驱, 论费穆和《小城之春》的历史意义, 上下 [A forerunner of modern Chinese film: on the historical significance of Fei Mu's *Spring in a Small Town*, parts 1 and 2]." 电影艺术 250, 251; 5, 6 期 respectively (1996): 分别载 73–78 and 34–42, respectively.

Li Shaobai and Hong Shi (李少白, 弘石). "品位和价值, 中国第一批长故事片创作概述 [An introduction and evaluation of China's first group of feature films]." 当代电影 38.5 期 (1990): 81–88.

Li Suyuan (郦苏元). "关于中国早期电影理论 [About film theories in early China]." 当代电影 61.4 期 (1994): 21–34.

——. "中国早期电影的叙事模式 [The narrative model of Chinese early cinemas]." 当代电影 57.6 期 (1993): 28–34.

Li Suyuan (郦苏元) and Hu Jubin (胡菊彬). [*A history of Chinese silent film* / English-language title: *Chinese Silent Film History*] 中国无声电影史. 北京: 中国电影出版社, 1996.

Li Youxin (李幼新). "李安, 赵文煊, Mitchell Lichtenstein 答客问——《喜宴》记者会 [Ang Lee, Winston Chao, and Mitchell Lichtenstein answer questions: the press conference for *The Wedding Banquet*]." 香港电影双周刊, 366 期 (1993): 20–21.

——. "台湾同志电影的两面: 《青少年哪吒》与《喜宴》 [Two faces of Taiwanese gay cinema: *Rebels of the Neon God* and *The Wedding Banquet*]." 香港电影双周刊, 364 期 (1993): 112.

Lin Yihua (临奕华), "一场欢喜一场空: 喜宴后感 [Delight and emptiness: feelings after seeing *The Wedding Banquet*]." 影响电影杂志, 35 期 (1993): 69–70.

Ling Wen (凌文), "隽永幽默背后的政治意识 [The political implications behind the poignant humor]." 香港电影双周刊, 374 期 (1993): 109.

Lu Deng (陆澄). "《喜宴》纯商业意味的电影 [*The Wedding Banquet*'s purely commercial flavor]." 香港电影双周刊, 376 期 (1993): 112–13.

Lu, Feii (卢非易). 台湾电影: 政治, 经济, 美学. [*Taiwan cinema: politics, economics, aesthetics*]. 台北: 远流出版事业股份有限公司, 1998.

Lu Hongshi (陆弘石). "任庆泰与首批国产片考评 [Evaluations of Ren Qingtai and first Chinese films]." 电影艺术, 2 期 (1992): 82–86.

Lu Xun (鲁迅). "我们现在怎么做父亲 [How we should be fathers today]." In 鲁迅全集, 第 5 卷 [*Lu Xun's Collected Works*, vol. 5]. 北京: 人民文学出版社, 1973: 116–30.

Luo Mingyou (罗明佑). "为国片复兴问题敬告同业书 [Some respectful suggestions to fellow members of the profession concerning the question of the revival of Chinese cinema]." 影戏杂志 1.9 期 (1930): no page numbers.

Luo Yijun (罗艺军). "电影的民族风格初探 [A preliminary discussion of national style in film]." Li Pusheng, Xu Hong, Luo Yijun (李晋生, 徐虹, 罗艺军), eds., 中国电影理论文选, (20–80 年代), 第 1 卷 [*Anthology of Chinese film theory*, vol. 1:268–69]. 北京: 文化艺术出版社, 1989.

Ma Junxiang (马军骧). "从《红高粱》到《菊豆》 [From *Red Sorghum* to *Judou*]." 二十一世纪, 7 期 (1991): 123–32.

——. "民族主义所塑造的现代中国电影 [The nationalist creation of modern Chinese cinema]." 二十一世纪, 15 期, 二月 (1993): 114–18.

——. "《上海姑娘》: 革命女性及〈观看〉问题 [*Shanghai Girl*: revolutionary womanhood and the problem of the 'gaze']." 当代电影, 36 期 (1990): 17–25.

Meng Tao (孟涛), ed., 《舞台姐妹》: 从提纲到影片 [*Two Stage Sisters*: from treatment to film]. 上海: 上海文艺出版社, 1982.

Mu Weifang (穆维芳). "《化身姑娘》 [*Tomboy*]." 陈播, ed., 三十年代中国电影评论文选, pp. 832–34. 北京: 中国电影出版社, 1993.

Mu Yun (慕云). "苍白的感情——我看《小城之春》 [A wan feeling—seeing *Spring in a Small Town*]." 新民晚报, 1948 年 10 [October] 月 3 日.

Ni Zhen (倪震). "黄土地之后 [After Yellow Earth]." 上海文艺出版社, ed., 探索电影记, pp. 196–205. 上海: 上海文艺出版社, 1987.

——. "《泰坦尼克号》: 电影工业的世纪总结 [*Titanic* sums up a century of cinema]." 大众电影 (1998), 6 期: 26–27.

Oral Cinema History Unit, Taipei Film Archive (国家电影资料馆口史电影史小组). 台语片时代 *(1)*. [*The era of Taiwanese-language films*, vol. 1]. 台北: 国家电影资料馆, 1994.

Shao Zhou (少舟). "孙瑜与电影《武训传》 [Sun Yu and the film, *The Life of Wu Xun*]." 电影艺术 215.6 期 (1990): 91–101.

Tan Chunfa (谭春发). "本是同根生, 主仆两处分 [An appreciation of *Twin Sisters*: mistress and maid from the same family]." 当代电影 57.6 期 (1993): 35–40.

Wang Rui (王瑞). "好莱坞电影与好莱坞现象 [Hollywood films and the Hollywood phenomenon]." 当代电影 58 期 (1994): 79–86.

Wang Wenhua (王文化). "《喜宴》在美国 [*The Wedding Banquet* in the United States]." 中国时报 [*China Times Express*], August 12, 1993.

Wang Yichuan (王一川). 张艺谋神话终结: 审美文化视野中的张艺谋电影 [*The end of the Zhang Yimou myth: aesthetic and cultural perspectives on Zhang Yimou's cinema*]. 郑州: 河南人民出版社, 1998.

Wang Yunman (王云漫). "李行导演美学观 [Director Lee Hsing's aesthetic point of view]." 电影欣赏 57.10, 期 (1992): 13–16.

Wang Zhimin (王志敏). 现代电影美学基础 [*Fundamentals of modern film aesthetics*]. Beijing: 中国电影出版社, 1996.

Wang Zhiqiang (王志强). "1995 年进口电影市场综述 [1995 market summary for film imports]." 张兆龙, ed., 中国电影年鉴 *1996*, pp. 203–205. 北京: 中国电影出版社, 1996.

Xie Fang (谢芳). 银幕内外 [*On and off-Screen*]. 北京: 世界知识出版社, 1986.

Xu Haofeng (徐皓峰). "张艺谋的《英雄》 [Zhang Yimou's *Hero*]." 电影艺术, 2 期 (2003): 4–9.

Yang Mo (杨沫). 青春之歌: 从小说到电影) [*Song of Youth: from novel to film*]. 北京: 中国电影出版社, 1962.

Yao Xiaolei (姚晓雷). "经典的结构与重建, 艺术中的 〈侠〉, 〈天下〉 及 〈英雄〉 ——也由从张艺谋的 〈英雄〉 说起 [Classic constructions and reconstructions: *xia, tianxia,* and heroism in art—speaking from Zhang Yimou's *Hero*]." 中国比较文学 51.2 期 (2003): 40–51.

Ye Longyan (叶龙彦). 春花梦露 [*Spring flowers and dreams of dew*]. 台北: 伯杨文化事业有限公司, 1999.

"*Yellow Earth*: full production script." "《黄土地》, 电影完整台本." 上海文艺出版社, ed., 探索电影记 [*A collection of exploratory films*], pp. 91–195. 上海: 上海文艺出版社, 1987.

Yi Dai (亦代). "现实主义电影论 [The theory of realist cinema]." 青青电影周刊 26.5 期 (1940): 4–7.

Yin Hong and Ling Yan (尹鸿, 凌燕). 新中国电影史 *(1949–2000)* [*A history of Chinese cinema: 1949–2000.*] 长沙: 湖南美术出版社, 2002.

Ying Xiong (应雄). "古典写作的璀璨黄昏, 谢晋及其家道主义世界 [The dazzling dusk of classical writing: Xie Jin's world of family values]." 电影艺术 211.2 期 (1990): 46–59.

——. "《农奴》: 叙事的张力 ['*Serfs*': narrative tension]." 当代电影, 36 期 (1990): 11–16.

Zeng Jingzhao (曾敬超). "阮玲玉 [*Center Stage*]." 吴中立, ed., 中华民国电影八十一年年鉴, pp. 36–38. 台北: 国家电影资料馆, 1992.

Zeng Yongyi (曾永义). 台湾歌仔戏发展与变迁 [*Development and changes in Taiwan's gezaixi*]. 台北: 联经出版事业公司, 1988.

Zhai Jiannong (翟建农). "样板戏电影的兴衰–文革电影: 20 世纪特殊的文化现象 [Ups and downs of new model opera films—the films of the Cultural Revolution period: a special cultural phenomenon of the twentieth century, part 1]." 当代电影 65.2 期 (1995): 37–43.

Zhang Baiqing (章柏青). "中国大片好自为之 [Chinese blockbusters need to get it together]." 大众电影 (1998), 5 期: 14.

Zhang Junxiang (张骏祥) et al. "白求恩大夫 [*Dr. Bethune*]," in China Film Press (中国电影出版社), ed., 中国电影剧本选集 [*Anthology of Chinese film scripts*], vol. 9. 北京: 中国电影出版社 (Beijing, 1981): 409–508.

Zhang Qiu (张秋). " 《英雄》, 张艺谋的转型 [*Hero*: Zhang Yimou's turning point]." 电影评价 2 期 (2003): no page number.

Zhang Wei (张卫). "民族题材影片我见 [My opinion on minority nationality films]." 电影艺术, 190 期 (1988): 51.

Zhang Yiwu (张颐武). "全球后殖民话境中的张艺谋 [Zhang Yimou in the context of global postcoloniality].” 当代电影 54 期 (1993): 18–25. Reprinted in 应雄, ed., 论张艺谋, pp. 54–68. (北京: 中国电影出版社, 1994).

Zhao Zhenjiang (赵震江), chief ed., 中国法制四十年 [*Forty years of the Chinese legal system*]. 北京: 北京大学出版社, 1990.

Zheng Dongtian (郑洞天). “ ‘大片’ 什么大?—读 《鸦片战争》 备忘录 [What's big about the “big film”?—a memo on reading *The Opium War*].” 中国电影家协会, ed., 论谢晋电影, pp. 569–571. 北京: 中国电影出版社, 1998.

Zhou Weizhi (周巍峙).“评 《白毛女》 影片 [On the film *The White-haired Girl*].” 王白石, 王文和, eds., 当代中国电影评论选 (上), [*Anthology of contemporary Chinese film criticism*, vol. 1], pp. 15–19. 北京: 中国广播电视出版社, 1987.

Zhou Xiangwen (周湘纹). “从 《孙中山》 论丁荫楠 [Discussing Ding Yinnan on the basis of *Dr. Sun Yatsen*].” 当代电影, 24 期 (1988): 79–89.

Chinese Film List

ENGLISH TITLE	CHINESE TITLE	DIRECTOR'S NAME	DIRECTOR'S CHINESE NAME	DATE
12 Storeys	十二楼	Eric Khoo	邱金海	1997
The Alishan Uprising	阿里山风云	Zhang Ying, Zhang Che	张英、张彻	1949
As Tears Go By	旺角卡门	Wong Kar-wai	王家卫	1986
Ashes of Time	东邪西毒	Wong Kar-wai	王家卫	1994
Ashima	啊诗玛	Liu Qiong	刘琼	1964
Azalea Mountain	杜鹃山	Xie Tieli	谢铁骊	1974
Beautiful Duckling	养鸭人家	Lee Hsing	李行	1965
The Best of Times	美丽时光	Chang Tsochi	张作骥	2002
A Better Tomorrow 1	英雄本色(1)	John Woo	吴宇森	1986
A Better Tomorrow 2	英雄本色(2)	John Woo	吴宇森	1988
The Big Boss	唐山大兄	Lo Wei	罗维	1971
Big Road	大路	Sun Yu	孙瑜	1934
The Birth of New China	开国大典	Li Qiankuan, Xiao Guiyun	李前宽 萧桂云	1989
Bitter Love	苦恋	Peng Ning	彭宁	1980
Black Cannon Incident	黑炮事件	Huang Jianxin	黄建新	1986

ENGLISH TITLE	CHINESE TITLE	DIRECTOR'S NAME	DIRECTOR'S CHINESE NAME	DATE
Blue Kite	蓝风筝	Tian Zhuang-zhuang	田壮壮	1993
A Borrowed Life	多桑	Wu Nien-jen	吴念真	1994
Both Sides Are Happy	两相好	Lee Hsing	李行	1962
Bridge	桥	Wang Bin	王滨	1949
Brother Wang and Brother Liu Tour Taiwan	王哥刘哥游台湾	Lee Hsing	李行	1958
Bugis Street	妖街皇后	Yon Fan	杨凡	1997
Bullet in the Head	義膽群英	John Woo	吴宇森	1985
The Burning of Red Lotus Temple	火烧红莲寺	Zhang Shichuan	张石川	1928
The Butterfly Murders	蝶变	Tsui Hark	徐克	1979
Center Stage	阮玲玉	Stanley Kwan	关锦鹏	1991
The Chinese Connection	精武门	Lo Wei	罗维	1972
Chungking Express	重庆森林	Wong Kar-wai	王家卫	1994
City of Sadness	悲情城市	Hou Hsiao Hsien	侯孝贤	1989
Come Drink With Me	大醉侠	King Hu	胡金铨	1966
Crossroads	十字街头	Shen Xiling	沈西苓	1937
Crouching Tiger, Hidden Dragon	卧虎藏龙	Ang Lee	李安	2000
Crows and Sparrows	乌鸦与麻雀	Cai Chusheng, Zheng Junli	蔡楚生 郑君里	1948
Darkness and Light	黑夜之光	Chang Tsochi	张作骥	1999
The Decisive Engagement	大决战	Cai Jiwei	蔡继渭	1991
Descendents of the Yellow Emperor	黄帝的子孙	Bai Ke	白克	1956
The Difficult Couple	难夫难妻	Zheng Zhengqiu, Zhang Shichuan	郑正秋 张石川	1913
Dingjun Mountain	定军山	No director		1905
Dr. Bethune	白求恩大夫	Zhang Junxiang	张骏祥	1963

ENGLISH TITLE	CHINESE TITLE	DIRECTOR'S NAME	DIRECTOR'S CHINESE NAME	DATE
Dr. Sun Yatsen	孙中山	Ding Yinnan	丁荫楠	1986
Drunken Master	醉拳	Yuen Woping	袁和平	1978
Drunken Master II	醉拳(2)	Lau Kar-leung	刘家良	1993
Durian Durian	榴莲飘飘	Fruit Chan	陈果	2000
Early Spring in February	早春二月	Xie Tieli	谢铁骊	1963
The Emperor and the Assassin	荆轲刺秦王	Chen Kaige	陈凯歌	1998
Enter the Dragon	龙争虎斗	Robert Clouse		1973
Eternal Fame	万世流芳	Maxu Weibang, Yang Xiaozhong, Zhu Shilin, Bu Wancang	马徐维邦 杨小仲 朱石麟 卜万苍	1943
Faraway Love	遥远的爱	Chen Liting	陈鲤庭	1947
Farewell, My Concubine	霸王别姬	Chen Kaige	陈凯歌	1993
Father and Son	父与子	Ng Wui	吴回	1954
Father and Son	父子情	Allen Fong	方育平	1981
Fist of Fury	精武门	Lo Wei	罗维	1972
Fists of Fury	唐山大兄	Lo Wei	罗维	1971
Five Golden Flowers	五朵金花	Wang Jiayi	王家乙	1959
The Game of Death	死亡游戏	Robert Clouse		1978
The Goddess	神女	Wu Yonggang	吴永刚	1934
The Greatest Civil War on Earth	南北和	Wang Tianlin	王天林	1961
Happy Together	春光乍泄	Wong Kar-wai	王家卫	1997
Hardboiled	枪神	John Woo	吴宇森	1992
Hero	英雄	Zhang Yimou	张艺谋	2002
Hollywood Hong Kong	香港有个荷里活	Fruit Chan	陈果	2001
Horse Thief	盗马贼	Tian Zhuang-zhuang	田壮壮	1985

ENGLISH TITLE	CHINESE TITLE	DIRECTOR'S NAME	DIRECTOR'S CHINESE NAME	DATE
House of Flying Daggers	十面埋伏	Zhang Yimou	张艺谋	2004
I Not Stupid	小孩不笨	Jack Neo	梁智强	2001
In the Mood for Love	花样年华	Wong Kar-wai	王家卫	2000
Judou	菊豆	Zhang Yimou	张艺谋	1990
The Kid	细路祥	Fung Fung	冯峰	1950
The Killer	喋血双雄	John Woo	吴宇森	1989
The Kunlun Column	巍巍昆仑	Hao Guang, Jing Muda	郝光 景慕达	1988
The Legend of Tianyun Mountain	天云山传奇	Xie Jin	谢晋	1980
The Life of Wu Xun	武训传	Sun Yu	孙瑜	1951
Lin Zexu and the Opium War	林则徐	Zheng Junli, Cen Fan	郑君里 岑范	1959
Little Cheung	细路祥	Fruit Chan	陈果	1999
Little Toys	小玩意	Sun Yu	孙瑜	1933
The Longest Summer	去年烟花特别多	Fruit Chan	陈果	1998
The Lost Kingdom-Gongle Opera Troupe	消失的王国-拱乐社	Li Xiangxiu	李香秀	1993
Love at Longshan Temple	龙山寺之恋	Bai Ke	白克	1962
Love Eterne	梁山伯与祝英台	Li Hanxiang, King Hu	李翰祥, 胡金铨	1963
Made in Hong Kong	香港制造	Fruit Chan	陈果	1997
Mambo Girl	曼波姑娘	Yi Wen	易文	1957
Mao Zedong and His Son	毛泽东和他的儿子	Zhang Jinbiao	张今标	1991
Money No Enough	钱不够用	Jack Neo	梁智强	1998
Mother's Happiness	儿孙福	Shi Dongshan	史东山	1928
My Son, Ah Chung	细路祥	Fung Fung	冯峰	1950
National Customs	国风	Luo Mingyou, Zhu Shilin	罗明佑 朱石麟	1935

ENGLISH TITLE	CHINESE TITLE	DIRECTOR'S NAME	DIRECTOR'S CHINESE NAME	DATE
The New Woman	新女性	Cai Chusheng	蔡楚生	1935
New Year's Sacrifice	祝福	Sang Hu	桑弧	1956
On the Hunting Ground	猎场扎撒	Tian Zhuang-zhuang	田壮壮	1985
One and Eight	一个和八个	Zhang Junzhao	张军钊	1984
The Opium War	鸦片战争	Li Quanxi	李泉溪	1963
The Opium War	鸦片战争	Xie Jin	谢晋	1997
The Orphan	人海孤鸿	Li Chen-feng	李晨风	1960
Orphan Rescues Grandfather	孤儿救祖记	Zhang Shichuan	张石川	1923
Oyster Girl	蚵女	Li Jia, Lee Hsing	李驾 李行	1964
Parents' Hearts	父母心	Ch'un Kim/Qin Jian	秦劍	1955
Police Story	警察故事	Jackie Chan	成龙	1985
The Puppetmaster	戏梦人生	Hou Hsiao Hsien	侯孝贤	1993
Queen of Sports	体育皇后	Sun Yu	孙瑜	1934
Raise the Red Lantern	大红灯笼高高挂	Zhang Yimou	张艺谋	1990
Rebels of the Neon God	青少年哪吒	Tsai Ming-liang	蔡明亮	1992
Red Sorghum	红高粱	Zhang Yimou	张艺谋	1987
Remorse at Death	生死恨	Fei Mu	费穆	1948
The Return of the Dragon	猛龙过江	Bruce Lee	李小龙	1972
Right a Wrong with Earthenware Dish	瓦盆申冤	Liang Shaopo	梁少坡	1909
The River	河流	Tsai Ming-liang	蔡明亮	1997
The Road Home	我的父亲母亲	Zhang Yimou	张艺谋	1999
Rumble in the Bronx	紅番區	Stanley Tong	唐季禮	1994
Rush Hour		Dan Ratner		1998
Rouge	胭脂扣	Stanley Kwan	关锦鹏	1987

ENGLISH TITLE	CHINESE TITLE	DIRECTOR'S NAME	DIRECTOR'S CHINESE NAME	DATE
Sacrificed Youth	青春祭	Zhang Nuanxin	张暖忻	1985
The Secret	疯劫	Ann Hui	许鞍华	1979
Serfs	农奴	Li Jun	李俊	1963
Shanghai Girl	上海姑娘	Cheng Yin	成荫	1959
The Show Must Go On	江湖儿女	Zhu Shilin	朱石麟	1952
Sing-Song Girl Red Peony	歌女红牡丹	Zhang Shichuan	张石川	1931
Six Scholars of the Western Chamber	六才子西厢记	Shao Luohui	邵罗辉	1955
Snake in Eagles Shadow	蛇形刁手	Yuen Woping	袁和平	1978
Song of the Exile	客途秋恨	Ann Hui	许鞍华	1990
Song of the Fishermen	渔光曲	Cai Chusheng	蔡楚生	1934
Song of Youth	青春之歌	Cui Wei, Chen Huaikai	崔嵬 陈怀皑	1959
Sons of the Earth	江湖儿女	Zhu Shilin	朱石麟	1952
Sons of the Earth	大地儿女	King Hu	胡金铨	1965
Spring in a Small Town	小城之春	Fei Mu; Tian Zhuang-zhuang	费穆 田壮壮	1948 2002
Spring River Flows East	一江春水向东流	Cai Chusheng, Zheng Junli	蔡楚生 郑君里	1947
Spring Silkworms	春蚕	Cheng Bugao	程步高	1933
Stealing a Roasted Duck	偷烧鸭	Liang Shaopo	梁少坡	1909
The Story of Qiu Ju	秋菊打官司	Zhang Yimou	张艺谋	1992
Street Angel	马路天使	Yuan Muzhi	袁牧之	1937
Taking Tiger Mountain by Strategy	智取威虎山	Xie Tieli	谢铁骊	1970
Third Sister Liu	刘三姐	Su Li	苏里	1960
To Live	活着	Zhang Yimou	张艺谋	1994

ENGLISH TITLE	CHINESE TITLE	DIRECTOR'S NAME	DIRECTOR'S CHINESE NAME	DATE
Tomboy	化身姑娘	Fang Peilin	方沛霖	1936
A Touch of Zen	侠女	King Hu	胡金铨	1971
Tragedy on the Pearl River	珠江泪	Wang Weiyi	王为一	1950
Troubled Laughter	苦恼人的笑	Yang Yanjin, Deng Yimin	杨延晋 邓一民	1979
Twelve Widows March West	十二寡妇征西	Hong Xinde	洪信德	1963
Two Stage Sisters	舞台姐妹	Xie Jin	谢晋	1965
Victory of the Mongolian People	内蒙人民的胜利	Gan Xuewei	干学伟	1950
Vive L'Amour	爱情万岁	Tsai Ming-liang	蔡明亮	1994
The Way of the Dragon	猛龙过江	Bruce Lee	李小龙	1972
The Wedding Banquet	喜宴	Ang Lee	李安	1993
White Gold Dragon	白金龙	No director		1933
The White-Haired Girl	白毛女	Wang Bin, Shui Hua	王滨 水华	1950
Woman, Demon, Human	人鬼情	Huang Shuqin	黄蜀芹	1987
Xue Pinggui and Wang Baochuan	薛平贵与王宝钏	He Jiming	何基明	1956
Yan Ruisheng	阎瑞生	Ren Pengnian	任彭年	1921
Yang + Yin: Gender in Chinese Cinema	男生女相:中国电影之性别	Stanley Kwan	关锦鹏	1997
Yellow Earth	黄土地	Chen Kaige	陈凯歌	1984
Zhou Enlai	周恩来	Ding Yinnan	丁荫楠	1991

Index

Abbas, Ackbar, 40–41, 132
adolescence, 144; fear about, 147
Adventures of Priscilla, Queen of the Desert, The, 219
aesthetics of display, 68
Ah Hock, 220
Ahmad, Aijaz, 172
Alishan Uprising, The, 188
allegory, 126, 127
Allen, Joseph R., 113
Allen, Robert, 50
Alliance Society, 224
Anagnost, Ann, 7, 21–22
Anderson, Benedict, 6, 21, 23, 39, 191, 192
Anderson, Marston, 78
androgyny, 115–16
Ang Lee, 10, 13, 47, 49, 52, 53, 66, 67, 69–74, 98, 137, 143, 169, 170, 175–79, 212, 231
Angkor Wat, 17
annals and biography mode of writing, 21
Anti-Japanese War of Resistance, 83, 226
Anti-Rightist Campaign, 228
Anti-Spiritual Pollution Campaign, 230
"appreciating sweetness," 22
arts: reformist, 49; traditional, 48
As Tears Go By, 129
Ashes of Time, 43–44
Ashima, 181
Asia Union Film and Entertainment, 69

Assayas, Olivier, 134
audience, 48; global, 48; regional-language, 48, 51; teahouse, 48, 55
audience-centered strategy, 55
August First Film Studio, 181
aura, 134
auto-ethnography, 188
Azalea Mountain, 62–64, 66, 136, 229

Bai Ke, 68, 190
Bakhtin, Mikhail, 149
ballet, model, 61
barbarians, 180; "cooked," 180, 182; "raw," 180, 182
Barlow, Tani, 112
Barmé, Geremie, 48
Barthes, Roland, 31
Basic Law of the Hong Kong Special Administrative Region, 231
Beautiful Duckling, 94–98, 228
Beer, Gillian, 77
Beijing Film Academy, 229, 230
Beijing Film Studio, 63, 91, 228
Beijing New Image Film Group, 163
Beijing opera. *See* opera
Bennett, Tony, 208
Berry, Chris, 111
Best of Times, The, 40
Better Tomorrow, A, 154
Bhabha, Homi, 7, 21, 222

Big Boss, The, 53, 198, 199, 201, 229
big film, 209, 210, 211. *See also* blockbusters; giant film
Big Road, 82, 201, 225
Birth of New China, The, 210
Bitter Love, 230
Black Cannon Incident, 176, 179–80
Black, David, 139
Bliokh, Vladimir, 224
Block 2 Pictures, 42
blockbusters, 205, 211, 232; mainland China, 209–10, 211
Bordwell, David, 43, 64–66
Both Sides Are Happy, 191, 193
Boxer Rebellion, 223
Braester, Yomi, 33
Bridge, 227
Brooks, Peter, 80–81, 91
Brother Wang and Brother Liu Tour Taiwan, 190, 193
brotherhood, 12, 135, 136, 137, 138, 143–44, 152–58; egalitarian, 143; as metaphor, 183; as redemption, 156; romance of, 137, 155. *See also* Confucian codes
Browne, Nick, 37–38
Bu Wangcang, 24
buddy films, 152
Bugis Street, 218–19
Bullet in the Head, 153–54
Burch, Noël, 50
Burning of Red Lotus Temple, The, 58
Butler, Judith, 7–8
Butterfly Murders, The, 230

Cai Chusheng, 130, 131
Cai Gurong, 81
Cannes Film Festival, 229
Cantonese. *See* language
capitalist roaders, 228
carnivalesque, 149–50
Carradine, David, 198
Carter, Jimmy, 229
Cathay Organization, 214
Cavell, Stanley, 120
CCP. *See* Chinese Communist Party

Cen Fan, 19
Censorship: in mainland, 54, 224; on Taiwan, 67
Center Stage, 108, 109, 129, 130, 131, 133, 134, 225, 231
Central Motion Picture Corporation, 30, 94–98, 175
Chan, Charlie, 200
Chan, Jachinson, 200
Chan, Jackie, 1–2, 12, 48, 52, 66, 129, 133, 137, 140, 143, 144, 145, 146, 150, 153, 158, 161, 168, 200, 229; adolescent image of, 12, 146, 147, 150; Chineseness of, 1–2; as global superstar, 1; Hong Kong identity, 2; as *kung fu* kid, 145, 149, 151; onscreen masculinity, 145, 200
Chang Cheh, 143, 155
Chang Hsiao-hung, 98
Chang Tso-chi, 39, 40
Chang, Grace, 133
Chang, Michael, 131
Chen Chengsan, 67
Chen Kaige, 54, 102, 106–107, 124, 231
Chen Mo, 88
Chen Shui-bian, 232
Chen Xiaomei, 174
Chen Xihe, 51
Chen, Donnie, 163
Cheng Jihua, 23
Cheng Yin, 111
Cheng Yu, 203
cheongsam, 120
Cheung, Maggie, 12, 108, 109, 129–34, 163, 212; star image, 130, 133
Chiang Ching-kuo, 231
Chiang Kai-shek, 12, 26, 112, 119, 190, 224, 225, 227
children, 110. *See also* women
China: elements of, 3; Greater, 5; reconfigurations of, 3
China Film, 205–206
China Film Art Research, 211
China Film Company, 24
China Film Co-Production Corporation, 69
China Film Corporation, 211

China Film Export and Import Corporation. *See* China Film
China United Film Company, 24
Chinarunn Pictures, 219
Chinese Communist Party (CCP), 58, 94, 182, 183; civil war with KMT, 226; Communist Revolution, 189, 190; establishment, 224; exploitation, 183; power structure, 128
Chinese identity. *See* Chineseness
Chinese-language film, 1
Chineseness, 3, 59, 69; in global world, 73
Choi Choseng. *See* Cai Chusheng
Chow Yun-fat, 140, 153
Chow, Rey, 14, 15, 21, 38, 121, 127, 128, 136, 188
Chu T'ien-wen, 30
Chua Beng Huat, 215, 217
Chungking Express, 41, 43, 45
Ciecko, Anne, 130
cinema of attractions, 11, 47, 48, 49–54
cinematic modes, Chinese, 2, 11
citizens: affiliations of, 7; rights of, 7
City of Sadness, 11, 29–38, 39, 78, 189, 190, 193, 231; construction of Taiwanese experience, 37; counter-history, 38; fictionalization of history, 18; and subaltern memory, 18; use of notes in, 36–37
civil war: between KMT and CCP, 225
civilizing project, 174, 182
Clark, Paul, 181
clash of civilizations, 5
collective identity, 9
Columbia Pictures, 69
Come Drink with Me, 53
commodifying gaze, 128. *See also* look
comradeship, 136
Confucian codes, 12, 71, 135, 138–44; cultural identity, 189; as ethnic symbol, 139; as masculinist, 139; performance of, 137; regulation of male behavior, 136; representation of past order, 139; as storytelling resource, 139; in PRC, 136; in Singapore, 136; on Taiwan, 136; transgression against, 137,152

Confucianism, 8; contestation of, 12, 91; government and, 135; patriarchal order, 177; reshaping of, 98; sexuality and, 18; women and, 113
coproductions, 4; PRC–Hong Kong, 53
costume: drama, 31, 224; spectaculars, 57, 58
Cowie, Elizabeth, 111
cross-border renaissance in film, 79
Crossroads, 82
Crouching Tiger, Hidden Dragon, 10, 11, 47, 48, 49, 66, 67, 69–74, 107, 137, 212, 232; cultural Chineseness of, 69, 70; lookalike films, 73
Crows and Sparrows, 82
Cua Lim, Bliss, 39, 41
Cui Shuqin, 132
cultural relaxation, 229
Cultural Revolution, 10, 20, 32, 33, 114, 170, 187, 188; launch of, 229; model ballet, 61; opera films during, 54
Curthoys, Ann, 31

Dai Jinhua, 102, 112, 113
Daoism, 47, 105–106
Darkness and Light, 40
daughter, 109–13; narrative role of, 113. *See also* women
Decisive Engagement, The, 210
deja desparu, 40, 42, 132
Deleuze, Gilles, 45, 174
Democracy Wall, 229, 230
Deng Xiaoping, 91, 229, 230, 231; death, 232
Descendants of the Yellow Emperor, 190, 193, 228
diaspora, Chinese, 2, 14, 194; cultural identity of, 49, 69, 73
Dietrich, Marlene, 120
Difficult Couple, The, 224
Dikötter, Frank, 180
Ding Yi, 60
Ding Yinnan, 210
Dingjun Mountain, 55, 56, 57, 224
Dirks, Nicholas, 31
distribution rights, 212. *See also* film industry

Doane, Mary Ann, 111
Docker, John, 31
documentary, 17. *See also* national history genre
Donald, Stephanie, 188
Doppelganger. *See* double
double, 154–55
doubling, 42, 43–44
Doyle, Christopher, 42
Dr. Bethune, 176, 179–80
Dr. Sun Yatsen, 210
Dresser, David, 24
Drunken Master, 144, 146–47, 229
Drunken Master II, 12, 137, 144, 147–51, 168
Duara, Prasenjit, 20, 23, 170–71
Durian Durian, 101

Early Spring in February, 114, 115, 125
Ebrey, Patricia, 189
EDKO Film, 69
Edwards, Louise, 112
Ehrlich, Linda, 80
Elite Group Enterprise, Inc., 163
Elsaesser, Thomas, 50, 54, 81
Emei Film Studio, 28
Eng, Robert Y., 167
Enloe, Cynthia, 110
Enter the Dragon, 198, 199, 200, 201
episteme, 172
Eternal Fame, 19, 23–25, 28, 226; as part of anti-Western tradition, 24
ethnic: constructions, 169; group defined, 171; identity, 169, 181; nation, 5
ethnicity, 10, 169–94; construction of, 171; cross-ethnic identification, 170; imported understandings of, 169–70; signifiers of, 171, 181–82
expressionist cinema, 66

Fabian, Johannes, 32
Face/Off, 137, 143, 158
family reunion, 99
family-home, 76, 98–107; as cinematic trope, 80; divided, 82–90; emptied out, 76, 98–107; links to national narrative,

82; new Confucian family, 96; reconstructed, 90–98; reenvisioning, 98
Fang Peilin, 84
Faraway Love, 82
Farewell My Concubine, 54, 124
Farquhar, Mary, 127
father: ancestral lineage, 141; good, 137; killing the, 137, 158–68; paternal powerlessness, 142; relationship with son, 100, 143; saving the good, 137, 144–52
Father and Son, 12, 76, 78, 79, 98–101, 142, 230; identity of Hong Kong and, 107
February 28 Incident, 35, 36, 190, 227, 231
Fei Mu, 89, 90, 130
Feii Lu, 39
femininity, 10
Fenghuang Film Studio, 99
Fengtai Studio, 57
Fifth Generation films, 32, 33, 34, 102, 103, 105, 109, 229, 230, 231; primitive passions in, 188
filiality, 12, 135, 137, 138–44, 147, 150, 152–58, 160. *See also* Confucian codes
film: as technology, 55
film industry: Communist control of, 83; global, 196–97, 204–13; in Hong Kong, 206–207; nationalization of, 227; in PRC, 205–206; on Taiwan, 206. *See also* imports; national cinema; piracy
film studies: English-language, 13, 14–15; transnational, 15
Fist of Fury, 198, 199, 201, 203
Five Golden Flowers, 181
five-year plan, first, 227
Fong, Allen, 78, 98, 99, 142
Fore, Steve, 147–51
foreign films, 4
foreigners, 175–80: in Chinese films, 168; Chinese relations with, 171; gaining of access, 176; othering of, 170; positive representations of, 170, 179
Forever Fever, 197, 213, 214, 219–21, 232
four modernizations, 230
Freud, Sigmund, 22, 126; psychoanalysis, 22–23

Fruit Chan, 100, 101
Fuery, Patrick, 138

Gallagher, Mark, 145
Game of Death, The, 199
Gang of Four, 230
gangster films, 138, 153–54, 230
Gaudreault, André, 50
Gelder, Ken, 134
gender: in cinema, 12, 108, 111; and nation, 10, 108, 109–10; transformation in modernization, 12. *See also* men; women
gezaixi, 11
ghost films, 18–19, 31; ghosts as wish fulfillment, 40; and linear time, 39. *See also* haunting
Ghost Story series, 58
giant film, 210, 211. *See also* big film, blockbusters
Gladney, Dru C., 187, 188
global capital flows, 3
globalization, 4, 10, 73, 196
Goddess, The, 119, 120, 125, 225
Godfather trilogy, 157–58
Goei, Glenn, 219
Golden Harvest, 148, 198
Golden Princess, 153
Gong Li, 12, 108, 109, 113, 124–29, 134; as metaphor for China, 128–29; sexualized body of, 126
Good Machine, 69, 175
Great Leap Forward, 228
Greater China Economic Circle, 207
Greatest Civil War on Earth, The, 191
Guangxi Film Studio, 102
Guattari, Félix, 174
Gunning, Tom, 50

Haiyan Film Studio, 25
Han Chinese, 188, 189; as big brothers, 13; ethnicity of, 189; intra-Han difference, 168, 170, 171, 189–94
Han Yingjie, 54, 66
Hang Shuqin, 113
Hansen, Miriam, 50, 68

happy endings, 12, 76, 81, 89, 91, 144
Happy Together, 42–43
Hardboiled, 154, 157
Hardt, Michael, 6
Harrell, Stevan, 171, 191
Harris, Kristine, 120, 122
Harvey, David, 45
haunting, 18–19; acting as, 134; double, 41, 46; haunted time, 19, 38–46; Hong Kong and, 41
He Jiming, 68
He Jingzhi, 60
healthy realism. *See* realism
Heaven and Earth, 218
Hero, 48, 49, 73, 107, 135, 136, 137, 159, 163–68, 195, 197, 205, 211, 212, 223, 232; as blockbuster, 168, 205
heroism, 140, 166, 167; reluctant, 144; transgressive male, 137
Hevia, James, 178
Hiep Thi Le, 218
historiography: historiological cinema, 17–38; as narrative mode, 20, 31; nation-state, 32; scientific status of, 31–32; subaltern, 34
history: counter, 32; official, 32, 33; revolutionary, 33; subaltern, 32; as truth or fiction, 31. *See also* historiography; memory
Hoberman, J., 167
Hoffman, John, 139
Hollywood Hong Kong, 101
Hollywood: film models, 195; impact on masculinity, 13; imports, 13, 197, 205, 206
Holm, David, 59, 61
Holocaust, 6
Home. *See* family-home
homogenization, 4, 5
Hong Kong, 10, 14; assertion of identity, 12–13; brotherhood, 13; cinema in 1970s, 65; as former colony, 19; gangsters, 13; gaze toward China, 79; handover to China (1997), 26, 40–41, 79, 99, 101, 107, 130, 132, 157, 207; and liminal state of adolescence, 144, 150; local in films,

Hong Kong (continued)
137; as outsider, 144; politicial identity, 102, 107; postcolonial postmodernity of, 38, 44–45, 46; refugees from mainland, 190, 226; as SAR, 19, 38, 43, 44; search for identity, 142, 144; as space of negotiation, 137
Horse Thief, 32, 170, 184–88, 192, 230, 231
Hou Hsiao Hsien, 18, 29–38, 39; cinematic techniques, 36
House of Flying Daggers, 10, 73
Hsiao-Peng Lu, Sheldon, 4
Hu Jingtao, 232
Hu Jubin, 50
Hu Ke, 187, 211
Hu Peng, 53
Hua Guofeng, 230
Hua Mulan (opera), 114
Hua Mulan, 112–13, 115, 131; and Confucian values, 113; Disney film about, 112; myth, 112–13, 125, 131
Huang Feihong, 53
Huang Zongjiang, 181
Humm, Maggie, 111
Hundred Flowers Campaign, 228
Huntington, Samuel, 5
Huters, Ted, 78

I Not Stupid, 216
Ibatan, 29–30
Ibsen, Henrik, 115
illness: as metaphor for social disease, 85
imports: from Hollywood. See Hollywood
In the Mood for Love, 11, 17, 18, 19, 38, 41, 42, 43–46, 232; as haunted film, 39, 41
individuals, 7. See also citizens
Internationale, 64
Internet, 3
interpellation, 7–8
Irma Vep, 134
Ivens, Joris, 226

Jameson, Fredric, 45
Jet Tone Production Company, 42
Jiang Qing, 54, 60, 228, 229, 230

Jiang Zemin, 231
jianghu. See underworld
Joint Declaration on Hong Kong, 41, 230. See also Hong Kong
Journey to the West, 56
Judou, 124, 125, 126, 127, 128, 159, 218, 231; banning of, 128

Karl, Rebecca, 28
Kenji, Mizoguchi, 36
Khoo, Eric, 215, 216, 217
Khoo, Olivia, 134
Kid, The, 100, 101, 102, 227
Killer, The, 13, 137, 144, 152–53, 154, 156, 158, 168, 231
Kim Soyoung, 39
King Hu, 10, 53, 54
KMT. See Kuomintang
Korea: modernization of, 39
Korean War, 227
kung fu films, 48, 53, 66, 67, 79, 213; as comedy, 145; combat in, 146; Confucian values and, 79; hero in, 148; as liminal space, 150; masculinity of, 150. See also martial arts
Kung Fu series, 198
Kunlun Studio, 226
Kuomintang (KMT), 26, 59, 85, 87, 120, 124, 192, 224, 225; Central Motion Picture Corporation, 94–98; civil war with CCP, 226; founding, 224; language policy on Taiwan, 192–93; nation-building project, 48
Kwai-cheung Lo, 137
Kwan Tak-hing, 53, 146
Kwan, Stanley, 108, 109, 129, 131, 132, 134, 140, 141
Kwok Wah Lau, Jenny, 127

Lacan, Jacques, 22
land reform, 227
language: among Han Chinese, 191; Cantonese, 26, 51, 192; Hakka, 193; Hokkienese, 192, 217; Japanese, 192; Mandarin, 26, 192, 193; official, 26, 192, 217; regulation

in films, 170, 192–93; Shangainese, 193; in Singapore, 193–94, 217; Singlish, 217, 219; spoken Chinese, 192; Taiwanese, 26, 51, 67, 192, 193; written Chinese, 191–92

Lau Kar-Leung, 148

law and film, 136

Law Kar, 81, 99

League of Left-wing Dramatists, 225

Lee Hsing, 93, 94, 95, 99, 137, 142, 190, 191

Lee Kwan-yew, 136

Lee Teng-hui, 3, 231

Lee, Bruce, 13, 48, 53, 54, 66, 100, 101, 102, 137, 196, 197–204, 213, 220, 221, 227, 229; as Asian American champion, 200; as China's first global film star, 196, 198; death, 198–99, 229; as diasporic China, 200; as Hong Kong, 199; international success, 196; masculinity of, 13, 197, 198, 201–202, 204, 209, 211; as Third World anti-imperialist, 200; as underdog, 200

Left-wing Film movement, 119

Legend of Tianyun Mountain, The, 230

Leung Ping-Kwan, 130

Leung, Tony, 163, 212

Lévi-Strauss, Claude, 31

Li Hanxiang, 53

Li Jun, 181

Li Lili, 130

Li Menwei, 130

Li Quanxi, 19, 25–28

Li Suyuan, 50, 51, 81

Li Xianglan, 24

Li Yiming, 181, 184

Li, Jet, 10, 163, 200, 212

Liang Qichao, 57

Liang Shanbo and Zhu Yingtai, 53

Lianhua Studio, 119, 130, 224

libidinal gaze, 12, 109, 111, 116, 120, 121, 126, 127. See also look

Life of Wu Xun, The, 62, 227

Lin Biao, 229

Lin Nien-tung, 53

Lin Zexu and the Opium War, 19, 25–26, 27

Lin Zhushan, 223

Little Cheung, 100, 101, 102, 107

Little Toys, 119, 122, 123, 125, 225

Litzinger, Ralph, 174

Liu, Cynthia, 177

Liu, Lydia, 112, 174

local: in Hong Kong films, 137; as transnational, 137

logic of the wound, 19–23

Loke Wan Tho, 214

Long March, 225

look: as cinematic trope, 109, 110. See also commodifying gaze; libidinal gaze; queer gaze; women

Lost World, The: Jurassic Park, 216

Louie, Kam, 140, 143, 152, 155, 167, 200

Love Eterne, 53, 228

Lowe, Lisa, 173

loyalty, 12, 135, 137, 138–44, 147, 152, 160. See also Confucian codes

Lu Feii, 93

Lu Hongshi, 48, 55

Lu Xun, 91, 92

Lu, Sheldon, 13, 14, 15, 130, 196

Lumière films, 223

Luo Mingyou, 119, 225

Luo Yijun, 52

Lyotard, Jean-Françoise, 45

Ma Junxiang, 80, 85, 111, 125

Ma Ning, 80, 81, 83, 86

Macau, return to China, 232

MacKenzie, John, 172

Mambo Girl, 133

Manchukuo Film Company, 24

Manchuria: establishment of film industry, 226

Mandarin. See language

Mandarin Duck and Butterfly School of literature, 81

Mao Zedong, 12, 19, 49, 59, 62, 77, 107, 224, 225, 227, 228; Talks at the Yan'an Forum, 59, 61, 62, 114, 225

Mao Zedong and His Son, 210

martial arts films, 9–10, 48, 49, 52, 53, 54, 57, 58, 69, 74, 135, 137, 138, 164, 201, 224; ban on, 225; conventions of, 70; global market for, 49, 66–74; god-spirit, 58; images of valor and, 140; links to opera, 71; stylized choreography of, 52; swordplay films, 70

Martin, Fran, 98

Marxism, sinicization of, 59

Marxism-Leninism, 77

masculinity, 10, 144; cinematic, 111; eroticization of, 202; heroic, 166; Hollywood, 209; Hollywood influence on, 13; *kung fu* films and, 150; machismo, 143; male bonding, 155; male codes, 138–44, 168; male exclusivity, 155; *mores* of, 137; and nation, 110; neo-*wu*, 201, 204, 208; new image of Chinese, 198; ordering nation and, 12; reinvention of, 137; traditional Chinese, 197–204; winning and, 164. *See also* Bruce Lee; Confucian codes; wen and wu dyad

masquerade, 111

Maxu Weibang, 24

May Fourth movement, 59, 68

Mazierska, Ewa, 45

Mee Pok Man, 216, 217, 218

Mei Lanfang, 52–53, 56

melodrama, 75, 76, 77–82, 91; family, 81, 94; father–son, 100; features of, 81; as genre, 81; melodramatic realism, 76, 82; as mode, 81; modern Chinese, 81; as signifier of modernity, 81; socialist, 103

memory: collective, 21; counter-, 29; oral, 30; subaltern, 18

men: in Chinese films, 135–68; privileging in relationships, 137. *See also* Confucian codes; father; masculinity

Meng Yue, 112, 115

Menglong Guojiang, 198

middle characters, 228

mimetic qualities of film, 19, 47

Mingxing Company, 86, 225

minority nationalities, 168, 172, 181; collective identity, 182; films, 170, 180–89,

228; Han Chinese relations with, 171; as little brothers, 13; maintenance as ethnic categories, 172; visual signifiers, 181–72

mise-en-scène, 76

modernity, 2; European-derived, 169, 171; globalized, 77; melodrama and, 81; realism and, 76, 77, 79; state-prescribed, 76; on Taiwan, 79

Money No Enough, 216

Moore-Gilbert, Bart, 172

Moscow Film Festival, 225

motherhood, 109–13; links to national, 110. *See also* women

Mui, Anita, 108, 132, 133, 149

Mulan. *See* Hua Mulan

multiculturalism, 3

Mulvey, Laura, 111, 116, 126, 127

My Son Ah Chung. See The Kid

narrative: role in foreign films, 55

nation: divided, 82–90; gendering of, 109–10; as male construct, 110; as people, 21; reconstructed, 90–98

national: concept of, 2; contested, 2, 5, 8; defining, 3, 5–8; identity, 2, 9, 169, 171; interface with transnational, 4; masculinity and, 144; narration of, 6; time and, 17–46; unity, 7. *See also* transnational

national cinema, 3, 8–13, 195; construction of, 14; expressive model of, 14; industry, 9; institutional approach to, 9; mainland cinema as Chinese, 14; multiplicity of, 14; and national culture, 9. *See also* film industry

National Customs, 119

national history genre, 17

nationalism: political, 48; territorial, 171

nation-state, 2, 5–6, 21, 208; China as modern, 9, 20, 22–23, 77; cinematic promotion of, 30; Confucianism and, 8. *See also* citizens; ethnic nation

Nazi Germany, 6

Needham, Joseph, 139

Negri, Antonio, 6

Neo, Jack, 215, 216–17, 219

New Cinema (Taiwan), 34–35, 193, 230
New Life movement, 112, 119
New Line Cinema, 151
New Taiwan Cinema. *See* New Cinema
New Wave cinema, 76, 78, 79, 98–107, 230
New Woman, The, 118, 119, 120, 121, 122, 123, 124, 125, 134, 225
New Year's Sacrifice, 78, 91–93, 228; approach to Confucianism, 91
Ng Ho, 148
Ng Wui, 100
Nielsen, Hanna Boje, 160
Nixon, Richard, 229
Norris, Chuck, 198, 203, 204
Northeast Film Studio, 60, 227
Nowell-Smith, Geoffrey, 90

Occidentalism, 174. *See also* Orientalism
Oedipal myth, 159
On the Hunting Ground, 187, 192
One and Eight, 32, 34
"open door" policy, 188
opera, 47; Beijing, 48, 54, 56; Cantonese, 48, 65; as common Chinese language, 49; communist appropriation of, 59; as influence on cinema, 48; military, 57; model, 58; regional, 56, 66–74; revolutionary, 11, 48, 49, 54, 58–66, 229; shadow, 11, 47–48, 49–54, 66–74; stars, 56; story cycles of, 56; Taiwanese *gezaixi,* 11, 49, 67, 228; traditional, 46
opera films, 11, 47, 49–54; as anachronism, 47; early, 51, 52, 55–58; as national film form, 56; revolutionary, 49, 54, 58–66; sinicization of cinema, 11, 54–58; Taiwanese, 49; yellow-plum-melody, 53
operatic: conventions, 57; mode, 11, 47–74
opium, trade in, 197
Opium War, The (1963), 19, 25–28, 29
Opium War, The (1997), 19, 22, 26, 28–29, 210–11, 212, 232
Opium Wars, 2, 19, 20, 223, 225; films, 10, 18, 19–29, 32, 139, 223; as wound, 22, 28
Orientalism, 5, 127, 169, 172, 173; internal, 173; as Western discourse, 169, 174

Orphan, The, 100
Orphan Rescues Grandfather, 141–42, 224; lineage in, 142
othering, 168, 169, 172, 187; of foreigners, 170; self-and-other model, 170, 171, 173, 174, 182–83, 188–89; trope of, 173
outsiders, 2. *See also* othering
Oyster Girl, 94, 228

painting, Chinese landscape, 38
Papke, David Ray, 157
Paradis Films, 42
Parents' Hearts, 100
past, the: as metaphor for the present, 32; narrating, 18; subaltern accounts of, 18. *See also* national history genre
patriarchy, 13, 136, 140, 176. *See also* Confucian codes
patriotic war films, 226
Patten, Christopher, 231
People's Liberation Army (PLA), 229
People's Republic of China (PRC), 3, 10, 11, 12, 229; founding of, 20, 53, 170, 227; lifting of martial law, 231
Philippines, 29
piracy, 197, 207–208; benefit to consumers, 209; damage to local industries, 207; as form of resistance, 209; in Greater China, 205, 207–208; prevention of, 212; Taiwanese moves against, 207; video, 209
PLA. *See* People's Liberation Army
Plaks, Andrew, 20
Police Story, 129, 133, 145
Popular Front (France), 79
Porter, Dennis, 173
postmodernity, 45
PRC. *See* People's Republic of China
propaganda, 20
Proust, Françoise, 39
publicity, 20
public–private divide, 109
Puppetmaster, The, 37

Qin Shi Huangdi, 195
Qipao. See cheongsam

Qu Qiubai, 49, 59
Queen of Sports, 201
queer gaze, 202. *See also* look

Raise the Red Lantern, 125, 126, 127, 128, 159, 218, 231; banning of, 128, 231
Rajadhyaksha, Ashish, 90
Rascaroli, Laura, 45
Ratner, Dan, 151
Rayns, Tony, 41, 203
realism, 29, 39, 72, 74, 75–107; changing contours of, 77; Chinese term for, 78; critical, 78, 79; as dominant Hollywood mode, 75, 76; as foreign concept, 78; healthy (Taiwan), 76, 78, 91, 93–94, 98, 228; link to national crisis, 77; links to modernity, 76, 79; melodramatic (*see* melodrama); as mixed mode, 79; neo-, 83; new, 83; as official mode of Chinese cinema, 11–12, 77, 90; origins in China, 81; poetic, 79; rejection of tradition, 91; representations of family-home (*see* family-home); revolutionary, 228; and Romanticism, 80; social, 77–78, 83; socialist (PRC), 76, 78, 79, 91, 92, 104; on Taiwan, 79; traditional, 93
Rebels of the Neon God, 98
reconstruction agendas, in cinema, 90
Red Guards, 229
Red Sorghum, 32, 124, 125, 126, 127, 128, 159, 231
Remorse at Death, 52, 227
Ren Qingtai, 55, 56, 57, 58, 61
Republic of China (Taiwan), 3, 12, 14; founding of, 170, 224. *See also* Taiwan
resistance: mimicry as, 222; in transnational environment, 204, 208
responsibility system, 230
Return of the Dragon, The. See Way of the Dragon, The
revolutionary realism, 228
revolutionary romanticism, 228
Reynaud, Bérénice, 133
Ri Koran. *See* Li Xianglan
Road Home, The, 142

Robertson, Maureen, 20
Roja, Carolos, 134
romance films, 224
Romance of the Three Kingdoms, 56
Romanticism, 77, 79–80; in China, 79; and realism, 80; revolutionary, 228
Rosenstone, Robert, 19
Rothman, William, 120
Rouge, 39, 40, 132
Ruan Lingyu, 12, 107, 108, 109, 113, 118–24, 125, 129–34; Cantonese identity, 131; as metaphor for China, 108, 128; patriotism, 126; roles, 119; star image, 119; suicide, 119–20, 132, 225
Rumble in the Bronx, 1; funding for, 1
Rush Hour, 2, 137, 144, 145, 151–52, 158, 168

Sacrificed Youth, 187
Said, Edward, 5, 127, 169, 172, 173
Sang Hu, 91
satire, banning of, 228
Saturday Night Fever, 220
Sayon's Bell, 188
Schein, Louisa, 173
Secret, The, 230
Sek Kei, 48
self-and-other model. *See* othering
Serfs, 170, 181–84, 185, 228
shadow opera. *See* opera
shadow poetry, 83
shadowplay, 49, 51, 59
Shanghai Dance School, 60
Shanghai Film Studio, 230
Shanghai Girl, 111, 125
Shanghai: Japanese occupation of, 19, 130, 132, 225; pre-war, 119, 130–31; under KMT, 119
Shaw Brothers, 53, 228
shengfan. See barbarians
Show Must Go On, The, 191
Shufan. See barbarians
Shui Hua, 60
sick man of Asia: China as, 196, 204
silent films, 55
Silverman, Kaja, 111

Simon, Frank, 29, 30

Singapore, 194; censorship in, 215; Economic Development Board, 215; film festivals, 218; film industry, 13, 21, 213–22; free trade economy, 213; Housing Development Board, 216; independence, 213, 214; International Film Festival, 216; Malay films, 214, 215; national imagery, 217–18; role in transnational film industry, 213

Singlish. *See* language

Sing-Song Girl Red Peony, 52, 225

"Sing-Song Girls, Les," 133

Sino-Soviet split, 228

Siu Leung Li, 150

Six Scholars of the Western Chamber, 67, 68

Snake in the Eagle's Shadow, 146

Sobchak, Vivian, 31

Social Darwinism, 77

socialist: realism (*see* realism); reconstruction, 91

Song of the Fisherman, 225

Song of Youth, 115, 116, 117, 118, 125, 136, 228, 233–34

"speaking bitterness," 18, 21–22. *See also* "appreciating sweetness"

special effects, 69, 212

spectacle, 48; Chinese, 55; foreign, 55

spectatorship: female, 111

Spring in a Small Town, 11, 76, 79, 83, 88–90, 227

Spring River Flows East, A, 82, 227

Spring Silkworms, 225

star image, 130

Stone, Oliver, 218

Story of Qiu Ju, The, 124, 128, 137, 144, 159–62, 168, 192, 231

Strange Tales of Liaozhai, 56

Street Angel, 11, 76, 82, 83, 86–88, 90, 226

Stringer, Julian, 131, 132, 153, 155, 156

Suleiman, Susan Rubin, 115

Sun Yat-sen, 224

Tailian Film Company, 27

Taiwan New Cinema. *See* New Cinema

Taiwan, 3, 10, 14, 223; autonomous identity, 67; censorship in, 67; end of utopian project, 79; film industry, 227; *gezaixi* opera, 11, 49, 67, 67; Han-Taiwanese, 67; inclusive cultural heritage, 68–69; independence movement, 190; indigenous population, 188, 190; Japanese occupation of, 35, 36, 67; KMT retreat to, 227; language problems, 192–93; martial law, 11, 191; as nation-state, 35; national reconstruction agenda, 92; nationalist perspective, 35; refugees from mainland, 190; Taiwanese language films, 67; *Taiwanren–waishengren* divide, 190. *See also* February 28 Incident

Taking Tiger Mountain, 229

Tambling, Jeremy, 42–43

Tan Xinpei, 56, 57

Tasker, Yvonne, 140

Teahouse. *See* audience

Teo, Stephen, 44, 53, 100, 133, 145, 191

tête-bêche, 44, 46

That's the Way I Like It. See Forever Fever

The River, 98

Third Sister Liu, 181

Three Kingdoms, The, 143, 155

Ti Lung, 140

Ti Wei, 206

Tian Zhuangzhuang, 83, 102, 184, 187, 192, 231

Tiananmen Square massacre, 128, 153, 157, 213, 231

Tibet: annexation of, 227; Chinese invasion of, 227; films about, 170, 184, 228

Tiger Tiger Productions, 219

time: cinematic, 10; cyclical, 21, 30

Titanic, 205, 211, 216

To Live, 124

Tomboy, 11, 76, 82, 83–86, 90, 140, 225

Tong, Janice, 45

Tong, Stanley, 152

Touch of Zen, A, 10, 53, 54, 66, 229

trade: free, 2, 27; in films, 204–13; international, 28; role in imperialism, 197. *See also* film industry; piracy

Tragedy on Pearl River, 79
transmission, 20. *See also* propaganda, publicity
transnational, 3, 4–5, 208; communication between Chinese territories, 196; development of cinema in China, 4, 5, 13, 196; film studies, 13–16, 195; investment, 222; markets, 222; projects, 195–96; resistance in transnational environment, 204; talent, 222. *See also* national
Travolta, John, 213, 220, 221
triads, Hong Kong, 2
tribute system, 13, 176, 178
Troubled Laughter, 230
Tsai Ming-liang, 98
Tsing, Anna, 195
Tsung-I Dow, 8
Tu Weiming, 5
Tung Chee-hwa, 232
12 Storeys, 216
Two Stage Sisters, 114, 115, 116, 125

underworld, 137, 152
United China Vision, 69
United Front, 224
United Nations: expulsion of Taiwan, 229; PRC as legitimate Chinese representative, 229
universalizing tendency, 173

vampires, 134
Victory of the Mongolian People, 184
Vincendeau, Ginette, 83
visual effects. *See* special effects
Vive L'Amour, 98
von Ranke, Leopold, 31

Walsh, Michael, 6
Wang Bin, 60
Wang Shujen, 207
Wang Shuyuan, 63
Wang Yiman, 131
Wang Yuejin, 126, 127
Wang Zhimin, 119
Wang, Q. Edward, 20–21, 31

Warner Bros., 198, 199
Water Margin, 56
Way of the Dragon, The, 198, 199, 201, 202, 203, 213
Wedding Banquet, The, 13, 98, 137, 143, 169, 170, 175–79, 231; ethnic dimension, 175
Wei Ping'ao, 202, 203, 204
wen and *wu* dyad, 140, 167, 200–201, 204
Wenhua Film Studio, 89
Western cinema, merger with Chinese aesthetics, 52
White Gold Dragon, 225
White, Hayden, 31
White-haired Girl, The, 11, 54, 60, 61–62, 114, 184, 227
Williams, Linda, 75, 101
Williams, Raymond, 80, 82
Woman, Demon, Human, 113
women: and children, 110; collective and, 110; construction of, 112; cosmopolitan, 12; motherhood and, 109–13; in PRC, 111–12; as refined courtesans, 132; representations in cinema, 12, 108–34; role of, 109; traditional role model, 112; woman-as-place, 108; women's films, 113; women's liberation, 109. *See also* libidinal gaze
Wong Fei-hung, 146–48, 151, 227
Wong Kar-wai, 17, 19, 38, 41, 42, 129; focus on time, 41, 42, 44
Woo, John, 53, 137, 138–39, 143, 144, 152–58, 161, 168; apocalyptic vision of Hong Kong, 157; move to Hollywood, 157, 158
Wood, Robin, 203
World Trade Organization (WTO): China's accession to, 206, 232; Taiwan's entry into, 206
World Wide Web. *See* Internet
wound, national, 23. *See also* logic of the wound; Opium War; "speaking bitterness"
WTO. *See* World Trade Organization
wu and *wen*. *See wen* and *wu* dyad
Wu Nien-jen, 30
Wu Tianming, 230, 231

Xi'an Film Studio, 184, 230, 231
Xi'an Incident, 225
Xia Yan, 64
Xie Fang, 12, 108, 113–18, 120, 125, 129; as
   metaphor for China, 129; patriotism, 126
Xie Jin, 19, 26, 28, 81, 210–11, 212, 232
Xie Jin Hengtong Film and Television
   Company, 28
Xu Haofeng, 164, 167
Xue Pinggui and Wang Baochuan, 67, 68,
   228

Yan Ruisheng, 224
Yan'an, 225, 226; Forum on Literature and
   Art, 59, 61, 62, 114, 225; solution, 59;
   story, 104, 106
Yang + Yin: Gender in the Chinese Cinema,
   140, 143
Yang Xiaozhong, 24
Yao Xiaolei, 167
Yasujiro, Ozu, 36
Yau, Esther, 126, 127, 188
Ye Longyan, 67
Yeh Yueh-Yu, 14
Yellow Earth, 10, 12, 29, 32, 33–34, 75, 76, 78,
   79, 98, 102–107, 230, 231; criticism of
   Maoist history, 104; emptiness aesthetic,
   105
Yeoh, Michelle, 130
Yihua Film, 84
yin and *yang*, 140
Yon Fan, 218
Yoshimoto, Mitsuhiro, 2, 3–4

Young, Robert, 173
Yuan Muzhi, 83, 86
Yuan Shikai, 224
Yue, Audrey, 44, 129, 134
Yuen Woping, 66, 69
Yuval-Davis, Nira, 109, 110, 140

Zeng Yongyi, 67
Zhang Baiqing, 209–10
Zhang Nuanxin, 187
Zhang Qiu, 167
Zhang Rui, 184
Zhang She, 54
Zhang Shichuan, 52, 58, 224
Zhang Wei, 185
Zhang Yimou, 10, 13, 49, 124, 125, 126, 127,
   128, 135, 136, 137, 144, 159–62, 168, 192,
   195, 197, 205, 211, 212, 213, 218, 231; red
   trilogy, 158–60
Zhang Yingjin, 9, 13, 188
Zhang Ziyi, 212
Zhang Zuolin, 57
Zhao Dan, 86
Zhao Ziyang, 173, 230
Zheng Dongtian, 210
Zheng Junli, 19, 25
Zheng Zhenqiu, 58, 77
Zhong Dafeng, 51
Zhou Enlai, 173; death, 229
Zhou Enlai, 210
Zhou Xuan, 133
Zhu Shilin, 24, 191
Zoom Hunt, 69